Conflict of Ages

The Great Debate
on the
Moral Relations of God and Man

by
Edward Beecher, D.D.

adapted and edited by

Phillip A. Ross

Original publisher
BOSTON:
Phillips, Sampson & Company.
London: Sampson Low, Son & Co.
1854
Entered according to Act 0f Congress, in the year 1853, by
EDWARD BEECHER,
In the Clerk's Office of the District Court of the District of Massachusetts.

Marietta, Ohio

Copyright ©2012 Phillip A. Ross
All rights reserved.

ISBN: 978-0-9839046-3-2
Edition: 2013.3.1

Published by

Pilgrim Platform
149 E. Spring St., Marietta
Ohio, 45750
www.pilgrim-platform.org

Biblical quotations are from the Authorized Version, in public domain, unless
    otherwise cited.

Printed in the United States of America

Edward Beecher (1803–1895)
Picture courtesy of The Harriet Beecher Stowe Center, Hartford, Connecticut.

BOOKS BY PHILLIP A. ROSS

The Work At Zion—A Reckoning, Two-volume set, 772 pages, 1996.

Practically Christian—Applying James Today, 135 pages, 2006.

The Wisdom of Jesus Christ in the Book of Proverbs, 414 pages, 2006.

Marking God's Word—Understanding Jesus, 324 pages, 2006.

Acts of Faith—Kingdom Advancement, 326 pages, 2007.

Informal Christianity—Refining Christ's Church, 136 pages, 2007.

Engagement—Establishing Relationship in Christ, 104 pages, 1996, 2008.

It's About Time!—The Time Is Now, 40 pages. 2008.

The Big Ten—A Study of the Ten Commandments, 105 pages, 2001, 2008.

Arsy Varsy—Reclaiming The Gospel in First Corinthians, 406 pages, 2008.

Varsy Arsy—Proclaiming The Gospel in Second Corinthians, 356 pages, 2009.

Colossians—Christos Singularis, 278 pages, 2010.

Rock Mountain Creed—The Sermon on the Mount, 310 pages, 2011.

The True Mystery of the Mystical Presence, John Nevin Williamson, Phillip A. Ross, Editor, 355 pages, 2011.

Peter's Vision of Chirst's Purpose in First Peter, 340 pages, 2011.

Peter's Vision of The End in Second Peter, 184 pages, 2012.

The Religious History of Nineteenth Century Marietta—Reflections, 120 pages, 2012.

Conflict of Ages, Or The Great Debate on the Moral Relations of God and Man, Edward Beecher, D. D., Phillip A. Ross, Editor, 524 pages, 2012.

Concord Of Ages, Or The Individual And Organic Harmony Of God And Man, Edward Beecher, D. D., Phillip A. Ross, Editor, 499 pages, 2013.

Dedicated to

Joseph Aloisius Ratzinger

also known as

Benedict XVI

who serves as

Bishop of Rome
the Sovereign of the
Vatican City State

and the leader of the

Catholic Church,

the largest branch of Christianity

in the hope for Christian Resolution

PREFACE

YOU have in your hands a dangerous book, dangerous because it deals with perhaps the most serious conflict in history, and I commend it with some trepidation. That conflict began in Genesis and has continued unabated through history. Many people believe it to be a conflict between believers and unbelievers, and a great many people, traditions and religions have framed the conflict in these terms. The Old Testaments prophets described the conflict as between the one true God and the many false gods, or the true prophet and the false prophets. Both conceptions are equally true, but the latter is to be preferred because the former suggests that those who oppose the God of the Bible don't believe anything, when in fact they believe as strongly as believers, but believe falsely.

And yet to even say that they believe falsely is not quite right, because what they believe has every bit as much logic, reason and experience to back it up as any argument provided by believers. And this is why this conflict has continued. It cannot be won by arguments, logic, reason or experience. In fact, it cannot be won by argument at all! It is not an intellectual or academic matter, though it involves intellectual and academic concerns. It is a matter of the heart, of faith and belief.

Those who don't believe and trust the Bible to be true, find it to be unbelievable and untrustworthy on the basis of sound logic, reason and experience. Don't get me wrong here! I'm not arguing against the veracity of Scripture. I'm arguing from the perspective of presuppositional antithesis, a Christian understanding forged by Cornelius Van Til and sharpened by Greg Bahnsen.[1]

---

1 Van Til, Cornelius. *The Defense of the Faith,* 3d ed.; Philadelphia: Presbyterian and Reformed, 1967. See also www.vantil.info. Bahnsen, Greg L. *Pushing the Antithe-*

Edward Beecher preceded both Van Til and Bahnsen, but he was aware to some extent of the equally logical, reasonable and experiential arguments coming from both sides of this chasm. Beecher does an admirable job of justifying both perspectives, and shows that both are in fact woven into Christian history. The fact of the presence of this conflict in Christian history should give us pause, particularly because both sides claim the Christian high ground. It involves the dispute between God's sovereignty and human free will.

I will let Beecher lay out the argument, which he does very well. But because I think that he has seriously failed in his final analysis, he also errs in his conclusion and remedy. And yet, there is great value to his work because he appears to be a serious believer in every respect. He did his best, which is all we can expect of anyone. And he is a creature of his time, as are we all. But because our time follows his by a century and a half we have more history to evaluate and better tools of evaluation. We have Van Til, Bahnsen and others to draw upon.

DISCOVERY

I stumbled upon this book quite by providence, as the old divines would say. I currently live in Marietta, Ohio, which is a unique place, as most every town undoubtedly is. Marietta's uniqueness comes from its founding in 1788 by an act of Congress, and its establishment on the most Western Frontier of the fledgling experiment known as the United States of America. Marietta is known for having the oldest church in Ohio—First Congregational Church, organized in Marietta in December of 1796.

I was working on a project regarding the Nineteenth Century religious history of Marietta, Ohio,[2] and discovered that the first honorary degree granted by Marietta College was given to Edward Beecher in 1841 (Doctor of Divinity). The leaders of Marietta College must have been pleased with Beecher's earlier book, *Statement of Anti-Slavery Principles* (1837), which encouraged a growing theme in American society at the time. Indeed, slavery has proven to be one of the most important and enduring themes of all American history.

The Beecher Legacy stands today as a crown jewel in the treasury of American culture, though it is full of conflict. The Beechers have

---

sis: The Apologetic Methodology of Greg L. Bahnsen, American Vision, 2007.

2   Summers, Thomas J. *The Religious History of Nineteenth Century Marietta—Reflections*, Pilgrim Platform, Marietta, Ohio, 2012, Phillip A. Ross, editor.

been a prolific, cantankerous, well-placed and very human family. It seems to have begun with Lyman Beecher, Edward's father. He survived three wives and was the most consistent person at the source of that legacy, firing up his children with the great concerns and big questions of life and history. For the most part Harriet Beecher Stowe has cornered the market on the Beecher legacy, to the paucity of the available treasure, I should add. Nothing against Harriet, but there is much more to this legacy than Harriet's work. All of the Beecher children were serious scholars, writers and theologians and are worthy of serious study and reflection.[3]

In my estimation, this book by Edward Beecher needs to be reconsidered from a slightly different perspective. Or, because he has been forgotten by history, it needs to simply be *considered*. He was consumed with both temporal (historical) and eternal concerns, and those concerns and his treatment of them may significantly contribute toward the renovation that is so needed by the Christian church in our day.

His book was originally published when America was deeply conflicted over the Great Awakenings and the New School/Old School controversies that set the stage for the American Civil War. During that same time Protestantism in general was also very displeased with "Romanism," Beecher among them, who published *The Papal Conspiracy Exposed* in 1855. It was during this time period, roughly the Nineteenth Century, that Christianity of most every stripe took a giant step decisively away from historic Christian orthodoxy, note the small "o" in *orthodoxy*.

Of course, depending on your tradition (Catholic, Orthodox or Protestant) you will see the roots of this departure differently. Of interest on this point will be the work of John Williamson Nevin, who decisively argued that the second generation Calvinists had already departed from the original Calvinism of Calvin, and which may be at the root of both the Great Awakenings and its detractors. You will find references in several footnotes in this book.

DEDICATION

People may wonder why I have dedicated this book to the current Roman Catholic Pope. Be assured that it is not to provide any sort of

---

3   For a brief description of the Beechers see: http://www.harrietbeecherstowecenter.org/hbs/beecher_family.shtml.

affront, nor to carry water from the wells of the Nineteenth Century spirit of anti-papalism, nor to further the flawed ecumenical efforts of the Twentieth Century. The ecumenism of the Twentieth Century built upon the errors of the Nineteenth. A different approach to ecumenicism is needed, and I have written much about these things through my own literature, so interested Christians can learn more there. But it may be that Edward Beecher has made a significant contribution to this cause, as well, if people can get beyond the errant presuppositions about him and about Christianity, and examine the issues with new eyes.[4]

I have dedicated this book to the Pope because he represents the largest group of Christians in the world today, and genuine ecumenism or Christian unity cannot avoid the inclusion of Roman Catholics. I also want the Catholic leaders to consider Beecher's argument, so I have edited his language a bit to make it less offensive. I think that Beecher's work may benefit the wholeness and unity of the Christian church by contributing to the correction, renewal and renovation of the Roman Catholic Church, the Orthodox church, the various Protestant churches including the various Reformed churches— even the Unitarian and Mormon churches, and even possibly Islam, which I understand to be another Christian heresy.

In the same way that I'm calling for this book to be reevaluated afresh in our day, we must also reevaluate each and all of the various denominations and movements that have made it into the Twenty-First Century. Of course, much such evaluation has been going on for some time as many people have come to realize that something very fundamental or basic has gone awry in Christendom and in the world. There are calls for reformation and revival coming from nearly every corner of the church and the world today.

Beecher was actually quite catholic in his outlook and treatment of the theology of his day. In particular, he identified a very basic theological problem and suggested a solution that is worthy of our best and most attentive consideration, though such consideration will be quite difficult for a number of reasons. But if he was right or even partly right—and that is the question that I hope to put on the table in our day by republishing this book—his work could provide serious grist for the ecumenical, catholic, Christian reformation and revival mill.

---

4   Jordan, James W. *Through New Eyes–Developing a Biblical View of The World*, Wipf & Stock, 2000.

It is important to understand the problem and see Beecher's solution in the context in which he presented it, and then in the way I propose to tweak it in the Appendix. He labored to frame the problem in its historical context. Consequently, it will help readers to have much Christian history and theology, including German theology, under their proverbial belts simply to perceive Beecher's systematic or holistic approach to the problem and his recommended solution—and mine.

In Beecher's day, the dominating problem that beset the churches was the ongoing argument between Calvinists and Arminians, or the Old School and the New School (or New Light) factions, or the Protestant churches and the newly founded Unitarian church. Beecher will show that these arguments can be traced back to the dispute between Augustine and Pelegius, and his analysis is sure to surprise and offend you, regardless of where you stand. Please bear with him—and me. Try to understand his argument and not simply dismiss him out of hand, so that you can consider the correction that I will suggest.

Be aware that I am not suggesting any sort of ecumenical union of Christian churches and denominations as if Christian unity is a matter of adding together all of the errors and idiocies of Christian history into a great administrative conglomeration and call it *unity*. But I am suggesting that our human understanding of God's Truth is cumulative, and that we need to embrace what is true according to the best measures of our contemporary tools and abilities, and to simultaneously abandon what is not. Genuine learning involves the willingness to admit our own errors and embrace ideas that are new to us.

Though Beecher is not up to speed regarding contemporary theology or science, we can learn much from his openness, keen wit, historical breadth and depth, and his unabashed commitment to Jesus Christ and to the history of Christ's church. Most people identify Beecher as a Unitarian or Arminian, but it seems to me that such an identification is short-sighted, inadequate and fails to understand the crux of his argument. As a staunch Calvinist myself, I implore you not to dismiss Beecher before you understand him.

Obviously, Beecher's work will not solve our internecine problems today because it is nearing two centuries since he first penned it, and there is much that has since happened and much that he simply didn't know. Nonetheless, there are indications in my opinion that his work was misunderstood and neglected by his Mainline contemporaries in the midst of the theological controversies of his own day—but adopted and adapted by many people who were fleeing the dissension that was destroying and dividing the churches.

Beecher demands that we ask, consider and answer the deepest questions about the thorniest problems, not to avoid them. He was solidly committed to the best understanding of both theological and scientific truth available to him, and he was willing to follow it wherever it led. Following Beecher's lead, I pray that all who read this manuscript will approach this book with as much patience and objectivity as they can muster. It is not an easy read, but it is worthwhile.

An additional reason to dedicate this book to Pope Benedict XVI is that he is German, and much of Beecher's scholarship was based on contemporary (in his day) German sources. It is likely that Pope Benedict is familiar with Beecher's German sources. He may also be familiar with this book, as well. I don't know. What I do know is that most Christian scholars today are not. My hope is that the most serious Christians today will be the most serious about fixing Christianity, which appears to be broken across the denominational spectrum. Many of the problems that Beecher intended to solve with this work, have been greatly exacerbated since it was first published in 1853.

I pray that the Pope (and others) will have the humility to receive this book in the spirit in which it is offered—in the simple hope for Christian resolution and advancement. Few are the denominations that don't believe that Christ has called His church into a unity of the highest caliber. But our world, and Christ's church, don't need any more revolutions, nor anymore reformations or revivals like those of the past. Those days are over. We cannot return to any previous time or historical epoch, and all such efforts in that direction are flawed. History does not flow backwards. The future always lies ahead in uncharted territory.

It would be difficult for the Pope to argue that the Roman Catholic Church is beyond correction, given the onslaught of sexual abuse suits it has received in the past thirty to forty years. I pray that he will see that the problem in the Church is larger than a few wayward priests, larger than a few wayward Protestant denominations, larger than anything the church has heretofore known. It seems to me that his admission of such things would help to significantly advance the establishment of Christianity.

The problems in every denomination go back to deep seated and long standing theological conflicts and rampant confusion about all sorts of things. But such thoughts are not for me to speculate about here. So, kindly join me in prayer that the best and most sublime Christian inspiration—with all of the various hopes and ideals that drove Beecher to write this book in the first place, and are driving me to republish it—will provide the context for its usefulness to all of God's many and diverse people—to the Pope, to Christ's Church and to the watching world.

Allow me to prepare you for some of Beecher's ideas and to then suggest some further analysis in the Appendix *after* you have read his arguments. He speaks much of "new-created minds" being at the source of the problem, but doesn't formally define the term. The term refers to the birth of individual human beings. The term is related to Beecher's solution to the problem, which he calls the *doctrine of preexistence*. Please don't rush to judgment or think that you understand what he means by this idea before you have seriously considered his argument in full.

I will argue that Beecher failed to adequately understand the Trinity, and that failure caused him to look for something that shapes human predilection such that God could not be blamed for creating people with an innate propensity to sin. Because of his commitment to individualism, he posited the idea of preexistence, such that people had earned God's damnation in some unknown previous state of existence. This way Beecher could hold the doctrine of total depravity without blaming God for creating people who cannot avoid sin. I believe that the Trinity better solves the problem without introducing a host of related difficulties.

I found myself thinking of this idea of preexistence as a kind of antediluvian human cultural remnant out of which God called Abraham. Abraham's father, Terah (whose Hebrew name means "Ibex, wild goat," or "Wanderer" and "loiterer") was a priest of a very ancient religion, possibly related to the god, Sin.[5] Abraham was called out of that

---

5   Stein, Robert H. "Sumer," ISBE 4:653-662. According to Sumerian myths, Sin was
    the child that resulted from Enlil's rape of Ninlil. Sin's wife was Ningal. Together
    they had three children, each of whom became prominent deities: Shimachu, the
    sun-god, Ereshkigal, queen of the underworld, and the youngest, Inanna (known as
    Ishtar in Semitic lands), who became Queen of Heaven. (from James W. Bell's *An-
    cient Sumeria*. http://www.jesuswalk.com/abraham/0_intro.htm). See also, Ross,
    Phillip A. *Peter's Vision of The End in Second Peter*, Pilgrim Platform, Marietta, Ohio,

culture to create a new culture that we know as Old Testament Judaism, which was to be a blessing to all nations, all peoples of the earth
(Gen. 12:2-3). The culture of Judaism got bogged down in self-cen-
teredness, whereupon Christ came to liberate the Gospel of God to
once again be a blessing to all nations, all peoples of the earth. Understanding Beecher requires an understanding of the "big picture" of
God's mission to the world. And my correction requires understanding
the role of the Trinity in that mission.

DELIVERY

My approach to putting this book together has been to reproduce
it in a way that maximizes its understandability without being a slave
to academic accuracy. And this has been quite a task because Beecher
was a scholar whose universe of discourse was quite broad, but the
academic standards of his day leave much to be desired. My intent is to
put Beecher's argument in the hands of contemporary Christians as
broadly as possible in order to encourage conversation and discussion
about it. However, I must forewarn you because it is a very big idea,
and fully worthy of your must careful consideration.

Regarding the text, Beecher's words have been preserved pretty
much as he wrote them. I have added or changed a word here and
there as a correction or improvement. The most significant change I
made was to substitute Beecher's idea of "misadjustment" with the
more contemporary language of "misunderstanding." He argues that
Christianity has been "misadjusted" since Augustine, and that this
"misadjustment" has produced various theological and philosophical
misalignments. I think that Beecher's idea will be more clearly communicated with the language of *misunderstanding*. At least, it is for me.

I have also changed the layout to better suit contemporary standards, by stretching out the text so that the reader is not simply presented with page after page of unformatted text and incredibly long
paragraphs—by pulling out quotations and providing more white
space. While Beecher was quite a scholar, his method of scholarship
(footnoting sources in particular) pales in comparison to contemporary
standards. Correcting this deficiency is certainly needed, but is beyond
my intentions here.

I have also added footnotes to provide identification and context
for the many people he mentioned. My footnotes are in the page font,

2012, chapter 8, "Lot's Lesons," section "Sodom," p. 69.

and Beecher's are in **Arial**. I am astonished and humbled by the many people he cited and referred to. My reading of Beecher has convinced me of how little I actually know, and how much there is to know.

Let me also remind the reader that this book, like my other books, is not intended to be a scholarly treatise. I'm not opposed to scholarship, but it can and often does impose categories upon those who engage in it that are oblique to the message of the Bible. Consequently, I hope to make Beecher's scholarship understandable and more readily available to those not inflicted with the scholarship gene. I'm more interested in the ideas of the book than its pedigree or historicity. That work can be done much better by others more qualified—and I hope it will be. There is always an optimal balance between detailed focus and breadth of scope to be sought.

Finally then, I am deeply grateful for my wife, Stephanie, and her work, support, encouragement, persistence and perseverance with me, especially as I have endeavored to write. I simply could not do what I do without her doing what she does.

May the Lord bless you as you read this book. Please consider it carefully and prayerfully. And if you make it all the way through it, join the conversation.

Phillip A. Ross
April 2012
Marietta, Ohio

Summary View of the Contents

Dedication... 1

Introduction.. 3

Nature Of The Conflict, End And Compass Of The
Work

Book I: The Conflict in its Principles

Chapter I: The Case Stated... 10

The steamship. The Question to be discussed: Is there a
misunderstanding of the moving powers of Christianity,
resulting in an inevitable logical conflict?

Chapter II: Presumptive Argument.. 12

Conflict of Old School and New School divines. Great
evils of the conflict. Existence of the same conflict in substance for fifteen centuries.

Chapter III: The Moving Powers of Christianity.................... 16

The powers essential to the practical working of the system. The principles of honor and of right. A full statement
of the fallen and ruined condition of man.

Chapter IV: The Principles of Honor and of Right................ 18

The origin of these principles. How developed. Opinions
of philosophers. Testimony of Scripture. Expositions of
Dr. Hodge, Prof. Stuart, Dr. Chalmers, Tholuck,
Melanchton and Calvin. The supreme importance and authority of these principles. Questions to be tested by them.

Chapter V: Statement of Moral Principles.................... 29

The obligations of great and powerful minds to inferior
and feeble minds. Application to God. Obligations of
God: as to the standard of responsibility; as to the mainte-
nance of the principles of justice in imputation and retri-

bution; as to the original constitutions and circumstances of his creatures. Support of these principles from Scripture and from Christian experience.

Chapter VI: Orthodox Authorities.. 37
How far the principles above stated have been recognized by the church. Testimony of Turretin, of the Princeton divines, of Dr. Watts, of J. Wesley, of the Westminster divines. Supreme importance of these principles.

Chapter VII: Facts as to human depravity.............................. 44
The second moving power is a thorough view of human depravity and ruin. Certain facts are obvious. Statement of them by Unitarian divines—Dr. Burnap, Pres. Sparks, Prof. Norton, Dr. Dewey. Their theory. Need of a deeper view virtually conceded.

Chapter VIII: Radical View Of The Ruin Of Man.................. 52
Necessity of depth and thoroughness. Points involved in a full view. Statements of Calvin. Synod of Dort. Confession of Helvetia. Confession of the Waldenses. French Confession. The Church of England. Confession of Belgia. Confession of Augsburg. Moravian confession. The Westminster divines. Exposition and remarks.

Chapter IX: Social And Organic Relations Of Man................ 62
Corrupting power of sinful family relations, and of depraved social and political organizations. Views of Dr. Burnap

Chapter X: Relations Of Man To Invisible Enemies.............. 65
A kingdom of fallen spirits revealed. Their power and wiles. Exposure of man to their influence.

Chapter XI: The Conflict A Reality..................................... 67
Each moving power is real, true, and well-sustained. Yet, as now adjusted, they are in direct conflict. Proof of this assertion.

BOOK II: THE CONFLICT IN EXPERIENCE

Chapter I: Laws Of Thought And Emotion Under The System... 71
Nature and design of Christianity. Interests involved. Depth of emotions excited. Tendencies to division and conflict.

Chapter II: Experiences Characterized................................. 73

Caused by the predominance, in different minds, of contending parts of the system. Resulting in reactions. Six enumerated.

Chapter III: First Experience; Or, The Philosophy Of Old School Theology.. 76

Its basis a belief of a depraved nature before action. Its origin a deep Christian experience. Illustrated by the case of Edwards. Scriptural testimony. Public formularies. Sources of its power.

Chapter IV: The Reaction.. 84

Not the result of carnal reason, but of the divine principles of equity and honor. These principles not denied. Effort to avert the conflict. A most remarkable position. Immeasurable interests involved. A failure.

Chapter V: The Reaction Irresistible...................................... 87

As The System Now Is. Virtual confession of Dr. Woods. Improper mode of representing the principles of honor and right. Attempt at defense by Dr. Hodge. His virtual confession. Course of Abelard, Pascal and others. Course of Dr. Chalmers. They improperly repudiate the application of the principles of equity and honor, as unauthorized rationalizing. In so doing they are at war with the Word of God.

Chapter VI: Second Experience; Or, The Philosophy Of Unitarian Theology.. 98

An entire recoil from the Old School theology. Its result is the rejection of radical views of human depravity. Its strength is in the principles of equity and honor. Early development of the system in New England. Case of John Adams, of Story, and of Channing. They argued logically from the true principles of honor and right. Extracts from Dr. Channing. He vindicates these principles. Inadequate replies. Power of the system.

Chapter VII: The Reaction.. 110

Testimony Of Dr. Channing And Others. Obvious Facts. Christian experience and Scripture react. Disappointment of the anticipations of Dr. Channing. Reasons. His altered views of Unitarianism. The increasing power of Christian experience and the Word of God decide the question.

Chapter VIII: Degradation Of Free Agency Itself................. 118

Original righteousness rejected. Position of Dr. Ware, Dr. Dewey, and Dr. Burnap. Hegelian theory.

Chapter IX: Third Experience; Or, The Philosophy Of Orthodox Universalism.. 123
Both moving powers retained. Relief sought in Universalism. Case of John Foster. His character, views and course. Extent of his influence.

Chapter X: The Reaction.. 130
Influence of the Bible and of a Christian experience. The nature of cruelty, the necessity of regeneration, and the causes of future misery. The tendency of moral causes.

Chapter XI. The Fourth Experience; Or, The Philosophy Of New School Theology.. 133
Both moving powers are retained, but the facts are modified by the principles. Its origin from holy men, for practical ends. Influence of Edwards and Fuller. Peculiarities of this theology. Appeal to the principles of honor and right. Controversy with the old theology. Extracts from Whelpley. Power of the system in revivals. Its auspicious general influences.

Chapter XII. The Reaction.. 140
Causes of a reaction are found in the consequences of denying a sinful nature before action. Either sin is caused by divine efficiency, as held by Dr. Emmons, or by an innocent though deteriorated nature and circumstances. Charge of a superficial view of depravity. Alarm of Dr. Nettleton and others. Charge that the conflict with the principles of honor and right is not averted. Arguments of Dr. Hodge. Princeton divines. Dr. Woods. Degradation of free agency results in some cases.

Chapter XIII: The Fifth Experience; Or, The Eclipse Of The Glory Of God.. 153
Cause of this experience, a full perception of the conflict, without relief. Tendencies to it in John Foster. Its full development. Its succession by the sixth experience. A full account of this experience deferred till the reconciliation has been presented.

BOOK III: The Reconciliation In Its Principles

Chapter I: The Problem Proposed................................ 161
The suggestion of a possible mode of reconciliation. The great importance even of this. Incidental evidence involved.

Chapter II: Method Of Procedure.............................. 164
Two supposable modes of solution. The adoption of the second.

Chapter III: State Of The Human Mind, And Conditions Of The Problem... 167
Power of illogical influences. Character of the persons addressed.

Chapter IV: The Essentials Of Harmony..................... 170
Retention of all the facts of the system. Full scope for Christian emotions and experience. The presentation of a perfect character of God.

Chapter V: The Misunderstanding............................. 177
Great power of a small misunderstanding. The misunderstanding stated. Its extensive and injurious influence. It is a mere assumption.

Chapter VI: The Readjustment................................. 184
It retains all the facts. It concedes all the principles. It harmonizes the combatants. Causes of the rejection of this view.

Chapter VII: The System As Adjusted....................... 188
It gives a radical view of human depravity, and averts Pelagian tendencies. It averts the degradation of free agency. It vindicates the measures of God. It elevates our conceptions of new-created minds. It gives a rational view of the kingdom of fallen spirits.

Chapter VIII: The Kingdom Of Fallen Spirits.............. 193
Importance of this part of the general system. Effects of the readjustment. The number of fallen beings not increased, but diminished, by the system of this world. Relations to the antiquity of the earth. Statements from Dr. Hitchcock; J. P. Smith; Babbage. Elevated point of view.

Chapter IX: Brief Summary Of The Whole Case........... 200
Original state of all new-created beings. The entrance of evil. The course of events. The final results.

Chapter X: A Presumption Rebutted......................... 203
It is alleged that this view has been considered and found insufficient. The allegation denied. The case stated. Illustra-

tion from the course of opinion with reference to the
Copernican system. Extract from Whewell.

BOOK IV: HISTORICAL OUTLINE AND ESTIMATE OF THE CONFLICT

Chapter I: General Outline.. 210

Importance and design of the discussions of other ages. Importance of a full history of this conflict. Sources of it. Outline of the field.

Chapter II: The Point Of Vision.. 216

Intellectual power and greatness of Augustine. Relations of present discussions to him. Views of Prof. Shedd, E. H. Sears, and others, concerning him. He is the point of vision.

Chapter III: Theological Speculations Before Augustine...... 221

State of things immediately after the apostles. Character of the first assaults on Christianity. The principles of honor and right become predominant. Tendencies to superficial views of depravity resulted. Theology of the Greek Church. Pelagius logically carried out existing tendencies to dangerous results.

Chapter IV: The Mountain-Top; Or, Augustine And His Experience.. 231

The necessity of a reaction. Augustine the providential agent. Not a mere logician. His depth of feeling and Christian experience. Not a mystic in a bad sense.

Chapter V: Augustine's Principles Of Equity And Honor..... 240

His elevated views of new-created minds. His high demands in their behalf. The extensive influence of these views in subsequent ages. His deep views of depravity. The inevitable conflict.

Chapter VI: Augustine's Theory Of Reconciliation.............. 247

A forfeiture of rights before birth. A kind of preexistence. Real preexistence rejected. His theory was, that all men existed and acted in Adam in a common nature.

Chapter VII: Response Of The Human Mind To The Theory Of Augustine.. 251

The fact of a forfeiture generally accepted. His solution ultimately and generally rejected. Various other contradictory solutions. The problem absurd and impossible, without real preexistence.

Chapter VIII: Different Modes Of Solution Considered........ 256
Augustine's solution rejected by the Princeton divines. Two forms of the theory of federal headship. Prof. Shedd resorts to a real self-determined choice or governing purpose before consciousness, and in Adam. Theory of Edwards is the personal identity of all men with Adam. Views of Haldane. Exposition of Augustine by Odo of Tournay, and Anselm.

Chapter IX: Disquiet Of The Human Mind....................... 270
The orthodox principles of equity and honor very elevated. The present state of man conceded to be indefensible, except on the ground of a forfeiture of rights. All solutions of the problem of forfeiture unsatisfactory. Final result, the idea of forfeiture rejected. In this no relief is found.

Chapter X: First Result Of Denying A Forfeiture Before Birth.. 277
Pelagianism the direct and logical result. Its first development. Its reappearance in various subsequent ages. Degradation of free agency its result. Elevation and truth of the principles which led to these inauspicious results. Julian of Eclanum, Dr. Channing, Whelpley, and J. Taylor, alike contend for these principles, and so far are correct and unanswerable.

Chapter XI: Second Result Of Denying A Forfeiture........... 284
Summary View Of The Contents. Before Birth. Resolution of human depravity through Adam into divine sovereignty. Cause of this modification of orthodoxy. Its chief development in New England. Hopkins leads the way. The younger Edwards, Dwight, Emmons, and the modern New England divines, follow. It does not give the desired relief. Views of Dr. Watts. Of the Old School divines. Of Unitarians.

Chapter XII: Other Ineffectual Efforts For Relief................. 292
Course adopted by the Semi-pelagians and the Roman Catholic Church. Course pursued by Arminius. Wesley and the Methodist divines. The theory of a forfeiture before birth is still the basis of their systems, and is not properly solved or defended. Calvinists, Lutherans, Arminians and Roman Catholics, here stand on common ground.

Chapter XIII: Estimate Of The Conflict...............................298

It has sprung from the honorable feelings of man, and the experience of Christians of deep piety; and yet has either given superficial views of human depravity, or else obscured the glory of God. The present state of things. Prospects of the future.

BOOK V: THE ARGUMENT

Chapter I: The Mode Of Proceeding.. 304
Question at issue, the truth of preexistence. Proof of the validity of arguments from the facts of the system. The necessity of first considering the alleged testimony of the Bible. Basis of the common doctrine, Rom. 5:12-19.

Chapter II: General View Of The Various Interpretations Of Rom. 5:12-19... 307
Vast and extended influence of the passage. Fundamental idea of the common interpretation. Various theories of the fall in Adam. No exposition of universal authority.

Chapter III: True Interpretation Of Rom. 5:12-19.................... 315
The sense of the passage is judicial, as the Old School divines contend. The death spoken of is natural death, as the primitive church contended. The sequence is merely typical, and not causative. Explanation of this statement.

Chapter IV: Use Of Language In Describing Sequences Of Apparent Causation... 319
They are denoted by the same forms of speech which are used to denote real causation. This mode of speech natural and universal. Case of miracles. Extract from Dr. Smalley. Use of illustrative comparisons.

Chapter V: Use Of Language In Describing Apparent Causation In Types.. 323
Explanation of sequences merely typical. Law of language, as before stated. Cases. The sprinkling of the blood of the paschal lamb. Atonement by sacrifices. Atonement by burning incense. Healing by the brazen serpent. Review of positions.

Chapter VI: Application Of The Preceding Principles To Rom. 5:12-19... 331

The judicial sense is authorized by Chrysostom, Theophylact, Grotius, Storr, Bloomfield, Knapp and others. Tholuck and Stuart concede that the words will admit of it. According to the preceding argument, the sequence is merely typical. The death is merely natural. Illustration of the type. Results.

Chapter VII: Appeal To Authorities.. 336
The judicial sense excludes the New School interpretation. Argument of Prof. Hodge and others in favor of that sense. Result, it is not asserted in the Word of God that the sinfulness of man was caused by the sin of Adam. Virtual coincidence on this point of Dr. Hodge and Dr. Emmons.

Chapter VIII: Import Of The Word *Death* In Rom. 5:12-19........ 347
Its import is natural death. Argument. Authority of the Greek Church. Internal evidence. The facts of the Old Testament. Argument from the antithesis refuted. The sequence is merely typical, whether we adopt the judicial sense, or that of the New School divines.

Chapter IX: Additional Evidence... 353
Analogy of the early types with which this is connected. Appropriateness and sublimity of the view. Root of the common errors. Genius and spirit of Paul demand this view. Moral arguments irresistible.

Chapter X: Case Of Melchizedek... 357
A striking illustration of the laws of typical interpretation involved in this argument. Paul speaks according to the appearance of things, and not according to the reality. Yet he uses the language of reality. Authority of Calvin, Barnes, Stuart, Bloomfield and others. True theory of typical language. Power of Rom. 5: 12-19, thus viewed.

Chapter XI: The Completion Of The Picture. 362
Decline and revival of typical interpretation. The habits of Paul's mind. The sentence of death. The case of Adam. That of his posterity. The antitype. Objections refuted. Paraphrase of the passage. Analogous typical comparisons.

Chapter XII: The Argument Reinforced. 370
General rule. The type is in the natural sphere; the antitype, in the spiritual. Appeal to Scripture. Rule of Fairbairn. To violate this rule overloads the type, and destroys the truth of

the comparison. It also violates all our ideas of justice, and causes a reaction. The final result, and appeal.

Chapter XIII: Survey Of The General Argument.................... 377

The deepest foundations of our religious belief. Principles applied to the being of a God; the evidences of revelation; the Newtonian system. The same mode of reasoning proves preexistence. Illustration in a single line of reasoning. Auxiliary arguments from the failure of all the common theories, and the inadequacy of the cause assigned for effects. Sufficiency of preexistence illustrated by the statements of the Princeton divines and Prof. Stuart. Arguments of Julius Mailer.

Chapter XIV: The Origin Of Evil.. 396

Allegation of Dr. Woods against preexistence, that it merely shifts the difficulty, but does not remove it. Reply. Further allegation that God has the entire control of all the feelings and acts of His creatures. Reply—a temporary limitation of control is implied in the greatness of God and His system, and the limited nature of created minds. This view honors God, and accords with the Bible. It explains the origin of evil, the need of development, and the origin of the present system. Dr. Woods is obliged to concede the principle, and does so in fact. The revealed character of God proves it.

Chapter XV: Argument From The System............................. 408

Outline of the argument. Preexistence unites in a sublime system the great scriptural facts, and harmonizes the action of all the parts. Facts to be united. The common theories fail. A true system of the universe much needed. Essentials of such a system. Common views of the church. A more full view essential. Statement of her real place in the system. Her work. Her worth to God and to the universe. Future in crease of the universe. Analogy of Marriage. Hypothesis of Bellamy. View of Pollok and of Chalmers. Inadequacy of all other systems. Point of the argument. Discriminations.

Chapter XVI: The Material System... 430

Importance of its relations to doctrine and practice. Errors caused by false views of it. Preexistence eradicates them. Tendency of the common doctrine to Gnosticism.

Chapter XVII: Results And Practical Tendencies.................... 435

1. To rescue Christianity from its present perilous position, and to restore to it its legitimate power. 2. To give dignity and elevation to the argument, and certainty to the conclusions derived. 3. To expose the verbal and superficial nature of alleged scriptural objections. 4. To produce sympathy with the whole spirit of the Bible. 5. To relieve difficulties, and introduce sympathy and mutual confidence into future discussions. 6. To avert Pelagianism, and to produce a deeper Christian experience. Favorable omens in the work of E. H. Sears, and in the recent rejection of Pelagianism by Unitarians. Dissent from some of his views. General con cessions as to the good tendencies of the doctrine of preexistence. Origin of the present state of things from ancient ecclesiastical Gnosticism. 7. Beneficial effects of the doctrine of preexistence will disclose themselves in all departments of life.

Appendix...459
Index...481

DEDICATION

My honored and beloved brethren in Christ, of every name.

I AM induced to dedicate this work to you, because its subject is one in which you all have a deep and common interest. You will doubtless observe that I do not address you as a controversialist, aiming to promote the interests of any existing theological party, but simply as a Christian brother, endeavoring to remove the causes of paralysis and division from our common Christianity, and thus to promote the interests of the church as a whole. I think also that you will not deny that the issue which I present to you is of sufficient magnitude to deserve and demand your candid and careful consideration. The great conflict of which I speak is, on the whole, the most prominent and important fact in the history of the church. So great a fact must have an adequate cause. Moreover, a cause powerful enough to produce, for so many centuries, such stupendous results, must also be powerful enough seriously to affect the adaptation of Christianity, as a system, to accomplish all that is involved in the great work of the conversion of the world. It is not enough that the existing system can do some good, or even much good; we need a system that shall give us the power intelligently to meet and logically to solve all of the great religious and social problems which we are called on to encounter in the great work of converting the world, and thoroughly reorganizing human society; for this work is not to be done, even in part, by infidel philosophy, but solely by the gospel of Christ, in its purity and power, as applied to all the relations of human society.

Animated by these considerations, I have endeavored to point out, as the cause of the conflict, an element foreign to the system, and which creates constant and powerful tendencies to pernicious errors in philosophy and in doctrine, divides the church, depresses

1

the tone of piety, and thus paralyzes the energies of Christianity, and unfits it to accomplish the great enterprise which it has undertaken.

Whatever, my Christian brethren, may be your ultimate conclusions concerning the truth of my views, I cannot but believe that every intelligent man will concede that they involve interests so great as to merit a thorough and prayerful consideration.

From this I do not shrink,—nay, I earnestly desire it. My prayer is, *Let God guide His church into all truth, and let the truth prevail.* I feel that such, too, are the momentous relations of the subject that He cannot be indifferent to it; and that if we seek His guidance in true humility, and free from the power of previous committals, it will be freely given. The most profound inquiry, conducted under His guidance, I do not fear. I fear nothing but a partisan spirit and sinful excitement, and those narrow and local views to which they give rise.

But so great is the power and the grace of our God and Savior, Jesus Christ, that I look for better things in you, and things that accompany salvation. God is giving increasing enlargement of views, fraternal affection, and Christian dignity, to the leading minds of His church in the various Christian denominations. Moreover, I think with great and constantly increasing pleasure of that widely-extended circle of sanctified and highly-educated minds, in every Christian body, whom it is my privilege and honor to call my beloved brethren in Christ. I rejoice in the thought of their intellectual and moral power and ample resources, and of the cheering fact that they are all consecrated to the service of our common Lord and Savior. I rejoice still more in the assurance that we are in daily communion with one common God and Father, who is over all, and in all, and through all; and that nothing is too much for us mutually to ask for each other, and to expect to receive through His grace, and the mighty working in us of the power of the divine and sacred Spirit.

May He, therefore, guide you into all the truth, till the light of the moon shall be as the light of the sun, and the light of the sun shall be seven-fold, as the light of seven days; till the watchmen shall see eye to eye, and together lift up the voice and sing, when the Lord shall turn back the captivity of His people, and cause all the nations of the earth to rejoice in His salvation!

Yours, in Christian affection,

E. Beecher, Boston, August 27, 1853.

Introduction

OF the heroes and the conflicts of war I do not propose to speak. It were, indeed, a more exciting theme. The vivid delineation of floating banners, flowing plumes, gorgeous apparel, glittering armor, and the stately march of embattled squadrons, agreeably stimulates and excites the imagination. The fierce onset of contending hosts, and the unutterable horrors of the conflict, arouse the deepest emotions of the soul.

A narrative of the conflicts of minds has not these advantages for popular effect. Such conflicts do not appeal to the senses, nor stimulate the imagination; nor is it easy to create, with respect to them, a popular excitement which shall be powerful and all-pervading. Nevertheless, all intelligent and thoughtful minds feel in them an interest deep and lasting, even though it be less exciting than that which is felt, for a time, in the conflicts of war.

Moreover, if in such intellectual conflicts the deep and honorable emotions of the heart can be unveiled, the interest rises, and often becomes intense.

The conflict of which I propose to write is, and ever has been, in its deepest recesses, a conflict of the heart. Not that gigantic intellectual efforts have not been abundantly put forth, but that the deepest and most powerful impulses have ever been those of the heart.

It has, indeed, often assumed a repulsive external aspect. In the huge volumes of the fathers, or of the scholastic divines, it has been presented in forms wearisome, and devoid of the decorations of rhetoric and the refinements of taste. In modern times, too, the technics of theology have sometimes rendered it mysterious and repulsive.

Yet beneath all this there has always rolled a deeper tide of pure and honorable emotion than has ever flowed from the heart of man on any other theme; moreover, the intellectual aspects of the conflict, viewed from a proper point of vision, have ever been majestic and sublime.

The subject of this conflict has been the greatest and most affecting that can interest or excite the human mind. It has been no less a theme than *The Moral Renovation Of Man*.[1] Through a long course of centuries, the Christian world has been divided into opposing parties on this great question.

On the one side have been the advocates of that system the peculiar characteristic of which is the doctrine of a supernatural regeneration rendered necessary by the native and original depravity of man, and effected according to the eternal purposes of a divine and mysterious sovereignty.

This system has always been exegetically developed from the epistle of Paul to the Romans, as its center and strength. At the same time, however, all other parts of the Word of God are appealed to in its support. Augustine[2] in ancient, and Calvin in modern times, have been preeminent in its development and defense. It has accordingly been called sometimes Pauline, at others Augustinian, and at others Calvinistic theology. It was substantially the theology of the Reformers, and of the Puritans. By the confession of all, it has exerted great power on the destinies of the world. Of its ablest opponents, some have honorably conceded that it has always elevated the tone of morals where it has prevailed. A leading historian of this age also concedes that it has led the van in the conflict for popular liberty. "For a century and a half," says Bancroft,[3] "it assumed the guardianship of liberty for the

---

1   Brown, William Lawrence, D.D. *A Comparative View of Christianity and the Other Forms of Religion*, Charles Tate, London, 1826, Vol II, Part IV, Chap. III, "The Great Object of Christianity is the Moral Renovation of Man, or His Sanctification."

2   Augustine of Hippo (354-430). According to Jerome, Augustine "established anew the ancient Faith." In his early years he was heavily influenced by Manichaeism and afterward by the Neo-Platonism of Plotinus. After his conversion to Christianity he developed a unique approach to philosophy and theology, accommodating a variety of methods and different perspectives.

3   Aaron Bancroft (1755-1839), born in Reading, Massachusetts to Samuel Bancroft and Lydia Parker, was an American clergyman. He served as a minuteman in the American Revolution, and was present, at the battles of both Lexington and Bunker Hill. He graduated from Harvard in 1778, taught, studied theology and spent three years as a missionary in Yarmouth, Nova Scotia. In 1785 he settled in Worcester,

English world." "In Geneva, in Scotland, wherever it gained dominion, it invoked intelligence for the people, and in every parish planted the common school."

Yet, in all ages, ever since the days of Celestius,[4] Julian[5] and Pelagius,[6] there have been, in large numbers, men highly estimable for intelligence and benevolence, and animated by a strong desire of urging society onward in the pursuit of moral excellence, who have, nevertheless, earnestly, perseveringly and with deep emotion, opposed this system, as being at war with the fundamental principles of honor and right, and hostile to the best interests of humanity. In the wide interval between these extremes, other intermediate parties have arisen, attempting in various modes, but hitherto without success, to reconcile the combatants, or in any other way to terminate the conflict. Indeed, these intervening parties have often contended violently among themselves, as well as with each of the extreme parties. The long duration and the astonishing vigor of this conflict indicate that it is not without some permanent and powerful cause. I propose, if possible, to discover that cause, and to state a mode in which all true Christians can, without any sacrifice of principle, be at harmony among themselves. I shall, in doing this, attempt to redeem the first-named system from a just liability to such attacks as it has sustained, by showing that all of its fundamental elements may be so stated and held as not to be inconsistent with the highest principles of honor and right.

I propose at the same time to do full justice to the motives and principles of those who in different ages have opposed it, as has been stated. So far as their principles of honor and right have been correct, it is my purpose to vindicate and defend them; at the same time, endeavoring to explain how it has happened that they have been brought into

---

Massachusetts as pastor of the Congregational church, and remained in the same post until his death in 1839. During the middle of his life his theological views shifted toward Arminianism and by his advocacy of liberalism he became a noted leader in the early period of the Unitarian schism.

4   Celestius was a follower of the Christian teacher Pelagius and the Christian doctrine of Pelagianism, which was opposed to Augustine of Hippo and his doctrine in original sin, and was later declared to be heresy.

5   Julian of Eclanum (386–455) was bishop of Eclanum, near today's Benevento (Italy). He was a distinguished leader of the Pelagians of 5th century.

6   Pelagius (354–420/440) denied the need for divine aid in performing good works. For him, the only grace necessary was the declaration of the law. Human beings were not wounded by Adam's sin and were perfectly able to fulfill the law apart from any divine aid.

conflict with the system which they oppose. I shall endeavor to point out a needless misunderstanding of the parts of the system, by which these principles have been brought into collision with the fundamental facts on which it is based.

To effect these purposes, it will become necessary to give a compendious view of the various efforts of the human mind, in different ages, to remove this antagonism. Such a view, properly given, will exhibit the deep interior emotions, as well as the logical and philosophical reasons, of that great controversy on this subject which has so long existed, and show the relations of its various parts to each other.

I earnestly desire, if possible, so to effect this as to remove the acerbities of feeling which have been caused by the controversies of the present or of past ages on this subject. The merely logical encounters of powerfully developed intellectual systems tend rather to irritation and alienation than to sympathy and confidence. Nevertheless, beneath every benevolent man's intellectual efforts on this subject there has been a deeply affecting personal experience, which, if known, would show, in a manner adapted to awaken deep sympathy, why he has reasoned as he has. Indeed, there is a great heart, not only of natural honor, but, still more, of sanctified humanity, which, from beginning to end, underlies this momentous controversy, the deep workings of which must be developed and appreciated, before the controversy can be properly understood. No honorable mind can see these workings uncovered, and not be touched with deep emotion in viewing the struggles of our common humanity, in endeavoring to resolve the deepest and most momentous problems of the present trying and mysterious system. This experience I aim to unfold, and thus, if I may, to create on all sides a feeling of sympathy and mutual interest, by pointing out those benevolent and honorable impulses, and that regard to truth,—mixed, it may be, with other motives,—by which the various parties have been actuated, and to produce a candid and united effort to eliminate error, and to develop the whole truth.

I am no less anxious to do what I can to save the minds of future inquirers from those painful and exhausting conflicts to which such multitudes have been exposed in ages past, by developing the entire range of the controversy, and sketching the outlines of the whole subject, and thus showing that from the greatest difficulties there is always a possible relief. I aim, moreover, to evince that, in order to a firm and decided defense of the whole Christian system, it is essential that we no longer confine the mind to those limited views of the relations of the church of God in eternity to His whole kingdom, in which it has hitherto generally moved, but that we should rather enter other and more extended fields of thought.

It is also my hope that I may furnish some small contribution to aid in advancing the future triumphs of the kingdom of Christ, by showing the relations of these more extended views to intellectual philosophy, education, and the proper organization of the ecclesiastical, civil and social system.

A due regard to the friends and advocates of certain opinions, which have been long received, but are here controverted, leads me to say that the views which I have presented are not set forth in haste. For more than twenty years, so far as I could judge, I have regarded them as substantially true. But I have, nevertheless, deemed it my duty often to review and reconsider them in the light of past as well as of existing controversies, and also of the word and providence of God. I have been, moreover, in part induced to defer their publication till this time, by a respect to the judgment of honored friends. Still, however, my chief motive for delay has been a desire no longer to watch this great controversy of ages in its present developments, and even to its close,— if, indeed, there should ever be a satisfactory close,—and to ascertain whether anything new could be suggested to give rational relief and unity to the mind of the community, and, at the same time, to mature my own thoughts, so that, if possible. I might avoid a crude and ill-digested presentation of so great a theme.

In reviewing the opinions of others, I have uniformly felt that men who have honestly labored to elucidate so difficult and trying a subject deserve sympathy and respect, and never severity, much less ridicule, even if their results may seem to us in many respects unreasonable or untrue. In this way only can a subject so difficult be treated, with any rational hope of benefiting all whom it concerns. May I not hope that, if any shall consider it their duty to review or to controvert any of my opinions, they will follow the same general principles?

Certainly, if any of my views are false, or any of my arguments unsound, they can be thoroughly exposed, and refuted with calmness, dignity, candor and kindness. Such honorable treatment is what I expect, if any effort shall be made to refute my views. But if, instead of this (which I will not anticipate), my arguments should be encountered with invidious remarks, or ridicule, or appeals to prejudice, then there will be sufficient reason to conclude, and all candid judges will conclude, that there is a conscious want (both desire and lack—Ed.) of anything better with which they can be opposed.

Is it not, however, to be hoped and expected that God, at length, will give to His people such faith in Himself, as the only perfect defender of the truth, that they will practically believe that no degree whatever of sinful feeling can be of any avail, in defending the doctrines of the Bible; nay, that, so far as it exists, it separates the soul from the great source of life and of truth, biases its judgment, and destroys the keenness and discrimination of its perceptions?

Is not the history of the church, in all ages, full of warnings on this point? How prone is depraved humanity, imperfectly sanctified, to be influenced by such considerations and emotions as God abhors! As hating sin, and infinitely exalted above its pollutions, He cannot but regard with utter repulsion any remaining pollutions of His people. He is entirely free from the narrowness of local interests, from envy, from rivalry, from ambition, from sectarian prejudice, from national bias, and from the errors of the age. He is light. He dwells in light; and the essential element of that light is love. How, then, can he who walks in the darkness of sin commune with Him?

He has assured us, moreover, that into this light His church, at length, shall come. To her it shall be given to put on fine linen, clean and white, which is the righteousness of saints. To her shall be given that full knowledge of God which is implied in the marriage supper of the Lamb. To her it shall be said, "Arise! shine! for thy light is come, and the glory of the Lord is risen upon thee!" (Is. 60:1). To her it shall be said, "The sun shall be no more thy light by day; neither for brightness shall the moon give light unto thee; but the Lord shall be unto thee an everlasting light, and thy God thy glory. Thy sun shall no more go down; neither shall thy moon withdraw itself; for the Lord shall be thine everlasting light, and the days of thy mourning shall be ended" (Is. 60:19-20).

If such things are near at hand, may we not hope, or rather, believe, that God will give to all of His own people, who may engage in this and other investigations, so much of His Spirit that they shall walk in His light and dwell in His love?

BOOK I

THE CONFLICT IN ITS PRINCIPLES

Chapter I: The Case Stated

IF into a community but little skilled in the laws of nature and the principles of mechanics a steamship were to be introduced, and if it were stated, as the common traditional direction of mechanics and philosophers, that the wheels should be so adjusted that they would revolve in opposite directions, it may be that the ignorance of the men of that community, and the force of traditional authority, would induce them, at first, to comply with the direction. But if, as would surely be the case, it was found by experiment that, when the wheels so adjusted were put in motion, the boat, so far from obeying her rudder, or taking an onward course, would do nothing but revolve incessantly round, without progress,—and, moreover, that her whole frame was unnaturally wrenched and strained by this method of procedure, and that, meantime, she had no power so to resist the winds and currents that they would not drift her wheresoever they would, —then, in all probability, the men in that community would repudiate the traditional direction which they had received, as inconsistent with the necessary and immutable laws of mechanics, and introducing discord and conflict into the system to which it was applied. And if, on adjusting the wheels so that they would both revolve in the same direction, it was found that the boat moved straight on in obedience to her rudder, and was able to resist the power of winds and currents, they would feel abundantly confirmed in their conviction of the essential falsehood of the traditional direction; nor could any amount of authority avail against this practical demonstration, taken from the working of the system itself.

An argument of the same kind, and of no less power, would rationally arise from the practical workings of a system of theology, against any traditional adjustment of its parts, if it had been found, on trial, to cause its main moving powers, in like manner, to work against each other,—thus introducing perpetual internal conflict into the very vitals of the system.

No question can be more interesting or important than whether there is good reason to believe that such a traditional misunderstanding has been introduced into the current system of Christianity; and whether, in consequence of it, the main moving powers of the system have been made, from age to age, to work against each other; and whether at this hour there is an internal conflict in the system, which no wit or skill of man can remove or overcome, till the traditional misunderstanding from which it springs has been repudiated. For, if such be the fact, never, till the misunderstanding is removed, will the moving powers of the system work together,—never, till then, will the internal conflict cease. Whether such is the fact is the question to be considered.

CHAPTER II: PRESUMPTIVE ARGUMENT

THAT this is the case, we may derive a presumptive proof from the history of certain recent wide-spread theological controversies among ourselves. No controversy in the theological world has excited a deeper interest among those who are reputed—and that justly —the decided friends of orthodoxy, than that between those who are familiarly called, in the Congregational and Presbyterian churches, "the Old School" and "the New School" divines.[1] These terms have, in themselves, little significance. Their import will be more fully disclosed as we proceed. It is sufficient here to remark, that New England has been the great fountainhead of the new divinity, and that the theological seminary at Princeton has been conceded to be the strongest citadel of the old theology. The two denominations among whom this conflict has been most fully developed have exerted, from the beginning, a very powerful influence in forming the character and shaping the destinies of this nation. The influence of the controversy has also extended to other denominations. If, then, we view our relations as a nation to the world, no one can properly say that this is merely a local controversy. Affecting deeply, as it does, the religious interests of this nation, it affects, also, those of the world. No one who is familiarly acquainted with those engaged in this controversy can deny that the great body on both sides are eminently pious, devoted, laborious, useful men. They profess, alike to be followers of the great reformers, and to regard with peculiar favor the system of doctrines developed by Calvin. They are, alike, the antagonists of formalism, and of ecclesiastical despotism, and the advocates of spiritual religion, of collegiate and popular education, of revivals of religion, and of the benevolent enterprises of the age. There is no good

---

1   The Old School-New School Controversy was a schism of the Presbyterian Church in the United States of America which began in 1837. Later, both the Old School and New School branches further split over the issue of slavery, into southern and northern churches. The Old School were Calvinists, and the New School were Arminians and Unitarians.

reason, therefore, why they should not have loved each other with a pure heart fervently, and no reason, so far as the great fundamentals of doctrine and practice are concerned, why they should not have been perfectly joined together in one mind and in one judgment. Brotherly love, in its elevated forms, is one of the happiest experiences of the human mind; nor is there any manifestation of which is more honorable to God, or more powerful to produce conviction of the divine origin of Christianity. How much, then, might these Christian brethren have enjoyed, how much might they have honored God, how much might they have blessed the world, if they had been united with the full power and fervor of common convictions and brotherly love!

And yet, instead of this, for years there has been between them an incessant controversy. In it, an incredible amount of intellect, emotion and energy, has been expended. Each party has been filled with alarm at the dangerous tendencies, or alleged pernicious influence, of some fondly-cherished principles of the other, as threatening either to subvert the gospel or to destroy its power. They have, therefore, conscientiously put forth great efforts to destroy the influence and arrest the progress of each other. As a natural and necessary result, in the course of this controversy there has been, in various ways, a vast amount of mental suffering. Pious men, deeply devoted to God, and earnestly laboring to effect the moral renovation and salvation of their fellow-men, have been cut to the heart by a keen sense of injustice, when suspicions have been created and disseminated, or even direct charges made, that they were unsound in the faith, and dangerous heresiarchs. Others have been pained and irritated by the charge of holding gross and exploded absurdities, dishonorable to God and ruinous to man. The amount of influence thus employed by good men to neutralize each other's power has been immense, nor has it failed to produce its natural effects. The internal struggles and convulsions thus produced in this large body of churches have wasted an amount of energy great almost beyond imagination. The Presbyterian church has been twice rent asunder. The New England Congregational churches, incapable, by reason of their organization, of such a division, have yet been, in fact, thrown into opposing parties, and agitated and torn by incessant and painful strife.

Meantime, in the eyes of intelligent spectators, riot familiar with theological debates, religion itself has been dishonored. How can it be otherwise, when such eminent men as have figured in these unhappy controversies, on both sides,—men who have had no superiors in the land,—have not only been arrayed in strife against each other, but have brought against each other charges of the most serious and injurious kind? We have, by custom, become familiar with this state of things, and do not at once apprehend its unspeakable evils. But, if we could suppose entire confidence and ardent brotherly love to have existed for the last century among the leading minds of these churches, and all their energies consecrated to the great departments of education, religious revivals, and benevolent enterprise, who can conceive how much greater the impulse that had been given to the cause of God, not only in our own land, but throughout the whole world!

And when these intelligent spectators ask, what are the points on which these good men are so divided, and in view of which they expend so much energy in destroying each other's power, it is very hard to give a reply which shall be brief, intelligible and satisfactory to the common mind. No one or two great, prominent, definite, intelligible scriptural doctrines can be stated by which a fundamental line of distinction can be drawn between them. They profess, in fact, to hold the same great revealed doctrines, and to differ only in certain modes of stating, explaining, and defending them.

Nor are developments of this kind limited to the last fifty or one hundred years, nor to the Presbyterian and Congregational churches of this land. The controversy has not, indeed, always been developed under its present names, nor with the same extent and system. But its essential elements have existed—as I shall soon show—as far back as the third or fourth century since Christ, and have been developed, in various forms, in each succeeding century, to this day, and in almost, if not quite, every Christian body.

It has been, moreover, in all ages, as it is now, a controversy among sincere Christians. It is, in this respect, entirely unlike the atheistic, pantheistic, infidel, and other controversies, in which all real Christians are on one side. But by this controversy, in all ages, as now, real Christians are divided against real Christians.

It is also worthy of special note, that this is a controversy in which no permanent and radical progress has as yet been made towards a final settlement. Good men are at this day as really and as thoroughly divided against good men as they ever were. At one time, the New School Theology (so called), proceeding from New England, seems to be carrying all before it in the Presbyterian church. Then there is a division, and a combination, not only without, but also within New England, to react upon it, and to restore the Old School theology to its original power. So has it been, in other ages and climes. Action and reaction have followed each other, but no substantial progress towards a termination of the controversy has ever been made.

Until at some future time this controversy shall cease, no one can tell how much it has weakened and paralyzed the whole church of God, and fatally destroyed its onward and impulsive power. Like the ship supposed, she has obeyed no rudder of universally admitted principle, but has drifted at the mercy of the winds and currents of controversy.

And yet no serious suspicion seems ever to have been awakened, that, after all, the difficulty lies, not in the alleged points of difference, but in some false adjustment, in which both parties agree, and by which the great moving powers of the system have been made to act against each other; and that, until this false adjustment is removed, there is a necessary and inevitable conflict in the system itself.

Is it not time, then, to consider this aspect of the case? Is not such a thing supposable? And does not this endless conflict of good men, with no progress, and no result but to cripple and neutralize each other, render the supposition in no small degree probable?

Such probability, however, is not all the evidence that the case demands, nor, happily, is it all that exists. It is possible, not only to show what are the two great moving powers of Christianity, but, also, to prove that they have been so adjusted that they do, in fact, work against each other, and thus produce necessary division and conflict in the system. Of this it now remains to adduce the proof.

CHAPTER III: THE MOVING POWERS OF CHRISTIANITY

BY the moving powers of Christianity, I mean those truths which in practice are of fundamental importance in the great work of moral renovation. Moral renovation is the great practical end for which the system of Christianity is designed, and in which it terminates. This work presupposes depravity in man, and a system of means ordained for its removal. Christ thus states His own views of His great aim and end. "I came not to call the righteous, but sinners, to repentance. The Son of Man is come to seek and save that which is lost" (Mt. 9:13, Mk. 2:7, Lk. 5:32). This is to be effected by producing in sinful man conviction of sin, a true and honorable sense of its evils, repentance and faith in Christ. But true repentance and confession of sin imply a conviction that the conduct of God towards the sinner has been in all things honorable and right, and that His own conduct towards God has been wrong, dishonorable, and without excuse. It is plain, therefore, that those are the great moving powers of Christianity which are essential in order to produce these results. It is no less plain that they are the two following:

1. A true and thorough statement of what is involved in the fallen and ruined condition of man as a sinner.
2. A full development of the honor, justice, and benevolence of God, in all His dealings with man, so made as in the first place, to free Him from the charge of dishonorably ruining them, and then to exhibit Him as earnestly and benevolently engaged in efforts for their salvation, through Christ, after they have been ruined by their own fault.

Of these two moving powers, each is equally indispensable in the great work of renovating and saving man. Till he is brought truly to see and deeply to feel his lost and ruined state, and the dangers to which he is exposed, he will make no effort to secure a salvation of which he feels no need.

Nor, on the other hand, can anyone sincerely and honorably confess and repent, if his views of God are such that he regards Him as, by unjust and dishonorable measures, the author of his ruin. He may feel slavish fear, but he will not feel genuine repentance, till he admits the charge that the entire guilt is his own, and believes that God can forgive him through Christ, and is earnestly and benevolently engaged in efforts for his salvation.

In these views, thus generally stated, we think that all true Christians will agree. They may differ in the manner in which they would develop the truths included under each of these great heads. But, that the practical working power of the system depends upon them, no one, we think, will deny.

These, then, are the two great moving powers of Christianity. These, to resume our original comparison, are the wheels which must be so adjusted as to work harmoniously together, before Christianity as a system can exert its full power. These, too, are the powers which, as we propose to show, have been made, by an unhappy misunderstanding, to work against each other, and hence the calamitous results that have been already set forth.

Before attempting definitely to state what is the alleged misunderstanding, it is important, in the first place, to prove that the conflict said to be caused by it really exists, and is unavoidable as the system is now adjusted. This will be made perfectly apparent by a mere statement of what is involved in a full development of each of these great moving powers.

Chapter IV: The Principles Of Honor And Of Right

WHAT, then, are the principles of honor and of right by which the conduct of God ought to be regulated in His dealings with His creatures, and especially with new-created minds? A knowledge of these is manifestly essential, in order to set forth that great moving power of Christianity, which I announced as the second, but shall consider as in the order of nature the first.

This is, as has been said, a full development of the honor, righteousness and benevolence of God towards His sinful creatures, so as, in the first place, to free Him from the charge of dishonorably causing their ruin, and then to exhibit Him as earnestly and benevolently engaged in efforts, through Christ, for their salvation when lost, so that he can truly say, "Thou hast destroyed thyself, but in me is thy help!"

The elements of this great moving power of Christianity are to be derived from those natural judgments, concerning the principles of honor and right, which God has made the human mind to form with intuitive certainty, and which He designed to be a divine disclosure to us of the principles by which He regulates His own conduct.

Inasmuch, however, as the mind of man is depraved, and there may be danger in trusting its unrevised and uncorrected decisions as to these principles, it is of great importance, for purposes of revision, carefully to study those developments of benevolent, honorable and just feelings, towards which the human mind, after regeneration, and under the guidance of the Holy Spirit, is found most directly to tend.

The results thus obtained we are again to verify, by comparing them, as far as may be, with the explicit statements of the Word of God.

This great moving power deserves particular attention. It is of fundamental importance in this whole investigation. No man will call in question what he concedes to be a real decision of God, however made; but there have been, and still are, those who think so much more of the verbal revelations of God than of any other, that they almost overlook the fact that the foundations of all possible knowledge have been laid by God in the consciousness and the intuitive perceptions of the mind itself. Forgetful of this fact, they have often, by unfounded interpretations of Scripture, done violence to the mind, and overruled the decisions made by God Himself through it, and then sought shelter in faith and mystery. To avert, therefore, such results, I shall proceed in the manner already suggested, to show that there are divinely-given convictions as to honor and right, and to state such of them as are required by the present discussion.

That there are, then, fundamental judgments concerning honor and right, which God has made the human mind to form with intuitive certainty, and which He designed to be a divine disclosure of the principles by which He regulates His own conduct, has been extensively held by leading divines and philosophers. Dr. Alexander[2] says, "That God, as a moral governor, has incorporated the elements of his law into our very constitution." He with great earnestness maintains, so his son assures us, "the intuitive perceptions of conscience as independent of every doctrine of theology, even the greatest." Other authorities might be quoted, but it is better to rest the case upon the testimony of God Himself, and not upon the decisions of uninspired teachers. The doctrine before us is an expressly revealed doctrine of the Word of God. Nor has it been revealed incidentally, and in unimportant relations; but formally, and as the basis of God's proceedings in the most important transaction of the present dispensation,—a transaction vitally affecting the interests of the greatest portion of the human race. I refer to the final judgment of all who have lived and died without a written revelation of the laws of God. That such will be judged and punished for their sins, is distinctly announced by the Apostle Paul (Rom. 2:12, 16). The reason which justifies this mode of proceeding is there distinctly declared to be that God has so constituted their minds that their intuitive decisions on questions of honor and right are, in fact, a law of God, although not revealed by a written revelation. Listen, then, to the divine statement:

---

2   Archibald Alexander (1772-1851), an American Presbyterian theologian and professor at the Princeton Theological Seminary. He served for 27 years as that institution's first principal from 1812 to 1840.

"For when the Gentiles, which have not the (revealed) law,
do by nature the things contained in the law, these, having
not the law, are a law unto themselves; which show the
work of the law written in their hearts,—their conscience
also bearing witness, and their thoughts the meanwhile accusing, or else excusing, one another" (Rom. 2:14).

It is not necessary here to go into a careful analysis of words or
phrases, for the main truth which I am considering lies on the very
face of the passage. God, it assures us, will judge the Gentiles at the last
day, though they have no revealed law, "Because they are a law unto
themselves, inasmuch as the work of the law is written on their hearts;"
that is, because he has so made their minds that a standard of judgment
is disclosed by their natural and intuitive perceptions and convictions
of honor and right. Indeed, so clear is the case, that leading commentators of all schools coincide in this interpretation.

Prof. Hodge[3] says, in commenting on the assertion that the Gentiles "do by nature the things of the law." When they practice any of
the virtues, or perform any moral acts, these acts are evidence of a
moral sense; they show that the Gentiles have a rule of right and
wrong, and a feeling of obligation; or in other words, that they are

"a law unto themselves. When the Gentiles are said to do by
nature the things of the law, it is meant that they have not
been taught by others. It is neither by instruction nor example, but by their own innate sense of right and wrong, that
they are directed. Having this natural sense of right and
wrong, though destitute of a law externally revealed, they
are a law unto themselves."

Prof. Stuart[4] declares that the import of the passage, as a reply to
the Jew, is,

---

3   Charles Hodge (1797-1878), the principal of Princeton Theological Seminary be-
    tween 1851 and 1878, was a leading exponent of historical Calvinism and was
    deeply rooted in the Scottish philosophy of Common Sense Realism.

4   Moses Stuart (1780-1852), an American biblical scholar who gradually made the ac-
    quaintance of German works in hermeneutics, first Johann Friedrich Schleusner,
    Seiler and Gesenius, and taught himself German. Known for his *Letter to Dr Chan-
    ning on the Subject of Religious Liberty* (1830), but more largely through the growing
    favor shown to German philology and critical methods.

"Although a heathen man has no scripture (and in this respect no law), yet he has an internal revelation inscribed on his heart, which is a rule of life to him, and which, if perfectly obeyed, would confer justification on him, as well and as truly as entire obedience to the written law could confer it upon you." As a matter of fact, however, he holds that neither Jew nor Gentile does so obey as to be justified. Prof. Stuart again says, "Those commit a great mistake who deny that men can have any sense of moral duty or obligation without a knowledge of the Scriptures. The apostle's argument, in order to convince the Gentiles of sin, rests on a basis entirely different from this." Again, the statement that the work of the law is written on their hearts means, in his judgment, "That the great precepts of moral duty are deeply impressed on our moral nature, and coexist with it, even when it is unenlightened by special revelation."

Dr. Chalmers[5] says of the apostle's reasoning, in verse 15, "There seem here to be two distinct proofs of the Gentiles being a law unto themselves. The first is from the fact of there being a conscience individually at work in each bosom, and deposing either to the merit or demerit of actions; the second, from the fact of their accusing or excusing one another in the reasonings or disputes which took place between man and man." This proves them to be in possession of a common rule or standard of judging; or in other words, that a law is actually among them. So true is it, even in its application to the Gentiles, that there is a light "which lighteth every man who cometh into the world" (Jn. 1:9). Again,

"There do exist, even in the remotest tracks of paganism, such vestiges of light, as, when collected together, form a code or directory of moral conduct. There are still to be found among them the fragments of a law, which they never follow but with an approving conscience, and never

5   Thomas Chalmers (1780-1847), a Scottish mathematician, political economist, and a leader of the Free Church of Scotland, was known for series of sermons on the relation between the discoveries of astronomy and the Christian revelation published in 1817. Within a year nine editions and 20,000 copies were in circulation. When he visited London Wilberforce wrote, "all the world is wild about Dr Chalmers."

violate but with the check of an opposing remonstrance, that by their own wilfulness and their own obstinacy is overborne,—in other words, they are a law unto themselves, and their conscience vests it with an authority, by bearing witness to the rightness and obligation of its requirements."

Tholuck[6] remarks,

"By the law written on the heart, Paul meant the conscience,—that which constitutes the bond of relationship between man and God, and which discovers itself as a sense of what is just and good." Again, "When the Gentile contemplated the law written within him as a commandment inscribed by God himself upon his heart, he might feel himself excited to obedience by a reverential awe of what is holy. This feeling, although it did not govern men's lives among the Greeks, comes yet nobly forward in many sentiments of the tragic poets. To cite one example, see the admirable chorus upon conscience in *Œdipus Tyrannus*."

In striking accordance with these views, Melancthon[7] has with great eloquence said,

"Wherefore our decision is this: that those precepts which learned men have committed to writing, transcribing them from the common reason and common feelings of human nature, are to be accounted as not less divine than those contained in the tables given to Moses; and, that it could not be the intention of our Maker to supersede, by a law graven on stone, that which is written by his own finger on the table of the heart."

Calvin,[8] commenting on this passage, strongly enforces the same views:

---

6   Friedrich August Gottreu Tholuck (1799-1877), known as August Tholuck, was a German Protestant theologian and church leader. His book, *Die wahre Weihe des Zweiflers* (1823), put him into the permanent position of the modern Pietistic apologist of Evangelical Christianity.

7   Philipp Melanchthon (1497-1560) was a German reformer and collaborator with Martin Luther. He was the first systematic theologian of the Protestant Reformation, and an intellectual leader of the Lutheran Reformation.

"Since all nations are spontaneously inclined to enact laws for themselves, it is too clear to be doubted that there are certain conceptions of justice and right which exist by nature in the minds of men." "He opposes nature to the written law, meaning that a natural light of justice illuminates the Gentiles, which supplies the place of the law by which the Jews are instructed, so that they are a law unto themselves."[9]

Nor have these views been promulgated solely by the apostle Paul. Our Savior, in His controversies with the Jews, assumed the existence of native and intuitive principles of right,—of divine authority,—and appealed to them, and called on His antagonists to do the same (Luke 12: 57).

"Yea, why, even of yourselves, judge ye not what is right?" The system of Christ, to use the words of Henry,[10] "has reason and natural conscience on its side; and, if men would allow themselves the liberty *of judging what is right*, they would soon find that all Christ's precepts concerning all things are right." Calvin says, on this passage, "Here Christ lays open the source of the evil, and touches, as it were with a lancet, the internal ulcer; they would not descend into their own consciences, and, before God, inquire within themselves what is right."

Abraham, moreover, in his plea for guilty Sodom, first adduced certain intuitive principles of right, and then, by the appeal, "Shall not the Judge of all the earth do right?" assumed not only that the mind of MAN was made intuitively to perceive the principles of right, but also that GOD was as truly bound by them as man; and God Himself, by His reply, sanctioned the assumption. He has also at other times sanctioned it, particularly in that impressive argument with the Jews, contained in the eighteenth and thirty-third chapters of Ezekiel, in which

---

8   John Calvin (1509-1564), born in France and fled to Switzerland, was an influential French theologian and pastor during the Protestant Reformation.

9   I do not quote the preceding authors to sanction the peculiar theory of anyone as to the nature and action of conscience, but only their great common doctrine, that God has so made the mind that it has in some way intuitive perceptions of honor and right (Beecher).

10 Matthew Henry (1662-1714) was an English commentator on the Bible and Presbyterian minister. His well-known six-volume *Exposition of the Old and New Testaments* (1708–1710) or *Complete Commentary*, provides an exhaustive verse by verse study of the Bible.

he appeals to the natural convictions of the human mind concerning what is honorable and right, in vindication of his own conduct against the charge that his ways were not equal. The conclusion of his argument is this, "Are not my ways equal, and are not your ways unequal? saith the Lord" (Ezk. 18:29). Thus he did not repudiate the standard of judgment before which they sought to try his ways; but admitting its authority as a natural revelation proceeding from himself, he joined issue with them, and declared that he could endure the scrutiny, and that they could not. Indeed, it is the highest, the crowning glory of God, that He can thus "overcome when he is *judged*" (Rom. 3:4).

It is proper that I should here call particular attention to the reason why I have so largely unfolded the scriptural evidence in favor of the position which I have laid down. I have done it for the sake of prominence and impression, and fixed attention. It is, because an appeal to the natural and intuitive principles of honor and right, such as I shall soon have occasion to make, is often regarded and treated as an improper and dangerous species of rationalizing. Of this we may see striking illustrations before we close this discussion. I deem it therefore important—nay, essential—to show that the position which I shall hereafter assume is not improper rationalism, but a doctrine of the Word of God, as clearly revealed as the doctrine of depravity itself. God Himself declares that the intuitive perceptions of the human mind, as to honor and right, are a revelation from the Creator,—a divine law, of supreme and binding authority. God Himself enjoins it on men, as a sacred duty, to judge by them. He does not feel honored by any defense which disregards them. Nay, He admits that His own conduct is amenable to judgment by these principles, and defends Himself by an appeal to the same.

I admit, indeed, that few have dared openly to deny that there are among men such intuitive principles of honor and right; but nevertheless, some, as we shall soon see, when pressed by their application to certain alleged acts of God, have denied that they are common alike to God and to man, and alike binding on both. Concerning this view, I would say, with emphasis, that it is a most unfounded and pernicious position. It is unfounded; for who has ever adduced, or can adduce, any evidence of its truth? It is most pernicious; for it destroys that which Tholuck so impressively calls "the bond of relationship between God and man." Indeed, it would subvert the very foundations of the government of God. How could we see or adore the glories of the divine character, how could we ever enter into rational and joyful communion with God, if He had so made our minds that our intuitive judgments of honor and right were, or could be, opposed to His own? How could we ever correctly judge of the honor or rectitude of His conduct, if the standard of honor and rectitude revealed by Him in the structure of our minds, did not agree with His own standard on the same points? Such a state of things would lay the foundation of necessary and eternal discord between Him and us, and that on the most important of all practical questions. We must therefore of necessity assume, not only that there are judgments concerning honor and right which God has made the human mind to form with intuitive certainty, but that they are common to God and to man. This is a fundamental doctrine of the Bible. To test any alleged acts of God by such principles, is not improper rationalizing. God not only authorizes, but even enjoins it as a sacred duty. To this point I call special attention.

It is no less plain, that whatever these principles are, their authority is supreme. No considerations of mere expediency or policy, whether individual or general, if opposed to them, ought to have any force; nor with God can they have any force. Though there is above Him neither judge nor judgment to which He is responsible, yet He has, in His own mind, an eternal and immutable law of honor and right which He cannot disregard, and He is His own omniscient judge. Should He not follow His own convictions of honor and of right, He could not retain His own self-respect, but would experience infinite self-condemnation and remorse; He would be the most miserable being in the universe. It is, therefore, an infinite necessity in God's own nature that He should obey the laws of honor and of right; and, beyond all doubt, He ever has, and ever will. A summary of these laws is nowhere explicitly and systematically set forth in the Word of God: they are rather from time to time assumed, as exigences occur.

Nor, so far as I know, has it been customary in setting forth the Christian system to attempt any formal statement of them. For this, obvious reasons may, in certain cases, account. Acts have been by some ascribed to God, which to say the least, are at war with our common ideas of equity and honor. In such cases, it is natural, as far as may be, to avoid a formal statement of these ideas.

If, however, the subject cannot be avoided, the same causes tend to produce a constrained and unnatural action of the mind. The supposed acts of God are assumed as a standard, and all principles are re-

jected that disagree with them; or, at least, it is said that, though true
with respect to man, they are not with respect to God; and that He is
not bound by them, though man is. Indeed, this has been done to a
great extent, as will be shown in the cases of Pascal,[11] Abelard,[12] and
others; and has, as might have been expected, revealed its tendencies
by its disastrous influences on the mind. An effort to eradicate from
the mind any real principle of honor and right does violence to our intellectual and moral nature. Such principles cannot be exterminated.
They will protest against the violence. The mind still yearns after
them, and cannot rest and be satisfied till they are assumed as true.

These principles, so far as involved in this inquiry, have reference
to the following points, among others:

1. The distinction that ought to be made between the innocent
    and the guilty.
2. The distinction that ought to be made between original con-
    stitution and responsible moral character.
3. The relations and obligations that exist between great and
    powerful minds and such as are more feeble and limited, and
    especially between the great self-sustained Mind and such as
    are inferior and dependent.
4. The obligations of the Creator to new-created beings, as to
    their original constitution, powers, circumstances, and proba-
    tion.

On all these points God has made the human mind to have decided intuitive convictions as to what is consistent with equity and
honor. These we are not violently to suppress by preconceived theories, or assumed facts. If any alleged actions of God come into collision
with the natural and intuitive judgments of the human mind concerning what is honorable and right on the points specified, there is better

---

11 Blaise Pascal (1623-1662) was a French mathematician, physicist, inventor, writer
    and Catholic philosopher. In 1646, he and his sister Jacqueline identified with the
    religious movement within Catholicism known by its detractors as Jansenism. Fol-
    lowing a mystical experience in late 1654, he had a "second conversion," abandoned
    his scientific work, and devoted himself to philosophy and theology. His two most
    famous works date from this period: the *Lettres provinciales* and the *Pensées*, the for-
    mer set in the conflict between Jansenists and Jesuits.
12 Peter Abelard (1079-1142) was a medieval French scholastic philosopher, theologian
    and preeminent logician.

reason to call in question the alleged facts than to suppose those principles to be false which God has made the human mind intuitively to
recognize as true. Moreover, we have divine authority for so doing;
since, in a debate with the Jews, involving these points, God does not
hesitate to appeal to these very principles, and to reason in perfect accordance with their common and obvious decisions (Ezek. 18: 1-4, 19,
22, 25, 29, and 33: 11, 17-20).

It has been already stated that aid is to be derived, in developing
and arranging the principles of honor and right, by considering those
manifestations of thought and conviction towards which the human
mind, when regenerated and sanctified, and under the guidance of the
Holy Spirit, most directly tends. It cannot be supposed that the
progress of true sanctification tends to make men unlike God in
thought, emotions and convictions; but, rather, to restore them more
fully to his lost image, and to prepare them for that intimate and perfect communion with Him for which the redeemed are especially designed.

How far the unregenerated mind can, in fact, be perverted in its
moral judgments by depravity, I shall not here undertake to decide.
But, so far as there is a liability of this kind, it is plainly removed so far
as the mind is sanctified, and thus restored to its normal state of sympathetic communion with God. In this state, its moral decisions ought
justly to be regarded as more and more evidently in harmony with
those of God.

The remaining source which I have specified, from which we can
derive aid in revising and perfecting our systematic enunciation of the
principles of honor and right, is to be found in the incidental assumptions and statements of the Word of God. Though there is not, as has
been remarked, any complete formal and systematic view of this subject given in the Bible, yet, in various occasional assertions and incidental statements, God has clearly set forth His own feelings and
views.

The fact that so much less intellectual effort has ever been expended in setting forth the demands of honor and justice on God, in
His dealings with new-created minds, than has been in stating and
proving the ruined condition of man, is, probably, the reason that no
public formularies have ever made any explicit statements on the subject. In consequence of this, and of the fact that it has not been common formally to discuss it in systems of theology, I shall not be able to

make full statements of conceded principles in the systematized formulas of others, as I propose to do on the subject of human depravity. I
shall, on the other hand, derive my statements from a careful examination and consideration of the sources of evidence already stated, and
then compare them with incidental statements by others.

CHAPTER V: STATEMENT OF MORAL PRINCIPLES

WHAT, then, are the principles of honor and right on the various points which have been specified?

1.   God has made us intuitively to perceive and feel, and therefore He also perceives and feels, that increase of powers to any degree of magnitude produces, not a decrease, but an increase, of obligation to feel and act benevolently towards inferiors,—that is, with an honorable regard to their true and highest good.

In proportion as a mind is strong, independent, and abundantly able to secure its own welfare, it is free from temptations to be absorbed in its own interests and cares, and is at leisure to think and feel and plan for others, whose welfare is not thus secure.

Moreover, as the powers of the superior mind increase, he has the greater ability to do good or evil to inferior minds. Of course, his obligation to use it for their good increases. Moreover, the influence of his example increases as his powers increase. Of course, he is bound by a proportionate obligation to make it such as all can safely imitate.

No moral principles are recognized as true with a clearer and more absolute intuition than those which I have now stated.

How is it in the parental relation? Do not all feel that the superior powers of parents create an obligation of the most touching and imperative kind towards a weak, defenseless, new-born infant? Do not such superior powers, and the fact that their example will exert a controlling influence, sacredly bind them in all things so to use their powers, and regulate their example, as to promote the highest good of the young heir of immortality who lies helpless in their arms? Would it not seem unspeakably horrible to allege their superior powers as a reason for doing otherwise?

If, therefore, God gives existence to inferior and dependent minds, is He, the Infinite Father—can He be—under any other or different obligations? Does He desire us to think of Him as not tenderly affected, and not bound by the appeal made to Him by a new-created mind, in view of the fearful eternity that spreads out before Him, so to exert His infinite powers, and so to order His infinite example, as shall most entirely tend to promote His eternal good? Does not every intuitive conviction, every honorable impulse of a benevolent mind, call for such an assurance concerning God, in order to be satisfied with His character? Is not this the dividing line between the divine and the satanic spirit? When, in this world, those who have gained wealth, knowledge and power, separate themselves in feeling and sympathy from the poor, ignorant and weak, and form select and exclusive circles, as if their superior powers and advantages imposed on them no obligation to sympathize with the sufferings and promote the welfare of those below them, can anything more perfectly illustrate the satanic spirit of him whose law is selfishness? Ought not the spirit of God to be entirely the reverse of this? Is it not? Could He be honorable or righteous if it were not so? Does anyone allege His right, as creator, to do as He will with His creatures? Within certain limits, He has this right. But creation gives no right to the creator to disregard or to undervalue the well-being of creatures, or to treat them contrary to the laws of their intellectual, moral and voluntary nature, on the ground that He created them. It is not enough to say, that, as He would treat them if He had not made them, so ought He now to treat them. On the other hand, the fact that He created them makes the most touching of all appeals to every principle of honor and right in the Almighty Creator to be their defender, protector, and friend.

If it is said that God, as the greatest of all beings, makes Himself and not His creatures His great end, it is enough to say, in reply, even if this were so,—on which I do not feel called upon now to express an opinion,—still, God cannot promote either His own happiness or glory, except by the observance of the principles of honor and right of which we are now speaking. Even if, therefore, He makes Himself His chief end, He must observe them. Nor could He make any other truly honorable minds happy if He were to disregard these principles, for the sake of any supposed greater good of which they are to partake. A truly honorable mind cannot conceive of a higher good, than that the God whom he loves and adores should fulfill to the highest conceivable degree of exactness, every demand of honor and right to every created mind, however small.

No personal honor, no exaltation, no amount of enjoyment, would bribe such a mind to be satisfied with a God who (even for His sake) had disregarded the principles of honor to anyone, even the least of all created minds. And it calls for a serious review of His opinions, if anyone is conscious of ascribing to God acts which make him fear to admit this principle in its full extent. God glories in defending the smallest and the feeblest of all His creatures.

2.   No man, unless compelled by some supposed necessity, would ever think of denying that the principles of honor and right and call upon God not to hold His creatures responsible or punishable for anything in them of which they are not the authors, but of which He is, either directly or indirectly, the creator, and which exists in them anterior to and independent of any knowledge, desire, choice or action, of their own. Whatever thus exists is a part of the original constitution conferred by the Creator on His creatures; and for this He is obviously responsible, and not they. His creatures are responsible only for that moral character which consists in or flows from their own voluntary use of the powers conferred on them by Him. To prove the truth of this statement, no argument is needed. It is one of the clearest and most absolute intuitive perceptions of the mind. God has so made our nature that we recognize its truth with a clearness and certainty that cannot be increased. This is distinctly recognized as the true ground of responsibility in the inspired volume (Scripture). It is so expressly stated by God, through the prophet Ezekiel. The sentence of death is denounced upon the soul that sins, and none else (Ezekiel, chapters 18 and 33). The coming judge of all declares, "My reward is with me, to give to every man according as his work shall be" (Rev. 22:12). The apostle Paul also announces that, before the judgment seat of Jesus Christ, every man shall receive according to what he has done, whether it be good or bad. But nowhere in the Word of God is it ever stated that a man is rewarded or punished for an involuntary constitution, which he received from God.

3. The principles of honor and right require of God, inasmuch as He demands of His creatures that they do what is right, and inasmuch as this demand is founded in the nature of things, that He should not Himself confound the distinction between right and wrong, by dealing with the righteous as with the wicked. The patriarch Abraham, in

his most eloquent and touching plea for guilty Sodom, assumed that the judge of all the earth would do wrong if He did this. "That be far from thee to do after this manner, to slay the righteous with the wicked; and that the righteous should be as the wicked, that be far from thee; shall not the judge of all the earth do right?" (Gen. 18:25). Did God repudiate this assumption of Abraham, that righteous man, whom He was not ashamed to call His friend? Nay, verily, He rather accepted and confirmed it by His approval. With reference to this point, Dr. Alexander, therefore, well says, "All intuitively discern, that, for a ruler to punish the innocent, and spare the guilty, is morally wrong" (p. 36). Still further; inspiration has decided that it is essential to true faith in God to believe, not only that He is, but that He is a rewarder of those who diligently seek Him.

4. The principles of honor and right demand of God not to so charge the wrong conduct of one being to others as to punish one person for the conduct of another, to which he did not consent, and in which he had no part. No decision of the human mind concerning honor and right can be clearer than this, and it is distinctly recognized by God as true. When the Jews, in the days of Ezekiel, charged Him with injustice, for punishing them for sins which they had never committed,—that is, for the sins of their fathers,—he did not admit the truth of the charge, and claim the right to so punish; but he indignantly, and in every variety of form, denied the fact alleged, and declared that the son should not bear the iniquity of the father, nor the father that of the son, but that every man should bear his own iniquity. "The soul that sinneth, it shall die. ... The righteousness of the righteous shall be upon him, and the wickedness of the wicked shall be upon him" (Ezk. 18:4, 20). Upon this ground alone did God rest His appeal to His accusers,—"Are not my ways equal, and are not your ways unequal?" (Ezk. 18:25, 29).

5. Since the creatures of God do not exist by their own will, and since they exist for eternity, and since nothing more vitally affects their prospects for eternity than the constitutional powers and propensities with which they begin their existence, the dictates of honor and right demand that God shall confer on them such original constitutions as shall, in their natural and proper tendencies, favorably affect

their prospects for eternity, and place a reasonable power of right conduct and of securing eternal life in the possession of all.

If, then, in the original constitution of any new-created mind, and entirely independent of his knowledge, desire, choice or agency, there is that which is really sinful (if the idea were not absurd, and the supposition were possible), and if he had no power to do good, and thus secure eternal life, such a creature would not be treated by the Creator according to the dictates of honor and right, nor would he be responsible for the sin so existing; for he would not be its author, but God, and for it God would be responsible.

Still further; if in the original constitution of a new-created mind, anterior to his choice or action, there is a radical derangement or corruption, resulting in a powerful tendency or propensity to sin, certain to result in ruin, whilst, at the same time, God had the power to create it without this derangement or corruption, so that its natural and proper development would tend towards eternal life, then such a mind is not dealt with rightfully and honorably.

He does not and cannot decide with what constitutional powers he shall exist. And yet nothing more vitally affects his prospects for eternity. If his original constitution is such that it naturally tends towards evil with great power, and thus creates a moral certainty of ruin, then existence is to him no blessing, but a curse; nor has the Creator dealt honorably or benevolently by him.

6. Not only do the demands of honor and right forbid the Creator thus to injure His creature in his original constitution, but they equally forbid Him to place him in circumstances needlessly unfavorable to right conduct, and a proper development of his powers.

What benevolent being, dealing with new-created minds committed to His care, would not feel bound to place them under a system of influences most favorably arranged for their highest good, and where all needless trials and temptations to sin and ruin would be avoided? Could any man defend himself on any principles of benevolence, honor or right, if he did not act on this principle? And when the great Creator is deciding on the circumstances of the new-created immortal minds called into being by His power, is it benevolent, honorable or right, for Him to act on any other principles?

If, now, in opposition to these views, any allege that God, for His own happiness or glory, or that of His creatures, may act on other principles, it is enough to say, as before, that it is not supposable that a perfect being could be made happy or glorious by acting on any other principles. The only grounds on which God, or any of His holy creatures, can be happy or glorious, as honorable and benevolent minds, in view of the ruin of any others, are those already stated. It must appear that God did not wrong them in their original constitution, but gave them a constitution honorably manifesting His sincere good will towards them as individuals, and tending towards eternal life. It must also appear that He did not wrong them in their situation and circumstances, but so placed them, that all things were, on the whole, as favorably arranged for all as possible. That, having thus placed them, He sincerely desired the highest good of all; and that He set before them good and evil,—life and death,—and demanded only faith and obedience that they should live. If, in such circumstances, any disbelieve His Word, and disregard His will and wishes, and perish, God is absolved, and the guilt is theirs.

These principles are so simple and obvious, that no one accustomed to regard benevolence, honor and right, would ever have thought of calling any of them in question, had not certain supposed facts seemed, at times, to make it necessary. But, notwithstanding this, these principles have been seen and felt to be true. They have been also incidentally, if not formally and systematically, acknowledged and announced, in all ages; and towards them, in their fulness, the mind of man has continually struggled, in proportion as it has become sensitive to the nature and demands of benevolence, honor and right. Nor will it ever rest, short of this ground. Indeed, why should it? Are not these views in accordance with the revealed character of God? Does not the Bible ascribe to Him all those traits from which all the principles that have been stated may be inferred? By His own testimony, He is love. He is the essence of honor, generosity, magnanimity. He has no pleasure at all in the death of any of His creatures. He exceeds all His creatures in the spirit of self-sacrifice for the good of others. He desires all to be saved. He is merciful, gracious, long-suffering, and abundant in goodness and truth, keeping mercy for thousands, forgiving iniquity and transgression and sin. He expostulates with His sinful creatures, saying, "Why will ye die?" (Ezk. 33:11). He says, "How shall I give thee up?" (Hosea 11:18). He laments, saying, concerning the lost. "O, that thou hadst known the things that belong to thy peace!" (Luke 19:42). He declares that men perish entirely by their own fault, and against His desires, efforts and warnings. "O, Israel! thou hast destroyed thyself, but in me is thy help found" (Hosea 13:9). It is not possible that a being whose feelings are such, and who makes such appeals, should act on any other principles than those already stated. If He were to give to any new-created mind a depraved natural constitution, disqualifying him for right action, and impelling him to sin, and then place him in circumstances of extreme temptation, how could He lament over him, declare that He had no pleasure at all in his death, entreat him not to die, but to turn and live, without manifest and gross insincerity? The fact, then, that God does, in all parts of the Bible, throw the entire blame of their ruin on men, and declares that it is contrary to His wishes, pleasure, and strenuous expostulations and efforts, is decisive proof that in all His dealings with them God has observed the principles of honor, right and benevolence, as they have been laid down. The Bible does not for a moment admit that men have in any respect been wronged. It always presents God as the injured party, and throws the whole responsibility of wronging him, and ruining themselves, on men.

Additional authority will be conferred upon the principles of honor and right thus set forth, if we will consult the inspired representation of the feelings, towards which a regenerate mind, under the influences of the divine Spirit, naturally tends. They are feelings of such deep interest in the welfare of others that they produce a disposition to forgo the exercise even of our own rights, rather than to be the occasion of tempting them to sin. If a Christian could eat meat in an idol's temple, or meat that had been offered to an idol, without injuring his own conscience, yet, as a truly benevolent person, he would readily abstain from it, rather than to expose a weak brother, by the power of the temptation of an example which he would misunderstand, to do violence to his own conscience; and, in general, true benevolence will lead us not only to avoid becoming to others an occasion of temptation to sin, but to do all in our power to avert from them such temptation, from any quarter whatever. Even if in any case the sinner who yields to temptation is criminal, and without excuse, still, no man acting under the full influence of the Christian spirit will excuse himself, if he has needlessly tempted or provoked him to the commission of the sin. It is the spontaneous impulse of a regenerate heart, in its highest exercises of holy love, to avert from others to the greatest extent temptations to sin, and to concentrate upon them to the highest degree in-

fluences that tend to lead them to holiness and eternal life. These feelings will not, indeed, forbid him to act on the principles of sovereignty
and justice towards such as have forfeited their rights wherever the
public good demands. Nor are such feelings in God inconsistent with
a dispensation of sovereignty and justice on similar grounds. But even
under such a dispensation, He inspires His people with a desire to do
all that they can to avert temptations, and to save all even of those who
have forfeited their rights, and might justly perish.

Can it be for a moment supposed that, as these feelings increase,
the Christian becomes more and more unlike God? Is it not reasonable
to believe that he becomes more and more His image? If, then, such
are the feelings of God even towards sinners, can He be satisfied, in
His dealings with new-created minds, with anything short of the principles of honor and right which have been stated? Moreover, if, as the
Christian crucifies all selfish desires, and comes under the full influence
of love he, in like manner, feels more keenly the principles of honor
and right already stated,—and this is the fact,—then is there not conclusive evidence that they are of God?

CHAPTER VI: ORTHODOX AUTHORITIES

AT this point, some of my readers are probably disposed to raise the inquiry, whether the preceding views of the intuitive decisions of the human mind as to the principles of honor and right have been, in fact, recognized as true in the church of God. To such I reply, they have. This will be made more fully to appear during the progress of this investigation. At present, it is enough to adduce some evidence on those points which are, of all others, to us the most immediately practical and important,—I refer to the demands of honor and right as to the proper constitution and circumstances of new-created minds.

The evidence which I shall adduce, in order to be above suspicion, will be derived from those who are high in reputation for sound and orthodox views.

It is derived from their discussions and decisions as to the constitution with which God made Adam, and the circumstances in which He placed him. In these discussions, they were incidentally called to meet, on its real merits, the great question, what was due from God to a new-created mind, and what was a fair probation of such a mind? The eminence of Turretin[13] as a champion of orthodoxy is unquestioned. What, then, teaches he on these points, viewing them as presented to God for practical decision, in the case of Adam?

He earnestly defends the position that God could not, consistently with His glory, make him otherwise than with a good constitution, well-ordered powers, and original righteousness, so that there should be in him no inclination to sin, no sinful propensities, and no conflict of the inferior against the superior powers; but, on the other hand, the love of holiness and of God, and a strong and constant

---

13 Francis Turretin (1623-1687) was a Swiss-Italian Protestant theologian known as a zealous opponent of the theology of Amyraldianism. He was an earnest defender of the Calvinistic orthodoxy represented by the Synod of Dort, and was one of the authors of the Helvetic Consensus, which defended the formulation of double predestination and the verbal inspiration of the Bible.

propensity to all that is right. He utterly denied that God could consistently make man with mere natural powers, which, although free from positive sin, tended to sin, and then produce a tendency to good only by a supernatural influence. In opposition to this, he held that on Adam, as a new-created being, God ought to confer an original righteousness properly belonging to his nature. Hence, in opposition to the theory of Bellarmin,[14] and many of the scholastic divines, that original righteousness was not an essential part of the nature of Adam, but merely a supernatural gift, he says:

> "If original righteousness was supernatural, it follows that it was the *natural* condition of Adam to be devoid of righteousness (or sanctity), and to be the subject of all those things which necessarily must exist in a person capable of holiness, and yet devoid of it; as, for example, ignorance, inclination to vices, concupiscence of the flesh, rebellion of the inferior part against the superior, and other things of the kind, which Bellarmin calls *diseases and weaknesses of nature.*
>
> "*But this cannot be said without ascribing them to him who is the author of nature, and who would thus be represented as the author of sin.*" (L. 5, Q. 11, § 9).

Against the same ideas he, in another place, thus argues:

> "if there was in man *any inclination to sin by nature, then God would be the author of it, and so the sin itself would be chargeable upon God,* as before proved" (L. 9, Q. 7, § 3).

As to the fallen angels, he says:

> "there is reason to assert that some protracted interval of time elapsed between the creation of the angels, which is the work of god, and their revolt, which is the work of evil spirits; otherwise, *if their first acts were sinful, the causation of sin would seem to be ascribed to God, as the next preceding efficient cause*" (L. 9, Q. 5, § 2).

---

14 Robert Bellarmine (1542-1621) was an Italian Jesuit, a Cardinal of the Catholic Church and one of the most important figures in the Counter-Reformation.

Thus clearly does Turretin inculcate the great truth that God is bound, by principles of equity and honor, to give to all new-created beings original constitutions, healthy, well-balanced and tending decidedly and effectually towards good. To make them either neutral, or with constitutions tending to evil, would be utterly inconsistent with the honor and justice of God, and would involve Him in the guilt and dishonor of sin. What can be more absolutely unequivocal and decided than this?

To the wide reach of these fundamental principles I would call particular attention, as well as to their decision and strength. The place occupied by the work of Turretin in the seminary at Princeton is well known. No protest has ever been issued by the professors there, or by the Presbyterian church, against these views. On the other hand, it will soon become apparent that the Princeton divines have themselves advanced similar views, and that in them they are sustained by the standards of their own church.

Views similar to those of Turretin may be found strongly expressed in the work of Dr. Watts[15] on the *Ruin and Recovery of Mankind*, in reply to Dr. J. Taylor.[16] In considering what is due from the Creator to a new-created being, he states, at some length, that He ought to confer on him a perfection of natural powers, both of body and spirit, considered as united and adapted to his present state. Even if they did not involve all the perfections which God can confer, or man produce by cultivation, yet, at least, they ought to be perfectly sufficient for his present well-being and station; that his bodily powers should be in perfect order, his reason clear, his judgment uncorrupted, his conscience upright and sensible; that he should have no bias to sin, but a bias to holiness, that is, to the love of God and of man; that there

---

15 Isaac Watts (1674-1748), an English hymn writer, theologian and logician, was brought up in the home of a committed religious Nonconformist. His father, also Isaac Watts, had been incarcerated twice for his controversial views.

16 John Taylor (1750-1826) was a successful businessman, poet and composer of hymns from Norwich, England. Ordained by dissenting ministers in Derbyshire. According to a family tradition, on settling at Norwich he went through Samuel Clarke's *Scripture Doctrine of the Trinity* (1712) with his congregation, adopted its view, and came forward (1737) in defense of a dissenting layman excommunicated for unitarian heterodoxy. In 1754 Taylor laid the first stone of the Octagon Chapel, Norwich and was described by John Wesley as 'perhaps the most elegant one in all Europe,' and too fine for 'the old coarse gospel.' He disowned all names such as Presbyterian, etc., claiming only that of *Christian*. His book, *Scripture Doctrine of Original Sin*, 1740, was against the Calvinistic view of human nature.

should be an entire subordination of the inferior to the superior powers,—indeed, that he should have a concreated (created at the same
time—Ed.) principle of holiness;—in short, that he should have the image of God, not merely naturally and politically, but morally. He
ought, he concedes, in order to have a trial, still to have free will, so as
not to be constrained to obey, and rendered incapable of sin; but at the
same time, he should have a superior propensity to good, and a full
sufficiency of power to preserve himself in a state of obedience and
love to his Creator. In a marginal note he thus proves that God ought
to give to a new-created mind a preponderating bias to holiness:

> "If the new-made creature had not a propensity to love and
> obey God, but was in a state of mere indifference to good
> or evil, then his being put into such an union with flesh and
> blood, among a thousand temptations, would have been an
> overbalance on the side of vice. But our reason can never
> suppose that God, the wise, just and good, would have
> placed a new-made creature in such a situation."

These statements are so clear that they need no comment. It is also
a matter of great interest that they have been fully endorsed by John
Wesley, the great founder of Methodism. When Dr. John Taylor
made his great assault on Original Sin, Wesley, as well as Watts, came
forth to its defense. On the points then at issue, he avowed himself as
at one with Dr. Watts and the Calvinists; and defended this position of
Dr. Watts, as a self-evident truth, and pronounced the argument of
Dr. Taylor against it to be utterly powerless and insufficient. He says :

> "This argument cannot be answered, unless it can be
> showed either, first, that in such a situation there would not
> have been an overbalance on the side of vice, or second,
> that to place a new-made creature in a situation where there
> was such an overbalance was consistent with the wisdom,
> justice and goodness of God. But, instead of showing, or
> even attempting to show this, you feebly say, 'I do not think
> the reason of man by any means sufficient to direct God in
> what state to make moral agents. But, however Adam's
> propensities and temptations were balanced, he had freedom
> to choose evil as well as good.' He had. But this is no an-
> swer to the argument, which like the former remains in its

full force. How could a wise, just and good God place his
creature in such a state as that the scale of evil should pre-
ponderate? Although it be allowed, he is, in a measure, free
still,—the other scale does not 'fly up and kick the beam.'"

Here Wesley perfectly accords with Turretin, as well as with
Watts, in holding that to make new-created beings either neutral, or
with a preponderance towards evil, would be highly unjust and dishonorable in God. The scales ought not to be merely balanced, but the
preponderance towards good should be decided and powerful.

Unless these original rights had been in some way forfeited, Dr.
Watts, also, regarded it as in the highest degree dishonorable in God
ever to disregard them.

The Princeton divines, in reality, advance similar views, although
not as openly, and with as much fulness and strength, as Turretin,
Watts and Wesley. First, they decide that to every new-created being
a probation is due. "Is it not necessary," they say, "that a moral being
shall have a probation before his fate is decided?" Again they state what
is essential to a fair probation. "A probation, to be *fair*, must afford as
favorable a prospect of a happy as of an unhappy conclusion." Their
ideas, however, of what is involved in such a fair probation, though
not fully stated, may be clearly inferred from the fact that they refer to
the probation of our first parents as a fair one. Their views of the moral
constitution necessary for such a probation are, no doubt, in accordance with the decision of the standards of their own church, as expressed in the following words of the larger catechism: "God endued
them with living, reasonable and immortal souls, made them after his
own image, in knowledge, righteousness and holiness, having the law
of God written in their hearts, and power to fulfill it, with dominion
over the creatures, yet subject to fall" (*Larger Catechism*, Q. 17.) This,
then, is the essential basis of a fair probation. The statement of the
Confession of Faith is, in essence, the same, except that it gives a more
expanded view of the state of the will of our first parents, asserting that
they "were under a possibility of transgressing, being left to the liberty
of their own will, which was subject unto change" (Chap. IV, § 2.)

These statements, it is plain, involve, in our first parents as the essential basis of a fair probation, a good original constitution, well-pro-
portioned powers, and a decided and powerful bias to good, resulting,
at first, in actual and perfect obedience to the law of God.

Satisfactory as is this implication of the views of the Princeton divines, yet they are exhibited still more clearly by their statements with respect to an original bias to evil. They teach us that it is the greatest of all calamities, and that it is utterly inconsistent with the existence of a fair and honorable probation.

> "What greater evil for moral and immortal beings can there be," say they, "than to be born contaminated in their moral nature, or under a divine constitution which secures the universality and certainty of sin, and that, too, with undeviating and remorseless effect? It is, as Coleridge[17] well says. 'an outrage on common sense' to affirm that it is no evil for men to be placed, on their probation under such circumstances that not one of ten thousand millions ever escaped sin and condemnation to eternal death."

On these grounds they elsewhere assert that men, if they have had no other or better probation than is involved in such a state of things, have, in reality, had no probation at all. Such a view, Prof. Hodge assures us, "represents the race as being involved in ruin and condemnation, without having the slightest probation" (*Commentary on Romans,* p. 227, 1st ed.). The Princeton reviewers, as we have seen, have decided that "a probation, to be fair, must afford as favorable a prospect of a happy as of an unhappy conclusion." Accordingly, as consistency requires, immediately after, in view of the supposition "that men are brought up to their trial under a divine constitution which secures the certainty of their sinning," they ask, with great emphasis, "Is this a fair trial?" (Theol. Ess., Vol. 1, p. 159).

In the preceding statements of Turretin, Watts, the Westminster divines, and the Princeton divines, is involved all that I have claimed on this point in my expose of the principles of honor and right. Indeed, the strength of their statements rather exceeds my own.

I shall not at this time add any further evidence that the principles which I have stated have been generally recognized as true by the church of God. At a subsequent time I shall resume the subject, and prove that the Reformers, as well as Augustine and other distinguished

---

17 Samuel Taylor Coleridge (1772-1834) was an English poet, Romantic, literary critic and philosopher who, with his friend William Wordsworth, was a founder of the Romantic Movement in England and one of the Lake Poets.

champions of orthodoxy, from age to age, have advanced as self-evident similar views as to the demands of the principles of honor and right upon the great Creator, with reference to new-created minds.

It would have been easy, instead of going into so much detail in proof of my positions, simply to have referred, in a general way, to Augustine, the Reformers, the Puritans, and their consistent and exact followers, as holding the views which have been set forth concerning the obligations of God to new-created minds. But, though the reference would have been well founded, it would have excited less attention, and awakened less interest.

It was not, however, for the public good that the thing should be thus lightly passed over. It has been the great evil of other ages that principles like these, although avowed, have not been consistently carried out. They need to be exalted, made prominent, and insisted on. If true at all, they are to all created beings the most fundamental and most momentous truths in the universe of God. They are like a full-orbed sun, in the center of all created existence. No system can be truly seen except in their light. No system can be true which actually contravenes them. For God is all glorious, all holy, all just, all honorable, all good. He cannot but observe the true principles of honor and of right. For, though he often dwells in the thick darkness, and deep clouds are His pavilion, yet now and evermore righteousness and judgment are the habitation of His throne.

Thus has one of the great moving powers of Christianity been developed and set forth. It is now necessary to set forth the other, as it has been stated by those held in the highest reputation as the true friends and defenders of the gospel. I refer to the great Reformers of the sixteenth century, and to those who glory in being deemed their true followers.

Chapter VII: Facts As To Human Depravity

IN order to present the conflict which is under consideration in its full strength, it is necessary to place in contrast with the principles of honor and right which have been developed the most radical view which has been extensively given of the fallen and ruined condition of man.

But, before doing this, it is expedient to prepare the way by a brief statement of some conceded facts, by which, even independently of the testimony of the Bible, the necessity of some such radical view is made apparent. The facts in question lie upon the surface of the history of this world, and are witnessed to by the observation and experience of all men. They are by no means such as our recent survey of the principles of honor and right would have led us to expect. For, if the demands of these principles on God, with reference to new-created minds, are such as have been stated, we ought *a priori* to expect to find in this world a race whose moral constitutions, powers and tendencies, should correspond with the principles which have been laid down, and whose history should illustrate and prove the existence of strong and predominant tendencies to good. We ought to expect that, although some might, through an abuse of freedom, fall into sin, the greater part would lead holy and perfect lives. That harmony, unity, brotherly love, pure morality, and an intelligent and devoted love of God, would characterize the great majority of men, giving a holy and lovely character alike to individuals and to communities. That pride, malice, envy, falsehood, contentions and wars, would be regarded as strange and painful anomalies in the history of this world.

It is needless to say that such anticipations, if formed by a visitor to this world, ignorant of its real history, would soon be dissipated by a painful view of the stern realities of actual human life. The Word of God, the consciousness of every Christian, and the dark records of vice and crime, of fraud and violence, of war and slavery, of remorse and woe. which fill the history of this world, too clearly and painfully testify that such ideal conceptions of human excellence must be regarded as nothing but the baseless fabric of a vision.

Indeed, so plain are the mournful realities, that the most eminent Unitarian divines do not hesitate to state them with an eloquence and power which cannot be resisted. That I may avoid even the appearance of exaggeration, I will state the facts in the words of such men as President Sparks,[18] Professor Norton,[19] Dr. Burnap,[20] and Dr. Dewey.[21] I will, moreover, take their statements from works designed to oppose the Calvinistic doctrine of depravity, that it may be the more evident how clear and undoubted are the real facts which exhibit the actual depravity of man. Dr. G. W. Burnap, of Baltimore, in an able work, designed to evince the rectitude of human nature, in opposition to the Calvinistic doctrine of depravity, does not hesitate to make the following clear and decided statement as to actual depravity:

> "The sinfulness of mankind no man in his senses has ever pretended to deny. 'No man liveth, and sinneth not.' No human being, with the exception of the Savior, has ever lived long enough to develop the moral nature, without being conscious of having done wrong.
>
> "The sinfulness of mankind has been demonstrated by the prevalence of wars, since the first recorded history of our race. War transforms a human being into a fiend, and leads to the commission of every crime, and is itself the greatest of all crimes. The number of people who have perished in war is, perhaps, ten times as great as now exists on earth. The quantity of property consumed and destroyed in war is, not unlikely, more than a hundred times as much as all mankind now possess.
>
> "The sinfulness of mankind has been demonstrated by the fearful amount of sensuality that has existed. The world

---

18 Jared Sparks (1789-1866) was an American historian, educator and Unitarian minister who served as President of Harvard University from 1849 to 1853.

19 Andrews Norton (1786-1853) was an American preacher and theologian. Along with William Ellery Channing, he was the leader of mainstream Unitarianism of the 1800s.

20 George W. Burnap, pastor of the First Independent Church of Baltimore, was a Unitarian minister. Among his books were *On Original Sin* (1844).

21 Orville Dewey (1794-1882) was an American Unitarian minister who prepared a course of lectures for the Lowell Institute of Boston, on the "Problem of Human Life and Destiny" and "Education of the Human Race."

has always been filled with the wretched victims of intemperance. It may safely be said, that most of the diseases which have afflicted mankind, and shortened human life, have been produced by the unlawful or excessive indulgence of the appetites.

"The sinfulness of mankind has been demonstrated by the social unkindness that has always prevailed, the cruel abuse of power which has reigned since the beginning of time, so pathetically described in the book from which our text is taken. 'So I returned and considered all the oppressions that are done under the sun; and, behold, the tears of such as were oppressed, and they had no comforter, and on the side of their oppressors there was power, but they had no comforter.' So much was the author's sensibility shocked and his pity moved, that he 'praised the dead which are already dead more than the living which are yet alive,' and thought it was better never to have been born than to have an existence in a world so full of injustice.

"The sinfulness of mankind is demonstrated by the existence of laws and courts and prisons and punishments. Their very purpose is to restrain man from sin, and to defend one man from the injustice of another. The evidences of man's sinfulness meet us at every turn, in the anger we witness, in the profaneness we hear, in the theft against which we bar our doors, in the conflagrations we behold by night lighted up by the incendiary's torch, in the wretched outcasts whom vice has driven forth to die of misery and want. Such are the overwhelming and undeniable evidences of the sinfulness of mankind."

Dr. Sparks, also, in his Letters to Dr. Miller,[22] in opposition to Calvinism,—a work of decided ability,—says, with reference to Unitarian divines,

"They preach that all men are depraved, deeply depraved, and sinners in the sight of God,—not by the will and appointment of their Creator, but by their own choice, their neglect of duty, and their obstinate disobedience. There is no theme, in fact, on which Unitarian preachers dwell more

---

22 *A Reply to The Review in which it is attempted to vindicate the church from the charges of that review,* by a Protestant Episcopalian, R.P. & C. Williams, 1821.

than on the moral depravity of man. This is the moral disease which they believe the religion of Jesus was intended
to heal" (p. 290).

The testimony of Prof. Norton to the facts of the case is still more
ample and unequivocal. In an article entitled "Views of Calvinism,"
containing an argument of great vigor against that system, he says:

> "If we look abroad, beyond the confines of Christianity, to
> the past history and present state of the world, we shall find
> that it is on the subject of religion that the most portentous
> and pernicious errors have prevailed,—errors of superstition
> and errors of virtual atheism,—on the one hand, conceptions
> of the spiritual world disastrously false, and, on the other, an
> abnegation of all but what is present and material."

These statements he confirms by a reference to Buddhism, "the
monstrous mythology and all-pervading superstitions of the Hindus,"
the systems of Mohammad and Confucius, and finally a great miscellaneous multitude of various superstitions and idolatries, into which any
proper religious belief or sentiment rarely enters. Of the followers of
these "most portentous and pernicious errors" he says: "These classes
constitute a great majority of mankind" (p. 209).

He then turns to the Roman Catholic and the Greek Orthodox
churches, and finds in them by far the greater part of those numbered
as Christians. Concerning them, he says: "Intelligent Protestants regard
the doctrines of either church as a mass of gross errors, accumulated
and consolidated during centuries of ignorance and superstition" (p.
210).

Passing from these to the Protestants, he represents the great majority of them as holding a system at war with reason and the character
of God,—a system which it is his main purpose, in two articles, to represent as pernicious in a high degree, yea, as even a system of blas-
phemy (p. 107).

As to the moral condition of Christendom, he uses the following
language:

> "Are we to conclude that it is the part of a wise man to turn
> away his eyes from the moral and religious ignorance, the
> debasement and annihilation of intellect, which exist in the

Christian world? Should we look with philosophical indifference on the vices and selfishness which spread through all
classes of society, on the physical and moral wretchedness of
the poor and the crimes which it generates, on oppression
and tyranny, and the maddening passions which they are
exasperating? Should we regard these things as the necessary
condition of humanity?"

With regard to the actual influence exerted even on Christian
communities by the simple, sublime and practical principles of Christianity, he uses the following unequivocal language:

"Is it impossible to render the practical operation of these
truths more general and effective? Is it impossible, when religion joins her voice to that which experience has been so
long uttering, to make men believe and feel, at last, that
their duty and their interest are the same; that the laws of
God are but directions which he has given us, in his infinite
wisdom and mercy, for attaining our highest happiness; that
it is better to be just and benevolent, honored and beloved,
than to be selfish, unjust and cruel, despised, distrusted and
hated; that it is unwise to sacrifice a great future good to a
present indulgence, which leaves behind it dissatisfaction
and repentance; and that he who submits the moral part of
his nature to the animal is degrading himself, and destroying his best capacities for enjoyment? Is it impossible that
the generality of men in a Christian land should be brought
to act as if they really believed these truths, and truths such
as these? Whether it be so or not, yet remains to be determined. The experiment has never been made."

Of course, the moral state of the heathen world is still worse.

To complete the dark picture, and to take away all excuse for this
state of things, he informs us that the reason of these mournful results
is not that the truths of Christianity are obscure, or beyond the comprehension of the masses of mankind:

"Are the truths for which we contend intrinsically difficult
to be understood? They are not so. They are as simple and
intelligible as they are sublime. The prospect which true re-

ligion opens to the mind has a beautiful and solemn
grandeur, to which that of the visible heavens affords but a
faint comparison; but it is with one as with the other,—we
need not travel far, nor search for our point of view, in order to behold all that is given us to see of the moral or of the
physical universe."

Such, then, according to Professor Norton, is the present wide-
spread moral depravity and degradation of the human race, after all
that God has done by the light of nature, by His providence, by revelation, and by the various and powerful means of grace, to sanctify and
elevate individuals and society; moreover, no one will pretend that the
state of things has been any better for six thousand years past.

Indeed, if all that Professor Norton says in the preceding passages
concerning Protestant communities were true, I do not see how to
avoid the conclusion that the picture which he gives of the prevalence
and power of error and actual depravity in the world is darker even
than that given by the Calvinists, whose doctrine of depravity he opposes. Truly, if these views are correct, the words of our Savior, "Strait
is the gate and narrow is the way that leadeth unto life, and few there
be that find it" (Matt. 7:14), are true to an extent far beyond what we
had supposed. But we regard this part of the picture as too deeply colored. In many portions of the Protestant world the true gospel has exerted great power in producing love, faith, self-denial, benevolent
enterprise, and a holy life. With this exception, we admit the correctness of the picture; and, if it is correct, then how deep and dark are the
shades of error and sin which rest upon and brood over this unhappy
world?

The testimony of Dr. Dewey is no less unequivocal and decided.
In a professed and formal statement of the Unitarian belief, elaborately
finished, he thus speaks :

"We believe in human depravity; and a very serious and
saddening belief it is, too, that we hold on this point. We
believe in the very great depravity of mankind,—in the ex-
ceeding deprivation of human nature. We believe that 'the
heart is deceitful above all things, and desperately wicked'
(Jer. 17:9). We believe all that is meant when it is said of the
world in the time of Noah that 'all the imaginations of men,
and all the thoughts of their hearts, were evil, and only evil

continually' (Gen. 6:5). We believe all that Paul meant
when he said, speaking of the general character of the heathen world in his time, 'There is none that is righteous, no,
not one; there is none that understandeth, there is none that
seeketh after God; they have all gone out of the way, there
is none that doeth good, or is a doer of good, no, not one;
with their tongues they use deceit, and the poison of asps is
under their lips; whose mouth is full of cursing and bitterness; and the way of peace have they not known, and there
is no fear of God before their eyes' (Rom 3:10-18). We believe that this was not intended to be taken without qualifications, for Paul, as we shall soon have occasion to observe,
made qualifications. It was true in the general. But it is not
the ancient heathen world alone that we regard as filled
with evil. We believe that the world now, taken in the
mass, is a very, very bad world; that the sinfulness of the
world is dreadful and horrible to consider; that the nations
ought to be covered with sackcloth and mourning for it;
that they are filled with misery by it. Why, can any man
look abroad upon the countless miseries inflicted by selfishness, dishonesty, slander, strife, war; upon the boundless
woes of intemperance, libertinism, gambling, crime; can
any man look upon all this, with the thousand minor diversities and shadings of guilt and guilty sorrow, and feel that
he could write any less dreadful sentence against the world
than Paul has written? Not believe in human depravity,—
great, general, dreadful depravity! Why, a man must be a
fool, nay, a stock, or a stone, not to believe in it! He has no
eyes, he has no senses, he has no perceptions, if he refuses to
believe in it!" (*Controversial Discourses*, pp. 16—18.)

What can be more explicit than this testimony to the deep and
general depravity of our race?

It ought, however, to be distinctly stated that Dr. Dewey, and indeed, all the writers whom I have quoted, earnestly repudiate the idea
that this development of sin implies in man a sinful nature in the obvious and literal sense of those words. They regard such an idea as highly
dishonorable to God, and as diminishing, or even annihilating, the
criminality of sin; nor, as we are informed by Dr. Dewey, do they
profess to believe "in what is technically called total depravity." The

origin of sin they ascribe to the perversion of free agency by limited, imperfect beings, in a world of temptation, bodily and mental.

There is, nevertheless, in this world an extent, a power, a preponderance and a stubbornness of sin, for which a solution so simple and obvious does not seem to account. This was felt and conceded, even by Dr. Dewey. Accordingly, while insisting that the origin of sin is plain, he says. "The extent to which these evils go is, doubtless, a problem that I cannot solve. There are shadows upon the world that we cannot penetrate; masses of sin and misery that overwhelm us with wonder and awe."

This very impressive and affecting statement of Dr. Dewey will now prepare us to see why there are so many who cannot rest content in the solution which he, and others of the same school, give of the origin of this state of things. The extent and the power of evil in this world are so great, even as conceded by Unitarians, that they cannot find an adequate solution of them in the mere free agency and temptation of uncorrupted minds. The facts stated are so unlike the action of upright and undepraved minds, that they at once suggest the idea that, in some way the human race has come into a fallen and ruined state, even before action. Certainly the dark and mournful facts which have been stated are not like the action of minds possessing a sound moral constitution, well-balanced powers, and predominating tendencies to holiness and truth.

Nor, in view of such facts, ought it to be deemed wonderful if efforts should be made to find a deeper and more radical cause for results so calamitous and so strange. The most thorough of these efforts I shall now proceed to consider. I shall show, moreover, that the impulse to the effort is in the highest degree honorable, even if it does happen to involve those who make it in a conflict with those principles of honor and right which they themselves avow and defend.

Chapter VIII: Radical View Of The Ruin Of Man.

IT is a principle of common sense and will, at least in theory, be conceded by all, that before the moral diseases of man can be thoroughly healed, their true nature, power and depth, must be understood. Moreover, in order to save him from the evils and perils of his present state, it ought to be fully known what those evils and perils are. If he has enemies, visible or invisible, it ought to be known who they are, and what is their power.

Under the influence of these convictions a large class of benevolent Christian minds have acted, in all ages. They have felt that the purest benevolence which can be exercised towards man demands the most full and faithful statement of his fallen and ruined condition as a sinner, however dark the views which may be thus presented. Those who have presented such views have commonly been men of deep Christian experience, like Augustine, the Reformers, the Puritans, and Edwards.[23] To such men the deep depravity of their own hearts is not merely a matter of doctrinal theory, but of profound experimental knowledge. To every statement of the Word of God, even the most humiliating, there is an unhesitating response within. Moreover, upon this deep inward knowledge of their fallen state is based, in their judgment, that whole work of new creation in righteousness of which they are no less conscious. In all cases, the knowledge of the first is regarded as the measure of the progress of the second.

Hence, the predominating influence under which they ever act is a desire of *thoroughness* in disclosing the ruined state of man before he is renovated by the grace of God. Fearful of healing slightly the

---

23 Jonathan Edwards (1703-1758) was a preacher, theologian, and missionary to Native Americans. Edwards is widely acknowledged to be America's most important and original philosophical theologians. His theological work is broad in scope, but he is often associated with his defense of Reformed theology (Calvinism), the metaphysics of theological determinism, the Puritan heritage and the First Great Awakening.

wounds of the people of God, they have earnestly sought to probe them to their deepest recesses. Believing the heart to be deceitful above all things and desperately wicked, they have felt that the danger was very great of being deceived by superficial views of the nature and extent of sin. Knowing that none but God can thoroughly search the heart, they have besought Him clearly to reveal to them its depths of evil. When God, as they believe, in answer to such prayers, and through His Word, providence and spirit, has given to such a full and experimental development of what they have sought, it has led them to insist much on three leading points, as all involved in a full view of the fallen and ruined condition of man.

1. His deep innate depravity as an individual.
2. His subjection to the power of depraved social organizations, called, taken collectively, the world.
3. His subjection to the power of unseen malignant spirits, who are centralized and controlled by Satan, their leader and head.

In considering the first point, they have not rested content with the mere fact that all men actually sin from the commencement of moral agency, but have sought to penetrate deeper, and to find in the antecedent nature of man a sufficient cause for this sad result, so uniform, yet so unreasonable. The consequence has been a very general belief of a properly depraved nature in man anterior to action of any kind. They have conceived of the human mind as a kind of seed-plot of sin, so to say, in which the seeds and germs and roots of sin were thick sown, and needed only exposure to the influence of the atmosphere and warmth of active life to cause them to germinate, spring up, and bear fruit.

The highest statements on these points were undoubtedly made by the Reformers and their immediate followers, in the sixteenth and seventeenth centuries. In their opposition to what they regarded the Pelagian tendencies of the Roman Catholic church, they transcended even the statements of Augustine, in some points. I refer, in particular, to their doctrine concerning the sinfulness of concupiscence (that is, propensity to sin) after baptism, and the predestination of the fall of Adam. In the Reformers, then, we shall find a sincere effort to make the most full and thorough development of the doctrine of human depravity that was possible, and from motives the most honorable and benevolent.

Let my readers, even if any of them reject the opinions of these men as stated, at least do them the justice to endeavor, for a time, to look at the system from their point of view. Let them regard the numerous Christian experiences of such men as I have described—men of the highest mental power, and of clear discrimination—as at least intellectual phenomena worthy of study, and consideration, and comprehension. Nor let anyone feel an illiberal repulsion from an honest effort to give a thorough statement of the reality and depth of the moral diseases of the human heart.

Moreover, if many of the facts as stated are, in reality, at war with the principles of honor and right, as I concede them to be, let them not rashly conclude that no adjustment of the system is possible by which the facts can be retained and that conflict can be removed.

But let us hear them speak for themselves. Calvin thus defines original sin: It is

> "a hereditary depravity and corruption of our nature, diffused through all parts of the soul, which, in the first place, exposes us to the wrath of God, and then produces in us those works which the Scripture calls the works of the flesh" (*Institutes,* II, 1, 8).

Of infants he says,

> "They bring their condemnation with them from their mother's womb, being liable to punishment, not for the sin of another, but for their own. For, although they have not as yet produced the fruits of their iniquity, yet they have the seed enclosed in themselves; nay, their whole nature is, as it were, a seed of sin; therefore it cannot but be odious and abominable to God. Whence it follows that it is properly considered sin before God, because there could not be liability to punishment without sin" (*Institutes,* II, 1, 8).

He also states, in general, that the corruption of nature precedes and gives rise to all sinful acts, and is itself deserving of punishment.

"Two things deserve distinct notice: first, that since we are
so vitiated and depraved in all parts of our nature, we are
justly convicted and condemned before God, to whom
nothing is accepted but justice, innocence, purity, ... Second, that this depravity never ceases to produce new fruits,
—that is. those works of the flesh before alluded to,—just as
a kindled furnace incessantly emits flame and sparks, or a
fountain constantly sends forth water" (*Institutes*, II, 1, 8).

He also contrasts actual sins, and indeed corrupt habits, with a depravity of nature, and, in reference to Rom. 3:10-18, says, "Men are
not such as are here described merely through sinful habits, but also by
a depravity of nature" (*Institutes*, II, 3, 2).

Calvin introduces this view of the ruined condition of man by a
statement of his motives. He regarded it as the chief wile of Satan, "by
concealing from man a knowledge of his disease, to render it incur-
able." In opposition to this, he aims to produce a knowledge of our
miserable condition, that shall cause earnest desires and efforts after a
true and thorough remedy. He plainly asserts, in doing this, that, anterior to all actual sin, there is in man a depraved nature, by which he is
exposed to the just anger of God, and from which a constant stream of
actual sins proceeds. Let us, for the present, look at this statement
merely as an effort at depth and thoroughness. As such, we cannot
deny that it is radical and fundamental.

From the following quotations, taken from public formularies, it
will be seen that the leading churches of the Reformers took substantially the same views, and, no doubt, for the same reasons.

The Synod of Dort assert that all men become depraved through
"the propagation of a vicious nature;" and after this thus proceed,

"Therefore, all men are conceived in sin, and born the children of wrath, disqualified for all saving good, propensity to
evil, dead in sins, and the slaves of sin; and, without the
grace of the regenerating Holy Spirit, they neither are willing nor able to return to God, to correct their depraved nature, or to dispose themselves to the correction of it" (Scott's
Synod of Dort, Chaps, III & IV § 2, 3).

In the latter confession of Helvetius this language is used:

"We take sin to be that natural corruption of man derived
or spread from those our parents unto us all; through which,
we being drowned in evil concupiscence, and clean turned
away from God, but prone to all evil, full of all wickedness,
distrust, contempt, and hatred of God, can do no good of
ourselves,—no, not so much as think of any" (*Harmony of
Confessions*, p. 163).

The confession of Bohemia, or the Waldenses,[24] says of original
sin, that it is

"naturally engendered in us and hereditary, wherein we are
all conceived and born into this world. ... Let the force of
this hereditary destruction be acknowledged and judged of
by the guilt and fault involved, by our proneness and decli-
nation to evil, by our evil nature, and by the punishment
which is laid upon it" (*Harmony*, p. 169).

Of actual sins, they say they are

"the fruits of original sin, and do burst out within, without,
privily and openly, by the powers of man; that is, by all that
ever man is able to do, and by his members, transgressing all
those things which God commandeth and forbiddeth, and
also running into blindness and errors, worthy to be punished with all kinds of damnation."

They declare that these things ought to be earnestly insisted on,
that men

---

24 Waldensians, Waldenses or Vaudois are names for a Christian movement of the
    Middle Ages, descendants of which still exist in various regions, primarily in North-
    Western Italy. In 1179, some Waldensians went to Rome, where Pope Alexander III
    forbade explanation or critical interpretation of the Bible without authorization.
    They disobeyed and began to preach according to their own understanding of the
    scriptures. When the news of the Reformation reached the Waldensian Valleys, they
    decided to seek fellowship with the nascent Protestantism. In 1532 they met with
    German and Swiss Protestants and ultimately adapted their beliefs to those of the
    Reformed Church and became the Italian branch of Reformed churches.

"may know themselves, that they are conceived and born in sin, and that forthwith, even from their birth and by nature, they are sinners, full of lusts and evil inclinations."

The French confession says of man:

"His nature is become altogether defiled, and, being blind in spirit and corrupt in heart, hath utterly lost all his original integrity. ... We believe that all the offspring of Adam are infected with this contagion, which we call original sin; that is, a stain spreading itself by propagation, and not by imitation only, as the Pelagians thought,—all whose errors we do detest. ... We believe that this stain is indeed sin, because that it maketh every man (not so much as those little ones excepted, which as yet lie hid in their mother's womb) deserving of eternal death before God. We also affirm that this stain, even after baptism, is in nature sin. ... (On this point, the Reformers contradict Augustine.) Moreover, we say that this frowardness of nature doth always bring forth some fruits of malice and rebellion, in such sort that even they which are most holy, although they resist it, yet are they defiled with many infirmities and offenses, so long as they live in this world" (*Harmony*, pp. 172-3).

The Church of England, in her Thirty-Nine Articles, says:

"Original sin is the fault and corruption of the nature of every man that is naturally engendered of the offspring of Adam. ... In every person born into this world, it deserveth God's wrath and damnation" (*Harmony*, p. 173).

In the confession of Belgium it is said:

"We believe that through the disobedience of Adam the sin that is called original hath been spread and poured into all mankind. Now, original sin is a corruption of the whole nature, and an hereditary evil, wherewith even the very infants in their mother's womb are polluted; the which, also, as a most noisome root, doth branch out most abundantly all kinds of sin in man, and is so filthy and abominable in

the sight of God that it alone is sufficient to the condemnation of all mankind" (*Harmony*, p. 175).

It is added, "Out of it, as out of a corrupt fountain, continual
floods and rivers of iniquity do daily flow."

The authors of the Confession of Augsburg say:

> "We mean, by original sin, that which the holy fathers and
> all of sound judgment and learning in the church do so call,
> namely, that guilt whereby all that come into the world are,
> through Adam's fall, subject to God's wrath, and eternal
> death, and that very corruption of man's nature derived
> from Adam."

In this definition they include what is called original sin imputed,
as well as original sin inherent. They define this corruption of nature
as involving want of all forms of original righteousness and concupiscence, and then add,

> "Wherefore, those defects and this concupiscence are things
> damnable, and, of their own nature, worthy of death. And
> this original blot is sin indeed, condemning and bringing
> eternal death even now, also, upon all them which are not
> born again by baptism and the Holy Ghost" (*Harmony*, p.
> 176).

The Moravian confession declares,

> "This innate disease and original sin, is truly sin, and con-
> demns under God's eternal wrath all those who are not born
> again through water and the Holy Ghost" (*Harmony*, p.
> 178).

The Westminster divines teach that

> "A corrupted nature was conveyed from our first parents to
> all their posterity. From this original corruption, whereby
> we are utterly indisposed, disabled, and made opposite to all
> good, and wholly inclined to all evil, do proceed all actual
> transgressions." Concerning this corruption of nature, they

say that "both itself and all the motions thereof are truly and properly sin."

To this they add,

"Every sin, both original and actual, being a transgression of the righteous law of God, and contrary thereunto, doth, in its own nature, bring guilt upon the sinner, whereby he is bound over to the wrath of God and curse of the law, and so made subject to death, with all miseries, spiritual, temporal and eternal" (*Harmony*, pp. 179, 180).

It is not my purpose at this time to enter into a full discussion of the precise import of all this language of the Reformers. It is, however, no more than equitable to guard it against a misunderstanding to which it is liable. It has sometimes been interpreted as if they meant to teach that the substance or essence of man, of which God is the creator, is itself sinful or sin. This idea was advanced by Flaccus Illyricus[25] in his controversy with Victorinus Strigelius,[26] and was also defended by Spangenberg.[27] Möhler[28] also regards this as the logical result of the

25 Matthias Flacius Illyricus (1520-1575) was a Lutheran reformer from Istria, present day Croatia. Affirming the natural inability of man, he adopted a position on sin as not being an accident of human nature, but involved in its substance, since The Fall. Promoting what Calvinists later called total depravity, Flacius insisted that human nature was entirely transformed by original sin, human beings were transformed from goodness and wholly corrupted with evil, so that without divine assistance there is no power even to cooperate with the Gospel when they hear it preached. Human acts of piety are of no value in themselves, and humans are entirely dependent on the grace of God for salvation. Those who agreed with him on this point, for example, Cyriacus Spangenberg, were termed Flaccians. Resisting ecclesiastical censure, he left Jena to found an academy at Regensburg.

26 Viktorin/Victorinus Strigel (1524-1569) was a Philippist Lutheran Theologian, who attended the University of Wittenberg to study philosophy and theology, and became a follower of Philipp Melanchthon.

27 August Gottlieb Spangenberg (704-1792) was a German theologian and minister, and a bishop of the Moravian Brethren. As successor of Count Nicolaus Ludwig Zinzendorf, he helped develop international missions, as well as stabilize the theology and organization of the German Moravian Church. For the first thirty years (1733-1762), his work was mainly in Germany, England, Denmark, the Netherlands, Suriname, Georgia and elsewhere. During the second half of this missionary period of his life, he went to Pennsylvania, where as bishop he supervised the Moravian churches and wrote as an apologist of the Church against the attacks of the Lutherans and the Pietists. He did much to moderate the mysticism of Zinzendorf.

28 Johann Adam Möhler (1796-1838) was a German Roman Catholic theologian. The liberal school of thought of which he belonged was discouraged in official circles.

original statements of Luther and his followers on original sin. But whether it is so or not, one thing is undeniable, that the Reformers always disclaimed it as a part of their doctrine.

A labored refutation of this error may be found in Turretin (Loc. 9, Quaes. 11). They held, he assures us, that the essence or substance of man, so far as created by God, was in itself negatively good; but, nevertheless, it was, in their view, devoid of original righteousness, and disordered by original sin as a moral disease, perverting the action of all the faculties. As the substance of the body is not itself disease, but is perverted and disordered in its action by disease, so the substance of the body and soul is not sin, but is perverted and disordered in its action by original sin. Moreover, Turretin defines original sin as neither an act nor as the substance of the soul, but as an "innate vicious habit." It is so called because it is a state of the body and soul predisposing to wrong action, just as acquired habits predispose to various modes of action. Of this he says,

> "It is compared to a disease, and is not merely a want of righteousness, but also a positive corruption, which introduces a universal derangement of nature and all its faculties, and is commonly described as involving folly, blindness and ignorance in the intellect, malice, contumacy and rebellion in the will, insubordination or want of sensibility in the affections, so that man becomes not only averse from good, but also prone to all evil."

This original sin, however, though not consisting in action, but preceding all knowledge and action, they regarded as criminal, and punishable to such a degree as to be a proper justification of eternal punishments, even in the case of unborn infants, as is distinctly stated in the French confession.

Such is a brief view of the depravity of man as an individual, which has been believed by some of the most devoted and experimental Christians whom this world has ever seen. In all of these statements it is apparent that they have benevolently aimed at the great end before mentioned,—that is, to give a thorough and radical view of the fallen

---

Protestants complained that he failed to grasp the Reformation as a movement, and focused on the doctrinal shortcomings, inconsistencies and contradictions of its leaders.

and ruined condition of man, so as to dissipate all the delusions of pride and self-confidence, and to prepare the way for a cure no less radical and thorough. They felt that the strength and obstinacy of their own inherent depravity was so great, and its resistance of all means of thorough cure so long-continued, that it must have its roots lower than any act of conscious choice, even in a depraved nature. So also the power of depravity, as developed in the history of the world was so great, both in resisting and rendering vain divine means and influences adapted to reform it, and in plunging man headlong into all depths of sin in its vilest forms, that they could not rest satisfied with a mere statement of the fact that men do voluntarily sin from the commencement of moral agency, but descended into the depths of a nature utterly depraved, anterior to all individual, personal action, for a cause permanent and powerful enough to produce such results.

To illustrate their ideas of the activity and of the power of this depraved nature, they resort to the most striking material analogies. It is like a glowing furnace, constantly emitting flames and sparks; a fountain sending out polluted streams. It is a seed or seed-plot of sin. Original sin, by which it is thus corrupted, is a stain or infection pervading all the powers of the soul. It is a noisome root, out of which do spring most abundantly all kinds of sin. They do not regard it as merely a propensity to sin, which is not of itself sinful, but assert emphatically that it is truly and properly sin, and exposes those in whom it is, even before they have acted at all, to the wrath of God and eternal death.

In coming to these results, they turned the clear gaze of their minds away, for a time, from other considerations, and regarded intently what they knew of human depravity by experience, by history, and by the Word of God, and sought to lay a foundation deep enough to sustain a doctrine that should come up to the fearful realities of the case. Nor does their language convey an idea at all too strong of the fearful power of the actual developments of human depravity in the history of this world,—even as stated by Unitarians,—or of the great truth, that there must be in man some adequate cause, before action, of a course of action so universal, so powerful, so contrary to right, to the natural laws of all created minds, and to his own highest interests.

But the question whether their statements are not liable to serious and unanswerable objections, so long as the moving powers of Christianity are adjusted as they are at present, will more properly come up for consideration here after.

CHAPTER IX: SOCIAL AND ORGANIC RELATIONS OF MAN

WE have seen how full are the statements of Turretin, Dr. Watts, John Wesley, and others, against the idea that a new-created being should be so made, or so circumstanced, that there should be an original bias or preponderance towards sin and ruin. If a new-created being has a sinful or morally deteriorated nature, there would seem to be, on these principles, the greater reason for not exposing him to the additional influence of circumstances tending to develop, strengthen and mature, his sinful propensities. We need, then, in order to judge of the conflict between principles, and facts, to consider the circumstances of man, as well as his nature and original propensities. If we stop short of this, we shall not adequately conceive the power of those causes, various and united, that tend to the ruin of man, as conceived by those who entertain the views under consideration. We see only the power of his personal depravity as an individual, and his weakness to resist allurements to sin. We ought, then, in order to complete these views, next to consider the fact, that, being thus depraved, man is subjected from his birth to the power of other sinful minds, united in depraved social arrangements and organizations, called, collectively, *the world*.

In the heathen world, and in sinful families of Christian nations, this subjugation to the power of evil social organizations begins from the time of birth. All the pollutions of idolatry, all the evil passions, actions and examples, of sinful parents, surround the child from his birth upward, and form the moral atmosphere in which he lives.

> "Superstitions exist that are the growth of ages; and idolatries that seem to have been adapted, with consummate address, to meet all that depraved nature craves; and these are so inwrought with the fabric of society as to make an integral part of every one of its institutions, and thus every earthly interest seems to demand that things should remain as they are."

On this subject Dr. Burnap has thus spoken, with great truth and eloquence:

"Society, from the same causes, is capable of becoming as vitiated as the individual, with this more calamitous consequence, that it reacts upon the individual, to make him more depraved than he could have become had he stood alone. Not only so, but the vices of society are more enduring than those of the individual. The vices of the individual die with him, but the vices of society are perpetuated from generation to generation.

"Under an arbitrary or a tyrannical government, all motives to a virtuous life are greatly weakened. Virtue has no reward, and vice is safe so long as it has the means to bribe the hand of justice.

"It is in vain to expect any high degree of moral attainment under a bad government. Take, as an example, the Ottoman empire. It occupies some of the fairest portions of the globe. But the very manner in which the government is administered corrupts and ruins everything. The whole organization of the state is nothing more nor less than a vast machine for extortion and robbery. The successive governors of the different provinces are generally court favorites, or mere adventurers, whose only hope of wealth and distinction is the favor of their sovereign, resulting in the opportunity of plundering, for a few years, one of the provinces of the empire. With this understanding, the sycophant takes possession of his government, and under the pretense of taxation, which he levies at his own discretion, the best citizens are sure to suffer the worst spoliation. The very appearance of thrift and wealth is dangerous, and all motive to industry and economy, to good morals and good management, is taken away. Those who are plundered seek first a refuge in hypocrisy and deception; or, having lost all, become the robbers and oppressors of those who are more defenseless than themselves.

"Can it be said that a human being, who is born and passes through life under such a government and in such a state of society, has a fair opportunity for right development? No more than a grain of corn thrown into a heap of stones or a thicket of brambles."

The power of corrupt social organizations is not at all exaggerated in this statement; and the same remarks may be extended to corrupt religious, educational and commercial organizations, which have in all ages exerted inconceivable power.

So, too, as far as the larger social circles, of which he is a part, in Christian nations, are worldly, ambitious, luxurious or sensual, he is led, by social power and rewards, and by the fear of shame, to follow the same course to which his depraved heart already impels him. Hence the fact that large cities are slaughter-houses of countless throngs of young men,—in theaters, at the gaming-table, the tavern, or the place of impure resort. Moreover, so far as business and politics are worldly and corrupt, so far they give a new impulse and greater development to his natural depravity. In some communities, the tendencies are all to ruin. In others, Christian families and churches to a certain degree counteract them; but still, even to this day, the predominant power of the organizations of this world has been to evil. They have tended to develop, mature, and confirm the native depravity which already exists in each man as an individual; and this alike in the higher circles of the wealthy, fashionable and powerful, and in the middle and lower walks of life. What Christian parent can send his child to the schools and colleges of our land, or into the stores of our merchants, or shops of our artisans, or even to the farms of our agriculturalists, without feeling that evil social influences, of vast power, will beset him on every side?

CHAPTER X: RELATIONS OF MAN TO INVISIBLE ENEMIES

WE have seen the social and organic relations of man. But even this, in the judgment of those who hold these views, does not complete the dark picture. They regard every man who is born under such social organizations as also exposed to the malice and wiles of powerful evil spirits, acting through them. This is not, indeed, a doctrine of nature; but, in their judgment, what nature does not teach is clearly revealed in the Word of God. This world, we are there informed, is the abode and theater of action for hosts of fallen spirits, who, whilst the generations of men die, live and plan, and acquire malignant wisdom, from age to age. They understand the depravity of man, and his moral weakness; and long experience has given them terrific skill in the science of temptation. Such systems of error as the depraved hearts of men are ready to adopt, they skilfully invent, promulgate and defend. Such organizations as are in spirit most opposed to the kingdom of God, they form, animate and sustain. Thus, not only by individual and transient suggestions, but through organized, established, and permanent systems of evil, do they "work in the children of disobedience," and "lead them captive at their will" (Eph. 2:2, 5:6). The fearful power exerted by these dark rulers of this world we are in no danger of over-estimating. None had a deeper conviction of it than our Savior. He was revealed and became incarnate to destroy the power of the devil and his hosts. When Paul was sent to the heathen world, his commission was, to turn them from the power of Satan to God. He regarded his chief conflict to be not so much with depraved man as with these dark hosts. Nor does prophecy give any hope of the conversion of the world till Satan is bound and cast into the abyss. Such is the fearful power of those spirits, in the midst of whose systems men, themselves so deeply depraved, are born and live. Not only, then, are men surrounded by corrupt human systems, but by powerful spirits of evil, skilled to animate and employ these systems for their ruin with the highest degree of energy.

65

Combine all of these statements, and we shall have a comprehensive and fearful view of the ruined state of man. Yet, fearful as it is, it is a view that has been, and, in its fundamental facts, still is, believed by some of the most devoted Christians ever seen on earth. They have been led to it by their own experience, by observation of history, and by the Word of God. So the Reformers, so the Puritans believed, and so the leading orthodox bodies of the present day substantially believe. Eminently devoted men, like Edwards, have commonly the deepest and most heartfelt conviction of these things. They regard them as obviously the views of the inspired writers. Accordingly, it is because God can and does save men, against such mighty causes of ruin, that, in the words of the apostle Paul, they extol the magnitude of his power. It is "according to the working of his mighty power which he wrought in Christ when he raised him from the dead and placed him at his own right hand in the heavenly places" (Eph. 1:19, 20). Those thus saved he describes as once "dead in trespasses and sins, walking according to the course of this world, according to the prince of the power of the air, the spirit that now worketh in the children of disobedience, and by nature the children of wrath, even as others" (Eph. 2: 1-3).

Such, then, is a development of the remaining great moving power of Christianity, as it has been and still is set forth by men deeply engaged in the great work of the moral renovation of man. At another time we shall consider the question, to what extent, and on what grounds, it is justly open to assault, as opposed to the principles of honor and right. But we will now look at it as a statement aiming at a thorough view of human depravity, and of the hostile forces which are arrayed against the renovation and salvation of man, and which are to be assailed and reversed by the power of God. It must be confessed that, on such a general view, it accords with the fearful energy with which depravity has been, in fact, developed in this world. It also presents a deep foundation for a system of redemption,—a system vast and sublime, and interlocking with the whole system of the moral universe. In its penetrating and revolutionary power it has proved itself deep and thorough. It presents to every individual a great work to be done, a great salvation to be secured. It provides powerful motives. It imparts energy. It creates a deep experience. It gives a profound and thorough character to all schemes of social reform. Moreover, it has ever been the great center of evangelical enterprise and power.

CHAPTER XI: THE CONFLICT A REALITY

SUCH, then, is a statement of the principles of equity and honor, on the one hand, and of the most radical view of the fallen and ruined condition of man, on the other. Each statement, it has been seen, is sustained by the testimony of men eminent for piety, and of the highest reputation as the defenders of orthodoxy. With regard to the fearful depth and power of human depravity, as actually developed, even eminent Unitarian divines give most explicit testimony. That only which is needed to complete the view is an account of the antecedent causes of such developments. This, as it has been just given, completes the common orthodox view of the two great moving powers of the Christian system. Can anything be more certain than that Christianity can never, as a system, operate harmoniously and with full power, except on two conditions,—first, that it shall, in theory, include what really belongs to them both, and, secondly, that it shall give ample room for the full and consistent development of each? For the radical elements of both belong to the system, and are alike essential to its perfect development and most salutary influence.

In contemplating them as they have been set forth, two things strike the mind as worthy of notice: one, that each, in its radical elements, is sustained by its own independent and indestructible evidence; the other, that, as Christianity is presently understood, there is no possibility of a full and harmonious development of them both. But on the other hand, one constantly conflicts with and tends to repress, and even to destroy, the other.

The evidence which sustains the principles of honor and right, as we have seen, originates from the fact that God has so made the mind that their truth is intuitively recognized and affirmed, and is, therefore, a divine revelation; and also from the distinct recognition of these principles in Christian experience and in the Word of God.

The truth of the fundamental facts concerning the ruined state of man is evinced by the combined testimony of the Word of God, of history, of observation, and of Christian consciousness.

But, that in some way these moving powers have been so misunderstood as to conflict with each other, is obvious from simply placing them, as above developed, side by side. To say the very least, the preceding statements as to the ruin of man do appear directly to conflict with the principles of honor and right which have been set forth, and tend directly to subvert and destroy them. He who holds that God, in the manner already set forth, gives existence to men with natures radically corrupt and depraved, anterior to any knowledge, desire or choice, of their own, with full power to do evil and none to do good, and then places them under the all-pervading influence of corrupt and corrupting social systems,—and, in addition to all this, subjects them to the tremendous and delusive power of malignant spirits, fearfully skilled in the work of developing, maturing and confirming original depravity,—cannot, at least, with any apparent consistency, say that the Creator has fulfilled towards them the demands of honor and of right, as they have been exhibited. How can he say that he has regarded their well-being as he ought, or that he has observed towards them the principles of justice? Has He not held them responsible for what exists in them through his own agency, and anterior to any desire, choice or action, of their own? Has He not conferred on them such original constitutions as most unfavorably affect their prospects for eternity, and render their right conduct and eternal life in the highest degree improbable? Has He not placed them in circumstances which are not reasonably and benevolently favorable to their eternal life?

He, then, who holds that God is the author of the facts alleged, finds himself constantly urged, by the demands of logical consistency, to evade, or else to call in question and deny, the real and self-evident principles of honor and right. On the other hand, he who holds to the genuine principles of honor and right will be no less powerfully urged to deny the facts alleged as to the ruined state of man, and to put forth all his energies to subvert and destroy them.

Nay, more; it would seem as if the preceding statement of the principles of honor and right had been specially designed to effect this end. It seems to oppose the statement of facts, as to the ruined state of man, deliberately, universally, radically, and step by step.

Moreover, undeniable facts prove the reality of the alleged collision. Each of these moving powers of the system thus put into opposition to each other has, in fact, created a party to represent and defend it, and to oppose and subvert the other.

It is also a fact worthy of distinct notice, that when, as has often been the case, individuals have tried to retain both powers in their system in full action, they have almost invariably run into self-contradiction; so much so, that few, if any writers of this class can be found who are exempt from the charge.

Finally, all attempts to harmonize these opposing powers have hitherto failed, and, as the system is at present understood, ever must fail. For, since each has in itself radical truth, which is sustained by its own evidence, it has a vital power which cannot be destroyed, nor can its defenders be thoroughly defeated; and, therefore, unless they can be harmoniously adjusted, division and conflict will be perpetual.

It is not possible, however, to convey a full idea of this momentous truth by mere general statements. We will, therefore, exhibit principles and facts more in detail to illustrate the reality of this conflict, and to show that, on existing grounds, it is interminable.

BOOK II

THE CONFLICT IN EXPERIENCE

Chapter I: Laws Of Thought And Emotion Under This System

LET us, then, proceed more fully to set forth what has been the actual operation of these powers, so misunderstood and in conflict, on the human mind. In doing this, I shall not, at present, follow the order of history. I shall, rather, look at the relations of the system to the human mind, its tendencies to produce deep divisions of opinions and feelings, and the different kinds of experience to which it naturally gives rise.

It will be seen at once that the opposing doctrinal positions which have been advanced are not points of mere speculation, but of deep practical, personal interest. Christianity does not meet man as a mere philosophical theory, nor as a speculation of some Socrates, Plato, Aristotle, or any other uninspired sage; but as an inspired message from God, invested with supreme authority, and pointing man to a final judgment, and to eternal destinies, to be decided in accordance with its principles and requisitions.

Nor does it relate, primarily, to theory, but to action. Its great end is to produce a moral change in man—in every man. It charges guilt on all. It calls at once for repentance, for a believing application for pardon through Christ, and for a holy life. Nor can the great points in question be avoided. Since they relate to conviction of sin, repentance, faith, and a holy life, they are, of course, involved in all preaching, in all prayer, and in all religious efforts.

Nor are the interests involved in these conflicting powers of secondary consequence, and therefore adapted to excite but little feeling. They involve all that man holds dear for two worlds, all that he can conceive of personal good or evil. Nay, more; they involve not merely individual well-being, but, what is infinitely more momentous, the character of God, and the eternal prospects of the universe under His omnipotent and all-pervading sway.

We need not wonder, then, that the developments of the human mind, under a system so misunderstood, and involving such interests, have been characterized by a fearful earnestness, and deep and intense emotion.

When such interests and emotions impel men, under such a system, it is absurd to suppose that division, of the deepest and most radical kind, can be averted. It never has been possible. It never will be. Each of the conflicting views is fundamentally true, and is sustained by powerful evidence. Each is intensely affecting to the feelings; and, such is the human mind, that it is to be expected that some will come entirely under the influence of one view, and others of the other. Moreover, if either gains the ascendency, it is large enough, and true and important enough, so to fill the field of vision, and to produce such an unwavering conviction of its truth, such an overpowering sense of its supreme importance, that it shall compel all that seems to be at war with it to give way, and summon the powers of logic, criticism and exposition to effect its purpose. More over, if either of these views thus takes possession of the mind, and fills and overwhelms it with emotion, it, of course, creates and gives character to a peculiar religious experience.

There are those, I know, who look with contempt upon such theological conflicts of the present and of past ages, and the next to superhuman efforts which men have put forth in the defense of their views. But conflicts on such themes as these are worthy of any other emotion than contempt. Nothing can be more sublime and affecting than this great controversy of ages truly viewed, as from some mountain-top of history we survey the reality and earnestness of the conflict, its extent and duration, the depth of emotion awakened by it, its fertility in varied intellectual results, and the relations of its solution to the future destinies of the world.

Let us, then, from such an eminence, endeavor to survey and develop some of the experiences which have sprung from the conflicting operations of these ill-adjusted truths.

Chapter II: Experiences Characterized

IT is not my present purpose to minutely consider all of the experiences to which the system of Christianity, as misunderstood, has given rise. I propose rather to exhibit in their bold outlines some of the more important of them, reserving others for future consideration.

In setting forth any experience, my purpose is, first, to present those true views in which are found the elements of its permanent vitality and power. After this, I shall then subjoin to each experience the reaction which has ever arisen against it from the truths which it has excluded, and with which it is in conflict. Of these experiences I shall now consider but six; others may be adverted to hereafter.

1. First of all will be noticed that in which a Christian experience, and a deep consciousness of the ruin of man, become so intense and powerful as to give the entire ascendency to the belief of the facts assumed in the most radical theory which has been stated of human depravity, and to suspend the power of the principles of honor and right to produce a disbelief, or even an essential modification of them. Such full faith has, indeed, sometimes led even to a rejection of those principles, at least in their relations to God; or, if not, to an evasion of them, or to a resort to the plea of mystery.

2. Next will be considered the feeling sense of the sacredness and momentous importance of the principles of honor and right in their relations to God, which gives the entire ascendency to those principles, and leads to an entire denial and rejection of the facts alleged, in setting forth in a radical manner the utter ruin of man.

3. I notice next an experience in which the fundamental facts and the moral principles are both retained without modification; but the mind seeks relief from their conflict in a system of ultimate uni-

versal salvation. Of this we have a deeply interesting illustration in the experience of the celebrated John Foster.[1]

4. Next to this will pass in review that class of experiences in which both the principles of honor and right and the essential facts are professedly retained; but still the principles are allowed to modify the facts, with the intention of removing all real conflict between them.

5. We shall then advert to an experience in which the principles and the most radical facts in question are both retained, without any perceived and satisfactory mode of modification or adjustment. In this case, the mind comes, for a time, under the oppressive and over-whelming consciousness of being apparently under a universal system which is incapable of defense, and under a God whom the principles of honor and of right forbid us to love and to worship.

6. Lastly, an experience will be noticed in which, as in the last, the principles and the most radical facts in question are both retained, but are harmonized by a new adjustment of the system, such that the painful conflict between fundamental truths is at an end, and God is seen in His full-orbed glory and loveliness, and is worshiped with un-divided affection and reverence.

I shall consider in the case of only the first four of these experiences the reaction to which they give rise; for the fifth experience is too terri-ble ever to be embodied in formal statements, or to become so general and permanent as to call for a reaction; and the sixth, if it is ever truly

---

1   John Foster was a Unitarian minister. *The Life and Correspondence of John Foster: with notices of Mr Foster as a Preacher and Companion* by John Sheppard, Author of 'Thoughts on devotion', etc.,ed. J. E. Ryland (2 vols, New York, 1846,). Also of note was his wife, Hannah Webster Foster of Little Cambridge (now All-ston-Brighton), the first American born woman to write and publish a novel. *The Coquette*, or the *History of Eliza Wharton* (1797), was a thinly veiled account (em-ploying fictitious names) of the seduction, betrayal and eventual death in childbirth of Elizabeth Whitman, the daughter of Reverend Elnathon Whitman of Hartford, Connecticut. Rev. Whitman was a distant relative of Reverend John Foster. Eliza-beth's seducer was thought to be Pierpont Edwards, son of Jonathan Edwards, of the the Great Awakening. The reputation of Pierpont's father as a moral arbiter added spice to the Whitman scandal. The scandal excited public attention. *The Coquette* was said to have been, next to the Bible, the most popular reading material of early nineteenth-century New England.

reached, is adapted to harmonize all the facts of the case with the principles of honor and right, and thus to render needless a reaction.

In this review of experiences, it is my earnest desire and aim, not merely to be impartial, but ever to regard with sympathy, and sincerely to honor, every response of the human soul to any part of the great system of truth, with whatever other errors it may have been connected. I am no less desirous to find a similar spirit in all of my readers. I do most earnestly deprecate the awakening in any mind of a spirit of partisan controversy. I rather desire, as I have already said, to do all in my power to create, on all sides, a feeling of sympathy and mutual interest, by pointing out those benevolent and honorable impulses, and that regard to truth,—mixed though it should be with other motives, by which the various parties have been actuated,—and to produce a candid and united effort to eliminate error and to develop the whole truth.

Chapter III: The First Experience, Or The Philosophy Of Old-School Theology

THE radical element of the first experience is the doctrine of real, responsible, punishable depravity in man, before voluntary action. Whether this depravity be called boldly a depraved or a corrupt nature, or, more mildly, innate or inherent depravity, it comes, at last, to the same thing. It is, as I have said, resorted to by Christian men to account for the fearful developments of actual depravity, which are so plain that even eminent Unitarian divines concede them, and state them with impressive eloquence and power. The mere power of choice and external temptation seem insufficient to explain a course of action so contrary to reason, so obstinate, so general, so ruinous. They, therefore, resort to the idea of a depraved and sinful nature anterior to choice and action. Those who hold this view also hold, so far as I know, without exception, the connected views of man's exposure to the full influence of corrupt social and organic relations, and of invisible malignant spirits of great power.

At first sight, it would be supposed that no one could be induced to believe that the great Creator could or would give to a new-created being such a nature, rendering it powerless to do good, and then place it in such circumstances. Yet many most excellent men have so believed and taught.

By what power, then, have they been brought to such conclusions? I answer, by the power of Christian experience. Nor is this an irrational ground of belief.

If a man is conscious that he has the plague, or a fever, or a consumption, he knows perfectly that he is not well. If by any medicine he is restored to perfect health, he knows what health is, and what is the normal and proper state of the body. In this case, no argument from divine benevolence, or the laws of honor and of right, against the existence of a diseased constitution, will ever convince him that he was not in fact sick with a malignant disease, affecting his whole constitution.

So there is a life of the mind. It involves an original and designed correlation to God, and such a state of the affections, passions, emotions, intellect and will, that communion with God shall be natural, habitual, and the very life of the soul. He who has been so far healed by divine grace as to reach this state has a true idea of the normal and healthy state of the soul; and, if he finds that there is that in the state of his moral constitution and emotions which seems to lie beneath his will and undermine its energy to follow the convictions of reason and conscience, and that by divine grace this is changed, and an energy, not only to will, but to do good, is supplied,—is it to be wondered at that, in some way, he should come to the conclusion that there is in his nature, or moral constitution, depravity or pollution anterior to the action of the will? Is it strange that he should deeply feel and express his moral impotence to do good, arising from such a cause, and, in his struggles against it, long for deliverance in the words of Paul, "O, wretched man that I am! who shall deliver me from the body of this death?" (Rom. 7:24).

Let us look into the experience of Edwards in one particular,—that is, as to a sinful propensity to self-admiration, which is always connected with a sinful desire for the praise and admiration of others, and leads to quick and bitter resentment if reputation is assailed. He who has been taught by God to know what spiritual chastity is will see in this action of the human mind, so natural, so powerful, so fearfully common, a kind of moral pollution, the loathsomeness of which he lacks words to express. He will long to exterminate this malignant and polluting disease of the soul, and to become in the sight of God spiritually chaste, humble, satisfied with the judgment and favor of God, and regarding it as a very small matter to be judged or censured by human judgments, and censure as no reason for ceasing to exercise towards all the utmost good will and Christian love and forgiveness. In this respect, Edwards, when tried by the most unreasonable and unkind rejection and dishonor from his own church and people, manifested one of the most beautiful examples on record of a mild, forgiving, Christ-like spirit. Why was it? If we look into his experience, we shall see that God had prepared him for it, by eradicating that bitter root of malignity, of which I have spoken. His experience I give in his own words:

> "I have a much greater sense of my universal, exceeding dependence on God's grace and strength than I used formerly to have, and have experienced more of an abhorrence of my own righteousness. The very thought of any joy arising in me, on any consideration of my own amiableness, performances or experiences, or any goodness of heart or life, is nauseous and detestable to me."

This is exactly the experience of one to whom God has shown, in its true light, the deep and unutterable pollution of that spiritual unchastity which is involved in that deep-rooted pride, which, like a cancer, seems to have struck its roots deeply into the human soul, and the extermination of which calls for so much providential discipline, and so many and so painful struggles, and which made the thorn in the flesh necessary to preserve the humility even of the apostle Paul.

Yet Edwards did not find this root of evil entirely exterminated in his soul; and so much had his moral sensibilities been quickened to see and feel its pollutions, that any tendencies to what he thus abhorred filled him with deep distress; therefore he proceeds to say:

> "And yet I am greatly *afflicted* with a proud and self-righteous spirit, much more sensibly than I used to be formerly. I see that serpent rising and putting forth its head continually, everywhere, all around me."

This one instance illustrates what takes place in such an experience, in many respects. It is a process which the apostles Paul and Peter compare to a crucifixion. The original depraved character is called *the flesh*, and is likened to a body composed of many members, each of which is to be crucified and destroyed. This radical process of regeneration and sanctification leads to a consciousness of depths of inward and hidden sinfulness, of which a deep innate depravity seems to give the only adequate account. The action of all the powers seems to be deranged and perverted by sin. The whole mind appears to be a wonderful system in ruins. The heart is felt to be deceitful above all things, and desperately wicked; and, as such, is hidden from the full knowledge of all but God.

This, no doubt, is what Prof. Hodge means, when he says, "Conviction of sin under this system is more than remorse for actual transgressions; it is also a sense of the thorough depravity of the whole nature, penetrating far beneath the acts of the soul, affecting its permanent moral states, which lie beyond the reach of the will."

Under the influence of such feelings, Edwards says: "It is affecting to think how ignorant I was, when a young Christian, of the bottomless, infinite depths of wickedness, pride, hypocrisy and deceit, left in my heart."

His more mature experiences cannot be understood, unless we consider by what principles he judged. His standard was this:

> "What must my soul become before it is capable of that pure and perfect sympathy with God in which its true life and health consists; and what are those moral states, habits and emotions, which must be eradicated in order to secure these results?"

All of these he sets down under the category of sinful states and emotions. All know that he became an eminently holy man. All know that through him God exercised an immense vital power in quickening the religious experience of the church. All know that no man in severe trials ever displayed more of the power of godliness than he. Being thus restored to spiritual health, was he not qualified to judge what was the moral state from which he had been raised by the grace of God? Let us, then, hear him state his own views of it. In his more mature experiences he thus speaks of himself:

> "My wickedness, as I am in myself, has long appeared to me perfectly ineffable, and swallowing up all thought and imagination like an infinite deluge, or mountains over my head. I know not how to express better what my sins appear to me to be, than by heaping infinite upon infinite, and multiplying infinite by infinite. Very often, for these many years, these expressions are in my mind, and in my mouth. 'Infinite upon infinite! Infinite upon infinite!' When I look into my heart and take a view of my wickedness, it looks like an abyss infinitely deeper than hell. And it appears to me that, were it not for free grace, exhalted and raised to the infinite height of all the fulness and glory of the great

Jehovah, and the arm of his power and grace, stretched forth in all the majesty of his power, and in all the glory of his sovereignty, I should appear sunk down in my sins, below hell itself; far beyond the sight of everything but the eye of sovereign grace, that can pierce even down to such a depth. And yet it seems to me that my conviction of sin is exceedingly small and faint. It is enough to amaze me, that I have no more sense of my sin. I know, certainly, that I have very little sense of my sinfulness. When I have had turns of weeping and crying for my sins, I thought I knew at the time that my repentance was nothing to my sin."

I am aware that, to some, this experience of Edwards will seem either mysterious or exaggerated. It is, nevertheless, an important fact, and deserves study. It is to be judged by the principles which have been stated, and of which I shall speak more fully in another place. It is enough, at present, to say that these very remarkable words are not to be set aside with contempt, as the exaggerated professions of an excitable mind, incapable of clear and discriminating thought. Their author was, confessedly, the great metaphysician of his age. None knew better than he, so far as experience is concerned, what sin and holiness were. And yet, such is his mature report of his own experience. I believe that there were real facts upon which his statements were based. What explanation ought to be given of them I shall consider in another place.

To Edwards, therefore, must it not have appeared evident that he had never, by conscious acts of choice, introduced all of this depravity into himself, but that his sins were, in some way, the development of something from the depths of his being, that had preceded his consciousness and choice? Would it not strongly incline him,—as a similar experience has thousands beside,—to the idea of a deeply depraved nature before actual sin?

Edwards, moreover, was no less distinguished by a deep sense of the reality and power of the malignant influences of evil spirits. He looked upon Satan as the great framer of systems of error, and the author of spurious and delusive religious affections; and he compares men to weak and silly sheep, constantly deluded, deceived, and combined in evil, or else frightened and scattered by his terrors. In the Word of God, and in all history too, as eloquently and logically set forth in his treatise on original sin, he found a constant illustration and proof of the truth of these views. In this experience he was but an exponent of a class of men found in all ages. To them has the law of God come home, as it did to Paul, and, under the influences of the divine spirit, their conviction of sin has been deep and agonizing, their regeneration has been thorough, their spiritual experience profound, and their new nature fully developed.

Out of such an experience grows an unwavering and unconquerable faith as to the most radical view of the great facts of man's ruin. If there is anything which they know with absolute certainty, it is the truth of these facts. Their own experience, history, and the Bible, coincide; the evidence is cumulative, manifold, irresistible. They not only believe, but, in fact, they *know*. They are not mistaken, and they know that they are not. Such is the legitimate tendency of an experimental knowledge of the truths of the case on regenerated minds. They know their original depravity, just as a man restored to health knows that he was diseased and is now in health. He knows past disease more absolutely by reason of its contrast with present health.

Evidence of the truth of such views of depravity they also find in the clear statements of the Word of God, and in the history of the world. Such views have, therefore, been very extensively held by the most powerful bodies of evangelical Christians, as appears from the quotations made from the creeds of the Reformation. Indeed, the *Princeton Review* alleges, and, so far as I know, correctly, that

> "there is not a creed of any Christian church (we do not mean separate congregation) in which the doctrine that inherent corruption, as existing prior to voluntary action, is of the nature of sin, is not distinctly affirmed. The whole Latin church, the Lutheran, all branches of the Reformed church, unite in the most express, nicely measured assertions of faith in this doctrine" (April, 1851, p. 324).

Moreover, men of the most eminent Christian character, in successive ages, such as the Reformers, the Puritans, Edwards, Chalmers, and the Haldanes,[2] have held these views. In their hands, too, deep and powerful results have been produced by the system.

Therefore is it that Dr. Hodge asserts, in the *Princeton Review*, that

> "it is an undeniable fact, that this system underlies the piety of the church in all ages. It is the great granitic formation, whose peaks tower towards heaven, and draw thence the waters of life, and in whose capacious bosom repose those green pastures in which the great Shepherd gathers and sustains his flock. It has withstood all changes, and it still stands. Heat and cold, snow and rain, gentle abrasion and violent convulsions, leave it as it was. It cannot be moved. In our own age and country, this system of doctrine has had to sustain a renewed conflict. It has been assailed by argument, by ridicule, by contempt. It has been pronounced absurd, obsolete, effete, powerless. It has withstood logic, indignation, wit. ... Still it stands" (*Princeton Review*, April, 1851, p. 319).

Indeed, we think that no one can fail to see that the religious depth that has been found in the Western church, and among the Reformers, and Puritans, and their followers, as compared with the superficiality of the Eastern church, under the auspices of John of Damascus,[3] and the Greek fathers, is owing to the more profound views of human depravity which were introduced into it by Augustine, and which gave a deep and vital character to its theology, but which never penetrated and vitalized the Eastern church.

---

2   Robert Haldane (1764-1842) was a Scottish churchman. In 1797 Haldane sold his castle, left the Church of Scotland and traveled around Scotland preaching. In December of that year he joined his brother and others to form the "Society for the Propagation of the Gospel at Home," which built chapels or "tabernacles" for congregations, supported missionaries, and maintained institutions for the education of young men to carry on the work of evangelization.

3   John of Damascus (645/676-749) was a Syrian monk and priest. Born and raised in Damascus, he died at his monastery, Mar Saba, near Jerusalem. A polymath whose fields of interest and contribution included law, theology, philosophy, and music, he is said by some sources to have served as a Chief Administrator to the Muslim caliph of Damascus before his ordination. He wrote works expounding the Christian faith, and composed hymns which are still used liturgically in Eastern Christian practice throughout the world. He is considered "the last of the Fathers" of the Eastern Orthodox church and is best known for his strong defense of icons.

No one, we think, in view of facts on the great scale, can deny that this system has exerted a deeper and more powerful influence on the world than any other. It has in it the elements of the greatest power, simply because it meets as no other system does the wants of the deepest forms of Christian experience, and through such channels the great river of moral power on earth must ever run.

And yet, powerful as it is, it has never acted in any community without meeting the counter influence of another power, springing from the deepest sources of intuitive human convictions and emotions. And, therefore, as we proposed, we shall proceed to consider the reaction to which this view of the system has ever given rise.

CHAPTER IV: THE REACTION

WE have stated the elements of power in the first view of the system; and, clearly, they are great, for a deep Christian experience has ever been the ruling power in God's kingdom. Yet we are obliged to add, that at no time, and in no community, have its triumphs been universal or permanent. Its advocates have been obliged to work against a steady, powerful and deathless reaction. Nor is the reason obscure.

As at present adjusted, it has never been able to prevent, or successfully to repel, a most powerful assault, prompted, not by human depravity and carnal reason, but by the divinely revealed principles of honor and of right. And to this assault its advocates have never made a reply which has had any decisive power.

And, indeed, at first one wonders how even the advocates of this doctrine can avoid seeing that it is in direct conflict with their own statements of the principles of equity and of honor. For instance; Turretin says of new-created Adam, that if there was in him "any inclination to sin by nature, then God would be the author of it, and so the sin itself be chargeable upon God." How much more is this true, if, in new-created beings, there is not merely an inclination to sin, but even a sinful nature before action, and an entire want of power to do right!

How explicit, too, are the statements of Dr. Watts, that it would be unjust for God so to form a new-created being that there should be in his nature a bias to evil. So, too, the Princeton divines tell us that "a probation, in order to be fair, must afford as favorable a prospect of a happy as of an unhappy conclusion;" and, by referring to the probation of Adam as a fair one, they teach us that a good moral constitution, well-balanced powers, and a decided bias to good, are essential to such a probation.

But are not men, by their concession, new-created beings? Do they not explicitly deny "any mysterious union with Adam, any confusion of our identity with his?" (Theol. Ess., I, 136). Is not God, therefore, truly the immediate creator of every man,—at least, so far as the spirit is concerned? Turretin, and the church at large, avow and defend this view.

Here, then, we have millions of new-created beings, commencing an eternal existence with sinful natures and a total inability to do good, even before thought or action. Can anything be more demonstrably at war with the principles of honor and of right which they avow than these facts?

Are we to suppose, then, that the advocates of this view have not seen this self-evident conflict, and have made no effort to obviate it? By no means. They have made strenuous efforts to defend the alleged facts on principles of equity and honor. Indeed, they take a ground that would, at least in part, sustain their position, if it were true. It is, however, a most remarkable ground; but, as it has been most extensively taken and held, and still is, it deserves careful attention.

The ground is this,—that all men, even before knowledge or action, and, indeed, before existence, have forfeited their rights as new-created beings, and have fallen under the just displeasure of God; and that the existence in them of a depraved nature, and of inability to do right, is a punishment inflicted on them by God, in accordance with their just deserts.

It is conceded by the Reformers and their followers that God cannot be defended on any ground other than this. They fully admit the demands of honor and right towards new-created beings, even to the highest degree. God is absolutely bound by them until they have been forfeited. But they allege that in the case of all men they have been forfeited: *And their whole defense of God turns upon this allegation.* If it can be made out, the defense may be valid. If it cannot be made out, the defense fails. And if it fails, it is no common failure. It involves God's honor and justice as to the eternal destinies of the countless millions of the human race.

With deep interest, then, we ask, when did all men make this alleged forfeiture, and incur this liability? The reply is, never in their own persons. Indeed, it was done before they existed, by the act of another, even of Adam.

But, in endeavoring by such a position to avoid collision with one law of equity and honor, do they not at once come into conflict with others? Is it not unjust and dishonorable falsely to charge the innocent, and to punish them for what they never did? Is it not unjust to decide that a new-created being has forfeited his right to a good moral constitution and propensities, and power to good, by an act which he never performed, and which took place hundreds or thousands of years before he was created?

Dr. Alexander says, that "all intuitively discern that for a ruler to punish the innocent is morally wrong." He also says, that "where we have intuitive certainty of anything, it is foolish to seek for other reasons." But who can be innocent of a sin in every possible respect, if those who are so accused did not exist when it was committed?

Of what avail, then, is it to avoid a conflict with one law of equity and honor, merely by coming into collision with others no less important and sacred? What are the naked facts alleged by the advocates of this view? They are these: that across the chasm of hundreds or thousands of years of absolute non-existence, the guilt and forfeiture of Adam's sin are transported, and ascribed to new-created beings, just beginning an immortal existence, and made the ground of punishing them with a depraved nature and inability to do good. Can such a procedure be made to accord with our intuitive convictions of equity and honor? Is it not punishing the innocent with infinite severity, and without a cause?

Nor is any relief gained by regarding such a sinful nature and inability to do good as coming on men not as a penalty, but as a consequence of Adam's sin, according to an ordinance of God as an absolute sovereign. Indeed, this is conceded and insisted on, as we shall see more fully hereafter, by all the leading divines of the Reformation, and by those who in modern days profess to walk most exactly in their steps. The sovereignty of God, as they have clearly seen and declared, implies no superiority to the laws of equity and honor. If their rights as new-created beings have not been forfeited, God has no right to disregard them.

But let us look at some of the efforts made to defend the alleged facts now under consideration. We shall then be able to judge what can be said to break the force of the principles of honor and right to which I have appealed.

CHAPTER V: THE REACTION IS IRRESISTIBLE, AS THE SYSTEM NOW IS

THE first point of attack has ever been, as we have already stated, the doctrine of the existence in a new-created being of a sinful nature, for which he is liable to just punishment, and that anterior to any knowledge, will or choice, of his own. How, it is asked, can it be honorable or right for God so to deal with any new-created being? To this question no one has ever been able to give any more satisfactory reply than those we have considered. These do not seem to have satisfied even all the friends of the doctrine of an inherent depravity of nature.

Indeed, a distinguished theological professor (Dr. Woods),[4] after setting forth what he asserts to be the faith of the church in all ages on this point, and surveying the discussions to which it has given rise, distinctly takes the ground of mere faith and mystery; that is, he comes distinctly to the conclusion that it cannot be vindicated on any principles of honor and right known to the human mind. Well may he say so. He expressly teaches that there is in the nature of man, anterior to knowledge or choice, a proneness or propensity to sin, which is "in its own nature sinful," "the essence of moral evil," "the sum of all that is vile and hateful." (*Woods' Works*, Vol. II, p. 336). He also teaches that God inflicts this "tremendous calamity" on all men for the sin of one man. This, he says, has been the belief of the church in all ages.

He then asks,

> "But how is this proceeding just to Adam's posterity? What have they done, before they commit sin, to merit

---

4   Leonard Woods (1774-1854) was an American theologian widely known for upholding orthodox Calvinism over Unitarianism. He was the pastor of the Congregational Church at West Newbury, Massachusettses, 1798, and the first professor of Andover Theological Seminary and between 1808 and 1846 in the chair of Christian theology.

pain and death? What have they done to merit the evil of existing without original righteousness, and with a nature prone to sin?" (Vol. II, p.315).

To feel the full force of this question, let it be once more stated that he regards this proneness of nature to sin as in itself sinful, yea, the essence of moral evil, the sum of all that is vile and hateful.

Surely, questions more momentous than these were never proposed. They affect all that man holds dear in all worlds, all that is holy and revered in God. They are, also, frankly and fairly stated. What, then, is his reply? It is a reply eminently worthy of profound attention. It touches the very vitals of Christianity. It shows, more clearly than words can utter it, the unfortunate, the defenseless condition of the system of Christianity when thus presented.

What, then, is the reply? In essence, it is simply this. It is utterly beyond our powers to show that such a proceeding on the part of God is either just or honorable.

"Here (he says) our wisdom fails. We apply in vain to human reason, or human consciousness, for an answer." Nay, more; he even admits that such conduct is "contrary to the dictates of our fallible minds." Yet he still insists that we ought not to judge at all in the case, but to believe that it is right, because God has done it. "God has not made us judges. The case lies wholly out of our province."

But if, as we have shown, God has made the human mind to form intuitive convictions of what is right and honorable in such cases if such convictions are a revelation of God Himself, if he appeals to them in his own defense, then plainly the case does not lie wholly outside of our province. How can we have any rational ideas of mercy in a case where, as God has made our minds, we must see that the most sacred principles of honor and right have been violated? Is such the basis of the greatest of all God's works, the redemption of the church?

That the human mind has strong intuitive convictions in this case, Dr. Woods concedes. The acts ascribed to God, according to our necessary convictions, appear dishonorable and unjust. But, to concede that, in this case, these moral intuitions are of divine origin, would be to abandon the argument. Nothing, therefore, remains but in some way to destroy their power, by giving them an evil name. This is commonly done by calling them "human reason," or "unsanctified philosophy," or "natural reason," or "carnal reason," and then warning all who revere God and love the truth not to be carried away with the subtlety of human reason, or by philosophical or metaphysical sagacity and adroitness. The following is an illustration of what I mean. Dr. Woods says:

> "It is no difficult task for the *subtlety of human reason*, to urge very plausible arguments against the common doctrine of man's innate moral depravity. But, so far as the doctrine is taught us by the inspired writers, it is our duty to hold it fast, however unable we may be to sustain it by *metaphysical reasoning*, or to remove the objections which *unsanctified philosophy* may set in array against it. It is a doctrine which is not to be brought for trial to the bar of human reason. Mere natural reason, mere philosophical or metaphysical sagacity, transcends its just bounds, and commits a heinous sacrilege, when it attacks this primary article of our faith, and labors to distort it, to undermine it, or to expose its truth or its importance to distrust" (Woods, Vol. II, p. 328).

I admit fully that the essential facts of human depravity, as I have set them forth, are of unspeakable moment, and that no revealed doctrine of the Bible is to be given up at the demand of unsanctified philosophy or carnal reason. But how does it appear that the intuitive decisions of the human mind as to honor and right, in view of the facts alleged, are unsanctified philosophy and carnal reason? How does it appear that they are not of divine origin, yea, the very voice of God through the human soul? Till this can be shown, it is not lawful to evade their power by resorting to mystery and faith in God.

Nor ought it to be forgotten that this style of reasoning is easily retorted. It is only necessary to assume that the theory in question is based upon a false interpretation of the Word of God, and then to warn all who fear God to avoid the sacrilegious audacity involved in doing violence to the divinely revealed principles of equity and honor, for the sake of sustaining the unfounded dogmas and crude speculations of human theories. If in this there would be no fair argument, as I concede,—if it would be but begging the question in debate,—why is the same style of argument any better on the other side of the question?

Dr. Hodge, an eminent leader of the Princeton divines, in view of the same alleged facts, at first assumes a ground of defense on the principles of justice. It would not be just, he tells us, to condemn men without a probation, either personally or in Adam. But a fair probation they have had. But even he must come at last to the same issue. His account of the matter is this: God's proceedings can be justified, because, before inflicting this tremendous evil, the race had a probation, through Adam as a representative; and that, since he sinned in this character, all men forfeited their original rights, and became obnoxious to penalty. Hence, the evils that come on men through his offense are not an arbitrary infliction, nor merely a natural consequence, but the infliction of a penalty.

But let us look a little more closely through these words at the real facts of the case, as held by Professor Hodge, and see if any real relief is gained. When, then, this penalty was originally denounced on them, had man transgressed any law? None; neither the law of Moses, nor the law of nature. Was there in them any innate depravity, on account of which they could be punished? None at all. The infliction of the penalty is antecedent to all these things. What, then, is this penalty? It is the greatest evil of which the mind of man can conceive. It is an entire forfeiture of the favor of God. It is the doom of commencing their existence out of fellowship with Him. It is to be utterly deprived of those original influences of the Spirit without which the mind cannot be developed in the image of God, but becomes inevitably sinful and corrupt, even before choice and action; and all this is denounced on all men before they have personally acted at all, and yet "it is of all evils the essence and the sum." That this is a fair statement of his views the following passage will show (Hodge on Romans, pp. 189, 190).

After considering some supposable causes of the penal evils that are asserted to come on the race through Adam, he decidedly rejects them, and thus proceeds:

> "No one of these causes, nor all combined, can account for the infliction of all the penal evils to which men are subjected. The great fact in the apostle's mind was, that *God regards and treats all men, from the first moment of their existence as out of fellowship with himself as having forfeited his favor.* Instead of entering into communion with them the moment they begin to exist (as he did with Adam), and form-

ing them by his Spirit in his own moral image, he regards them as out of his favor, and withholds the influences of the Spirit.

"Why is this? Why does God thus deal with the human race? Here is a form of death which the violation of the law of Moses, the transgression of the law of nature, the existence of innate depravity, separately or combined, are insufficient to account for. Its infliction is antecedent to them all; *and yet it is of all evils the essence and the sum.* Men begin to exist out of communion with God. This is the fact which no sophistry can get out of the Bible, or the history of the world. Paul tells us why it is. It is because we fell in Adam; it is for the offense of one man that all thus die. The covenant being formed with Adam, not only for himself, but also for his posterity,—in other words, Adam having been placed on trial not for himself only, but also for his race,—his act was, in virtue of this relation, *regarded as our act.* God withdrew from us, as he did from him; in consequence of this withdrawal we begin to exist in moral darkness, destitute of a disposition to delight in God, and prone to delight in ourselves and the world. The sin of Adam, therefore, ruined us; it was the ground of the withdrawing of the divine favor from the whole race; and the intervention of the Son of God for our salvation is an act of pure, sovereign and wonderful grace." And again: "The infliction of a penalty supposes the violation of law. But such evil was inflicted before the giving of the Mosaic law; it comes on men before the transgression of the law of nature, or even the existence of inherent depravity. It must, therefore, be for the offense of one man that judgment has come upon all men to condemnation."

Now, it will be observed, that the whole of this attempted vindication of God in inflicting such a penalty turns simply and only upon the assumed fact that "He regarded as our act" the act of Adam,—an act which it is at the same time conceded was not our act. It is conceded that we had not sinned in any sense; we had not violated the law of Moses, nor of nature, nor of Paradise, and there was in us no innate depravity. Nay, we did not even exist. Yet before our existence the penalty on us was denounced, and before any action of ours it is inflicted,—a penalty which "is of all evils the essence and the sum," and inflicted solely on the ground that God regarded as ours an act which was confessedly not ours.

The question by such a defense is merely shifted; but it returns with augmented force. On what principles of honor or of right is God to be justified in regarding as ours an act which was not ours, and on such a ground inflicting on us the greatest of all conceivable evils? Is not the imputation in question an additional act of injustice, instead of a just ground of inflicting a penalty so severe?

On this point Prof. Hodge has thrown no light. No light can be thrown upon it. So long as he holds such views, he must at last—as in fact he does—come to the ground of mystery and faith taken by Dr. Woods. That venerable father, conceding, as he does, that such facts are against our natural intuitions of honor and right, is obliged to say, "Here our wisdom fails. We apply in vain to human reason and human consciousness for an answer. We are perplexed and confounded, and find no resting-place until we seize the sublime truth, that 'God's ways are not our ways, nor his thoughts our thoughts,' and that all his acts and all his appointments are right." Prof. Hodge must, and does at last, join Dr. Woods in thus rejecting the testimony of our intuitive convictions of honor and right, and in retreating beneath the shelter of mystery and faith.

With reference to these dealings of God with our race, he distinctly says that they cannot be "explained on the common sense principles of moral government. The system which Paul taught was not a system of common sense, but of profound and awful mystery" (*Princeton Review*, April, 1851, p. 318).

Still, there are certain things from which they both shrink; and, in so doing, they, in at least one particular, admit the authority of these same natural intuitions, which they have just rejected. Dr. Woods regards as unauthorized and appalling the position that infant children, who are not guilty of any actual sin, either outwardly or inwardly, will be doomed to misery in the world to come, merely for sinful propensity,—forgetting that elsewhere he had declared it to be the very essence of all depravity.

Dr. Hodge also repudiates the doctrine "that eternal misery is inflicted on any man for the sin of Adam, irrespective of inherent depravity or actual transgression." But why should even these views be repudiated, or regarded as appalling?

Have they not been taught and defended by the same plea of faith and mystery to which Dr. Woods and Dr. Hodge resort, in opposition to the most obvious principles of equity and honor? We shall soon see that they have been. Why, then, do they repudiate them, or regard them as appalling?

Is it not merely because they are at war with those intuitive principles of honor and of right which God has made the mind to form? But are not the other facts, defended by both, really against those principles? Dr. Woods concedes that they are "contrary to the dictates of our minds" (Vol. II, p. 315), but attempts to weaken the force of the concession by calling them "fallible minds." But if our intuitive decisions are fallible in one case, why not in another? It certainly is an intuitive perception of the human mind—if there is any—that to regard that as our act which is not our act, and, on this ground, to inflict on us, before knowledge or action of any sort, a penalty which "is of all evils the essence and the sum" is as much at war with the principles of honor and of right as any act whatever can be. Therefore, if this intuition is delusive, what ground is there for trusting any other? True, it seems to us appalling and unjust in the highest degree to sentence a human being to eternal misery who has never acted at all, whether it be done on the ground of a propensity of which he is not the author, or an act which he never performed. But our intuitions of right are no more clear against such acts as those which Dr. Woods and Dr. Hodge condemn, than they are against those which they justify in God. If they are fallible in one case, why not in the other?

After all, the course of Abelard, Pascal and others, was the only thoroughly consistent course. They boldly took the ground that God did condemn innocent beings to endless misery for Adam's sin, and that on this subject our ideas of honor and right are not to be trusted, because they are not common to us and to God.

Listen to Pascal:

> "What can be more contrary to the rules of our wretched justice than to damn eternally an infant, incapable of volition, for an offense in which lie seems to have had no share, and which was committed six thousand years before he was born? Certainly nothing shocks us more rudely than this doctrine; and yet, without this mystery,—the most incomprehensible of all,—we are incomprehensible to ourselves."

Yes. He reverently believed the tremendous fact alleged, and thousands of others have done the same,—on the ground that, though at war with our necessary and intuitive convictions of justice, still those convictions are "wretched," and not worthy of confidence. "Such, indeed," said they, "are our views of justice, but they are not the views of God."

Listen next to Abelard:

> "Would it not be deemed the summit of injustice among men, if anyone should cast an innocent son, for the sin of a father, into those flames, even if they endured but a short time? How much more so, if eternal? Truly, I confess this would be unjust in men, because they are forbidden to avenge even their own real injuries. But it is not so in God, who says, 'Vengeance is mine, I will repay;' and again, in another place, 'I will kill, and I will make alive.' For God commits no injustice towards his creature in whatever way he treats him,—whether he assigns him to punishment or to life. ... In whatever way God may wish to treat his creature, he can be accused of no injustice; nor can anything be called evil in any way, if it is done according to his will. Nor can we, in any other way, distinguish good from evil, except by noticing what is agreeable to his will" (Opera. Paris, 1616, p. 395).

So, then, Abelard deemed it just in God to cast an "innocent" child into eternal flames for the sin of Adam; and that, in whatever way God should treat any of His creatures, it would be just.

Is not this a distinct avowal of the doctrine so sublimely repudiated by Abraham, the friend of God, when he appealed to the eternal principles of right, as conceived of by the human mind, as binding God also? "That be far from thee to do after this manner, to slay the righteous with the wicked; and that the righteous should be as the wicked, that be far from thee. Shall not the Judge of all the earth do right?" (Gen. 18:25). And did not God sanction this appeal?

But, at all events, Abelard was consistent. Entangled in the Roman Catholic system, from which he could not fully extricate himself, he ascribed to God acts at war with the intuitive moral convictions of the human mind; and what else could he do, except to say that, however such acts might seem to man, they appeared right to God, since in his idea and in reality right consisted simply in following his own will. Thus did Abelard virtually reject our ideas of right, as false and unworthy of confidence.

But, on this ground, there is no standard by which the creatures of God can judge of his character; and it would be absurd to ask, "Shall not the Judge of all the earth do right?" (Gen. 18:25), for certainly he will always do what he in fact wills to do, and this, according to Abelard, is the standard of right. Just as if there were no essential difference between benevolence and malevolence, between a purpose to produce a happy universe and a purpose to produce a miserable one! Just as if God could make it right to treat the innocent and the guilty as if there were no difference in their character; or to make a law, and then punish with eternal misery all who obey, and reward all who break it; or to hate all who love and honor Him, and to love all who hate and dishonor Him! But enough. Nothing but the supposed necessity of defending acts of gross injustice falsely ascribed to God could ever have driven a man like Abelard—one of the most independent thinkers of his age—upon ground so truly appalling.

And yet, even Dr. Chalmers, at this late day, has taken a similar ground. He adopts it "as the truth of the case that an individual is justly culpable for an iniquitous deed, done, not by himself, but by another, who lived nearly six thousand years ago." And yet he admits that "his own moral sense is altogether unable to apprehend it." This is not all. His moral sense is altogether against it.

In principle, however, Dr. Woods, Dr. Hodge, Pascal, Abelard and Dr. Chalmers, all stand on the same ground. In order to defend certain alleged acts of God, which are at war with the intuitive convictions of the human mind as to honor and right, they all reject—though not all to the same extent—the authority of those convictions, and call the application of them to those acts an improper rationalizing.

Now, in reply to this charge of improper rationalizing, it is enough to say that, as has been abundantly shown, it is a doctrine of the Word of God, revealed as plainly as the doctrine of depravity, that such intuitive convictions of the human mind are, in fact, a revelation, and a law of God Himself; and that their authority is supreme, and that God adopts them as the rule of His own conduct, and admits that He is bound by them, and declares that He always observes them, and is ready to have all His acts tested by them. Therefore, in denying that

He has done such acts as these divines ascribe to Him, we not only stand on Scripture ground, but, still more, we obey an explicit requisition of God, and do Him the highest honor.

The intuitive convictions of the minds of created beings, as to honor and dishonor, right and wrong, are the most important in the universe. They are the voice of God Himself in the soul. On them all just views of God depend. On them, as a basis, His universal and eternal government must ever rest. Shake them, and you shake the very foundations of His kingdom; for righteousness and judgment are the habitation of His throne.

Moreover, so long as anyone clearly sees what he regards as acts of God to be at war with these fundamental principles of equity and honor, genuine, honest and honorable conviction of sin, confession and repentance, are impossible. To thinking minds in this state it is of no avail to resort, by a familiar analogy, to the case of a man who has fallen into the ocean, and to whom a rope is thrown. In vain are they told that he will not waste his time in speculating whether he was thrown overboard honorably, or dishonorably, or accidentally, but will at once lay hold of the rope, that he may be saved. To those who speak thus they will say, "You do not reflect that a spirit cannot lay hold of the rope of salvation without repentance, and that true repentance implies a sincere confession that the conduct of God has been honorable and right, and that of the sinner dishonorable and wrong; and this is the very point on which we have difficulties which we long to remove, in order that we may confess sincerely and honorably, and not hypocritically, and under the influence of selfish fear."

The only practical course, so long as these views are retained, is to suppress or prevent, if possible, such an action of the moral nature. Within certain limits, this is possible. The influence of early education, and a reverence for sacred things, may keep the minds of many at rest. If objections are raised, the consideration of them may be declined, on the ground that the system of Christianity "is not a system of common sense, but of profound and awful mystery," and that it is not to be tried before the bar of reason. They can be taught to withdraw their minds from all such questions, and fix them on the facts as developed in experience and in the Scripture, and to aim at practical results. As the system in question now stands, this is clearly the wisest course for its advocates. For, so far as the minds of men can be called away from such points, and fixed on the legitimate evidences of their guilt and ruin, many will be alarmed, and brought to seek salvation in Christ. And, to a very considerable extent, by organization, and the pressure of denominational public sentiment on the mind from childhood, this can be done.

Nevertheless, since these facts are within the proper province of the mind, a universal and permanent suppression of the action of the instinctive convictions of the human race as to honor and right is not possible, and, if it were, it is not in accordance with the purposes of God that it should be effected. He has done nothing at war with those principles of honor and right that He has implanted in the human mind; and, therefore, He does not fear to have His system judged by them. Nay, there is reason to believe that He has allowed these principles to be embodied as at present they are in the Unitarian body with a view to this result.

Chapter VI: The Second Experience Or The Philosophy Of Unitarian Theology

WE come, next, to the development of the second of those experiences of which I have spoken, as originating from the influence upon the human mind of the conflict of the great moving powers of Christianity. It is an entire recoil from Old School theology to the other extreme. It is an experience in which a feeling sense of the truth and importance of the great principles of honor and right, in their relations to God, so far gains the ascendency as to lead to the entire rejection of the radical facts which have been stated concerning human depravity and the ruined condition of man.

This experience has found a more consistent and complete development among the Unitarians of New England than ever before; for, in the case of those like Pelagius, Socinus,[5] and Dr. J. Taylor, it existed, as will hereafter appear, in connection with a greater or less number of inconsistent truths, but here its influence has extended logically through the whole system.

It is obvious that the orthodox views of the doctrines of regeneration, the atonement, the Trinity, and other parts of their system, naturally correspond with their views of human depravity. The great end of their system is to restore man from the state of sin and ruin into which he has fallen. Of course, a renunciation of their views as to that state of sin and ruin naturally leads to an effort at a self-consistent readjustment of the whole system of Christianity. Nowhere has this effort been more consistently and thoroughly carried out than in New England.

When we consider the original character of the Puritan fathers of New England, and their strong attachment to the faith of the Reformers, it may seem surprising that a defection from their principles so extensive, and including a body of men of so much intellectual

---

5   Faustus Socinus developed Socinianism or unitarianism in the Minor Reformed Church of Poland during the 1500s, which was also embraced by the Unitarian Church of Transylvania during the same period.

power, should have occurred as it has in the very heart of New England.

With some, a ready and familiar solution of the fact is, to refer it to the depravity of the human heart, and its aversion to the humbling truths of the gospel. But, although I am as fully assured as anyone can be of the deep depravity and deceitfulness of the human heart, I can not believe that this solution can furnish a full, adequate and truly philosophical account of the matter. I do not believe that this great mental movement and revolution will ever be properly understood, until it is seen and conceded that the influence of an important part of the truth of God was one of the most powerful causes which was concerned in producing it. I refer to that part which I have already developed in the statement which I have made of the principles of equity and of honor, in the dealings of God with new-created minds.

The reality and truth of those principles, it will be remembered, has been in all ages fully conceded, or, rather, asserted by the orthodox; and the only ground of justifying God, in not applying them to men in this world, was the allegation that He imputed to them the sin of Adam, and regarded them as having thus forfeited all their rights. The invalidity of this justification I have already set forth. Is it to be wondered at that the free and powerful minds of New England could not always be held by such views, or that they should at last recoil from the whole system which was made to rest upon them? Even before the full and open development of Unitarianism, many of the strongest and most thinking minds were reacting against the system which this view presented to them. They could not but regard it as dark, dreadful and unjust. The case of John Adams—afterwards President of the United States—is a striking illustration of the truth of these remarks.

After leaving college it was his original design, as we learn from his diary, to prepare for the life of a clergyman; but doctrinal difficulties prevented. Under date of August 22, 1756, he thus writes,—being at that time engaged in teaching a school in Worcester, and having just decided to commence the study of the law:

"22, Sunday. —My inclination, I think, was to preach; however, that would not do. ... The reason of my quitting divinity was my opinion concerning some disputed points." He was at this time a young man, having only completed his twentieth year. By consulting the record of the preceding Sabbath, we can look deeply into his heart, and see how he was affected by one of these "disputed points,"— the doctrine of the imputation of Adam's sin. Though but a youth, he writes with strong common sense, and with the clearness and force that distinguished his maturer years:

> "If one man or being, out of pure generosity and without any expectation of returns, is about to confer any favor or emolument upon another, he has a right and is at liberty to choose in what manner and by what means to confer it. He may confer the favor by his own hand, or by the hand of his servant; and the obligation to gratitude is equally strong upon the benefited being. The mode of bestowing does not diminish the kindness, provided the commodity or good is brought to us equally perfect, and without our expense. But, on the other hand, if one being is the original cause of pain, sorrow or suffering, to another, voluntarily, and without provocation, it is injurious to that other, whatever means he might employ, and whatever circumstances the conveyance of the injury might be attended with. Thus, we are equally obliged to the supreme Being for the information he has given us of our duty, whether by the constitution of our minds and bodies, or by a supernatural revelation. For an instance of the latter, let us take original sin. Some say that Adam's sin was enough to damn the whole human race, without any actual crimes committed by any of them. Now, this guilt is brought upon them not by their own rashness and indiscretion, not by their own wickedness and vice, but by the supreme Being. This guilt brought upon us is a real injury and misfortune, because it renders us worse than not to be; and, therefore, making us guilty on account of Adam's delegation, or representing all of us, is not in the least diminishing the injury and injustice, but only changing the mode of conveyance."

Judge Story,[6] too, that great luminary of American jurisprudence, though educated in the Calvinistic faith, before he finished his college life turned from that system,—under the influences of similar causes,—

---

6   Joseph Story (1779-1845), an American lawyer and jurist who served on the
    Supreme Court of the United States from 1811 to 1845. Remembered for his opin-
    ions in Martin v. Hunter's Lessee and The Amistad, along with his magisterial *Com-
    mentaries on the Constitution of the United States*, 1833,

and, with his classmate, the world-renowned Channing,[7] became the earnest advocate of an opposing system.

If the principles of honor and of right which I have stated are true, then, however much we may regret the results to which these and other eminent men came, it is both disingenuous and uncandid to deny that, so far as they followed them, they were actuated by noble and sublime principles.

I am aware that, in view of the results to which they came, it has happened that, by a natural association, any application of the principles themselves, in these relations, is very often regarded with a kind of fear and distrust. Whenever anyone begins to speak of forming a judgment on the doctrine of imputation and human depravity by referring to the principles of honor and right as they apply to God, fears are entertained, at once, of the worst results. They are warned of the danger of such speculations, and of our incapacity to judge of the divine dispensations, and of the necessity of confiding in the statements of God.

These cautions, together with education and Christian consciousness, are sufficient to restrain many minds. But many are so deeply affected by a conviction of the truth and importance of the principles in question, and are so much agitated by the seeming conflict of the common views of depravity with them, that they cannot rest. The character of God is the sun of the moral world. To them these views seem fatally to darken it, and to fill the universe with gloom. This they cannot endure. At length, after many painful struggles, they first reject the facts concerning human depravity and ruin, from which such results seem to flow; and, finally, the whole system which grows out of them. Such appears to have been the case with Dr. Channing, who, at first, was taught to believe and seemed to hold the usual doctrine of human depravity. Step by step he proceeded, till he had renounced not merely human depravity, but the other doctrines connected with it,

---

7   Dr. William Ellery Channing (1780-1842) was the foremost Unitarian preacher in the United States in the early Nineteenth Century and, along with Andrews Norton, one of Unitarianism's leading theologians. In opposition to traditional American Calvinism, he preferred a gentle, loving relationship with God. He opposed Calvinism for "proclaiming a God who is to be dreaded. We are told to love and imitate God, but also that God does things we would consider most cruel in any human parent, were he to bring his children into life totally depraved and then to pursue them with endless punishment" (Channing 1957: 56). He became the primary spokesman and interpreter of Unitarianism when he preached the ordination sermon of Jared Sparks in Baltimore in 1819 titled "Unitarian Christianity."

including that of evil spirits. But, even in those who thus reject the whole system, there is no point on which they feel so deeply as on the conflict of the common doctrine of depravity with the principles of honor and right in the divine Being. Their attention has been turned strongly and predominantly to these principles. Their deepest experience has arisen from a contemplation of them, and from an earnest desire and firm purpose to repudiate all alleged facts that represent the supreme Ruler of the universe as dishonorable and unjust.

Almost the entire force of the argument of Dr. Ware[8] against Dr. Woods depends upon his appeal to the moral attributes of God as inconsistent with the Calvinistic doctrine of imputation, original sin, and total depravity.

Moreover, the strength of the feelings of Unitarians against the doctrine of the Trinity seems to be chiefly owing to its connection with the orthodox doctrine of depravity. Accordingly, Dr. Channing says,

> "We find Trinitarianism connecting itself with a scheme of administration exceedingly derogatory to the divine character. It teaches that the infinite Father saw fit to put into the hands of our first parents the character and condition of their whole progeny; and that through one act of disobedience the whole race bring with them into being a corrupt nature, or are born depraved. It teaches that the offenses of a short life, though begun and spent under this disastrous influence, merit endless punishment; and that God's law threatens this infinite penalty; and that man is thus burdened with a guilt which no sufferings of the created universe can expiate, which nothing but the sufferings of an infinite being can purge away. *In this condition of human nature Trinitarianism finds a sphere of action for its different persons.*"

Notice, now, the depth of emotion which is caused by the conviction that for God to deal thus with His creatures is dishonorable and

---

8   Henry Ware (1764-1845), a preacher and theologian influential in the formation of Unitarianism. In 1805 he was elected to the Hollis Chair at Harvard, precipitating a controversy between Unitarians and Calvinists. He helped in the formation of Harvard Divinity School and the establishment of Unitarianism there in the following decades, publishing his debates with eminent Calvinists in the 1820s.

unjust. He proceeds to say, of such views, that they look upon them with "horror and grief."

> "They take from us our Father in heaven, and substitute a stern and unjust Lord. Our filial love and reverence rise up against them. We say to the Trinitarian, touch anything but the perfections of God. Cast no stain on that spotless purity and loveliness. We can endure any errors but those which subvert or unsettle the conviction of God's paternal goodness. Urge not upon us a system which makes existence a curse, and wraps the universe in gloom."

Let no one suppose that there is any affectation of feeling here. It is a true and genuine experience of a mind highly endowed with the noblest sensibilities of our nature. Beyond all doubt, his feelings were sincere, honorable and deep.

Nor were these words the sudden result of oratorical excitement and enthusiasm; although a part of that eloquent discourse which fully opened the great controversy. We find the same views in a private letter, dated Boston. December 29, 1812:

> "I have spent this evening with our dear _____, and she put into my hands your letter on the subject of religion, to which you referred in the last which I received from you. I read it with sorrow. I saw that your mind was yielding to impressions which I trusted you would repel with instinctive horror. I know that Calvinism is embraced by many excellent people, but I know that on some minds it has the most mournful effects; that it spreads over them an impenetrable gloom, that it generates a spirit of bondage and fear, that it chills the best affections, that it represses virtuous effort, that it sometimes shakes the throne of reason. On susceptible minds the influence of the system is always to be dreaded. If it be believed, I think there is ground for a despondence bordering on insanity. If I, and my beloved friends, and my whole race, have come from the hands of our Creator wholly depraved, irresistibly propense to all evil, and averse to all good,—if only a portion are chosen to escape from this miserable state, and if the rest are to be consigned by the Being who gave us our depraved and

wretched nature to endless torments in inextinguishable flames,—then I do think that nothing remains but to mourn in anguish of hearty then existence is a curse, and the Creator is _____.

"O, my merciful Father! I cannot speak of thee in the language which this system would suggest. No! thou hast been too kind to me to deserve this reproach from my lips. Thou hast created me to be happy; thou callest me to virtue and piety, because in these consists my felicity; and thou wilt demand nothing from me but what thou givest me ability to perform" (*Channing's Memoirs*, Vol. I, p. 353).

It is true that the Reformers do not teach that God directly creates in man a sinful nature; but they do teach that, on account of the sin of Adam, He creates the soul without original righteousness, withholds from it divine influences, places it in a body and in a world of temptation, so that it inevitably becomes corrupt before action, and, being propense to all evil, and averse to all good, is developed in nothing but absolute and entire depravity. Do not such doctrines as these fully justify the feelings of Dr. Channing?

The principles of Turretin, of Watts, of Wesley, of the Princeton divines, of the Presbyterian church, and of the Reformers, as to the claims of new-created minds on God, will abundantly justify such feelings, unless God can be released from those claims by imputing to men a sin which was committed by another long before they were created; and shall we wonder that Channing was not satisfied or relieved by such a defense? Plainly, then, the system had been so adjusted as to bring into collision the real facts as to human depravity, and the principles of honor and right; and he clung to the principles, and, seeing no way to reconcile them with the facts, he rejected the facts.

This was, indeed, a calamitous result, but it sprang from the action of some of the noblest principles of our nature. Nor on the great scale will it be in vain. The existence of the Unitarian body is a providential protest in favor of the great principles of honor and of right.

It was not the purpose of Dr. Channing to color or exaggerate the opinions of Trinitarians in the representation which we have quoted, nor, in my judgment, has he done it. The statements of the creeds of the Reformation are stronger and more deeply colored than his. In another place he refers to the fact that later representations are somewhat softened; but he is not even so satisfied with them.

> "This system, indeed, (he remarks) takes various shapes, but in all it casts dishonor on the Creator. According to its old and genuine form, it teaches that God brings us into life wholly depraved, so that under the innocent features of childhood is hidden a nature averse to all good, and prepense to all evil—a nature which exposes us to God's displeasure and wrath, even before we have acquired power to understand our duties, or to reflect upon our actions. According to a more modern exposition, it teaches that we came from the hands of our Maker with such a constitution, and are placed under such influences and circumstances, as to render certain and infallible the total depravity of every human being from the first moment of his moral agency; and it also teaches that the offense of the child who brings into life this ceaseless tendency to unmingled crime exposes him to the sentence of everlasting damnation. Now, according to the plainest principles of morality, we maintain that a natural constitution of the mind unfailingly disposing it to evil, and to evil alone, would absolve it from guilt; that to give existence under this condition would argue unspeakable cruelty; and that to punish the sin of this unhappily constituted child with endless ruin would be a wrong unparalleled by the most merciless despotism" (I, p. 543).

This statement, too, is fully justified by all the orthodox authorities to whom I have referred, unless God can be absolved from the claims of honor and right, by imputing to millions of new-created minds a sin which they never committed, and then inflicting on them, by way of punishment, a corrupted moral constitution, certain to plunge them into sin and misery.

It is apparent that the force of these statements of Dr. Channing depends upon the assumption of our power and duty to test any alleged facts by the intuitive principles of honor and right, and that these principles are invested by God with just and supreme authority. But, not to leave an assumption so fundamentally unsustained, in his piece entitled "Moral argument against Calvinism," he formally investigates the subject. The statement of Calvinism which he there gives is taken substantially from the Westminster divines, and is not exaggerated.

> "Calvinism teaches that, in consequence of Adam's sin, in eating the forbidden fruit, God brings into life all his posterity with a nature wholly corrupt, so that they are utterly indisposed, disabled and made opposite to all that is spiritually good, and wholly inclined to all evil, and that continually. It teaches that all mankind, having fallen in Adam, are under God's wrath and curse, and so made liable to all miseries in this life, to death itself, and to the pains of hell forever."

In the light of this doctrine he presents; also, both here and elsewhere, the related doctrines of predestination, election, reprobation, and endless punishment. Against this doctrine, in such relations, he arrays the argument "that a doctrine which contradicts our best ideas of goodness and justice cannot come from the just and good God, or be a true representation of his character."

In reply to the allegation that our capacities are limited, and we, therefore, incompetent to judge, he admits the limitations of the human mind, but denies that on this account we are to distrust or call in question those moral intuitions which God created it necessarily to form. To confide in these, he asserts, is to confide in God, not to dishonor Him. We cannot reason, if we distrust our primitive and necessary laws of belief. Nor can we judge in morals, if we distrust our necessary moral intuitions. Herein he exactly agrees with Dr. Alexander. He proceeds to say that there is indeed much that we do not now know, and shall know hereafter. Nevertheless,

> "no extent of observation can unsettle those primary and fundamental principles of moral truth which we derive from our highest faculties operating in the relations in which God has fixed us."
>
> "God, in giving us conscience, has implanted a principle within us which forbids us to prostrate ourselves before mere power, or to offer praise where we do not discover worth.—a principle which challenges our supreme homage for supreme goodness, and which absolves us from guilt when we abhor a severe and unjust administration. Our

Creator has consequently waived his own claims to our veneration and obedience any further than he discovers himself to us in characters of benevolence, equity, and righteousness. He rests his authority on the perfect coincidence of his will and government with those great fundamental principles of morality written in our souls."

This conclusive argument is conducted with great eloquence and ability on the ground of natural reason, without reference to the Scriptures. The result of it, as applied to Christianity, is thus stated:

"We know that this reasoning will be met by the question, What, then, becomes of Christianity? for this religion plainly teaches the doctrines you have condemned. Our answer is ready,—Christianity contains no such doctrines."

Thus, then, the principles of honor and right have formed around themselves a party, and, being carried out logically to their full results, have destroyed all belief of any radical view of the facts in which the ruin of man consists.

Let no man despise this argument, or think fairly to meet it by alleging that human pride, or carnal reason, or hatred to the truth, is its moving power. It is not so. Its moving power is to be found in those great principles of honor and right which are a part of that natural law of God which he has inscribed on the soul of man, and which is rightfully invested with His own supreme authority.

Moreover, as an argument it is adapted to operate with immense power on a rational mind; and, unless some different understanding of the system of Christianity can be made it is unanswerable, and logically fatal to the scheme; nor will it ever be possible to prevent a large class of minds from feeling its power and yielding to its influence. It has in it a principle of vitality which cannot be destroyed. Unless it is recognized, and the system so stated as to harmonize with it, it will surely cause eternal conflict and division. The radical doctrine of depravity will still live; for it is true, and cannot die. But it is impossible that the human mind, especially after it has been so educated and elevated as to feel the generous and honorable spirit of Christianity, should not respond to such an appeal.

How, then, has this argument been met? Attempts have been made to meet it in two ways. Some retain the facts unmodified, and resort to faith and mystery. Others modify the statement of facts, in order to remove the alleged discord between them and the principles of honor and right. I shall consider these modifications in a subsequent experience giving rise to the New School theology. At present it is sufficient to consider the course of those who do not attempt to modify the facts. As we have seen, they concede that their equity and honor cannot be shown, according to any known principles of the human mind. Accordingly, they take refuge in faith and mystery. They deprecate all attempts to compare the facts in question with the principles of honor and right, as a kind of skeptical rationalism. They deny that we have any right to subject these doctrines to the scrutiny of reason. They declare that such a process is sacrilegious, and leads to Pelagianism, Unitarianism, and Infidelity. Indeed, the ground assumed often painfully recalls to our memory the sneer of Hume, that the friends of Christianity are very indiscreet in exposing it to the scrutiny of reason, a test which it is by no means able to endure. We know, indeed, that there are facts which are to be taken solely on divine authority. But if any statement, designed as the basis of conviction of sin and repentance, is palpably at war with natural right, it is not merely profitless to resort to the plea of mystery and faith, but for many minds, it is dangerous. When they hear that God regards as ours an act which was confessedly not ours, and punishes us for it by a penalty great beyond conception, rejecting us from His fellowship, and giving us a nature depraved before knowledge or choice, they find no relief in the statement of Professor Hodge, that Christianity is "not a system of common sense, but of profound and awful mystery." After Dr. Woods has conceded that such facts are contrary to the moral convictions of our minds, and cannot be justified on any known principles, it is no relief to be told that the whole subject is a mystery, and that it is our duty to believe that all is right from a regard to the veracity and rectitude of God. There are limits to the duty of faith in alleged mysteries. If there were not, there could be no defense against absurdities the most gross, promulgated under the cover of the Bible. The advocates of Transubstantiation take refuge behind the shield of mystery; but all Protestants agree in the decision that a dogma which does violence to the intuitive convictions of the human mind, through the senses, shall not be sheltered by the plea of mystery and faith. So there are certain first truths on which all reasoning rests. Without them we cannot evince the being of a God, or establish the divine origin or authority of the Bible. The intuitive convictions of the human mind as to honor and right are of no less authority. Without them we could form no idea of the moral character of God. If any statements are directly at war with these, the resort to mystery and faith in their defense is not legitimate. That millions of non-existent beings should be considered as performing Adam's act, and on this ground be punished for it, before they have known or done anything, or that any created being should deserve punishment for a nature existing in him anterior to any knowledge, will, or act of his own, will ever and universally be regarded as at war with the divinely inspired principles of honor and right, by all who are left to their natural and spontaneous convictions. The idea of an original constitution corrupted, and sure to result in sin, will no less earnestly be rejected. Nothing but a supposed necessity of the sternest kind will ever lead anyone to disregard such first truths, and to take refuge under mystery.

Chapter VII: The Reaction, Testimony Of Dr. Channing And Others, Obvious Facts

SUCH are the elements of strength in this scheme of doctrine; and, certainly, as the system is now understood, they are irresistible in a logical encounter with the opposing position. Why, then, does not this scheme prevail, and carry with it the whole Christian community? That it does not do this, that it never has done it, is plain. Why is it so?

The reason is one similar to that mentioned in the case of Old School theology; it is that it meets everywhere a powerful reaction. This reaction arises from facts, from Scripture, and from Christian consciousness.

The reaction of facts is clear and decided. Recall the statements made by leading Unitarian divines as to the sinfulness of man and the history of this world. What can be more dark than the views given by Professor Norton? Dr. Dewey confesses that the extent of human depravity "is a problem that he cannot solve, and that there are shadows upon the world that we cannot penetrate,—masses of sin and misery that overwhelm us with wonder and awe." Let any man study the interior history of governments in all ages; of war, of slavery and the slave trade; of idolatry; of all pursuits in which the mainspring has been the love of money; of morals, not only in the pagan, but also in the Christian world; of sensualism and licentiousness,—and he will be obliged to say, with Dr. Dewey,

> "We believe that the world now, taken in the mass, is a very, very bad world; that the sinfulness of the world is dreadful and horrible to consider; that the nations ought to be covered with sackcloth and mourning for it; that they are filled with misery by it. Why, can any man look abroad upon the countless miseries inflicted by selfishness, dishonesty, slander, strife, war; upon the boundless woes of intemperance, libertinism, gambling, crime;— can any

man look upon all this, with the thousand minor diversities
and shadings of guilt and guilty sorrow, and feel that he
could write any less dreadful sentence against the world
than Paul has written? Not believe in human depravity,—
great, general, dreadful depravity! Why, a man must be a
fool, nay, a stock or a stone, not to believe in it! He has no
eyes, he has no senses, he has no perceptions, if he refuses to
believe in it!"

Moreover, we find in the recorded experience of Dr. Channing
himself that, with all his efforts to infuse into men elevated and honorable convictions of their own nature, and to arouse them to cor-
respondent action, he found a general, steady and powerful
indisposition to respond to the appeal.

Under the date of November, 1833, he has given us an interesting
discussion of the spirit of society in this world. He develops truly and
eloquently the great law of love to God and to man, and then thus
proceeds:

"Need I ask you whether a love thus grounded and nour-
ished is the spirit of society? Is it the habit of society to
meditate on the great purposes for which each human being
was framed? Has society yet learned man's relation to God,
his powers, his perils, his immortality? Are these the
thoughts which circulate in conversation, these the convictions which are brought home to you in your ordinary intercourse? Need I tell you how blind the multitude yet are
to what is nearest them and concerns them most deeply, to
their own nature,—how they overlook the spiritual in man,
—how they stop at the outward and accidental,—how few
penetrate to the soul, and discern in that responsible, immortal being, an object for unbounded solicitude and love?
The multitude are living an outward life, discerning little
but what meets the eye, valuing little but what can be
weighed or measured by the senses, estimating one another
by outward success, conflicting or cooperating with one
another for outward interests. The consciousness of what is
inward, and spiritual, and immortal,—how faintly does it stir
in the multitude! Man's solemn, infinite connections with
God and eternity are unacknowledged or forgotten; and so

little are they comprehended, that, when urged on the conscience as realities, as motives to action and as foundations
of love, they are dismissed as too unsubstantial or refined to
exert a serious influence on life. Thus the spirit of society is
virtually hostile to those great truths in regard to human nature on which Christian love is built, and without which we
cannot steadfastly and disinterestedly bind ourselves to our
race."

How far does this differ from the orthodox view of such scriptural
statements as these, that men, until regenerated, are "without God in
the world," and act under the influence of "the carnal mind, which is
enmity against God, because not subject to the law of God" (Rom.
8:7).

Again; after unfolding the demands of the law, as to universal, all-
embracing love of man, independently of wealth, social position, rank
or birth, he thus proceeds:

"Thus universal, all-comprehending, is the love which
springs from just views of man's nature and relation to God.
And is this the spirit of society? Does society breathe and
nurture this, or does it inculcate narrowness, exclusiveness,
and indifference towards the great mass of mankind? Do we
see in the world a prevalent respect for what all human beings partake? On the contrary, do not men attach themselves to what is peculiar, to what distinguishes one man
from another, and especially to outward distinction; and is
there not a tendency to overlook, as of little value, those
who in these respects are depressed? Do they not worship
the accidents, adventitious, unessential circumstances, of the
human being,—birth, outward appearance, wealth, manner,
rank, show,—and ground on these a consciousness of a superiority which divides them from others? Can we say of
that distinction, which is alone important in the sight of
God, which is confined to no condition, which is to outlive
all the inequalities of life, and which, far from separating,
binds those who possess it more and more to their race,—I
mean moral and religious worth,—can we say of this, that it
is the object of general homage, before whose commanding
presence all lower differences among men are abased? The

influence of outward condition in attracting or repelling men's sympathies and interest is one of the most striking features of modern society, and gives mournful proof of the faint hold which Christianity has as yet gained over the hearts and minds of men. ... Who can deny that, on the whole, the spirit of society is adverse to this enlarged, all-embracing spirit of Christ? ... Such is the spirit of society. Christianity teaches us to feel ourselves members of the whole human family; society, to make or keep ourselves members of some favored caste. Christianity calls us to unite ourselves with others; society, to separate ourselves from them. Christianity teaches us to raise others; society, to rise above them. Christianity calls us to narrow the space between ourselves and our inferiors, by communicating to them, as we have ability, what is most valuable in our own minds; society tells us to leave them to their degradation. Christianity summons us to employ superior ability, if such we have, as a means of wider and more beneficent action on the world; society suggests that these are a means of personal elevation. Christianity teaches us that what is peculiar in our lot or our acquisitions is of little worth, in comparison with what we possess in common with our race; society teaches us to cling to what is peculiar, as our highest honor and most precious possession. Fraternal union, sympathy, aid, is the spirit of Christianity; exclusiveness is the spirit of the world. And this spirit is not confined to what is called the highest class. It burns, perhaps, more intensely in those who are seeking than in those who occupy the eminences of social life. It is a disposition to undervalue those who want what we possess, to narrow our sympathies to one or another class, to forget the great bond of humanity. This spirit of exclusiveness triumphs over the spirit of Christianity, and, through its prevalence, the great work given to every human being, which is to improve his less favored fellow-being, is slighted. The sublime sphere of usefulness is little occupied. A spirit of rivalry, jealousy, envy, selfish competition, supplants the spirit of mutual interest, the respect, support and aid, by which Christianity proposes to knit mankind into a universal brotherhood."

If the essence and root of sin is selfishness, as opposed to the law of love, does not this state of things seem to justify the conclusion that men must have in them powerful native tendencies to such deep depravity? Is this like the action of a race whose original constitutions, as they enter upon this life, are pure and uncorrupted?

At first, he was full of hope as to the power of the Unitarian movement to renovate society. But the stern teachings of experience at last taught him that even to the call of that system there was not that readiness to respond that ought to be expected from a race of men naturally tending to all that is good and noble. In a letter to Blanco White, dated Sept. 18, 1839, he says:

> "I would that I could look to Unitarianism with more hope. But this system was, at its recent revival, a protest of the understanding against absurd dogmas, rather than the work of deep religious principle, and was early paralyzed by the mixture of a material philosophy, and fell too much into the hands of scholars and political reformers; and the consequence is a want of vitality and force, which gives us little hope of its accomplishing much under its present auspices, or in its present form. When I tell you that no sect in this country has taken less interest in the slavery question, or is more inclined to conservatism, than our body, you will judge what may be expected from it. Whence is salvation to come? This is the question which springs up in my mind continually. Is the world to receive new impulse from individual reformers, or from new organizations? Or is the work to go on by a more silent, unorganized action of thought and great principles in the mass? Or are great convulsions, breaking up the present order of things, as in the fall of the Roman empire, needed to the introduction of a reform worthy of the name? Sometimes I fear the last, so rooted seem the corruptions of the church and society. But I live in hope of milder processes."

To me, the solution of all this seems to be clear;—sincere, earnest and indefatigable, as were the efforts of Dr. Channing, the force of the radical and originating causes of such widespread actual human depravity was deeper and greater than his system would allow him to understand and consistently to believe, and therefore it steadily defied and resisted his most earnest and philanthropic efforts.

He did not, indeed, despair; but most of his hopes lay in the uncertain future. In the year 1839, in the preface to the third Glasgow edition of his works, he thus sets forth his hopes as a social reformer:

> "These volumes will show that the author feels strongly the need of deep social changes, of a spiritual revolution in Christendom, of a new bond between man and man, of a new sense of the relation between man and his Creator. At the same time, they will show his firm belief that our present low civilization, the central idea of which is wealth, cannot last forever; that the mass of men are not doomed hopelessly and irresistibly to the degradation of mind and heart in which they are now sunk; that a new comprehension of the end and dignity of a human being is to remodel social institutions and manners; that in Christianity, and in the powers and principles of human nature, we have the promise of something holier and happier than now exists. It is a privilege to live in this faith, and a privilege to communicate it to others. The author is not without hope that he may have strength for some more important labors; but if disappointed in this, he trusts that these writings, which may survive him a little time, will testify to his sympathy with his fellow creatures, and to his faith in God's great purposes towards the human race."

In another place he says, in the same year:

> "I live as did Simeon, in the hope of seeing a brighter day. I do see the gleams of dawn, and that ought to cheer me. I hope nothing from increased zeal in urging an imperfect, decaying form of Christianity. One higher, clearer view of religion rising on a single mind encourages me more than the organization of millions to repeat what has been repeated for ages with little effect. The individual here is mightier than the world; and I have the satisfaction of seeing aspirations after this purer truth. ... I believe,—I trust,—that a better age of theological literature is dawning upon us. The human mind is beginning to throw off the weight

of authority which has crushed it for ages; and, although its first strength may be put forth in vehement wrestling with errors, in the subtleties of controversy, perhaps in rushing from one to another extreme, yet, if left to the free use of its powers, and to the quickening influences which God is pouring upon it through nature, through events, through revelation, and through a more secret and inward energy, it will at length arrive, in one and another gifted individual, to that state of calm, intense and deep meditation and feeling, from which all living and life-giving works on morals and religion are to proceed. One such work may be enough to give a new aspect to theology, to introduce modes of viewing and studying it as superior to those which now prevail as those are to the antiquated scholastic subtleties and jargon which once bore its name."

In the anticipations of such results, to be produced by the power of truth and love, I am happy to sympathize with this distinguished philanthropist. But, in my judgment, the turning point of the whole revolution will be, so to adjust the system that the highest and most perfect enunciation of the principles of equity and honor in God shall not hide or extenuate the reality or the depth of the depravity and the moral ruin of man. When the depth of the moral malady of the race is fully understood, and so set forth as to imply no dishonor in God, then will that great revolution be attained, the hope of which Dr. Channing was never willing to abandon, but to which he still clung, in the midst of the severest disappointments and the most gloomy prospects.

But, at present, I am concerned simply with the facts which a long course of philanthropic effort compelled Dr. Channing reluctantly to admit.

In view of such facts, we ask, as before, is it possible that a race of beings in whom there is no native and inherent depravity, whose original constitutions are healthy and well balanced, and in whom there are preponderating tendencies to good, should for a long course of thousands of years have presented such results as these? It cannot be.

This view of the mournful facts of history and observation must naturally prepare the way for a more affecting and impressive study of the Word of God. In that are found most vivid statements of the original, universal and deep depravity of man,—a depravity so absolute that men are said to be dead in trespasses and sins, and by nature the children of wrath. This state of things is asserted to be as universal and ab-solute as the need of the redemption of Christ. "We thus judge," saith the apostle Paul, "that if one died for all, then were all dead; and that he died for all that they who live should henceforth live not unto themselves, but unto him who died for them and rose again" (2 Cor. 5:14–15). The universal necessity of a moral regeneration, or new cre-ation, is seen to result from these facts, and to be clearly stated in the Word of God.

These views are illustrated and confirmed by the statement of the experience of the inspired writers,—an experience utterly unlike that of any other human writers except such as have derived a similar experi-ence from the Word of God.

In addition to this, it is a fact that multitudes in every age do be-come conscious, in their own experience, of a great and radical moral change, which fully corresponds to these statements of the Word of God, in their most obvious sense and deepest extent. They are made to see in the character of God, and in His law, the true standard of holi-ness; they are deeply convinced of their own sinfulness and moral im-potence; they become conscious of a great moral change, corresponding in all respects to that set forth in the Word of God; they now receive a new and spiritual understanding of that sacred book; the new creation therein revealed towers upwards like a mountain towards heaven, radiant with glory, full of new and enrapturing spiritual life. Even one individual book, like the Epistle to the Ephesians, seen and felt in its spiritual glory, is enough to satisfy the soul of the divine, the supernatural origin of the Word of God. In it the new-born soul mounts up as on the wings of an eagle, until it sits down with Christ in heavenly places, amidst the glories of heaven.

Is it to be wondered at that causes so powerful as these should cause a constant reaction against the results which by a strict logic are made to flow from the principles of honor and right by Unitarian di-vines? In evangelical conviction of sin, and regeneration, there is a liv-ing power; and in the certainty which it gives of the deep meaning and exact truth of the Bible on the subject of human depravity, there is an energy of resistance to opposite doctrines which nothing can over-come or destroy.

Chapter VIII: Degradation Of Free Agency Itself

ONE result of the Unitarian views is altogether undesigned, and was little foreseen by the leaders of that system. Indeed, it is not peculiar to their system, as we shall show in considering some forms of the New School theology. It is the virtual degradation of free agency itself, in their efforts to elevate the existing nature of man. They assert that God creates men from age to age with such moral constitutions as the claims of equity and honor demand. But the history of this world, as they state it, contradicts the idea that men are born holy, or with powerful and predominating tendencies to good. Therefore they take the ground of Dr. Ware:

> "Man is by nature—by which is to be understood as he is born into the world, as he comes from the hands of the Creator—innocent and pure; he is by nature no more inclined or disposed to vice than to virtue, and is equally capable, in the ordinary use of his faculties, and with the common assistance afforded him, of either."

Thus, in order to account for the actual sinfulness of man in this world, Unitarians are compelled to abandon the highest standard as to what is due from God to new-created minds. They abandon the idea of minds created with original righteousness, and, therefore, with strong predominant and effective tendencies to good, as unphilosophical or even impossible. They take the ground that God has given to men as necessarily limited, ignorant, imperfect, new-created beings, all that the nature of free agency will allow. Thus, Dr. Dewey says:

> "It is in the very nature of a moral and imperfect being to err; not to sin willfully, malignantly,—that is not necessary,—but to err through ignorance and impulse, to fall into excess or defect, and so to fall into sin. And it is in the

power of such a being to sin intentionally. Man has done both. And misery has followed as the consequence, at once, and corrective, of his errors. Where, now, is the mystery or difficulty? ... An imperfect, free moral nature is, in its essential constitution,—is, by definition, peccable; it is liable to err; and its erring is nothing strange nor mysterious. The notion of untempted innocence for such a being is, I hold, a dream of theology. His very improvement, his very progress, ever implies previous erring."

The essential principle of this defense of God, in view of the conceded and fearful sinfulness of man, is, that God has given to him as good original constitutions as the nature of free agency admits of. Indeed, it would seem logically to result in the principle that sinning is a general necessity of all finite moral beings, as such, and is an essential part of a moral education, designed to result in stable virtue.

Dr. Burnap presents similar views. He teaches us that "every human soul comes from the hand of God pure, as was Adam; without, indeed, any decided character, but capable of virtue and holiness, though exposed to temptation and sin." He explains his sin by the fact that he is free, has strong appetites and impulses, bodily and mental, is ignorant, is surrounded by temptations, and yet is under law. Thus he inevitably falls into sin. Then comes in the power of habit, and the law of development, to strengthen and confirm these evil results. (See the whole of Discourse XXI.)

In another place he makes the following clear and explicit statements :

"It is God's will that man should commence his career at nothing, without positive character, though innocent; without knowledge, without experience: weak, and subjected to urgent wants and strong necessities; with passions within and many and mighty temptations without. His ignorance is liable to be deceived, his passions to be excited, his interests to be miscalculated, and, of course, he is liable to sin. In comparison to God, in his best estate, he has the weakness of infancy. Is it not to be expected that a being thus endowed and thus conditioned should sometimes sin? All that can be expected of man is that his career should be progressive; that his choice should be fixed on good after

wavering a while. Man being free, the only way in which
his character can be established is by fixing his deliberate
and habitual choice on good. Accordingly, this seems to be
the whole purpose of the present life. This world is a state of
discipline, having in view this very end,—the production in
man of a holy character."

This view accounts for the universal sin of this world by the necessary nature of free agency and of a state of probation, as designed to
form a holy character. Of course, as in a great majority of cases there is
an entire failure to secure this result, we are compelled to entertain
very low ideas of the possibilities of free agency.

The obvious tendency of these views is to degrade the essential
nature of free agency itself, and of the universe as based on it. It no less
diminishes the guilt and evil of sin. Indeed, it approximates very
closely to the idea of the Hegelian school,—that sin, though an evil, is
yet a necessary and useful means of moral development.

Dr. Burnap seems to have been aware that his views would appear
to be open to this objection; for he states it, and endeavors to show
that his views do not tend to it.

> "To the doctrine of this discourse I am aware that it may be
> objected, that it is calculated to lower the standard of the
> gospel, to diminish our apprehensions of the evil of sin, to
> make it less burdensome to the conscience, and to disparage
> the importance of the mission of Christ as a remedy for the
> sinfulness of mankind. Serious and religious minds may fear
> that it tends to the development of such a religious philoso-
> phy as that so widely propagated of late in Germany by
> Hegel, which represents sin as not only incident to human
> nature, but one of the appointed means of its development
> and perfection."

In his reply he concedes and endeavors to show that sin is not by
any means so great an evil as it is represented by the orthodox. He
then adds: "But it does not follow, because no sin is an infinite evil,
and no sin can merit an infinite punishment, that it is no evil at all, and
does not deserve any punishment. Nor does it follow, because punishment is remedial and inflicted for the purpose of curing sin, that it is as
well to sin and suffer for it, as to keep the law of God and avoid both

the sin and the suffering." He speaks of it, however, chiefly as an evil to the sinner, and sums up his views in the following brief statement:

> "The condition of man, then, here on earth, as in a state of moral probation, amounts to this. God has given him two chances for happiness;—one, through sinless obedience; the other, through repentance and reformation,—in short, through moral discipline. Human imperfection renders the first impossible, and therefore God has kindly provided the second."

This involves, of course, the doctrine that the nature of free agency is such, that to form a perfect character through sinless obedience is, in the nature of things, impossible. It cannot be done except through a process of sinning, and of consequent moral discipline and repentance. Certainly such views, even if they differ in some respects from those of Hegel,[9] do, nevertheless, so depress our ideas of the evil of sin, that men of deep Christian experience, who know its evils and its power, will be likely to feel that there is very little to choose between the two views.

Of course, there will be men of deep Christian consciousness who will feel that such views imply a false standard of the true life and health of the soul. They do not, in their view, probe its diseases thoroughly; they cannot, therefore, effect a radical cure. Whenever a standard is taken so low as to represent the fearful and gigantic developments of human depravity in this world as the result of human limitation, ignorance and frailty, in a mind naturally pure, and not of deep innate depravity, the highest vitality and power of religion is rendered impossible. Until it aims at a radical regeneration, it has no adequate end: it effects nothing of any moment, and, in the great conflict with the real and earnest and gigantic depravity of earth, it will be trodden under foot and despised.

Hence, although such views are derived from and depend upon the true and powerful principles of honor and right as applied to a misunderstood system of Christianity, yet the steady testimony of fact, the Bible and Christian consciousness, produces a constant reaction,

---

9   Georg Wilhelm Friedrich Hegel (1770-1831), a German philosopher, and one of the creators of German Idealism. His historicist and idealist account of reality as a whole overturned European philosophy and was an important precursor to Continental philosophy and Marxism.

which, on a great scale, has prevailed against them, and ever will prevail. Even the power of the most obvious first truths will not ever avail universally to eradicate from the minds of men a belief of the great fact of innate human depravity in its most profound and radical form, and of its connected facts. They are sustained by independent evidence of their own so strong that they will live. But equally powerless will argument be universally to eradicate the views of those who reject those facts because so presented as to war with honor and right. Unless, therefore, in some way these truths shall be harmonized, there is a foundation laid for endless conflict and division.

CHAPTER IX: THIRD EXPERIENCE; OR, PHILOSOPHY OF ORTHODOX UNIVERSALISM

WE now come to a third and most interesting experience. It is one which results from holding unmodified, and with full faith and deep sensibility, both the most radical facts concerning human depravity and the principles of honor and of right.

Upon a certain portion of such minds the power of the principles of honor and right is so great, that, although they cannot cease to believe the facts as to human depravity, yet they shrink from carrying out the system of Christianity to its full and scriptural results, and take refuge in the doctrine of universal salvation. It is well known that the prevailing opinion of the great body of evangelical Christians, in all ages, has been opposed to this doctrine. This has resulted from a full conviction that the testimony of Scripture is decidedly against it. Yet, so urgent and powerful are the principles of honor in some minds, that, in view of the common doctrine concerning the alleged dealings of God with man through Adam, they have been unable to rest in any result short of universal salvation. But it is not till after many struggles and much suffering that they finally come to this conclusion. The experience of such has found an eloquent utterance in the words of the truly eminent John Foster.

Of the intellectual and moral eminence of this distinguished man it is unnecessary that I should speak. He occupies an unquestioned place among the most powerful writers of the English language. His friend and biographer, J. E. Ryland, says of him, "He had that intellectual magic which summons from all points of the compass the most sudden and happy illuminations of thought. Images arose on all sides at the master's bidding; nor did he hesitate to call them from the

loftiest region or the lowest." John Sheppard,[10] another intimate friend
and pupil, says of him,

> "Few spirits can have passed away from earth endowed with
> more of intellectual grasp and penetration, to meet the
> wonders and grandeurs of regions immense and untra-
> versed; few, also, I believe, with a more profound persua-
> sion that, as creatures, however endowed, admired or
> dignified, in ourselves we are nothing."

But, vast as were his powers, they did not elevate him in spirit
above the feeblest and most lowly of our race. His feelings ever tended
to sympathy with the weak and the oppressed. Hence his biographer
says of him,

> "He was remarkable for civility and kindness to small
> tradesmen and work people; he used to complain that
> women were generally underpaid, and would often give
> them more than they asked. He abhorred driving a bargain
> with poor people. When sometimes shown small wares
> brought to the door for sale, on being told the price, he
> would say, O, give them a few pence more! See! there's a
> great deal of work here; it must have taken some time to
> make.' And he would turn the article—whatever it might be
> —in every direction, and find out all the little ingenuities
> and ornaments about it."

These small facts reveal great principles. They give us an insight
into a great and noble spirit. They reveal a mind so keenly sensitive to
the principles of honor and of right that over it their influence must
have been supreme. They furnish, therefore, the key to the experience
which we are about to disclose and illustrate.

The occasion on which Foster expressed his views was this:

In the year 1841 a young minister wrote to him a statement of his
inquiries and difficulties on the subject of the eternity of future punishments. In reply, he concedes the almost universal judgment of divines in affirmation of the doctrine, and that the testimony of Scripture

---

10 Sheppard, John. *Christian encouragement; or, Attempts to console and aid the distrssed
    and anxious*, 1800. *Essays designed to afford Christian encouragement and consolation*,
    1833. *Thoughts, chiefly designed as preparative or persuasive to private devotion*, 1829.

for it is "formidably strong." Yet, solely on the basis of what he calls "the moral argument," he rejects the doctrine. On what, then, is this argument based? Plainly, on a view of the facts concerning the origin of man's depravity.

By this I mean that the facts which have been stated as held by the orthodox concerning the conduct of God towards new-created minds, both with regard to their original constitutions and their circumstances, so deeply affected and pained his benevolent spirit, that, seeing no way to answer the arguments which sustained the system of which those facts were a part, he sought relief in the doctrine of universal salvation.

That this process was not a logical vindication of God, in the acts in question, is plain; but it gave at least this relief, that it represented God as not adding an eternal and still greater wrong to that of which he appeared already to have been guilty. But of this I shall speak again. My present object is to show how the mind of Foster sought relief under a system so misunderstood as to bring the conduct of God towards man into actual conflict with the principles of honor and right.

In his reply to the young clergyman, he first illustrates the fearful idea of eternity, and then thus proceeds:

> "Then think of *man*,—his nature, his situation, the circumstances of his brief sojourn and trial on earth. Far be it from us to make light of the demerit of sin, and to remonstrate with the supreme Judge against a severe chastisement, of whatever moral nature we may regard the infliction to be. But still, what is man? He comes into the world *with a nature fatally corrupt*, and powerfully tending to actual evil. He comes among *a crowd of temptations adapted to his innate evil propensities*. He grows up (incomparably the greater proportion of the race) in great ignorance; his judgment weak, and under numberless beguilements to error, while his passions and appetites are strong; his conscience unequally matched against their power,—in the majority of men, but feebly and rudely constituted. The influence of whatever good instructions he may receive is counteracted by a combination of opposite influences almost constantly acting on him. He is essentially and inevitably unapt to be powerfully acted on by what is invisible and future. In addition to all which, there is the *intervention and activity of the great tempter and*

destroyer. In short, his condition is such that there is no hope of him, but from a direct special operation on him of what we denominate grace. Is it not so? Are we not convinced? Is it not the plain doctrine of scripture? Is there not irresistible evidence, from a view of the actual condition of the human world, that no man can become good, in the Christian sense, can become fit for a holy and happy place hereafter, but by this operation, *ab extra*? But this is arbitrary and discriminative on the part of the sovereign agent, and independent of the will of man; and how awfully evident is it that this indispensable operation takes place only on a comparatively small proportion of the collective race!

"Now, this creature, *thus constituted and circumstanced*, passes a few fleeting years on earth,—a short, sinful course, in which he does often what, notwithstanding his ignorance and ill-disciplined judgment and conscience, he knows to be wrong, and neglects what he knows to be his duty, and consequently, for a greater or less measure of guilt, widely different in different offenders, deserves punishment. But endless punishment! hopeless misery through a duration to which the enormous terms above imagined will be nothing! I acknowledge my inability (I would say it reverently) to admit this belief, together with a belief in the divine goodness,—the belief that 'God is love,' that his tender mercies are over all his works. Goodness, benevolence, charity, as ascribed in supreme perfection to Him, cannot mean a quality foreign to all human conceptions of goodness. It must be *something analogous in principle to what he himself has defined and required as goodness in his moral creatures*, that, in adoring the divine goodness, we may not be worshiping an 'unknown God.' But, if so, how would all our ideas be confounded while contemplating him bringing, of his own sovereign will, a race of creatures into existence in such a condition that they certainly will and must, —must, *by their nature and circumstances,*—go wrong and be miserable, unless prevented by especial grace, which is the privilege of only a small proportion of them, and at the same time affixing on their delinquency a doom of which it is infinitely beyond the highest archangel's faculty to apprehend a thousandth part of the horror!"

On page 290 he presents similar views:

"It would be a transcendently direful contemplation, if I believed the doctrine of the eternity of future misery. It amazes me to imagine how thoughtful and benevolent men believing that doctrine, can endure the sight of the present world, and the history of the past. To behold successive, innumerable *crowds carried on in the mighty impulse of a depraved nature, which they are impotent to reverse,* and to which it is not the will of God, in his sovereignty, to apply the only adequate power, the withholding of which consigns them inevitably to their doom; to see them passing through a short term of mortal existence (absurdly sometimes denominated a *probation*), *under all the worlds pernicious influences, with the addition of the malign and deadly one of the great tempter and destroyer,* to confirm and augment the inherent depravity, on their speedy passage to everlasting woe;— I repeat, I am, without pretending to any extraordinary depth of feeling, amazed to conceive what they contrive to do with their sensibility, and in what manner they maintain a firm assurance of the Divine *goodness and justice.*"

In these passages we cannot but notice the clear and eloquent manner in which he combines the three great elements which I have set forth as constituting the ruined condition of man; deep personal depravity anterior to action, exposure to corrupt worldly social combinations and influences, and the fearful wiles of evil spirits.

We notice, also, the full faith with which he sets them forth. Scripture, experience, history, and his own observation and Christian consciousness, appeared to him to unite their testimony to sustain this view of facts.

At the same time, he was keenly alive to the demands of the principles of honor and right, and could not avoid seeing their contrariety to such alleged facts. The effect upon his mind he states in these affecting words, concerning the system of this world,—"To me it appears a most mysteriously awful economy, overspread by a lurid and dreadful shade."

Who does not see here the elements of an experience precisely similar to that of Dr. Channing? The facts contemplated by Foster appeared to Channing, also, to present an "awful economy, overspread by a lurid and dreadful shade." Of course, such minds as these must find relief somewhere from such a state of things. Channing renounced and denied the facts; Foster's mind was unable to resort to this mode of relief. The facts he could not deny. The principles of honor he could not renounce. Hence, though he saw that it was at war with the almost universal opinion of the church and the clear words of Scripture, he overruled the laws of interpretation, and rejected, on purely moral grounds, the doctrine of the eternity of future punishment.

And are there not still other minds who feel these difficulties, as well as Foster and Channing? And will not such an appeal, presented with such eloquence, exert great power on many such minds? Dr. Woods seems to be of this opinion. He says, "The thoughts suggested in the letter, together with the influence of the author's name, are adapted to unsettle the faith of multitudes." Such an influence was no doubt deeply felt in England. Foster says:

> "A number (not large, but of great piety and intelligence) of ministers within my acquaintance have been disbelievers of the doctrine in question, at the same time not feeling themselves called upon to make a public disavowal."

How many more there may have been, or may still be, in the same state of mind, of course no one can tell. But the belief that many real Christians held such views caused in England, as is well known, a great reluctance, even among the believers of the doctrine, to introduce it as a test in the Evangelical Alliance. I know of no reason to be confident that the views of Foster will not also make converts even among the evangelical ministers of our own land, so strong is the appeal to the principles of honor and right, in view of the facts of human depravity as extensively held. I am aware that many suppose that a more correct theory of free agency,—as applied to the facts of depravity,—would have relieved Foster, and is, among us, a defense against the spread of his views. Of this we can better judge after considering the next experience.

There is not, however, in my judgment, any good reason to believe that the improved views in question would have given the needed relief to Foster. He appears to have considered the course of reasoning on which they rest, and to have derived from it no relief.

He says in his journal, No. 485: "The very intelligent Mr. G. reasoned against the Calvinistic doctrine of original depravity" (that is, its most radical form) "evidently, I perceived, from his feeling respecting that of eternal punishments. Believing this last, he was anxious—as a kind of palliation of its severity—to make man as accountable a being as possible, by making his vice entirely optional, and so making all his depravity his crime." Foster, then, had looked at the principles of the system that resolves all moral depravity in man into voluntary action, and did not find in it the requisite relief. He did not regard it as a true view of the real facts of the case. Nor did it hold him back from his appeal against the doctrine of future eternal punishment.

But, whether this appeal shall extensively avail or not to shake the belief of the Christian community in that doctrine, still it shows with what fearful power the principles of honor and right operate upon some of the most finely constituted minds of our race. It shows, also, that sympathy, and not severity, is due to all such minds, even if they fall into error, when struggling under the painful pressure of a system involving truths so great, and yet so radically misunderstood. It evinces no less clearly that a proper readjustment of these truths is the only radical relief. It is in vain to attempt to suppress or to exterminate the influence of the principles of equity and of honor, or the efforts of men to find relief from the conflict which exists between them and the facts concerning human depravity as commonly held. It is not without deep anguish and fearful struggles that such men as John Foster are impelled to force their way, by overruling scriptural testimony, to such results. There is an awful and affecting solemnity and earnestness in his words, which clearly indicates that his soul had been agitated to its lowest depths. It is affecting to think how many other minds of a like kind may have encountered struggles, similar at least in kind, if not in their results. Moreover, until the system is better adjusted, there will be a powerful tendency to the results at which Foster arrived.

Chapter X: The Reaction

POWERFUL as is the appeal of John Foster, it is by no means adapted to control the convictions of the universal Christian community. Its power lies in the appeal to the principles of honor and right; but there are other truths that will still assert their claim to be heard, and react against it. The Bible will ever powerfully react.

In the next place, there is a Christian experience which so reveals the malignant nature of sin as to throw it out of the pale of lawful sympathy, as in its essential nature cruel, and tending to cruelty in the highest degree, so that to punish it implies in God no cruelty, but the reverse.

Cruelty is that disregard of the feelings of others, or that infliction of suffering on them, which arises from the want of a proper benevolent interest in their welfare. It is not enough to prove cruelty that pain is caused. This is often done from the most benevolent purposes. In the education of children, to spare the rod is often cruel; to inflict it, mercy.

But especially to cause pain, however intense, by defeating malevolent and cruel purposes, is not cruelty. If the plans of a seducer, or an assassin, or a slanderer, are exposed, and a retributive tide of moral emotion turned against them, they suffer. So is it—so must it ever be —when all sin is disappointed and exposed. The suffering thus caused is not a kind of suffering which can be felt alike by good and bad, as is the burning of material fire, or the tortures of the inquisition. Such physical tortures could be continued even after sorrow, regret, penitence, confession, and reformation.

Such are the physical ideas which many entertain of the sufferings of hell. They came from that church which created and administered the inquisition,—that tremendous engine of cruelty,—and which consigned to endless misery all who refused to enter her pale, however holy they might be. Such a church would need to conceive of a hell whose torments should depend on material fire, against which holiness is no defense. Such ideas, too, have extensively infected the imagination of the Protestant world.

But such is not the suffering caused by the exposure and punishment of sin. It is not merely positive or physical. Much of it is the result of the disappointment of sinful purposes, involving cruelty in their essential nature, and in all their tendencies towards God and man. Against suffering thus caused the law of moral sympathy in holy minds does not reject.

A profound Christian experience, moreover, reveals the fact that the radical character of all men is selfishness, as opposed to the law of love; and that this tends to cruelty, and is the great source of the cruelty that fills this earth. The great design of the gospel is by regeneration to remove this root of cruelty and misery. But, if it is not removed in this world, but is left forever to increase in strength, and to disclose its natural results, it will encounter God, be exposed and justly abhorred, and thus be rendered unutterably miserable; and yet, by a kind of misery which is in its nature so malignant that it will repel all sympathy, and array against itself the reaction of benevolent justice. In short, the root of future misery will be the just defeat and exposure of the spirit of cruelty, by infinite love, armed with infinite power. This suffering will endure so long as selfishness, its cause, endures. To remove that cause is the great object of regeneration. The system of this world is adapted to produce that change. Future suffering, consisting, as it does, in malignant passions, is not adapted to produce it, but the reverse. There is, therefore, no reason why the future suffering of such as die in sin should ever end.

A profound Christian experience naturally suggests this view, and it is so plainly sustained by the Word of God that all doubt is removed.

On the other hand, the law of God, by forbidding selfishness and enjoining love, is seen to be, in effect, a prohibition of cruelty; and its penalty a defense of the universe against such as refuse to love God and his creatures, but give themselves up to a spirit of selfishness, which, in its very essence and tendencies, is cruel towards God and all his creatures, and deserves to be exposed and abhorred in all who will not renounce it and return to the law of love.

In addition to these considerations, as has already been stated, it is seen that Foster does not furnish the needed relief at the right point. The real difficulty is that God should give to any new-created beings corrupt moral constitutions, and then place them in circumstances of so great moral disadvantage. It is no relief to this to say that God will not punish them forever for the sins which originate in such a constitution and circumstances. This would be no compensation for wronging them at the outset. And, knowing by religious experience what sin is, and to what it tends, they choose to believe the Word of God as to its future results, and to take refuge in faith and mystery with reference to those dealings of God which are so hard to understand and defend, as to the original constitutions and circumstances of the human race, rather than to disregard the plain teachings of the Bible as to future punishment. Even Foster conceded that the obvious language of the Bible was strongly adverse to his views. This, to the largest portion of true Christians, will ever be decisive. God knows best what will be the future state of sinners. He has a complete view of the whole case. It is wisest and safest, as well as our duty, to trust Him. Thus will the great body of the Christian community continue to reason.

It is not to be expected, however, that all even of true Christians will be able to find relief in this course. Others will not improbably feel impelled to obtain relief by rejecting the doctrine of future eternal punishment. Nor, till there is a better understanding of the facts and principles of the system, will this powerful tendency to conflict and division cease. The doctrine of the eternity of future punishments will not ever be generally repudiated, so clear are the revelations of Christian consciousness as to sin, and so strong is the Scriptural argument by which the doctrine is sustained. On the other hand, till some better understanding is found, it will be impossible to prevent some, even of the most pious, from seeking relief by following in the steps of John Foster.

Chapter XI: The Fourth Experience; Or, The Philosophy Of New School Theology

WE come now to an experience of great interest and importance, in consequence of the controversies to which it has given rise, and the extended results which still flow from it. It is that experience in which, in some form, a constant appeal is made to the principles of honor and right, to modify or correct certain parts of the Old School doctrine of the ruined state of man, whilst, at the same time, an earnest effort is made fully to retain and inculcate the real and essential facts of human depravity, yet so as to accord alike with those principles and with the Word of God.

It derived its origin from no predisposition to subject the doctrines of God's Word to any processes of cold and heartless rationalism. Its present developments originated with one of the holiest men whom God has ever raised up to illuminate and bless the church and the world. The deep Christian experience of Edwards has already called forth our grateful recognition of the goodness and sanctifying power of God, as manifested in him. We now add that it was this holy man who gave the first impulse to the great movement which we are now considering.

The occasion of its commencement was the interruption of the plain, direct and faithful preaching of the gospel, which had been caused by the doctrine of the entire inability of the sinner to perform the spiritual duties of repentance and faith, upon which his salvation was suspended by God. This doctrine was carried out logically.

In New England, to a great extent, the practice of urging sinners to immediate repentance and faith, as reasonable and practicable duties, had ceased. In place of it, men were directed to use the means of grace with moral sincerity, and to pray to God that He would interpose and do for them that which they were unable to do for themselves. Unconverted men were encouraged to enter into either a full or a partial covenant with the church, and to cherish the idea that thus, at least to a certain extent, they were doing their duty. In this way, although the doctrine of entire depravity and absolute inability was retained in theory, it was virtually denied in practice. The consciences of sinners were thus quieted, and urgent calls to immediate repentance had almost entirely disappeared. Meanwhile, errors of various kinds were rolling in like a flood.

In England, in some circles, as we learn from the narrative of his own experience by Andrew Fuller,[11] this same doctrine of the absolute inability of the sinner to perform spiritual duties had produced almost an entire cessation of preaching the gospel, in any form, to the impenitent. Fuller says of himself, "My father and mother were dissenters of the Calvinistic persuasion; and were in the habit of hearing Mr. Eve, a Baptist minister, who, being what is here termed high in his sentiments, or tinged with false Calvinism, had little or nothing to say to the unconverted. I therefore never considered myself as any way concerned in what I heard from the pulpit." Again he says: "With respect to the system of doctrine which I had been used to hear from my youth, it was in the high Calvinistic, or rather, hyper-Calvinistic strain, admitting nothing spiritually good to be the duty of the unregenerate, and nothing to be addressed to them in a way of exhortation, excepting what related to external obedience. Outward services might be required, such as an attendance on the means of grace, and abstinence from gross evils might be enforced; but nothing was said to them from the pulpit in the way of warning them to flee from the wrath to come, or inviting them to apply to Christ for salvation." Of himself, when he first began to preach, he says: "Those exhortations to repentance and faith, therefore, which are addressed in the New Testament to the unconverted, I supposed to refer only to such external repentance and faith as were within their power, and might be complied with without the grace of God. The effect of these views was, that I had very little to say to the unconverted; indeed, nothing in a way of exhortation to things spiritually good, or certainly connected with salvation." Around him, too, on every side, fatal errors were triumphant.

---

11 Andrew Fuller (1754-1815) was an eminent Baptist minister, born in Cambridgeshire, and settled at Kettering. He was a zealous defender of the governmental theory of the atonement against Hyper-Calvinism on the one hand and Socinianism and Sandemanianism on the other, but he is chiefly distinguished in connection with the foundation of the Baptist Missionary Society.

Here, then, was an emergency, and in meeting it Edwards was God's chosen instrument in America, and Andrew Fuller in England. The great principle from which this reaction against the paralyzing and ruinous errors which have been stated derived its life and energy was, that the inability ascribed to the sinner in the Bible was not an absolute inability, caused by the want of natural powers, but solely a voluntary and inflexible aversion to duty; or, to use the technical terms adopted to express these ideas, it was not a natural, but a moral inability, consisting in a fixed unwillingness to do what God requires. Of course, so far from excusing the sinner, it did but enhance his guilt. Neither did it furnish any reason why the sinner should not be urged, by every possible motive, to the immediate performance of his duty. This at once gave directness, pungency and power to preaching, and led the way in extending those great revivals of religion which began under the preaching of Edwards. The principles were first developed by Edwards, and carried out and applied by Hopkins, Bellamy, and others of kindred views. In England, Fuller at first began to investigate the same questions without aid, but, being directed to the works of Edwards, adopted his principles and results. Edwards, inconsistently, still held to a sinful nature, but Hopkins consistently developed from these principles, and from the treatise of Edwards on the nature of true virtue, the doctrine that all sin and holiness consist in voluntary action, and that the essence of holiness is disinterested benevolence, and of sin is selfishness. He also rejected the doctrine of imputation, or of a forfeiture of the rights of the human race by the sin of Adam. Thus were the foundations of New School theology laid by men of deep Christian experience, and in view of ends of the highest moment. It was the theology of revivals.

When Unitarianism subsequently developed itself, the advocates of this system constantly endeavored so to present it as to escape the pressure of hostile arguments derived from the principles of honor and of right, by rejecting all that appears to be irreconcilable with them. Under such influences, the system has reached its present condition. The advocates of these views have had no disposition to relinquish or to weaken the doctrine of depravity. On the other hand, the voice of their own Christian consciousness, the Word of God, and the testimony of history, have confirmed them in its belief and defense. But they have, nevertheless, made unwearied efforts to reconcile it with the principles of equity and honor, so as to remove, if possible, the conflict which had, in the case of the Unitarians, led to results which they regarded as alike mournful and calamitous.

Briefly stated, then, their fundamental peculiarities are these: They deny the imputation of Adam's sin to his posterity,—that is, they deny that God regards as their act that which was not their act, and that on this ground He inflicts on them the inconceivably severe penalty alleged by the Old School divines. They also deny the existence in man of a nature in the strict sense sinful and deserving of punishment anterior to knowledge and voluntary action, and teach that all sin and holiness consist in voluntary action. As a natural result, they also deny the doctrine of the absolute and entire inability of the sinner to do the duties required of him by God. The inability asserted in the Scriptures they hold to be, according to just laws of interpretation, merely a fixed unwillingness to comply with the will of God, which is not inconsistent with a real and proper ability to obey, but derives its character of inexcusable guilt from the existence of such an ability.

Anyone who will read the writings of the advocates of this scheme will see at once that they resort as confidently to the principles of honor and of right for the defense of their peculiar views as either John Foster or the Unitarians. The only difference is, either that they do not apply them to the same doctrines, or else not to the same extent. They do not from a regard to them, with Foster, reject the eternity of future punishment, nor, with the Unitarians, the doctrine of depravity,—but they do attempt so to modify the old statements of the latter doctrine, in view of them, as to represent the conduct of God towards his creatures in their fall as neither dishonorable nor unjust, and the doctrine of eternal punishment as not at war with benevolence and justice, and, therefore, as not incredible.

These views, as they passed out of New England into the Presbyterian church, were encountered with the most decided hostility, and the doctrines of the old theology were inculcated, often in forms the most repulsive and odious to the New School divines.

As was natural in such circumstances, the emotions and the language of the advocates of these views, in refuting what they regarded as so injurious, were often no less vivid and powerful than those of the Unitarians in refuting what they regarded as the pernicious errors of orthodoxy. We have considered the language of Dr. Channing. Compare with this the language of Whelpley,[12] in his celebrated *Triangle*. Speaking of the course of events in the city of New York, he says:

> "You shall hear it inculcated from Sabbath to Sabbath, in many of our churches, that a man ought to feel himself actually guilty of a sin committed six thousand years before he was born; nay, that, prior to all consideration of his own moral conduct, he ought to feel himself deserving of eternal damnation for the first sin of Adam."

This, it will be seen, is the identical doctrine that Pascal and Abelard undertook to defend, at the sacrifice of our moral convictions of honor and right. Listen, now, to the emotions with which it is repudiated by this eloquent writer, as at war with equity and honor.

> "I hesitate not to say that no scheme of religion ever propagated among men contains a more monstrous, a more horrible tenet. The atrocity of this doctrine is beyond comparison. The visions of the Koran, the fictions of the Sadder, the fables of the Zendavesta, all give place to this:— Rabbinical legends, Brahminical vagaries, all vanish before it."
>
> "The idea, that all the numerous millions of Adam's posterity deserve the ineffable and endless torments of hell, for a single act of his, before any one of them existed, is repugnant to that reason which God has given us; is subversive of all possible conceptions of justice."

Concerning the doctrine of man's natural inability to do his duty, he uses the following strong expressions: "It is an insult to every man's unbiased understanding,—to the light of his conscience."

In like manner, the idea that God gives us a depraved and punishable nature anterior to knowledge and choice is by the same writer repudiated, on the same ground. The connection of these doctrines with that of a limited atonement he thus sets forth:

---

12 Whelpley, Samuel. *Letters addressed to Caleb Strong ... showing, that retaliation, capital punishments, and war, are prohibited by the gospel, 1818. The triangle. A series of numbers upon three theological points, enforced from various pulpits in the city of New York, 1832. Lectures on ancient history : comprising a general view of the principal events and aeras in civil history, from the creation of the world till the Augustan age, 1816.*

"The whole of their doctrine, then, amounts to this: that a
man is, in the first place, condemned, incapacitated, and
eternally reprobated, for the sin of Adam; in the next place,
that he is condemned over again for not doing that which
he is totally and in all respects unable to do; and, in the third
place, that he is condemned, doubly and trebly condemned,
for not believing in a Savior who never died for him, and
with whom he has no more to do than a fallen angel."

Of these doctrines he says that "they are calculated and tend to
drive men to skepticism, deism, atheism, libertinism, nay, to madness."
The reason is, that by "them the first principles of immutable and eternal justice are supervened and destroyed."

He exposes the pretext that our moral intuitions—which condemn
such views—are carnal or unsanctified reason; and recognizes in them
the voice of God. A similar strain of remark is very frequent in the advocates of these views. Indeed, they are directly adapted to call into exercise some of the deepest and most powerful emotions of the soul.

It cannot be denied that, in many respects, these views give great
relief to the mind; and their appeal to the moral sense of the community is powerful, and, to no small extent, effectual.

This system has not had so long a history, nor has it acted on so
wide a scale, as the older system. But during its existence it has effected
an incalculable amount of good. It has exerted a penetrating and powerful influence on the Old School theology. It has acted as a counter-
poise against its tendencies to paralysis and inaction, and rendered it
more direct and aggressive in its appeals to sinners. It early exploded
the idea that unregenerated men could properly be received as members of churches, or assume the office of preaching the gospel. It elevated the standard of piety and activity in the clergy and in the
churches. It aroused and developed great intellectual activity in theological investigations. Its great idea is, the power and duty of holy action. It has accordingly communicated an impulsive energy to every
interest and department of society.

It has, moreover, been instrumental in arousing the attention of
multitudes to religion, and exciting them to earnest efforts, and leading them to true repentance and faith. And, in connection with its development, and under the influence of its advocates, the modern

system of benevolent enterprise came into existence and was matured and established. The system, therefore, contains in itself many elements of great, varied and lasting power. Yet it has not succeeded in uniting the Christian community; nor, thus far, does it seem to be approximating towards it. It has not superseded a reaction; it has always been violently opposed, and is no less so now than at any other time.

Chapter XII: The Reaction

THE reasons of the reaction which has been referred to I now proceed to unfold. The denial of a depraved nature—in the proper sense—before action, is regarded by many as either leading to a doctrine of divine efficiency in the production of sin, which, in their view, reason and the moral sense repudiate; or else to the doctrine that the cause of man's entire actual depravity is an innocent nature. and circumstances.

It is obvious that, assuming the fact of the universal and entire actual depravity of the human race, as soon as they begin to act, some cause ought to be assigned for a result so contrary to reason, interest and right. But, after rejecting the theory of imputation and of a sinful nature, in the proper sense of the term, nothing seems to remain but an innocent nature so affected by the fall of Adam as always to lead to sin, or else a stated exercise of divine efficiency to produce sinful voltions in every human being, from the beginning of his existence. Accordingly, some have taken one of these grounds, and others have taken the other.

With regard to the second of these schemes, it is plain that it really denies that there was any influence or agency in the sin of Adam to produce universal sin, except that it was merely the condition on which God suspended the determination of His own stated mode of action in causing sin or holiness. If Adam had obeyed, then God, by direct efficiency, would have statedly caused obedience in all his posterity; but, as he sinned, God statedly causes sin. This view is adopted and defended as necessary, on account of a theory of free agency, which denies to any moral agent the power of choice, except through the agency of God to cause him to choose, and which asserts the exercise of the same divine agency in sinful as in holy choice. Some eminent men have, I concede, reconciled their reason and a moral sense to this view.

The considerations which chiefly recommend it are its simplicity, its entire rejection of a depraved nature in any form, its complete resolution of all sin into voluntary action, and its apparent tendency to exalt the sovereignty of God. Some of the bold language of Scripture also seems, at first sight, to sustain these views. But it never has been able to recommend itself to the universal Christian community. In fact, it results in this: that God, as a sovereign, and for general ends, first caused Adam to sin, and then, because he sinned under the power of this divine efficiency, he proceeded by a like efficiency to cause all of his posterity to sin in all their actions, and always continues so to do, except when he sees fit to cause holy actions by the same divine energy.

This view is properly rejected by numerous opponents, on the ground that it would be unjust to reward or punish volitions so created; that it tends to destroy a sense of accountability, and that it is inconsistent with all just ideas of free agency and the liberty of the will.

We come back, then, to the idea of a deteriorated constitution, which, though not sinful or punishable, is yet the certain, uniform, and universal cause of sin.

To this view the Old School divines object on two grounds: first, that, however plausible the argument from the principles of honor and right, it nevertheless denies, under the name of physical depravity, what are the actual facts in all men, as stated in Scripture and revealed by experience,—that is, real depravity and strong sinful propensities anterior to knowledge and action,—and that hence it gives a defective and superficial view of the real nature and power of original sin and total depravity. There is, as I have before said, an experience which tends to lead to the belief of such deep original depravity. An example of this we gave in the case of Edwards. The depth of depravity in the regenerated heart seems to such, bottomless,—far, far below anything introduced by a wrong and intelligent main purpose. History and observation seem to confirm these views.

It was a spiritual consciousness of this fact which so deeply alarmed Dr. Nettleton,[13] in view of the doctrine under consideration. He felt that the very foundations of orthodoxy were destroyed; and yet he could not make a logical defense against the arguments of Dr. Tay-

---

13 Asahel Nettleton (1783-1844), an American theologian and Congregational pastor who was highly influential during the Second Great Awakening. The number of people converted to Christianity as a result of his ministry is estimated at 30,000. He attended Yale College (1805-1809) and was ordained in 1811. He is most notably known for his participation in the New Lebanon Conference in 1827 during which he opposed the teachings of Charles Finney and Lyman Beecher.

lor, from the principles of honor and right, against physical depravity anterior to knowledge and choice. Nor can anyone do it whilst the system of Christianity remains on its present basis. Yet the feelings and the experience will remain, and in many minds will overrule all arguments against them, even as they did in the case of Dr. Nettleton. They will also cause deep apprehension and alarm. Those who deny real inherent criminal depravity, anterior to voluntary moral action, will be regarded as abandoning original sin, and as on the high road to Pelagianism and Unitarianism. That they have no such purpose, their opponents, if candid, will concede; yea, that they intend to hold fast to the great cardinal doctrines of depravity and regeneration in the fullest sense. Yet, since they have abandoned the plea of mystery, and adopted the principles of honor and right, they regard them as having launched their system on a logical current, the tendencies of which they have not calculated, and the issue of which they do not foresee. They see, either consciously or unconsciously, that the alleged principles of honor and right, as the system now is, directly tend to sweep away the true and deep doctrine of depravity and satanic influence, and to leave only a nominal and superficial depravity, which will not finally differ much from the position of sober Unitarians.

It is a consciousness of this tendency which has aroused the Old School divines to oppose the progress of this system with so much earnestness and perseverance. Their feelings are clearly stated in the following letter of Dr. Nettleton to Dr. Woods. (Memoir, pp. 291—4.) Speaking of those who hold these views, he says,

> "They admit that there is a tendency or propensity to sin in the very constitution of the human mind, but they deny that this tendency is sinful." In consequence of this, he says, "They adopt a new theory of regeneration. It has been said by some that regeneration consists in removing this sinful bias, which is anterior to actual volition; this they deny. But, whether we call this propensity sinful or not, all orthodox divines who have admitted its existence have, I believe, united in the opinion that regeneration does consist in removing it. ... No sinner ever did or ever will make a holy choice prior to an inclination, bias or tendency, to holiness. On the whole, their views of depravity, of regeneration, and the mode of preaching to sinners, cannot fail, I think, of doing very great mischief. This exhibition overlooks the

most alarming features of human depravity, and the very essence of experimental religion. It is directly calculated to prevent sinners from coming under conviction of sin. ... The progress of conviction is ordinarily as follows:— Trouble and alarm, 1. On account of outward sins. 2. On account of sinful thoughts. 3. On account of hardness of heart, deadness and insensibility to divine things,—tendency, bias, proneness or propensity to sin, both inferred and felt; and this the convicted sinner always regards, not merely as calamitous, but as awfully criminal in the sight of God. And the sinner utterly despairs of salvation without a change in this propensity to sin; and while he feels this propensity to be thus criminal, he is fully aware that, if God by a sovereign act of his grace does not interpose to remove or change it, he shall never give his heart to God, nor make one holy choice. If the sinner has not felt this, he has not yet been under conviction of sin, or felt his need of regeneration."

Of those who adopt the views which he is opposing he says:

"They do in effect tell their hearers and their readers what the most godly Christians certainly find it the most difficult to believe,—that their propensity to sin, however strong it may be, is not criminal, but only calamitous; that they need not be alarmed at this awful propensity to sin; that they need not, for God does not, regard it with displeasure. ... Every step in the progress of conviction and conversion is in direct opposition to these sentiments."

He then states strongly the tendency of such views to produce spurious conversions, and adds:

"Piety never did and never will descend far in the line of such sentiments. Were I to preach in this manner, I do solemnly believe that I should be the means of healing the hurt of awakened sinners slightly; of crying peace, peace, when there is no peace, and of throwing the whole weight of my ministerial influence on the side of human rebellion against God."

No one can properly refuse to honor the deep experimental feeling which prompted these remarks, and the sincerity and earnestness of the protest against the views in question. Nor are such sentiments and feelings confined to Dr. Nettleton. Many sympathize with him. Dr. Woods, in his lectures recently published, has enforced similar views. The same is true of the writers in the last series of the *Panoplist*. On this ground we explain their fear of rationalism, and of the intuitive principles of the Scotch philosophers; for their great difficulty is to refute the argument from the intuitive principles of honor and right, against a depraved nature before choice. The Princeton divines pursue the same strain of argument, and so do all who sympathize with them in New England; especially Dr. Dana, in his letter to Professor Stuart, and in his recent Appeal.

Nor is this all. It is still further alleged that so long as the doctrine of a deteriorated nature, resulting in the universal certainty of a consequent actual and total depravity, is retained, there is no real relief gained in respect to the alleged conflict with the principles of honor and right.

This objection to this view is sustained by the allegation that the chief difficulty lies more in the thing done than in the mode of doing it.

The thing done is this, as is agreed on both sides. God, in consequence of Adam's act,—an act preceding the personal existence of all men,—has, in some way, brought it to pass that all men, without fail in any one case, do sin and come into a state of utter and endless ruin, unless they are saved from it by supernatural and special grace. Moreover, it is conceded that it was God's purpose and design to effect this, and in some way He established a system or a constitution by which it has been effected. In this fact, it is said,—a fact conceded by both sides, —the main and great difficulty lies. In removing this difficulty, Professor Hodge says that every theory that denies imputation is less effectual than the doctrine of imputation. Under this statement he includes the theory of a depraved and criminal nature before action, a deteriorated constitution leading to sin, and a divine system or constitution leading to sin. Professor Hodge says :

> "How is it to be reconciled with the divine character, that the fate of unborn millions should depend on an act over which they had not the slightest control, and in which they

had no agency? This difficulty presses the opponents of the doctrine (of imputation) more heavily than its advocates."

These views are sustained by the Princeton reviewers. God, they say, must produce such results either on the ground of justice or of sovereignty. The defenders of imputation take the ground of justice. Their opponents that of sovereignty. This, they say, greatly aggravates the difficulty.

> "Is it more congenial with the unsophisticated moral feelings of men that God, out of his mere sovereignty, should determine that because one man sinned all men should sin, that because one man forfeited his favor all men should incur his curse, or because one man sinned all should be born with a contaminated moral nature, than that, in virtue of a most benevolent constitution, by which one was made the representative of the race, the punishment of the one should come upon all?"

Against the theory of mere sovereignty Professor Hodge alleges that, "It represents the race as being involved in ruin and condemnation, without having the slightest probation." The same allegation is made elsewhere by the Princeton reviewers (*Princeton Theological Essays*, vol. II. p. 159).

This allegation, of course, leads them to state what are the principles of honor and right, as it respects a new-created being. We have already stated them, but will refer to them again. First, that to every such being a probation is due. "Is it not necessary (they say) that a moral being should have a probation before his fate is decided?" Again, they state what is essential to a *fair* probation, and, in so doing, they distinctly recognize the binding force of two of the most stringent of the principles of honor and right which I have laid down. I mean those that relate to the original constitution and circumstances of a new-created being. Concerning these I assert that honor and right require that they be such as to render a favorable result of probation to each individual hopeful, and not utterly improbable and hopeless. In accordance with this, they say, "A probation, to be *fair*, must afford as favorable a prospect of a happy as of an unhappy conclusion."

Is this condition complied with, say they, if God either gives a depraved nature, before action and trial, in consequence of a single act of Adam, done ages before they were born, and in which they did not participate, or if, before action or trial, he introduces into their original constitution predisposing causes of sin, so powerful and certain in their operation that they are sure to ruin all, unless counteracted by a divine interposition transcending all human power, and then exposes the possessors of such natures, even from their earliest years, through life, to the influences of sinful organizations; and to all this superadds the fearful wiles of Satan and his hosts? Or, if we resort to the idea of merely a divine constitution, intentionally so ordained as in some way to effect the same results, is the case any better? In the judgment of the Princeton divines, not at all. They say, "Men are brought up to their trial under a 'divine constitution,' which secures the certainty of their sinning; and this is done because an individual sinned thousands of years before the vast majority of them were born? Is this a fair trial?"

Again, they say,

> "What greater evil for moral and immortal beings can there be than to be born 'contaminated in their moral nature,' or under a divine constitution which secures 'the universality and certainty of sin,' and that, too, with undeviating and remorseless effect? It is, as Coleridge well says, 'an outrage on common sense' to affirm that it is no evil for men to be placed on their probation under such circumstances that not one of ten thousand millions ever escaped sin and condemnation to eternal death."

It will, perhaps, be asked, how much better is that to which the Princeton divines resort as a justification of God, in producing the facts in question? This let every man decide for himself. They resort to the idea that we had a fair probation in Adam. God (they say) appointed Him our federal head, and made a covenant with Him, including us. His probation He regarded as our probation; his sin as our sin; his act as our act. Hence, from the beginning of our existence, He regards us as covenant breakers and rebels, withholds divine influences from us, and leaves us to the consequent and necessary corruption of nature, to actual sin, and to final ruin, unless grace interposes. I have already given my views of this effort at justifying the alleged facts, and need, at present, to make no more remarks. I recur to it here for the sake of saying that, according to the Princeton divines,—and in this they are correct,—all the Reformers, had it not been for the assumption of such a probation, trial, failure, and condemnation in Adam, would have felt it impossible to justify God in bringing men into existence with depraved natures. Speaking of mark, they say, "he, in common with all the reformers, almost without exception, and the whole body of the reformed, constantly make the distinction between imputed sin and inherent corruption; maintaining that the latter *could not be reconciled with God's justice without the admission of the former.*"

This theory, it is interesting to notice, leads to modes of speech which seem to be designed to pay homage to the sense of honor and justice which God has implanted in the mind. Men are, therefore, spoken of as having been once upright; as having had a fair probation; as having failed in the trial; as having broken the covenant, and revolted from God; as having corrupted their natures, and justly exposed themselves to the anger of God. These forms of speech plainly evince what are the demands of honor and right, and are adapted to turn away the eye from the painful realities of the case; and thus enable those who think to justify God by them, and are affected by them, as if it were possible that the real facts could correspond with them, to see clearly that the theories of a corrupt nature before action, or a deteriorated nature always sure to lead to sin, or a divine constitution adapted and sure to lead to sin, are unjust to new-created minds.

But, on the other hand, those who resort for relief to the theory that all sin consists in voluntary action, and that men, as free agents, have truly a real, though never exercised, power to avoid becoming sinful from the first, see just as clearly that every possible form of the doctrine of imputation fails to justify the great conceded facts of human depravity. The idea of a mysterious unity of all men in Adam, so as to make one great moral person, thus making the sin of Adam truly and properly that of every man, they reject as absurd, and in this the Princeton divines agree with them. The literal transfer of the moral character and personal guilt of Adam to all men, they reject; and so do the Princeton divines. The doctrine that God, by any constitution or covenant whatever, can justly or honorably regard Adam's sin as the sin of thousands of millions who are and were confessedly innocent of it, as not being in existence when it was committed, and on the ground of such an unjust judgment inflict on them that which is of all evils the essence and the sum, they also very properly reject, though here their Princeton brethren do not agree with them.

What, then, is the result? Two large bodies of most intelligent and pious men reject reciprocally each other's grounds for justifying the facts in question. It is certainly supposable, and not at all improbable, that both sides are correct in the allegation that the views of their opponents do thus war with honor and right.

At all events, it is plain that the New School views do not so meet and satisfy the sense of honor and right, in the advocates of the doctrine of imputation, as to remove deep conflict and division. A similar retort is made by Dr. Woods against the New School divines, in view of the fact that they reject the idea that God gives to his creatures a nature which is, in the proper and literal sense, sinful before action, as dishonorable to Him, and at war with equity. To this Dr. Woods replies that the doctrine in question is not at all worse than the doctrine that God gives to all men deteriorated natures, which, even if not strictly sinful, are yet sure to lead them into sin and ruin. This, it will be seen, is in accordance with the principles of Dr. Watts, Wesley, and the Reformers, that it is dishonorable and unjust (if there has been no forfeiture of rights) to give to a new-created being a preponderating bias to sin. Dr. Woods urges his retort at great length. I will give a specimen of his mode of reasoning.

In replying to the charge that it is unjust for God "to bring moral corruption and ruin upon the whole human race merely on account of one offense of their common progenitor, and without any fault of theirs," he says:

> "And is there not just as much reason to urge this objection against the theory just named? Its advocates hold that God brings the whole human race into existence without holiness, and with such propensities and in such circumstances as will certainly lead them into sin; and that he brings them into this fearful condition in consequence of the sin of their first father, without any fault of their own. Now, as far as the divine justice or goodness is concerned, what great difference is there between our being depraved at first, and being in such circumstances as will certainly lead to depravity the moment moral action begins? Will not the latter as infallibly bring about our destruction as the former? and how is it more compatible with the justice or the goodness of

God to put us into one of these conditions than into the other, when they are both equally fatal? It is said that our natural appetites and propensities and our outward circumstances do not lead us into sin by any absolute or physical necessity; but they do, in all cases, certainly lead us into sin. and God knows that they will when he appoints them for us. Now, how can our merciful Father voluntarily place us, while feeble, helpless infants, in such circumstances as he knows beforehand will be the certain occasion of our sin and ruin? ... What difference does it make, either as to God's character or the result of his proceedings, whether he constitutes sinners at first, or knowingly places us in such circumstances that we shall certainly become sinners, and that very soon? Must not God's design as to our being sinners be the same in one case as in the other; and must not the final result be the same? Is not one of these states of mankind fraught with as many and as great evils as the other? What ground of preference, then, would any man have? ... Let intelligent, candid men, who do not believe either of these schemes, say whether one of them is not open to as many objections as the other. It is said that all the feelings of our hearts revolt at the idea that God gives us a depraved, sinful nature at our birth, and that no man can believe this without resisting and overcoming his most amiable sensibilities; and do not our moral feelings equally revolt at the idea that God creates us without holiness, and gives us at our birth such appetites and propensities as he knows will forthwith bring us into a state of depravity? And have we not as much occasion to resist and overcome our amiable sensibilities in one case as in the other?" (Woods, Vol. II, pp. 359–361).

The appeal of Dr. Woods to those who do not believe either of these schemes had already been fully met, as will be remembered, by Dr. Channing. After condemning the older form of the doctrine, which involves a depraved and punishable nature before action, he condemns, with no less severity, "the more modern exposition, that we came from the hand of our Maker with such a constitution, and are placed under such influences and circumstances, as to render certain and infallible the total depravity of every human being, from the first moment of his moral agency." Concerning this view, he says, "That to give existence under this condition would argue unspeakable cruelty, and that to punish the sin of this unhappily constituted child with endless ruin would be a wrong unparalleled by the most merciless despotism."

It is plain, then, that no real available and general harmony is effected by the positions of the New School party. Indeed, as we see, they satisfy neither the Unitarians, as zealous advocates of honor and right, on the one hand, nor the thorough defenders of the innate depravity and utterly ruined condition of man, on the other. Both of these parties agree that a conflict with the principles of honor and right exists as truly in the new scheme as in the old. And, in addition to this, the Old School divines regard the denial of a real, inherent criminal depravity, anterior to action, as virtually an abandonment of the doctrine of original sin, and as leading ultimately to Pelagianism and Unitarianism.

But, on the other hand, the New School party relying, justly, on the self-evident principles of equity and honor, reject the theory of imputation and forfeiture on which the Old School party base their entire justification of God. In this they are sustained by the unanimous concurring opinion of the Unitarian party. Both of these parties agree that the fundamental position of the old theology is utterly indefensible.

With reference to the New School theology, I would here also say that it has, at least as held by certain minds and in certain circumstances, a tendency to degrade our conceptions of free agency. To escape the pressure of the argument against the theory of a deteriorated moral constitution, that it is at war with equity and honor in God, some, who profess to hold the doctrines of the New School divines, take the ground that the moral constitutions of men are as good as the nature of free agency will allow. In this way they arrive at the same virtual degradation of free agency of which I have spoken when considering the tendencies of Unitarian theology. This is, virtually, a denial that there has been any fall of the race. But, certainly, it is a very low and unworthy conception of the capabilities of free agency to suppose that the mournful and deeply corrupt moral developments of this world are a fair illustration of its natural tendencies and results in the best and most uncorrupted minds.

Even that Hegelian view of the necessity of moral evil as a means of education, which Dr. Burnap was not willing to adopt,—though his views seem to approximate to it,—has an unpleasant similarity to the views of Dr. Bushnell. He teaches that

> "if a child was born as clear of natural prejudice or damage as Adam before his sin, spiritual education, or, what is the same, probation, that which trains a being for a stable, intelligent virtue hereafter would still involve an experiment of evil; therefore, a fall and bondage under the laws of evil."

Again, of Christian virtue he says:

> "It involves a struggle with evil, a fall and rescue. The soul becomes established in holy virtue as a free exercise only as it is passed round the corner of fall and redemption, ascending thus unto God through a double experience, in which it learns the bitterness of evil and the worth of good; fighting its way out of one, and achieving the other as a victory."

It would seem, according to this, that such is free agency that a process of sinning is an indispensable part of a finished spiritual education in all minds. This certainly degrades free agency to the lowest point of the scale, and represents moral evil as a necessary means of moral education at all times, and in all worlds. But, if evil is thus necessary for such an end, how can a proper sense of its moral ill-desert be consistently retained?

This error may, perhaps, have arisen from generalizing as true of all minds what is sometimes true of depraved minds. If inherent depravity exists, to act it out is sometimes overruled to effect a cure. But, that sin is not necessary to develop undepraved minds, the case of the unfallen angels and of Christ plainly shows.

On the whole, after thus considering the diverse systems which have resulted from an attempt to modify the facts so as to accord with the principles of honor and right, the following conclusion appears to be established: that though, so far as they rest on these principles, they all have indestructible elements of power, yet they always give rise to a powerful reaction. Hence, though in certain aspects they have a decided logical advantage over the old system, yet it also, in other aspects, has a great power of assault, as opposed to them. The deep depravity of man, even before action, seems to find a response in facts in human consciousness and in the Word of God. In particular, a deep Christian experience leads naturally to its belief. The moral wants of man and Christian experience will ever give power to the deepest views of depravity; and when the conclusions derived from the principles of honor and right begin to render the New School system superficial, there will be a reaction in some of the most experimental minds to deeper views. But, since these profound views cannot be harmonized with reason and the moral sense, as the system is now understood, the exercise of these powers with reference to them will be proscribed, and refuge will be sought in faith and mystery. From this result other minds will again earnestly and decidedly react, and thus the conflict will be eternal.

Chapter XIII: Or, The Eclipse Of The Glory Of God

WE now come to an experience which, in its full development, is less common than either of those which have been considered; but towards which, nevertheless, there are often strong tendencies. It is that experience in which the principles of honor and right, and also the facts concerning the depravity and ruin of man, are both retained, and yet without the perception of any satisfactory mode of modification and adjustment. In this case the mind comes, for a time, under the oppressive and overwhelming consciousness of existing, apparently, under a universal system which is incapable of defense, and under a God whom the principles of honor and of right forbid us to worship.

We will first look at the tendencies to this state as illustrated in the experience of an eminent theological writer, whose views we have before considered; we refer to the celebrated John Foster. In a letter to that distinguished scholar and divine. Dr. Harris,[14] President of Cheshunt College, Foster thus expresses himself:

> "I hope, indeed may assume, that you are of a cheerful temperament; but are you not sometimes invaded by the darkest visions and reflections, while casting your view over the scene of human existence, from the beginning to this hour? To me it appears a most mysteriously awful economy, overspread by alurid and dreadful shade. I pray for the piety to maintain an humble submission of

---

14 John Harris (1802-1856). At the age of fifteen he joined the Independent Church, and began to preach as a member of the Bristol Itinerant Society. In 1836 he wrote his essay, *Mammon, or Covetousness the Sin of the Christian Church*, which won a prize of 100 guineas offered by Dr. Conquest, which brought him into notice; thirty thousand copies being sold within a few years. In 1838 he received the degree of doctor of divinity from Brown University, America, and was appointed president and professor of theology in Cheshunt College; and in 1850, when the Independent colleges at Highbury, Homerton, and Coward, near London, were united, Dr Harris was elected principal of the New College that was formed.

thought and feeling to the wise and righteous Disposer of
all existence. But, to see a nature created in purity, qualified
for perfect and endless felicity, but ruined at the very origin,
by *a disaster devolving fatally on all the race,*—to see it in an
early age of the world estranged from truth, from the love
and fear of its Creator; from that, therefore, without which
existence is a thing to be deplored,—abandoned to all evil,
till swept away by a deluge,—the renovated race revolving
into idolatry and iniquity, and spreading downward
through ages in darkness, wickedness and misery,—no Divine dispensation to enlighten and reclaim it, except for one
small section, and that section itself a no less flagrant proof
of the desperate corruption of the nature;— the ultimate,
grand remedial visitation, Christianity, laboring in a difficult progress and very limited extension, and soon perverted
from its purpose into darkness and superstition, for a period
of a thousand years,—at the present hour known and even
nominally acknowledged by very greatly the minority of
the race, the mighty mass remaining prostrate under the in-
fernal dominion of which countless generations of their ancestors have been the slaves and victims,—a deplorable
majority of the people in the Christian nations strangers to
the vital power of Christianity, and a large proportion directly hostile to it; and even the institutions pretended to be
for its support and promotion being baneful to its virtue,—
its progress in the work of conversion, in even the most favored part of the world, distanced by the progressive increase of the population, so that even there (but to a fearful
extent, if we take the world at large) the disproportion of
the faithful to the irreligious is continually increasing,—the
sum of all these melancholy facts being, that thousands of
millions have passed, and thousands every day are passing
out of the world, in no state of fitness for a pure and happy
state elsewhere; O, it is a most confounding and appalling
contemplation!"

It is perfectly apparent that there was a powerful tendency in Foster's mind towards the state which has just been described. In looking
over the scene of human existence, he found himself sometimes in-
vaded by "the *darkest visions and reflections.*" The whole of the present
dispensation appeared to him "*a most mysteriously awful economy, over-*

spread by a lurid and dreadful shade." He still held fast to the belief that
God is wise and righteous. But it cost him many struggles to retain
this aspect of his character, in view of the apparent facts of the case. "I
pray for the piety," he says, "to maintain an humble submission of
thought and feeling to the wise and righteous Disposer of all existence." But a connected view of the system as a whole, including the
fall of the race in Adam,—their deep individual depravity, their subjection to corrupt social organizations and to the malign power of evil
spirits, and their mournful history in all ages, was to him "a most confounding and appalling contemplation."

His biographer, J. E. Ryland,[15] represents him as having here "advanced within the awful shadow of a subject which seems partially to
have obscured his perception of the ultimate ground of moral responsibility." I do not think that this is a full statement of the case. The experience of Foster originated from the difficulty of reconciling the
facts of the system, as a whole, with God's obligations, as a being of
honor and justice, towards successive generations of new-created
minds. And it is plain that, if he had not found relief in some way, he
would have come into the dark shade of a system which he could see
no mode of reconciling with honor and right; and, under the government of a God whose character, as he saw it, he could not rationally
reverence and adore.

I know that the human mind will earnestly struggle against coming into such a state. Yet, if the system logically leads to it, we ought
not to wonder that minds which have a strong regard to logical consistency are sometimes forced into it. It was in view of such results that
Dr. Channing said of Calvinism, "I know that on some minds it has
the most mournful effects; that it spreads over them an impenetrable
gloom." Such would have been its lasting influence on Foster, had he
not in some way found relief. But he immediately proceeds to state in
what manner he found it possible to avoid such an entire eclipse of the
character of God.

> "And it would be a transcendently direful contemplation, if
> I believed the doctrine of the eternity of future misery. It
> amazes me to imagine how thoughtful and benevolent men,

---

15 John Edward Ryland (1753-1825) was a founder of the Baptist Missionary Society,
    maintaining a close friendship with both Andrew Fuller and William Carey, and
    consistently advocated the claims of the Society.

believing that doctrine, can endure the sight of the present world and the history of the past. To behold successive, innumerable crowds carried on in *the mighty impulse of a depraved nature, which they are impotent to reverse*, and to which it is not the will of God in His sovereignty to apply the only adequate power, the withholding of which consigns them inevitably to their doom,—to see them passing through a short term of mortal existence (absurdly sometimes denominated a *probation*) under *all the world's pernicious influences, with the addition of the malign and deadly one of the great tempter and destroyer, to confirm and augment the inherent depravity*, on their speedy passage to everlasting woe,—I repeat, I am, without pretending to any extraordinary depth of feeling, amazed to conceive what they contrive to do with their sensibility, and in what manner they maintain a firm assurance of the Divine goodness and justice."

We are now prepared to see what are the causes of the experience which we are considering, when it is fully developed. They are these: to have, from Christian experience and from the Word of God, a conviction of the radical facts as to the ruin of man, as clear and unwavering as the belief of one's own existence; and, at the same time, to have an equally unwavering belief of the principles of honor and right, and of the demands made by them on God with reference to new-created beings, and to see the conflict between them, without any apparent mode of reconciliation.

This is not the experience of a skeptic, or of a caviller. It sometimes takes place after years of deep and joyful Christian experience have purified the soul, and produced a full conviction of the inspiration of the Word of God. which nothing can shake.

In this state of mind, and whilst keenly sensitive to those demands of honor and right which pressed upon Foster, let the following things be true: that, after a careful examination of all the theories of the Old School and the New School divines for vindicating the fall in Adam, and its results, they are rejected as insufficient; that an experience of the deep depravity of the heart, and the study of history and the Bible, render impossible the adoption of the Unitarian theory; that the theory of John Foster is wholly irreconcilable with the obvious tendencies of things, and the explicit testimony of the Word of God; that in the rejection of the Bible there would be no relief, since the depravity of man, and his tendencies to irremediable misery, are as clear by the light of nature as by revelation; that, moreover, there is no rational ground for the rejection of the Bible, but full and ample grounds for its reception as an inspired communication from God;— let these things be true, and the things of which we speak will be the unavoidable result.

The mind of any refined and educated man, and especially of a Christian man, recoils from the thought that God can be other than holy, just and good. Hence, Dr. Channing says, "We can endure any errors but those which subvert or unsettle the conviction of God's paternal goodness. Urge not upon us a system which makes existence a curse, and wraps the universe in gloom!"

Yet views of the conduct of God may be presented, and for a time believed, which are, in fact, at war with the principles of honor and right, and which present to the mind a malevolent God; and a consistently logical mind cannot escape the influence on its feelings of what it really believes. Although no Christian will ever, in fact, believe that God is dishonorable and unjust in His dealings with His creatures, yet His alleged acts may be such that He cannot rationally be seen in any other light. Then is the sun of the universe for a time eclipsed, and the whole system seems, to use the words of Foster, "to be overspread by a lurid and dreadful shade." How many ever pass in fact into this dark valley, I have no means of determining. It is not an experience that men are disposed to make public. I knew one man, of eminent piety, and distinguished as a clergyman, who had had trials of great severity from tendencies to such views. I have, however, a full knowledge only of what I have learned by experience. For a time the system of this world rose before my mind, in the same manner, as far as I can judge, as it did before the minds of Channing and Foster. I can, therefore, more fully appreciate their expression of their trials and emotions. But I was entirely unable to find relief as they did. The depravity of man, neither Christian experience, the Bible, nor history, would permit me to deny. Nor did reason or Scripture afford me any satisfactory grounds whatever for anticipating the restoration of the lost to holiness in a future state. Hence, for a time, all was dark as night.

If anyone would know the full worth of the privilege of living under, worshiping, loving and adoring a God of honor, righteousness and love, let him, after years of joyful Christian experience, and soul-satisfying communion with God, at last come to a point where His lovely character, for a time, vanishes from his eyes, and nothing can be rationally seen but a God who is selfish, dishonorable, unfeeling. No such person can ever believe that God is such; but he may be so situated as to be unable rationally to see Him in any other light. All the common modes of defending the doctrine of native depravity may have been examined and pronounced insufficient, and the question may urgently press itself upon the mind, Is not the present system a malevolent one? And of it no serious defense may appear.

Who can describe the gloom of him who looks on such a prospect? How dark to him appears the history of man! He looks with pity on the children that pass him in the street. The more violent manifestations of their depravity seem to be the unfoldings of a corrupt nature, given to them by God before any knowledge, choice or consent, of their own. Mercy now seems to be no mercy, and he who once delighted to speak of the love of Christ is obliged to close his lips in silence, for the original wrong of giving man such a nature seems so great that no subsequent acts can atone for the deed. In this state of mind, he who once delighted to pray kneels and rises again, because he cannot sincerely worship the only God whom he sees. His distress is not on his own account. He feels that God has redeemed and regenerated him; but this gives him no relief. He feels as if he could not be bribed by the offer of all the honors of the universe to pretend to worship or praise a God whose character he cannot defend. He feels that he should infinitely prefer once more to see a God whom he could honorably adore, and a universe radiant with His glory, and then to sink into non-existence, rather than to have all the honors of the universe forever heaped upon him by a God whose character he could not sincerely and honestly defend. Never before has he so deeply felt a longing after a God of a spotless character. Never has he so deeply felt that the whole light and joy of the universe are in Him, and that when His character is darkened all worlds are filled with gloom.

Yet, during all this strange experience, he feels that he is in fact doing no dishonor to the true God. He knows that all true goodness, honor and love, in himself, came from the Word and Spirit of that God; and asks, could He thus have trained me, if He were not good, honorable and full of love? Could He have trained me to hate himself?

In contrast with this it would be appropriate finally to place the experience of one who retains all the radical facts as to human depravity, and the system that grows out of it, but passes from the deep gloom of the last experience into the sunshine of the divine glory, by discovering a mode in which these facts can be so adjusted as to harmonize with the principles of honor and right in God. The transition in my own case was as if, when I had been groping in some vast cathedral, in the gloom of midnight, vainly striving to comprehend its parts and relations, suddenly before the vast arched window of the nave a glorious sun had suddenly burst forth, filling the whole structure with its radiance, and showing in perfect harmony the proportions and beauties of its parts. But the rational basis of such an experience needs first to be seen, before the experience itself can be understood.

BOOK III

THE RECONCILIATION IN ITS PRINCIPLES

Chapter I: The Problem Proposed

THE reality, the nature and the power, of the great conflict which I have undertaken to consider, are by this time sufficiently apparent. Who can estimate the amount of emotion and of suffering which the system of Christianity, as thus misunderstood, has caused in minds eminent alike for intellectual power and for benevolence?

How sad to think of its influence for years upon such a mind as that of Foster! How affecting the conflicts which it causes in the minds of ingenuous young men, trained to the love of free thought, and sensitive to the principles of equity and honor, when they find themselves impelled by these principles either to reject facts revealed by Christian consciousness and the Bible, or else to see dark clouds arising to eclipse the character of God! Under the present system they can take no position in which the action of their minds will not be, in some respects, forced, unhealthy and unnatural. To reject the thorough doctrine of depravity, leaves the deep moral wounds of their nature unprobed and unhealed, and perpetuates the sufferings which pride, when not properly understood and eradicated, always causes. To retain the doctrine of depravity in its fulness, and to war against honor and the principles of right in its defense, or by sophistry to evade their demands, or to sink into deep gloom with Foster,—either, though less pernicious in its results, is nevertheless a course the necessity of which is deeply to be deplored. To spend centuries in a conflict on such points, without progress, is certainly a mournful waste of energy, enjoyment and usefulness.

But a full idea of the magnitude of this conflict cannot be gained, till its historical development, through a long series of centuries, has been surveyed. To this survey it would seem to be natural and appropriate now to proceed.

I am induced, however, to defer such a survey for the present, by the conviction that a consideration of the mode in which the system of Christianity can be so readjusted as to remove the conflict is essential to a thorough and profound understanding of the various historical developments of that conflict.

But, before entering directly upon the solution of the problem thus presented, to avert all misunderstanding, it is necessary first to state how much I propose at this point of the investigation to undertake. I propose, then, at this time, merely to show that there is, at least, one supposable mode in which the system can be so adjusted that both of the great moving powers of Christianity may be retained and fully developed, and yet made to act together in perfect harmony.

A full and argumentative consideration of the evidence of its truth does not fall within the scope of my present purpose. At another time I propose to resume that point, and to enter carefully into a consideration of that part of the subject. But, as a preparatory step, it is sufficient for my present purpose to show that the solution which I shall suggest is possible. It is no doubt true, as will soon appear, that the mere statement of it will incidentally effect much more than this; but I aim not so much at argument as at statement and exposition.

For we are not to suppose that, in a case like the present, it is of no importance to establish merely the possibility of the mode of reconciliation in question. It will avail to show that the full belief of the truths on both sides, which have been brought into conflict, is not of necessity unreasonable. It will prove that they do not of necessity come into collision with each other. It will evince that there is at least one way in which they can be harmonized. If we can also show that there can be no other way, then doubtless the mode suggested is the true way. If we do not know this, and if we see no reason why there should not be other modes in which it can be done, then we are authorized to say that either in the mode suggested, or in some other way, they can be harmonized.

I shall begin, therefore, by simply proposing a possible mode of reconciliation, and defer to a future time a full consideration of the question whether it is in fact the real mode.

At the same time, I would again advert to the truth that, in many cases, the mere fact that a certain adjustment of the parts of a system will harmonize the action of the whole is reasonably deemed to be a very strong presumption, or even a sufficient proof, that that is the true arrangement. If a certain number of wheels, levers and axles, were known to belong to one machine, and if, after repeated trials of various modes of combination, the parts of the machine had never worked harmoniously together, then the mere fact that a mode of combination which had at last been pointed out would remove the conflict and develop the full power of the machine, would be regarded by all as a sufficient proof that it was the true and proper mode of combination. I cannot, therefore, even state the present solution, without furnishing evidence of this kind, of greater or less degree of strength.

CHAPTER II: METHOD OF PROCEDURE

THERE are two modes in which we may suppose that a problem of this kind can be solved. One by a direct and specific divine revelation in language; the other by a study of the principles and component parts of the system itself. We are obliged to resort to the latter mode in order to prove the being of a God, and the divine origin and inspiration of His Word. It cannot, therefore, be an unsafe mode of proceeding, since it is at the basis of all our belief in a God and in revelation.

For the present, I shall consider the problem now before us in the second mode, on the assumption that we are allowed by the Word of God to solve it by simply considering the principles and component parts of the system, and are not bound by any verbal statements of revelation to adopt any particular theory on the subject.

To illustrate my meaning, I would refer to the true theory of the solar system. It is now conceded that there has been no solution of this system given in the Word of God. The great Creator has made it known only by disclosing to the human mind the principles and facts which, when viewed as a system, involve its truth. By the study and comparison and arrangement of these, it was at last discovered. God, by making the system as He did, and by placing the requisite principles and facts in the possession of men, did virtually, though not verbally, reveal to them the true laws of the universe. Newton, by studying and combining what God gave to men, at last interpreted the revelation.

So I shall assume that, in this case, God has given to us the principles and facts, which, viewed in their relations, do reveal to us the true mode of harmonizing the great moving powers of Christianity. These principles and facts He has given to us, not in any one mode, but in various modes. He has so made the mind that it gives us, by its intuitive perceptions, those great intellectual and moral principles which are at the basis of all possible knowledge. He has so made the body, and the material system around us, that they are to us a great and inexhaustible library of facts, principles and laws. He has given us, by His providence, as developed in history, sacred and profane, rich and varied stores of truth. There we see His great moral system in operation. There we study the various theories of man with reference to it, and watch their results as reduced to practice. But, above all, God has revealed to us in His Word facts and principles of the highest moment, and most extended relations. He there transcends the bounds of sense and of time. He places before us the inhabitants of other worlds, and their relations to us. He discloses His own plans, in their eternal relations, and our connection with them. He unfolds to us the great fact that all things in this world center and terminate in the redemption of the church. He discloses to us, moreover, the final and glorious destinies of the church in eternity.

All the principles and facts placed before us, in these various ways, in fact belong to one and the same great system, the center of which is that high and holy One of whom and through whom and to whom are all things.

Moreover, in my present inquiries, I shall assume that God has so presented to us this system, taken as a whole, that by a careful study of it we may learn the great law of its harmonious action; and that the Bible has said nothing designed to foreclose this mode of inquiry, or to confine us, by express verbal revelation, to any particular theory on the subject.[1]

I know that this position has been denied, and will be disputed. In its proper place, therefore, I shall fully consider such denials, and endeavor to exhibit the real relations of the Bible to the subject. At present, however, I shall assume as correct the position concerning the Bible which I have laid down, reserving the proof of its truth to another place.

On this assumption, then, I shall proceed to present what is certainly a possible mode of removing all conflict between the moving powers of Christianity; that is, between those thorough views of innate human depravity, and subjection to the powers of evil, which are recognized as true and scriptural by men of a profound Christian experience, and the highest principles of honor and right, which a well-

---

1   The "system taken as a whole" cannot be considered apart from humanity taken as a whole, which is fundamental to the idea of the Trinity. See *The True Mystery of the Mystical Presence*, John Nevin & Phillip Ross, Pilgrim Platform, Marietta, Ohio, 2011.

ordered mind intuitively perceives to be true, and obligatory upon God as well as upon men.

Chapter III: State Of The Human Mind, And Conditions Of The Problem

BEFORE engaging in an undertaking as serious as that proposed, it is important to call to mind the great fact that sound logic and true benevolence are but a part of the influences by which the human mind is, or ever has been, in fact, controlled in forming its opinions. Even, therefore, if I should succeed in presenting a solution in which truly logical and benevolent minds would be united, it would not follow, of course, that all division would cease, but only that it would cease among candid and reasonable good men. This is not possible as things now are, and therefore to make it possible is my great aim.

But in a large portion of the religious community there are committals from which it is hard, if not impossible, for them to escape. I refer to the votaries of the Church of Rome in particular. That body was early committed to a false theory, and, by reason of her claim to infallibility, is cut off from alteration or retraction. Moreover, upon the minds of many, various illogical influences still exert great power. These flow sometimes from the imagination, sometimes from the association of ideas, sometimes from pecuniary or social interests, sometimes from a bad heart. Moreover, the solution before me will touch and affect a wide range of such influences and interests. It is not, therefore reasonable to demand of me that I shall succeed in presenting a solution which will, in fact, avert division among all men, of all moral characters, and in all states of mind, but that I shall present a solution adequate to avert division among benevolent and reasonable minds. Nor is it a condition that I shall be able at once to suspend the power of illogical influences proceeding from constitutional peculiarities, or pecuniary or organic interests, even among good men.

In some good men the imagination is so inordinately predominant that they are so governed by taste and poetry as to be almost insensible to the force of logic. Others are so impelled by imaginative emotions that they have no affinity for enlarged, calm and comprehensive logical views. In others the association of ideas has imparted to everything that has been, during their education, linked in with the system of the gospel, such an aspect of holiness, that even errors are invested with all the sacredness of the truths with which they have been associated. Not only the Church of Rome, but all state churches, and great denominational organizations, exert an influence, upon the standing and means of support of all their members, so powerful that it tends to arrest or overrule the free action of the logical power, by an influence which is, in its essential nature, rather intimidating than illuminating or reasoning. In others, emotions of reverence and gratitude to great and good men of past ages, emotions in themselves very proper, are so inordinate as to render them incapable of admitting that any of their views can be erroneous. National prejudices, moreover, and denominational commitments, and the general state of society in any age, exert a great control over the action of the logical power. It is not a condition of the problem before me that I shall be able at once to suspend the influence of such causes, and to unite all men in one common view. It only requires that I give a reconciliation which is sound in principle, and will finally be recognized as such by all rational, impartial, and unbiased minds.

Much less do the conditions of the problem require, as I have before said, that I shall be able to suspend the blinding power of a sinful aversion to the truth, or to neutralize the influence of a moral repulsion from the divine character which no reasonable view of things can harmonize with God. There is such a thing as hating the truth by reason of sin. Of this our Savior spoke when He said that men love darkness rather than light, because their deeds are evil. Pride and selfishness cannot be practically and heartily harmonized with the true principles of honor and right, for they are not themselves honorable and righteous. But those who are truly humble, benevolent and penitent, are disposed to see the truth. They are not indisposed to justify God, and to condemn themselves as sinners. There is. therefore, no moral obstacle in the way of a clear perception of truth in the minds of such. What they shrink from is not just humiliation and self-condemnation, nor any just views of the divine sovereignty, but allegations which, in their most candid and humble hours, seem at war with the honor and rectitude of God. From these they recoil, from the very fact that they love Him with supreme affection, and cannot endure to see His glory obscured. Our problem, then, has respect to such minds as these, and not to such as are in spirit still opposed to God. It is in vain to try to satisfy the feelings of worldly, proud, conceited, selfish minds, continuing such, or to harmonize them with statements of their own deep depravity and guilt, and of the right of God to deal with them in accordance with the principles of a wise and benevolent sovereignty. Sinful feelings are essentially unreasonable, and lead to a dislike of the truth itself, however stated, and the difficulty caused by them cannot be remedied till they are removed.

But those difficulties which are felt by truly sanctified, humble and reasonable minds, and the more in proportion as they become holy, humble and reasonable, are entirely of another kind; and it is of the removal of these that we now propose to speak.

The problem, therefore, has reference to benevolent, candid, humble, logical, well-balanced minds, who, though keenly sensitive to all proper appeals to their feelings, are yet not governed by the association of ideas, nor by the imagination, nor by mere emotion, but desire to maintain a proper consistency and harmony between their intellectual and moral views and their emotions, and who cannot rest in systems made up of incongruous and self-contradictory positions.

Chapter IV: The Essentials Of Harmony

I HAVE stated the character of the minds among whom I regard it as possible to produce harmony. Let us proceed to consider the essential elements of harmony among such minds. First of all, then, I remark, that, in order to secure this result, it is obviously indispensable to retain all the facts which really belong to the system as a great whole. This is essential in order to avoid partial and one-sided views. The universal system may be compared to a machine composed of many wheels, which may be put together in various ways, by omitting one or more of the wheels; but yet, there is always evidence that the true way has not been discovered, so long as all the wheels are not included, each in a place that makes it contribute to the common result to be produced by their joint action. Or, to resort for an illustration to a common game among children, the parts of the system are like the letters which compose a word, and are given out in confusion, to be united by the discovery of the word to which they belong. Other words may be spelled by a part of them, but if any are omitted it is a proof that the true word has not been discovered.

In like manner, if any of the real and great facts of God's system are omitted, no matter if the rest are so united as to make a system of some sort, it is plainly not the true system, nor can it harmonize such minds as those to whom my reasoning is directed. They will desire to take not one-sided, but enlarged and comprehensive views, and to include all the known or discoverable facts of God's system. To illustrate by an example: there are those who reject the Bible, in reality, on account of its deep views of human depravity, or of future punishment, or of Satanic agency. Others, retaining it in name, on various grounds drop many of its doctrines. To a truly benevolent, logical and well-balanced mind, such a course can give no relief. It is merely rejecting a large portion of the most important and best authenticated facts of the system; and it results of necessity in limited, defective and one-sided views.

The system, therefore, which satisfies a truly logical and well-balanced mind, will retain all the facts of the Bible, of history, of science, and of the philosophy of the human mind and body, as being, in fact, harmonious parts of the true system of which it is in pursuit.

Moreover, in order to produce harmony, the system must be such as to give full and free play to all the convictions and emotions which it is the design of Christianity to call into existence. In particular, it must allow the process of conviction of sin, humiliation and confession, to advance with such power, and to such an extent, as thoroughly to probe and radically to heal the moral diseases of the mind. The theory of sin and the facts concerning human depravity must be so stated as to aid, and not to impede, the full development of the deepest forms of Christian experience. For the work of sanctification is the chief work of the Spirit of God, and, till its full demands are met, the most powerful portion of Christian minds will never rest. In all ages the channel of power has been that of deep conviction of sin, penitence and self-abasement before God. Any views which permanently obstruct this channel will cause a rise in the streams of Christian emotion, till they are swept away. The fundamental facts as to the fallen and ruined state of man must be, therefore, retained with the utmost fulness.

Nor must the full power of the invisible spiritual enemies of the human race to flatter and deceive to be hidden, so as to allow of delusive views of human power and self-originated progress. On the other hand, the need of a supernatural divine agency must be recognized as essential, in order thoroughly to purify the soul, and to restore it to its normal relation to God.

The reason for this is obvious. There is a correlation between the mind and God, which is the basis, so far as the mind is holy, of a sympathetic communion, designed and adapted to fill all the capacities and develop and perfect all the powers.

This is not merely natural, like the vision of the sun; but it is suspended on a manifesting power in God,—such that He can reveal or hide himself, as He will.

This sympathetic communion cannot be perfect until the soul is entirely cleansed from sin; for holiness in man is essential to a true conception of holiness in God, as well as to sympathy with it. Every one that loves knows God, and he who loves not knows not God; for

God is love. Nor can perfect love in God be comprehended, except by
that perfect love which casts out fear (1 John 4:8, 18).

Hence, as a matter of experience, seasons of deep conviction of
sin, mourning and self-loathing, precede seasons of eminent and joyful
communion with God. It is this process of moral cleansing which fits
the soul for communion with God. It also renders peculiar manifestations of divine favor safe to the Christian, since it increases the depth
of his humility before God, and his conviction that he owes all that he
has of moral excellence to the grace of God.

Edwards says of himself:

> "Often, since I lived in this town, I have had very affecting
> views of my own sinfulness and vileness; very frequently to
> such a degree as to hold me in a kind of loud weeping,
> sometimes for a considerable time together; so that I have
> often been forced to shut myself up. I have had a vastly
> greater sense of my own wickedness, and the badness of my
> heart, than ever I had before my conversion. It has often ap-
> peared to me that, if God should mark iniquity against me, I
> should appear the very worst of all mankind; of all that have
> been since the beginning of the world to this time; and that
> I should have by far the lowest place in hell."

To this the editor subjoins in a note the following judicious remarks:

> "Our author does not say that he had more wickedness and
> badness of heart since his conversion than he had before;
> but that he had *a greater sense thereof*. Thus a blind man may
> have his garden full of noxious weeds, and yet not see or be
> sensible of them. But should the garden be in great part
> cleared of these, and furnished with many beautiful and
> salutary plants; and, supposing the owner now to have the
> power of discriminating objects of sight: in this case, he
> would have less, but would see and have a sense of more.
> And thus it was that St. Paul, though greatly freed from sin,
> yet saw and felt himself as 'the chief of sinners.' To which
> may be added, that the better the organ and clearer the light
> may be, the stronger will be the sense excited by sin or holi-
> ness."

This is but a natural result of the illuminating power of the divine Spirit, whilst engaged in the work of thoroughly purging the soul from the pollutions of sin.

It is an experience like that of an eminent ancient saint, who exclaimed, "I have heard of thee by the hearing of the ear, but now mine eye seeth thee; wherefore, I abhor myself, and repent in dust and ashes!"

The natural result of such seasons of mourning for sin is divine comfort and communion in a still higher degree; and such was, in fact, his experience.

He says, in describing other parts of his religious life,

"I have sometimes had a sense of the excellent fulness of Christ, and his meetness and suitableness as a Savior; whereby he has appeared to me far above all, the chief of ten thousands. His blood and atonement have appeared sweet, and his righteousness sweet; which was always accompanied with ardency of spirit, and inward strugglings and breathings, and groanings that cannot be uttered, to be emptied of myself, and swallowed up in Christ.

"Once, as I rode out into the woods for my health, in 1737, having alighted from my horse in a retired place, as my manner commonly has been, to walk for divine contemplation and prayer, I had a view, that for me was extraordinary, of the glory of the Son of God, as Mediator between God and man, and his wonderful, great, full, pure and sweet grace and love, and meek and gentle condescension. This grace, that appeared so calm and sweet, appeared also great above the heavens. The person of Christ appeared ineffably excellent, with an excellency great enough to swallow up all thought and conception,—which continued, as near as I can judge, about an hour; which kept me the greater part of the time in a flood of tears, and weeping aloud. I felt an ardency of soul to be, what I know not otherwise how to express, emptied and annihilated; to lie in the dust, and to be full of Christ alone; to love him with a holy and pure love; to trust in him; to live upon him; to serve and follow him; and to be perfectly sanctified and made pure, with a divine and heavenly purity. I have several other

times had views very much of the same nature, and which
have had the same effects."

Such is the process by which the soul is conducted towards perfect
holiness, and which it is essential that nothing be allowed to interrupt.

But it is no less important that nothing shall be mingled with such
views as shall misrepresent God, and make the system, logically viewed
as a whole, a source of torture to the sanctified and fully developed
mind, exquisite in proportion to the degree of its sanctification. There
is nothing of this kind in God, when truly seen; but false theories have
often introduced such elements.

The decisive point of trial of every system, therefore, is, can it give
a view of depravity such as to include all sin, and so deep and powerful
as to go to the bottom of the human malady, and purge it fully out,
and give a consciousness of life and health, and of restoration to its true
and normal state; and moreover, reveal to man the true system of this
world, and yet, at the same time, disclose to it a God such in attributes
and acts that, in its most holy state, it can perfectly love Him, without
doing violence to any of its regenerated powers and honorable emotions?

Human depravity is a matter of fact and of consciousness; and, in
order to heal it, we must take it as it is, in all its extent and magnitude.
And any system that cannot go to the bottom of a regenerated consciousness, cannot radically heal the soul; and till the mind is thus
healed, it is in vain to present to it a theoretically perfect view of God,
for it must first be radically sanctified before it can experimentally
know and commune with such a God.

On the other hand, however deep a system is in its theory of human depravity, if, in fact, it misrepresents the feelings or the acts of
God, it must fill a truly regenerated and fully developed mind with
deep distress, because it cannot fully love God without doing violence
to its regenerated nature. Let us illustrate this by a familiar scriptural
analogy. The church is united to God in such relations that she is
called the bride, the Lamb's wife.

Suppose, then, that a truly benevolent king, deeply interested in a
young woman of low rank but of distinguished natural talent, and yet
proud, ambitious, selfish and cruel, had undertaken to correct her de-
fects and educate her to become his wife, and had so far revolutionized
her character as to make her humble, unaspiring, full of disinterested

love, forgiving, compassionate and sensitively honorable, and then had espoused her to himself,—could anything fill her with deeper anguish than to have facts stated concerning Him, on evidence apparently con-clusive, which, if true, would prove that in his general administration he was cold-hearted, selfish, cruel, and devoid of all sympathy in the sufferings of his subjects?

Would not the very fact of her own moral renovation—her love, tenderness, sympathy, and sensitive honor—fit her for keener suffering than she could have endured in her original ambitious and unfeeling state? Would any personal favors from him satisfy her? Would she not say, "How can I love one so unlike the character which He has taken so much pains to form in me? O, why, why has He trained me to hate himself?"

Yet the fact that He had so trained her would lead her to feel that there must be some error about the alleged facts.

"His true character," she would say, "must accord with that which He has taken so much pains to form in me."

And so, if acts and states of mind are ascribed to God which, in fact, logically imply that He has acted wrong fully towards His crea-tures, or that He is cold-hearted, cruel and unfeeling, it fills the regen-erated mind with unutterable distress. And yet, statements have, in fact, too often been made, which legitimately imply this.

God can, indeed, even under such a system, so reveal Himself, by special grace, that His real character shall be truly seen and felt in such a manner as to be independent of opposing theories, and to suspend their power. Or, the mind may for a time defend itself by false logical processes, or by statements addressed rather to the imagination than to the reason.

Thus, the logical tendencies of the system may for a time be sus-pended, as seeds often lie long in the soil with out vegetating.

But, as education and general culture and Christian sympathy and honor advance, the real nature of the theory will be disclosed, and the mind cannot but see and feel the logical tendencies of the facts alleged; and, as soon as this comes to pass, it is in anguish; for the system is then seen to be such that it cannot find a God whom its regenerated powers can truly, honorably and fully love; nay, the only God which it can logically find it feels bound to hate.

How, then, can a harmony and reconciliation be effected between the facts which are essential in order to reveal the true character and condition of man, and effect his thorough moral renovation, and such a character of God as a regenerated mind can reasonably honor and love?

CHAPTER V: THE MISUNDERSTANDING

IN order to answer the question before us, the natural course is carefully to examine the system of Christianity as it now is, and thus to ascertain, if possible, what is the cause of the misunderstanding. It is not, of necessity, anything obvious and prominent. Powerful systems are often easily and fatally misunderstood by a small cause. The movement of a part of the iron track of a railroad only a few inches from its true position is enough to put the whole system out of order, and to produce terrific scenes of confusion, ruin, suffering and death. A small motion, easily and quickly performed, can ruinously misadjust the wheels of a steamboat.

So, in the great system of the universe, a single false assumption, plausible in its aspects, and made without due examination and consideration of its necessary and inevitable effects, may, by falsely adjusting its moving powers, throw the whole system into confusion, and plunge millions into endless ruin. Such a plausible but unfounded assumption I now proceed to state.

That, then, which I regard as having produced the great and fatal misunderstanding of the system of Christianity, the effects of which I have endeavored to exhibit, is the simple and plausible assumption *that men as they come into this world are new-created beings*. That they are *new-born* beings, is plain enough; that they are, therefore, *new-created* beings, is certainly a mere assumption. True, it is a plausible assumption; and so was the old theory that the sun revolved around the earth. Was it not obvious, it was said, to the eyes of all, that such was the fact? Moreover, was there not, apparently, clear Scriptural evidence of it? Did not the Bible speak of the sun as rising and setting? Did not Joshua cause it to stand still? Such was the reasoning of good men, even so late as the time of Turretin. On this point Dr. Hitchcock[2] says:

---

2 Edward Hitchcock (1793-1864) was a noted American geologist and the third President of Amherst College (1845–1854).

"Until the time of Copernicus, no opinion respecting natural phenomena was thought more firmly established, than that the earth is fixed immovably in the center of the universe, and that the heavenly bodies move diurnally around it. To sustain this view, the most decided language of Scripture could be quoted. God is there said to have *established the foundations of the earth, so that they could not be removed forever*; and the sacred writers expressly declare that the sun and other heavenly bodies arise and set, and nowhere allude to any proper motion in the earth. And those statements corresponded exactly to the testimony of the senses. Men felt the earth to be immovably firm under their feet; and when they looked up, they saw the heavenly bodies in motion. What bold impiety, therefore, did it seem, even to men of liberal and enlightened minds, for anyone to rise up and assert that all this testimony of the Bible and of the senses was to be set aside! It is easy to conceive with what strong jealousy the friends of the Bible would look upon the new science which was thus arraying itself in bold defiance of inspiration, and how its votaries would be branded as infidels in disguise. We need not resort to Catholic intolerance to explain how it was that the new doctrine of the earth's motion should be denounced as the most fatal heresy; as alike contrary to Scripture and sound philosophy; and that even the venerable Galileo should be forced to recant it upon his knees. What though the astronomer stood ready, with his diagrams and formulas, to demonstrate the motion of the earth; who would calmly and impartially examine the claims of a scientific discovery, which, by its very announcement, threw discredit upon the Bible and the senses, and contradicted the unanimous opinion of the wise and good,—of all mankind, indeed,—through all past centuries? Rather would the distinguished theologians of the day set their ingenuity at work to frame an argument in opposition to the dangerous ideology, that should fall upon it like an avalanche, and grind it to powder. And, to show you how firm and irresistible such an argument would seem, we need no longer tax the imagination; for Francis Turretin, a distinguished Protestant professor of theology, whose writings have, even to the present day, sustained no mean reputation,

has left us an argument on the subject, compacted and arranged according to the nicest rules of logic, and which he
supposed would stand unrefuted as long as the authority of
the Bible should be regarded among men."

But, after all these plausible appearances in external phenomena
and in the Scriptures, the theory in question was a mere assumption,
and its influence, so long as it was retained, was to throw the whole
system of the material universe into confusion. Therefore, notwithstanding the reasonings and prejudices of good men, and the anathemas of the Roman Catholic Church, it has long since been rejected,
and consigned to the locality in the moon where the great Italian bard
located the forged decretals, upon which, in their day, was erected the
portentous structure of Roman Catholic despotism.

Such, too, may soon be the destiny of the plausible but unproved
assumption that men, as they enter this world, are new-created beings.

But, it may be asked, what is the injurious influence of this assumption? How does it misunderstand and disorganize the system of
the moral universe? To this I reply; by an absolute necessity it gives an
immediate and definite direction to the powerful principles of honor
and of right, such that they energetically war against and tend to destroy any radical doctrine of original and inherent depravity. That
there are powerful principles of honor and of right, with respect to
new-created beings, we have shown. We have also shown that the reality and validity of these principles, in their highest form, has been
decidedly and earnestly maintained by the most orthodox portions of
the church, as well as by others. And what do these principles demand?
As stated by myself, and avowed by Turretin, Watts, Wesley and the
Princeton divines, and confirmed by the churches of the Reformation,
they demand that God shall give to all new-created beings original
constitutions, healthy and well-balanced, and tending decidedly and
effectually towards good. To make them either neutral or with constitutions tending to sin, would be utterly inconsistent with the honor
and justice of God, and would involve Him in the guilt and dishonor
of sin. Moreover, God is bound to place new-created things in such
circumstances that there shall be an over-balance of influences and
tendencies on the side of holiness, and not of sin. Such are the conceded demands of the principles of equity and of honor. If there should
be any doubt of the absolute truth and entire accuracy of these state-

ments, let my readers refresh their memories by reading once more the fifth (p. 29) and sixth (p. 37) chapter of the first book of this work.

If, then, in view of such principles, we assume that men are new-created beings, what are the inevitable consequences? It follows, by a logical necessity, if God is honorable and just,—which all assume,—that they have uncorrupt moral constitutions, and predominant propensities to holiness, and are in circumstances tending to develop and perfect these tendencies. If not so, what becomes of the honor and justice of God? But if so, then what fragment is there left of any radical doctrine of human depravity, or of corrupt human or satanic influence?

But such wholesale inferences as these, though perfectly logical and irresistible so long as the premises are retained, make war as directly upon facts, common experience and history, as upon the fundamental doctrine of depravity in the Word of God.

What, then, is to be done? Only two resources remain. One is, to justify the Creator by devising some mode in which new-created beings, long before they are created, or have known or done anything, can forfeit all their rights, and come under his just displeasure; the other, to release God from the elevated claims of the principles of equity and honor, as above stated, by the plea that such is free agency that they involve an impossibility,—that is, by so degrading the nature of free agency as to bring it down so very low that it will reach the deep moral depression of the atrocious developments of men, and of evil spirits through men, in this world, and accept them as the natural and necessary developments of free agency.

But, by resorting to either of these alternatives, the conflict is not removed, but rather augmented. The doctrine of a forfeiture of rights by the imputation of Adam's sin can never escape the charge of involving, not merely injustice, but falsehood also. According to it, it will ever be said, God first falsely accuses new-created beings, and then, on the basis of this false accusation, inflicts a penalty of infinite and inconceivable severity,—a penalty which is of all evils the essence and the sum.

One would think that the worst enemy of Christianity could not desire to place it on a worse basis, or in a more indefensible position than this. The redemption of the church is the chief work of God. In it He aims to reveal in its highest degree the glory of His grace. And yet, as God has made the mind, it cannot but regard it as based on an act of

God dishonorable and unjust in the highest conceivable degree. Is this a proper basis of a system of free, pure, wonderful, sovereign grace?

On the other hand, the doctrine that free agency is of necessity so imperfect as to involve such atrocious developments as those which make up the history of this world, is at war with well-known facts. It was not such in the innumerable hosts of holy angels, who have never deviated from the reverent worship and service of God, but are still glorious in holiness and flaming fires of love, and intent with all their powers to do His will. And who has any shadow of right to say that the great majority of the whole created universe are not such to this day? It was not so in the case of our great exemplar,—the man Jesus Christ; for, though He was in all points tempted as we are, yet was He without sin. Amid trials of every form, and of intense severity, He remained holy, harmless, undefiled, separate from sinners.

But, if the necessary nature of free agency does not involve such results of sin and misery as fill this world, and there has been no forfeiture of original rights, then God cannot be justified in bringing such results to pass, merely as a sovereign, either by His own direct efficiency, or by a series of natural causes, acting through the body or the soul, or both; and this is conceded, or rather strongly asserted, by all the leading Old School authorities. So that, on this ground, the actual facts of this world, and of revelation, are such that they logically lead us to the result that the present system is indefensible, and that God does not deserve the honor, reverence and worship, of His creatures. Nor is it any relief to resort, with Foster, to the idea of universal salvation; for, in addition to the fact that the doctrine is at war with Scripture, and the natural tendency of things, it is no defense of God against the charge of wronging men in their original constitution and circumstances, to say that He does not add to it a still greater, even an infinite wrong.

It is perfectly plain, then, that the simple and plausible assumption that men, as they come into this world, are new-created beings, does so direct the action of the great, the omnipotent principles of honor and right that they do act with constant and fearful energy against the other great moving power of Christianity. This is the simple and unnoticed motion by which the great wheels of the ship of Christianity are made to revolve in opposite directions. That they do so revolve, I have shown by an appeal to facts. By the statements just made I have shown how that effect is produced; nor, so long as the assumption in question is made, is it possible to avoid the result.

It appears, then, that the whole conflict which we have been considering arises from the assumption that men, as they come into this world, are new-created beings. The principles of honor and of right, as we have stated them, relate solely to new-created beings, who have had no probation, but who are to have one, in which they are to decide by their own action their destinies for eternity. In all ages, the binding force of these laws has been felt to rest on this consideration. If any person has been created with a moral constitution tending to good, and well circumstanced, and honorably, and affectionately dealt with by God, and then has made an ungrateful return, by disobedience and revolt, then all concede that he has forfeited his original rights. If such a person is punished, or dealt with on principles of sovereignty, all feel that it is right.

Now, as it regards men, it is always merely *assumed*, on all sides, that they are, as they enter this world, new-created beings. This is certainly, in a case of so much moment, a remarkable fact. It cannot be explained on the ground that it is a self-evident truth; for it is not. Never has it been regarded as such in the world at large. Indeed, a large proportion of the human race, if not the majority, have always believed in some form of the doctrine of the preexistence of man.

Nor is it because this assumed truth has no powerful logical relations; for, in fact, it is, as I have proved, involved in all the reasoning of the opposing parties in the great conflict which I have described: nor have the advocates of equity and honor any power in argument against the other party which does not depend upon this assumption.

Nor is it because this assumed truth is clearly revealed; for it is not. Indeed, it can be conclusively shown that it is not revealed even indirectly, much less directly and obviously.

Nor is it because the evidence of the assumed truth has ever been carefully considered and proved to be sufficient; for no such thing has ever been done. In short, it is the most remarkable case of an illogical assumption of a fundamental truth, during a controversy of ages, of which I have any knowledge. The only thing that has prevented its proper exposure has been the fact that it has been so generally, not to say all but universally, assumed on both sides of the question. This assumption is involved in the doctrine that the cause of human depravity is the sin of Adam, and that on this account all men are born with either inherent depravity, or deteriorated or deranged moral constitutions. These things, of course, imply that their depravity is not the result of their previous action in a preceding state of existence, but that they come into this world as new-created minds. This is plain to a demonstration; for, if men caused their own original depravity in a former state, then it was not caused by the sin of Adam. But, if Adam caused it, then they did not cause it in a former state, but are new-created beings.

But, if they are new-created beings, then all the demands of honor and right are in full force towards them. Accordingly, Pelagius and his compeers and successors, in view of these principles, have always denied that man is, in fact, born with a deteriorated moral constitution, and asserted that he has such a one as the principles of honor and right demand for a new-created being. This is the fundamental element of Pelagianism. The same principles lead to the denial of man's exposure and subjection to powerful malignant spirits. This, it is alleged, is not consistent with the demands of honor and right towards new-created beings. The same principles would also lead to a denial of man's exposure to corrupt human organizations, if the facts were not too notorious to be denied. Those who hold these views, however, do, in fact, make every effort that they can to present in lighter shades the dark colors of depraved human society and organizations. The system thus developed is clearly logical, in view of the premises; but it wars with the facts of history, Christian consciousness and the Bible.

On the other hand, those who assert innate depravity, or a deteriorated moral constitution, in view of fact, Scripture and Christian consciousness, at once come in conflict with the demands of the principles of honor and right towards new-created minds.

Chapter VI: The Readjustment

IF, as I have shown, the moving powers of the system are at once and of necessity misunderstood because of the assumption that men enter this world as new-created minds, then, by the denial and rejection of this assumption, can the system be at once readjusted.

If, in a previous state of existence, God created all men with such constitutions, and placed them in such circumstances, as the laws of honor and of right demanded,—if, then, they revolted and corrupted themselves, and forfeited their rights, and were introduced into this world under a dispensation of sovereignty, disclosing both justice and mercy,—then all conflict of the moving powers of Christianity can be at once and entirely removed.

Each party can retain the truth for which they have so earnestly contended, and yet not war with that which now opposes it. The advocates of the deepest views of human depravity can hold to their views, and yet not war with the principles of honor and of right. The warmest advocates of these principles can retain them in full, and yet not conflict with the great facts of human depravity and ruin. Let us first look at the case of the Old School divines.

It has already become apparent that the great result at which the most orthodox leaders have aimed has been to justify God in His dealings with man by showing that there was a forfeiture of the rights of the human race anterior to their birth into this world. We have seen that, on the supposition that they come into this world as new-created beings, it is impossible to justify such a forfeiture. But no such difficulty attends the supposition that the forfeiture in question occurred not in this world, but in a previous state of existence, by the voluntary and personal revolt of each individual from God. That is a real forfeiture, and one that does not implicate God.

Let us next consider the case of the most strenuous advocates of the principles of honor and right. They very properly contend that God cannot give to new-created beings a corrupt or sinful nature. Yet they do not deny the general depravity of man,—so mysterious, at least in its extent and power. This view fully vindicates God from the charge against which they protest, and throws on man the entire blame of any deterioration or corruption in his nature with which he enters this world. It also fully explains the mysterious depth and power of depravity; nor does it, in so doing, depreciate or degrade the nature of free agency itself. In like manner can it be shown that there is, in reality, no important principle or fact, for which the various opposing parties contend, that cannot be secured without conflict, on this assumption. It is, therefore, entirely effectual to harmonize the system,—which is the end for which I propose it,—and is, on this ground at least, worthy of universal acceptance. Moreover, as there is no middle ground between the two assumptions, that men enter this world as new-created beings, or that they do not, it appears to be the only assumption that can restore harmony.

I am well aware that there is, in many most excellent persons, a disposition to revolt from this view. But I feel assured that it is not so much from thorough investigation, as on the ground of an unexpressed but powerful state of general feeling, that has been created by the course of events in past ages. To the production of this state of feeling I am well aware that men of eminent religious character have largely contributed.

But it is no less true that good men aided in the formation of the dogmas of Rome, and of her despotic organization. It is one of the mysteries of God's providence, that His great enemy has been allowed to effect so much by means of good men. Is it, then, at all improbable that, by his agency,—even through good men,—a prejudice has been created against the truth on this point also?

If there is, in fact, a malignant spirit, of great and all-pervading power, intent on making a fixed and steady opposition to the progress of the cause of God,—and, if he well knows that there is one truth of relations so manifold, important and sublime, that on it depends, in great measure, the highest and most triumphant energy of the system of Christianity,—then, beyond all doubt, he would exert his utmost power in so misleading the church of God as to fortify them in the strongest possible manner against its belief and reception. He would as early and as far as possible pervert and disgrace it. He would present it in false and odious combinations, and thus array against it the full power of that most energetic faculty of the human soul, the association of ideas. He would fill the church and the ministry with a prejudgment against it, not founded on argument, and yet so profound as to make its falsehood a foregone conclusion, and that to such an extent as entirely to prevent any deep and thorough intellectual effort on the subject. He would, after succeeding in this, paralyze them with an effeminate timidity with reference even to any serious and thorough discussion of the subject; so that even men who are in general the boldest advocates of free inquiry shall tremble and grow pale at the thought that anyone with whom they are associated shall dare to avow an open and firm belief of the proscribed truth.

But, if the Bible is to be trusted, there is such a spirit employing from age to age his utmost energies in opposing the cause of God; and it is and ever has been true, in fact, that this sublime and momentous principle of widely-extended relations, and of immense power in all its relations,—a principle that can restore perfect harmony to the system of Christianity,—has been treated, for long and gloomy centuries, in just the manner that I have described. On no subject that I have ever examined have minds which in general were elevated, free and liberal, manifested to such an extent the power of an irrational prejudgment, or of sensitive and paralyzing timidity. I will not say that this has been universal, for I have evidence to the contrary. But yet, as the causes that have tended to such a result have been of universal operation, they have exerted a wide spread and almost universal power. Nor will I positively affirm who is the author of this state of things. It is enough to say that it has, to my own mind, in view of its history, a striking resemblance to the workings of that great and sagacious spirit, who in so many other respects has deceived and deluded the nations, in his most skilful efforts to oppose the progress of the kingdom of Christ, and to fortify and extend his own dark domains.

For it appears that an effectual harmonizing principle of the Christian system is found in the assumption that all men, by a revolt from God in a previous state of existence, incurred a forfeiture of their original rights as new-created minds, and are born into this world under that forfeiture. It also appears that to evolve and defend the idea of such a forfeiture is that at which the orthodox leaders of the church have been aiming, for century after century. Indeed, they have—and very properly so far as this point is concerned—made the whole system of Christianity, as involving the redemption of the church, the glory of God and the eternal welfare of the universe, to rest upon a forfeiture of rights by all men before birth. Before them was early placed the idea of it which I have presented; an idea, simple, intelligible, rational, perfectly adequate to meet and explain every fact of the case, involving no violation of a single principle of honor or right, and capable of a development reflecting the highest glory on God.

And yet things were so managed, from an early period, that step by step the mind of the church was misdirected on this subject, early committals were entered into, and prejudices created; so that, when the great conflict came on which first tried to sound the depths of this great question, all things were prepared to involve the orthodox world, under the lead of Augustine, in a wrong decision, which since that time has never been thoroughly reconsidered. From that time to the present, whenever the view which I have presented has been brought forward, it has been, to a great extent, timidly or passionately rejected, without thorough and adequate investigation. Meantime, when the difficulties of the Augustinian theory have been found too great to be endured, other theories of forfeiture have been devised, which are no better. I shall endeavor hereafter clearly to evince that every one of these theories of forfeiture involves God, and His whole administration, and His eternal kingdom, in the deepest dishonor that the mind of man or angel can conceive, by the violation of the highest and most sacred principles of honor and right, and that on the scale of infinity and eternity. And yet their authors were most excellent men, and were aiming at most benevolent ends. The same, however, was true of most of the early advocates of some of the worst principles of the Church of Rome. To me both cases appear strangely like subtle delusions of the great mastermind of falsehood and fraud.

If the facts which I have already adduced do not seem to any to justify this strong language, then I would only ask them to suspend their final judgment until they have heard the whole statement of the case. If they are not convinced before I close this inquiry, then let them freely, if they see fit, charge my language with extravagance and excess. For my own part, I feel that, strong as my assertions are, yet the words of truth and soberness were never more truly spoken than in this case. Moreover, I have felt that no less than this was due to a principle so vitally affecting the glory of God, and yet so long and so extensively dishonored, trodden under foot, and despised.

CHAPTER VII: THE SYSTEM AS ADJUSTED

I HAVE, in the preceding chapters, shown at large that the assumption that men enter this world as new-created beings at once causes the principles of honor and of right to act against any doctrine of original and inherent depravity; and that any effort so to degrade the capabilities of free agency as to account by it for the sinful developments of this world is at war with reason and with facts. I have also shown that as soon as we drop this assumption, and enter upon a former sphere of existence, in which all the laws of honor and of right were in all respects fully observed towards all new-created minds, every difficulty is at once removed. In this sphere of existence every man was the unreasonable and inexcusable author of his own corruption and ruin. From this sphere all men come into this world under a dispensation of wise and benevolent sovereignty, established for the more full development of the excellence of God, and the attainment of great public ends by the redemption of the church.

I propose now to consider a little more in detail the effects of this readjustment on the system as a whole.

I have before stated that, to insure harmony, it is essential not only to retain all the facts of the system, but so to, adjust all its parts as to give full and free play to all the convictions and emotions which it is the design of Christianity to call into existence. I adverted in particular to the process of deep conviction of sin, and purification from it, as the great end of the system; and to the necessity of presenting to a mind thus purified a God whom it could consistently love. I also specified the importance of a clear view and a feeling sense of the presence and power of our invisible spiritual enemies, and of our need of the sustaining, invigorating and sanctifying influences of the divine Spirit. To secure all these results, the system, as well-adjuster, directly tends. We retain all the facts of the system, because we exhibit in full power the great and fundamental doctrine which leads to them,—that all men are in a fallen state, and have forfeited their original rights, and are under the just displeasure of God, and exposed to His righteous judgments. This, as all must concede, has ever been regarded by the orthodox as the fundamental basis of the Christian system, and out of it grows the whole economy of redemption. The whole Christian doctrine concerning God the Father, the Son and the Holy Spirit, atonement, regeneration, the means of grace, the church, and eternal retributions, naturally grows out of it in undiminished, yea, rather in augmented fullness and glory. All of the teachings of God, through the human mind, the material system, providence, His Word and His spirit, it gratefully and confidingly receives. It mutilates nothing, it rejects nothing, in the great and majestic temple of universal truth.

But, to be more particular:

1. We escape the constant and powerful tendency which exists under the old theory to give a superficial view of the great facts of man's depravity and ruin.

A rational regard to the honor and justice of God is not under this view, creating constant tendencies towards Pelagian ideas. On the other hand, we are at once enabled to penetrate deeply and philosophically into the lowest recesses of human depravity, even as they are disclosed in the experience of the most profound and spiritual minds.

The old orthodox writers, in order to convey their ideas of a sinful state in man preceding and causing actual transgression, often familiarly call it a sinful habit, just as they call a foundation for holy acts a holy habit of soul. But, if men enter this world as new-created beings, there cannot, in reality, be in them anything to correspond to the words "sinful habit." For they have not acted at all; and a good God cannot create sinful habits. But, under the system as readjusted, these words describe the very thing which precedes wrong action, and causes a propensity to it. Men are born with deeply-rooted sinful habits and propensities. We are enabled, also, to understand the power and obstinacy of those evil propensities of which the holiest men are most deeply sensible, and why so intense a furnace of trial is needed in this world, to purge out the dross of sin. This view of the system, therefore, without dishonoring God, opens the way to a deep and thorough conviction of sin, and thus to the highest attainments in sanctification. In short, this theory enables us to understand and to explain such an experience as that of Edwards, and to see that it could be founded on facts.

2. We escape the constant and powerful tendency, to which I have
before referred, to degrade the nature of free agency itself, by supposing that such facts as occur in this world are the natural and necessary
results of the best minds which God could make, in their normal state.

There has been in the church, in all ages, a strong desire to believe
in the possibility of an elevated state of original righteousness. But,
with any even tolerably elevated standard of excellence, any man must
see that the human race are, from their earliest developments, in a very
degraded state. What can be more dark than the picture of them given
by Dr. Channing and Prof. Norton? Yet, if we deny preexistence, and
maintain the divine justice, we are driven towards the conclusion that
a free agent is such a being that God could do no better for him, on
account of the essential nature of free agency. From this fatal and
melancholy tendency the system, as readjusted, entirely relieves us.
Moreover, it gives us what the church has sought in vain. The idea
that men were once upright *in Adam* is merely a shadow of relief, but
has in it no reality. There is no reality except in the idea that men were
once, in their own persons, actually upright, but fell before they entered this world; and that, therefore, their sins here are not the natural
result of mere free agency.

3. We do not ascribe to God any facts at all at war with the highest principles of honor and of right. Nay, more; we open the way for
the presentation of His character in new and peculiar forms of loveliness and grace. Nor is this all. If I may use the language of painters, we
change the ground color of the whole view of the universe. If we look
at this natural world through a colored medium,—whether it be red,
yellow, blue, purple, or black,—the whole aspect of the scene is
changed. Every object appears in an unnatural hue, and we long once
more to see all things in the pure white light of heaven. But the old
theory is a dark-colored medium. Seen through it, the whole universe
appears, to use the heart moving words of Foster, to be "overspread by
a lurid and dreadful shade." Well do I understand the import of those
words, and well do I remember my joy when that dark medium was
broken, and I was by divine grace enabled to see all things in the pure,
natural and radiant light of the true glory of my Savior and my God.

And now, instead of a God dishonorably ruining His creatures,
the mind can find a God who has devised, at the expense of great self-

denial, a system merciful towards the fallen, and benevolent towards the universe. It can find a God whom its regenerated emotions, and its highest conceptions of honor and right, do not forbid it to worship; and light irradiates, and joy unspeakable fills the soul. Such are the principles on which the last experience to which I have adverted is based. Such was the character of God, which, like a radiant sun, rose upon my mind when involved for a time in midnight gloom, and filled my soul with sacred joy and peace.

4. We arrive at a sphere of existence in which we can carry up to the highest point our conceptions of the rectitude of the original constitutions of all new-created beings, and of God's sincere good will towards them, and sympathetic and benevolent treatment of them.

I do not mean that we can historically retrace and set forth the actual course of events in God's dealings with new-created beings; but I do mean that there is nothing to forbid the highest conceptions concerning such dealings that can flow from the attributes of infinite wisdom, justice, honor and love.

The importance of preexistence, as averting a theoretical degradation of the nature of free agency itself, cannot be overestimated. Such degradation, I have shown, is the inevitable result of endeavoring to defend God on the assumption that He has given to men, as they are in this world, as good constitutions as the nature of free agency will allow. If free agency, in its best estate, results in such a history as that of this world,—in such a development of universal and desperate depravity, resulting in vice, crime, woes, idolatry, and moral pollution, to an extent almost inconceivable,—then it depresses and darkens our ideas of the universe itself. Indeed, what motive can God have to create free agents, if free agency, in its own nature, is capable of nothing better than it has disclosed in this world? But, if this world is but a moral hospital of the universe, —if in it are collected, for various great and public ends, the diseased of past ages, the fallen of all preceding generations of creatures,—then we are at once relieved from such depressing views of free agency itself. A new-created, upright mind, may still be an elevated and glorious object, and reflect the highest honor on the great Creator.

Moreover, of all preceding generations of created beings it may still be true that incomparably the greatest part have retained their integrity. Compare, now, with a view so elevated and cheering, the gloomy and depressing theory that a free agent is necessarily a being of so low a grade that he cannot be fully developed, and come to the knowledge of good and evil, and arrive at mature and stable virtue, without the experience of sin. Concerning such views, Möhler has well said that they make any doctrine of a fall a foolishness, and make "an entrance into evil necessary, in order to serve as a self-conscious return to good." This idea, he remarks, "exalts evil itself into goodness."

Hagenbach[3] also says, concerning certain such speculators, who seemed to concede that men are in a fallen state, that the kind of original sin which they seem to establish is identical with the finite character of the nature and consciousness of man, which is a matter of necessity. Thus, the idea of sin and responsibility is destroyed, and a doctrine introduced which would prove fatal to all true morality. According to this theory, no being can be properly educated, except through a process of sinning. "Education must first seduce that man who is in a process of mental development, before it can lead him to virtue" (Blasche, quoted by Hagenbach, § 295).

This is the lowest and most depressing conception of the nature and capabilities of free agency. From all temptation to conceptions of this dark and gloomy aspect we find a relief in the theory of preexistence. The fallen minds around us may be no more a fair specimen of what new-created, upright minds should be, than the inmates of a hospital are of the normal and healthy state of the body.

We now see that new-created minds may have been in a high degree beautiful and well-ordered, so that, even in their perfections, there may have been an incidental occasion for sin. We can see that God loved them all, and that no one ever fell and perished, except against His expostulations, and without causing Him sincere grief.

5. It presents the scriptural doctrine concerning a kingdom of fallen spirits in a light much more rational, intelligible and impressive.

But, as this is one of the most difficult and delicate points in theology, it deserves a separate and formal consideration.

---

3   Karl Rudolf Hagenbach (1801–1874) was a Swiss church historian.

CHAPTER VIII: THE KINGDOM OF HOSTILE SPIRITS

THE doctrine concerning a kingdom of hostile spirits is, certainly, not a neutral doctrine. If it is not true, no doctrine ought to be more decidedly rejected. If it is true, none ought more earnestly to be defended. If it is true, this world can never be understood till its truth is admitted. If it is true, as the apostle John says, that those most powerful civil and ecclesiastical organizations, which are set forth under the symbol of a beast, and a harlot riding thereon, were framed, and are animated, by the God of this world, the spirit that works in the children of disobedience,—if His power must be broken before they are destroyed, and if he must be bound before the church can reign, then all views of the power of evil in this world, and all measures designed to encounter it, must be superficial, if they over look and ignore these and similar great facts.

And yet the supposition that men are new-created beings, and are exposed to the power of such spirits, although either disabled by innate depravity, or enfeebled by deteriorated moral constitutions, is so repugnant to every principle of honor and right, that there has been a steady tendency to disbelieve and deny the whole doctrine concerning evil spirits, because it involves such results.

But, by the readjustment which I have suggested, the whole aspect of the doctrine is changed. The system of this world, viewed from this new point of vision, implies not that any new subjects are added by it to the kingdom of darkness, but that multitudes are redeemed from it who were already in it when the system was established.

To gain a clear and consistent conception of this aspect of the case, we must enlarge our views of the amount of time that may have elapsed since the creation and fall of those angels who founded the kingdom of error and of sin. In many minds, a belief has existed of the comparative recency of the creation of this world. It has also been believed that the creation of the angels, and the fall of a part of them, but little preceded the creation of this world. In this case, the dispensation of this world could not grow out of a state of things which had come into existence during the lapse of millions of preceding ages.

No room, therefore, has been left, after the original fall of the angels, for organizing and extending a kingdom of falsehood, fraud and seduction; and for its augmentation in the course of ages, by tempting individuals in various worlds, and in the successive orders of new-created spirits.

Now, although no one is authorized to say positively that such was the course of events, no more ought he to assume, without proof, that it was not.

And now, at length, we are in a position to know that, at least so far as the material creation is concerned, it is not as recent as has been supposed. There is internal evidence to the contrary in the very structure of the globe. Many millions of years must have elapsed since this earth was created. Indeed, on this point the language of geologists is very strong and decided, as the following extracts from Drs. Hitchcock and J. P. Smith will evince. The argument from the time needed to deposit the various strata of the of rocks is thus stated by Dr. Hitchcock:

> "It is certain that, since man existed on the globe, materials for the production of rocks have not accumulated to the average thickness of more than one hundred or two hundred feet; although in particular places, as already mentioned, the accumulations are thicker. The evidence of this position is, that neither the works nor the remains of man have been found any deeper in the earth than in the upper part of that superficial deposit called *alluvium*. But, had man existed while the other deposits were going on, no possible reason can be given why his bones and the fruits of his labors should not be found mixed with those of other animals, so abundant in the rocks to the depth of six or seven miles. In the last six thousand years, then, only one five-hundredth part of the stratified rocks has been accumulated. I mention this fact, not as by any means an exact, but only an approximate, measure of the time in which the older rocks were deposited; for the precise age of the world is probably a problem which science never can solve. All the means of

comparison within our reach enable us to say, only, that its duration must have been immense."

Again, he says:

"Numerous races of animals and plants must have occupied the globe previous to those which now inhabit it, and have successively passed away, as catastrophes occurred, or the climate became unfit for their residence. Not less than thirty thousand species have already been dug out of the rocks; and, excepting a few hundred species, mostly of sea shells, occurring in the uppermost rocks, none of them correspond to those now living on the globe. In Europe, they are found to the depth of about six and a half miles; and in this country, deeper; and no living species is found more than one twelfth of this depth. All the rest are specifically and often generically unlike living species; and the conclusion seems irresistible, that they must have lived and died before the creation of the present species. Indeed, so different was the climate in those early times,—it having been much warmer than at present in most parts of the world,—that but few of the present races could have lived then. Still further; it appears that, during the whole period since organized beings first appeared on the globe, not less than four, or five, and probably more—some think as many as ten or twelve—entire races have passed away, and been succeeded by recent ones; so that the globe has actually changed all its inhabitants half a dozen times. Yet each of the successive groups occupied it long enough to leave immense quantities of their remains, which some times constitute almost entire mountains. And, in general, these groups became extinct in consequence of a change of climate; which, if imputed to any known cause, must have been an extremely slow process."

Again, he says:

"The denudations and erosions that have taken place on the earth's surface indicate a far higher antiquity to the globe, even since it assumed essentially its present condition, than the common interpretation of Genesis admits. The geologist can prove that in many cases the rocks have been worn away, by the slow action of the ocean, more than two miles in depth in some regions, and those very wide, as in South Wales, in England. As the continents rose from the ocean, the slow drainage by the rivers has excavated numerous long and deep gorges, requiring periods incalculably extended. I do not wonder that, when the skeptic stands upon the banks of Niagara river, and sees how obviously the splendid cataract has worn out the deep gorge extending to Lake Ontario, he should feel that there is a standing proof that the common opinion, as the age of the world, cannot be true, and hence be led to discard the Bible, if he supposes that to be a true interpretation. But the Niagara gorge is only one among a multitude of examples of erosion that might be quoted, and some of them far more striking to a geologist. On Oak Orchard creek, and the Genesee river, between Rochester and Lake Ontario, are similar erosions, seven miles long. On the latter river, south of Rochester, we find a cut from Mount Morris to Portage, sometimes four hundred feet deep. On many of our south western rivers we have what are called canyons, or gorges, often two hundred and fifty feet deep, and several miles long. Near the source of Missouri river are what are called the Gates of the Rocky Mountains, where there is a gorge six miles long and twelve hundred feet deep."

To these he adds nearly two pages more of similar cases. After adducing much other evidence, he thus concludes:

"Now, let this imperfect summary of evidence in favor of the earth's high antiquity be candidly weighed, and can anyone think it strange that every man, who has carefully and extensively examined the rocks in their native beds, is entirely convinced of its validity? Men of all professions, and of diverse opinions concerning the Bible, have been geologists; but on this point they are unanimous, however they may differ as to other points in the science. Must we not, then, regard this fact as one of the settled principles of science?"

Equally striking, or even more so, are the statements of Dr. J. P. Smith in the supplementary notes to his learned treatise entitled *Geology And Scripture*. After considering certain volcanic formations, he says:

> "It would seem perfectly impossible for any person, but moderately acquainted with the visible phenomena of volcanic regions, to escape the impression that myriads of ages must have been occupied in the production of these formations, before the creation of man, and the adaptation of the earth's surface for his abode" (p. 367, Bonn's edition).

Of another formation he says,

> "Ages innumerable must have rolled over the world, in the making of this single formation" (p. 373).

He also quotes Babbage,[4] as saying in his *Ninth Bridgewater Treatise*, "It is now admitted by all competent persons that the formation of those strata which are nearest the surface must have occupied vast periods, probably millions of years, in arriving at their present state" (p. 72).

And are we to suppose that in all of these past ages there were no intelligent beings in existence? Were there no angels great in might, and swift to do His will?

There is, indeed, no reason to believe in the existence of the human race on this earth before the time assigned in the Mosaic record. But the existence of some of the angels from the beginning of the creation, and the creation of other intelligent spirits from that time onward, in other parts of the Creator's kingdom, to see His works and execute His plans, are in the highest degree reasonable and probable.

Therefore, after the first creation of the angels, the fall of Satan and his fellows may have taken place in ages far remote; and through them the kingdom of darkness may have been extended by moral conflict, wiles and temptation, from age to age. Moreover, the final destruction of this kingdom, by a system of moral exposure, may be one of the great ends of this present and final dispensation.

---

4   Charles Babbage (1791-1871) was an English mathematician, philosopher, inventor and mechanical engineer who originated the concept of a programmable computer. Considered a "father of the computer." See Appendix: The Bridgewater Treatise, p. 459.

In perfect accordance with this view is the prominence given in the Bible to the conflict of the two great kingdoms of light and of darkness, and of the relations of the events of this world to that conflict. Listen to the words of inspired apostles: "For this purpose the Son of God was manifested, that he might destroy the works of the devil." "He must reign till he hath put all enemies under his feet Then cometh the end, when he shall have put down all rule and all authority and power" (1 Jn. 3:8. 1 Cor. 15: 24, 25).

It would seem, from passages like these,—and they are numerous, —that the destruction of the kingdom of darkness, and of its king, was one great end of the manifestation of God in human form. To destroy his works He was revealed. When all the power and rule and authority of this kingdom are put down, then comes *the end*.[5]

It is true that in the process of subduing this kingdom He also redeems the church, and that this also is a primary end of the system.

But, in fact, the great end, which includes both, is so to prostrate Satan's kingdom, and to establish God's, that God shall be all and in all. And it is by redeeming the church, as we shall hereafter more fully show, that He secures both results.

Now, if we take enlarged views of the antiquity, origin and progress, of the kingdom of Satan, we shall see that in it may have been found, among spirits seduced by him and his angels, after their own original fall, the materials out of which the church is formed, and that the triumph of God may be vastly augmented by this fact.

He may rescue millions from his grasp by means of the system of this world, and by their redemption develop such an amount of moral power as utterly to prostrate both the king of darkness and his kingdom.

It is not my purpose, at present, to assert these things as facts, but simply to remove those narrow views of the previous history of creation, which would, without evidence, exclude the propriety or possibility of such a supposition.

I aim to show that by the proposed readjustment of the system the whole aspect of the doctrine concerning a kingdom of hostile spirits, and man's exposure to it, is changed; and that the system of this world, viewed from this point of view, implies not that any new subjects are

---

5   For a discussion of the teleological implications of the end of the world see *Peter's Vision of Christ's Purpose in First Peter* (2011) and *Peter's Vision of The End in Second Peter* (2012), Phillip A. Ross, Pilgrim Platform, Marietta, Ohio.

added to that kingdom, but that multitudes are redeemed from it who were in it when the system was established.

Having now reached this point of view, we are enabled to take still more elevated and enlarged views of the dispensation of this world in its relations to the past and the future history of the universe. For it is a fair conclusion, from the statements of the Word of God, that the antecedent history of God's kingdom extends back for ages of ages, and that the results of all this anterior history of the universe are concentrated and brought to a crisis in this world, and that all the future history of the universe will diverge from the results of the dispensation of this world. The great idea is, evil entered in ages past, and introduced a kingdom hostile to that of God. The conflict of these kingdoms comes to its crisis here; and then comes the end of this dispensation, and the eternal state of the universe begins.

CHAPTER IX: BRIEF SUMMARY OF THE WHOLE CASE

FOR the sake of a definite and vivid impression, I will now endeavor to concentrate in one summary view the result of the preceding discussions. That result is this: that, by supposing the preexistent sin and fall of man, the most radical views of human depravity can be harmonized with the highest views of the justice and honor of God. The doctrines of the innate depravity of man, and his exposure to corrupt social organizations, and to the power of evil spirits, sustain entirely different relations to the principles of honor and right, as we reject, or as we adopt, the idea of preexistence. If we reject it, the alleged facts and the principles come into immediate and inevitable conflict.

But if all men have existed and sinned, before this life, in another state of being, then it is easily conceivable, and worthy of belief, that, when first created, all the demands of honor and right as to their constitution and circumstances were fully met, and that, since in those circumstances they sinned, the fault was entirely their own, and not at all God's. Moreover, it is easily conceivable, and worthy of belief, that the result of a course of sinning should be to leave in their minds that predisposition to sin which we, in common cases; designate by the name *sinful habit*, but which is in this case called *original sin*; which is no part of the original constitution of the mind, but was introduced into it by the sinner himself; so that for it he, and he only, is responsible; which is not an act, but a permanent result of previous acts, and appears as simply a strong predisposition, or tendency, or propensity to sin.

It has also been shown to be supposable that the fall of Satan and his angels took place in the far remote ages of past eternity, and that since their fall other spiritual beings have been seduced to join them in their revolt, and have come under the despotism of Satan, forming a vastly extended kingdom of fallen souls. It is still further supposable that God saw fit to destroy the power of Satan and his hosts by a system of disclosures, in which he should enter this kingdom, and, by a material system, regenerate and rescue from his grasp a large portion of his subjects, and destroy him and the rest by those disclosures of moral power that should proceed from this work of redemption. It may be that, not only this world, but the whole existing material system, were created with reference to this end, and that this is the basis of the analogies of things material and spiritual. That for the same end the incarnation and atonement of Christ were predetermined, and the results of the whole work ordained before the foundation of the world.

All this, on the supposition now under consideration, may be true: and, if it may be true, then there is no necessary collision between the facts as to human depravity and the principles of honor and right which have been stated; for, if these were all observed at the time of the original creation and trial of man, and if they then, on a fair and honorable probation, forfeited their rights, and fell under the penalty of God's law, and were justly exposed to endless ruin, then the entire aspect of God's dispensations towards this world is radically changed. The principles of honor and right which pertain to new-created minds having been observed, and all claim to divine favor having been forfeited by each for himself, then all fall into the hands of God as clay of the same lump, to be dealt with on such principles of sovereignty as the interests of His universal kingdom may demand. And now the whole aspect of this world changes. Man is the author of his original depravity, and not God. No addition is made by the system to the number of fallen minds, but, on the other hand, unnumbered multitudes are delivered by it from a fallen state. What men enjoy in this world is a gracious gift of God to them, beyond their deserts. What they suffer is less than they deserve, for it is of the Lord's mercies that they are not consumed. The multitudes who are saved owe eternal life to the free grace of God. All who are lost perish entirely by their own original revolt from God, persisted in during this life.

But, on the other supposition, none of these things is true. If men are new-created beings, then all the laws of honor and right towards them, as such, are in full force. They have done nothing before they come into existence in this world to forfeit the favor of God. If any of them perish, it is the addition of so many new-created souls to the number of the lost. To create them sinful before knowledge or action, if it were possible, and then expose them to the malignant influences of corrupt society and satanic wiles, would be at war with the principles of honor and of right. And any dispensation or constitution of

God which brings them into this world with deteriorated and corrupted constitutions, and places them in circumstances of immense social disadvantage, and exposed to the organized and fearfully powerful
temptations of Satan, for aught that I can see, comes into direct collision with those principles of honor and right which God Himself has
implanted in the soul.

Here, then, we arrive at what I have referred to from the beginning,—a possible adjustment of the two great moving powers of
Christianity. There is between them no necessary opposition. They
may be so adjusted as to work together in harmony. But the assumption that this is our first state of existence at once misunderstands them,
and causes one to work against the other with tremendous power. And
it is this counter-working of the two great wheels of the system which
has produced those lamentable divisions among good men, to which I
have already so fully adverted.

CHAPTER X: A PRESUMPTION REBUTTED

I HAVE already expressed my views as to the antecedent course of speculation in the church on the subject of preexistence. But, as references may still be made to it, in order to prejudice the views which I have advanced, I propose, before I proceed further, to anticipate any prejudgment which may arise in any mind from this quarter.

It may, then, be said—as, in fact, it has been said to me—that this view is no novelty; that it has been suggested again and again, for centuries; and that, after full and mature consideration in all its relations, it has been rejected as not furnishing the requisite relief. But, if there were in it any self-evidencing power of truth, it would before this have been received, at least by all regenerated and reasonable minds, even as the true doctrine of the solar system has been by all candid and learned inquirers.

To this I reply, that though it is true that the fundamental idea has been suggested in various ages past, yet it is not true that it has ever been fully and maturely considered in all its relations. On the other hand, it has been treated just as was the true theory of the solar system, for many long centuries after that was proposed; that is, it has been merely proposed and suggested, but the system to which it belongs, and of which it is a logical part, has never been wrought out and explicated. There is, as I shall endeavor to show, a view of the character of God, which properly belongs to this system, which has never been properly developed and introduced as an element in systems of theology.

All know with what energy the mind of the church has been developed on such subjects as the Trinity, the Atonement, and the eternal purposes of God. This subject deserves, at least, as thorough a discussion as these, or any other; for no other involves questions, or principles, or results, of greater moment. And yet there never has been in any age a period of mental energy expended in a full and radical discussion of this question. On the other hand, almost the en

tire intellectual energy of all ages has been expended in setting forth
and defending the opposite system.

Such being the facts, till this view has been fully considered there
can be no presumptive argument against it from the fact that it has not
been generally adopted. The theory that the sun, and not the earth,
was the center of the solar system, was rejected for ages, simply because it was not thoroughly looked into, although often suggested;
and has been adopted only within a few centuries, and solely in consequence of a general, profound and radical investigation of it, in all its
relations to existing facts. Before this, the mathematical talent of the
world was employed to expound and defend the geocentric theory,
with its cycles and epicycles.

The following extract from "Whewell's *History of the Inductive
Sciences*" will place this subject in its true light:

> "The doctrine of Copernicus, that the sun is the true center
> of the celestial motions, depends primarily upon the consid-
> eration that such a supposition explains very simply and
> completely all the obvious appearances of the heavens. In
> order to see that it does this, nothing more is requisite than
> a distinct conception of the nature of relative motion, and a
> knowledge of the principal astronomical phenomena. There
> was, therefore, no reason why such a doctrine might not be
> discovered,—that is, suggested as a theory plausible at first
> sight,—long before the time of Copernicus; or, rather, it was
> inevitable that this guess, among others, should be pro-
> pounded as a solution of the appearances of the heavens.
> We are not, therefore, to be surprised, if we find, in the ear-
> liest times of astronomy, and at various succeeding periods,
> such a system spoken of by astronomers, and maintained by
> some as true, though rejected by the majority, and by the
> principal writers."

He then proceeds to show how the application of mathematical
talent to the geocentric theory (that which places the earth in the center) gave it an apparent superiority, by means of the theory of ec-
centrics and epicycles, to the heliocentric theory (that which places the
sun in the center). He then adds,

"It is true that all the contrivances of epicycles, and the like, by which the geocentric hypothesis was made to represent the phenomena, were susceptible of an easy adaptation to a heliocentric method, when a good mathematician had once proposed to himself the problem; and this was precisely what Copernicus undertook and executed. But, till the appearance of his work, the heliocentric system had never come before the world, except as a hasty and imperfect hypothesis; which bore a favorable comparison with the phenomena, so long as their general features only were known; but which had been completely thrown into the shade by the labor and intelligence bestowed upon the Hipparchian or Ptolemaic theories by a long series of great astronomers of all countries."

He then proceeds to state at some length the evidence of the fact that, whilst all the mathematical talent of the world was employed in developing and defending a false theory of the universe, yet the true theory had been often and clearly suggested. He remarks,

"It is curious to trace the early and repeated manifestations of this view of the universe. Its distinct assertion among the Greeks is an evidence of the clearness of their thoughts, and the vigor of their minds; and it is a proof of the feebleness and servility of intellect in the stationary period that, till the period of Copernicus, no one was found to try the fortune of this hypothesis, modified according to the improved astronomical knowledge of the time.

"The most ancient of the Greek philosophers to whom the ancients ascribe the heliocentric doctrine is Pythagoras; but Diogenes Laertius makes Philolaus, one of the followers of Pythagoras, the first author of this doctrine. We learn from Archimedes that it was held by his contemporary, Aristarchus. 'Aristarchus of Samos,' says he, 'makes this supposition, that the fixed stars and the sun remain at rest, and that the earth revolves round the sun in a circle.' Plutarch asserts that this, which was only a hypothesis in the hands of Aristarchus, was proved by Seleucus; but we may venture to say that, at that time, no such proof was possible. Aristotle had recognized the existence of this doctrine by arguing against it. 'All things,' says he, 'tend to the center of the

earth, and rest there, and therefore the whole mass of the
earth cannot rest except there.' Ptolemy had in like manner
argued against the diurnal motion of the earth: such a revolution would, he urged, disperse into surrounding space all
the loose parts of the earth. Yet he allowed that such a supposition would facilitate the explanation of some phenomena, Cicero appears to make Mercury and Venus revolve
about the sun, as does Martianus Capella at a later period;
and Seneca says, it is a worthy subject of contemplation,
whether the earth be at rest or in motion: but at this period,
as we may see from Seneca himself, that habit of intellect
which was requisite for the solution of such a question had
been succeeded by indistinct views and rhetorical forms of
speech. If there were any good mathematicians and good
observers at this period, they were employed in cultivating
and verifying the Hipparchian theory.

"Next to the Greeks, the Indians appear to have possessed that original vigor and clearness of thought from
which true science springs. It is remarkable that the Indians,
also, had their heliocentric theorists. Aryabatta (A.D. 1322),
and other astronomers of that country, are said to have advocated the doctrine of the earth's revolution on its axis;
which opinion, however, was rejected by subsequent
philosophers among the Hindus.

"Some writers have thought that the heliocentric doctrine was derived, by Pythagoras and other European
philosophers, from some of the oriental nations. This opinion, however, will appear to have little weight, if we consider that the heliocentric hypothesis, in the only shape in
which the ancients knew it, was too obvious to require
much teaching; that it did not, and could not, so far as we
know, receive any additional strength from anything which
the oriental nations could teach; and that each astronomer
was induced to adopt or reject it, not by any information
which a master could give him, but by his love of geometri-
cal simplicity on the one hand, or the prejudices of sense on
the other. Real science, depending on a clear view of the relation of phenomena to general theoretical ideas, cannot be
communicated in the way of secret and exclusive traditions,
like the mysteries of certain arts and crafts. If the philoso-

pher did not see that the theory is true, he is little the better
for having heard or read the words which assert its truth.

"It is impossible, therefore, to assent to those views
which would discover in the heliocentric doctrines of the
ancients traces of a more profound astronomy than any
which they have transmitted to us. Those doctrines were
merely the plausible conjectures of men with sound geo-
metrical notions; but they were never extended so as to embrace the details of the existing astronomical knowledge;
and perhaps we may say that the analysis of the phenomena
into the arrangements of the Ptolemaic system was so much
more obvious than any other, that it must necessarily come
first, in order to form an introduction to the Copernican."

Now, I freely admit that the common theory of the moral system,
at first sight, did seem to be suggested by some passages of Scripture,
just as was the geocentric theory of the material universe. Moreover, it
seemed to account for the fundamental facts of the Christian system,
just as the geocentric theory seemed to account for the phenomena of
the solar system. Hence, it being hastily assumed that the Bible teaches
it, all the energy of evangelical divines has been put forth to explain
and defend it. It has, indeed, not been denied that the theory of preexistence would also explain the facts of native and entire depravity, and
relieve some difficulties. But it has been for the most part summarily
rejected, just as was the heliocentric theory, and for the same reason.
Eminent divines have never thoroughly considered its scriptural relations, and undertaken and thoroughly executed the problem of developing the system to which it belongs, so as to embrace the details of
the existing theological knowledge.

Perhaps, too, in this, as in the other case, the energetic investigations of the advocates of the old system were allowed to exist, as an introduction to a new and better system. We have, at least, been enabled
by them to see what is the best that can be said in its behalf; and we
have had full and ample opportunity to study its operation on individuals and on society.

It would have been well if the theory of preexistence had suffered
merely from neglect, as above stated. But, in addition to this, prejudice
was awakened against it, by the errors and eccentricities of some of its
early defenders. Of these, perhaps no one was more conspicuous than

Origen.[6] He, by his unsound views on many points, and by associating preexistence with a false philosophical theory of the universe, created in many minds a prejudice against the idea itself. To this I shall advert again, in its place.

Thus have I endeavored to state the principles of the reconciliation of the contending powers of Christianity which I propose. We are now prepared to enter upon a consideration of a historical analysis of the course of the great conflict which has been spoken of as existing during a long series of ages.

---

6   Origen Adamantius (184/185–253/254) was an early Christian Alexandrian theologian, and one of the most distinguished writers of the early Church. He excelled in multiple branches of theological scholarship, including textual criticism, biblical interpretation, philosophical theology, preaching, and spirituality. Some of his teachings were controversial. Notably, he frequently referred to his hypothesis of the preexistence of souls. He believed that in the beginning all intelligent beings were united to God; he also held out the possibility that in the end all beings would be reconciled to God in what is called the *apokatastasis* or "restitution." His views on the Trinity, in which he saw the Son of God as subordinate to God the Father, became controversial during the Arian controversy of the fourth century, though a subordinationist view was common among the ante-Nicene Fathers.

BOOK IV

HISTORICAL OUTLINE AND

ESTIMATE OF THE CONFLICT

Chapter I: General Outline

WHEN we turn from the interests and controversies of the present generation, and undertake to survey those of past ages, we seem at first to be entering upon a boundless ocean, of difficult and perilous navigation. But, after a little experience, we find that the ocean is not illimitable, and that its navigation is by no means as difficult or hazardous as at first appeared. We soon find a compass and a chart; and, aided by the favoring gales of the spirit, we safely and happily complete our voyage. We find, too, that such a voyage is not in vain. We find more than dry dogmas and obsolete creeds to bring home with us, as the fruits of our adventures. We find that the history of thought and emotion in the church of God, in all ages, has a vital relation to the condition and interests of the present age; and that the future is not to be separated from the past by an abrupt interval, but to have its roots in it, and to grow out of it with a mature and healthy growth.

We have seen that the careful study and development of the false theories of the material universe was, in the judgment of Whewell, an important preparation for the development of the true theory. In like manner, it may be true that the energetic investigations of false theories of the system of the moral universe were needed, and were designed by God as an introduction to a new and better system. We have, at least, thereby been enabled to see what is the best that can be said in behalf of those theories, and have had ample opportunity to study their intellectual and moral influences on individuals and on society.

So far as I know, no complete and philosophical history of this great conflict of ages has ever been written, although many and important elements of it are contained in the various learned and able histories of the church, and of dogmatic theology, which have from time to time appeared.

Whenever such a history shall be fairly written, it will, I am assured, clearly evince that the principles of honor and of right, as I have stated them, have been recognized in every age; but that, so long as it has been assumed that this is our first state of existence, the course of events has been this: First, that these principles have, in some minds, given rise to superficial views of human depravity, which are not adapted to produce a deep Christian experience. Then, that against these views, from time to time, men, actuated by a profound Christian consciousness, have reacted, and endeavored to promulgate and defend deeper views of the great facts concerning the depravity of man, and his exposure to unseen and powerful spirits of evil but that, nevertheless, in so doing they have made a painful war upon the most obvious and sacred principles of honor and right; and that every effort to remove this contrariety, made during the course of more than fifteen centuries, has been in vain. The study of such a history would be eminently salutary. It would enable us to avoid all *a priori* and abstract theorizing, and to consider the simple question, what, in fact, have been the developments of the human mind, under the common assumption that this is our first state of existence, and that the fall of Adam is, in some way, the cause of the sinfulness of the human race. Such a review would powerfully confirm our previously announced conclusion, that the conflict of principles, which I have in this work asserted to exist, is a reality; that the two great working powers of Christianity are in fact misunderstood, and do work against each other; and that they can never be made to work together, on the assumption that this is our first state of existence.

A history of the kind to which I have adverted ought to contain a full view of the manifestations and phases of this great controversy, as seen in at least the following theological developments:

1. The doctrines and speculations of the period anterior to Augustine, on the sinful condition of man and his redemption through Christ.
2. The great Augustinian and Pelagian controversy.
3. The Semipelagian[1] controversies, till the tenth century.

---

1 Semipelagianism was developed as a compromise between Pelagianism and the teaching of Church Fathers such as Saint Augustine, who taught that man cannot come to God without the grace of God. A distinction is made between the beginning of faith and the increase of faith. Semipelagian thought teaches that the latter half—growing in faith—is the work of God, while the beginning of faith is an act of free will, with grace coming into play later. It was labeled heresy by the Western Church in the Second Council of Orange in 529.

4. The controversies of the Schoolmen[2], upon the same topics, until the Reformation.

5. The discussions and decisions of the Reformers.

6. The debates and decisions of the council of Trent, and the subsequent controversies in the Roman Catholic church, e. g. in the case of Baius, of Molina, and of the Jansenists.

7. The Arminian[3] controversy in Europe and America.

8. The Socinian controversy on these points, soon after the opening of the Reformation.

9. The assaults of the celebrated Arian,[4] Dr. J. Taylor, on the doctrine of original sin, and the rejoinders of his English antagonists.

---

2   Scholasticism is a method of critical thought which dominated teaching by the academics (scholastics, or schoolmen) of medieval universities in Europe (1100-1500) and a program of employing scholarship to articulate and defend orthodoxy in an increasingly pluralistic context. It originated as an outgrowth of, and a departure from, Christian monastic schools.

3   This controversy is the one that was addressed by the Dutch Reformed churches at the Synod of Dort in 1618–1619, a meeting to which Protestant representatives from Reformed churches in other countries were invited, pertaining to the points of contention raised by the Arminian party in its publication of five articles of Remonstrance in 1610. These were rejected by the Synod in the Canons of Dort, the essence of which is commonly referred to as the Five Points of Calvinism. These debates go back in some form to Augustine of Hippo's debate with the Pelagians in the Fifth Century on theological cornerstones of soteriology, including depravity, predestination, and atonement.

4   Arianism developed about 320, in Alexandria, Egypt, and concerned the person of Christ. It is named after Arius of Alexandria. He was exiled to Illyria in 325 after the first ecumenical council at Nicaea condemned his teaching as heresy. It was the greatest of heresies within the early church that developed a significant following, and almost took over the church. Arius taught that only God the Father was eternal and too pure and infinite to manifest on the earth. Therefore, God produced Christ the Son out of nothing as the first and greatest creation. The Son then created the universe. Because the relationship of the Son to the Father is not natural, it is, therefore, adoptive. God adopted Christ as the Son. Though Christ was a creation, because of his great position and authority, he was to be worshiped and even looked upon as God.

10. The development of New England theology on sin, holiness and human depravity, by Edwards, Hopkins, Emmons[5] and others, in reply to the Arminians and J. Taylor.
11. The more recent Unitarian controversies on human depravity, in Europe and America.
12. The further developments of New England theology on sin and holiness, by Dr. N. Taylor and the New Haven divines.
13. The controversies in New England and the Presbyterian church, to which they gave rise.
14. The more recent controversy of Professor Park and the Princeton divines.

If any one, on looking over this formidable outline of a wide extended field of controversy, should fear lest the mind should be wearied and confounded by the multiplicity of names and conflicting theories, let him, for a moment, rise above names, and consider the things in debate, and he will see that they are few and simple. On the one side he will find, under the influence of Christian consciousness, Scripture and history, a constant effort to state thoroughly the entire ruin of man, its origin from Adam, and its remedy in Christ. On the other he will find the annunciation, with greater or less fulness, of the principles of honor and right, in their relations to God, and His dealings with men; and efforts, under their influence, either utterly to disprove, or to modify and soften, the facts alleged, concerning the utter ruin and gracious recovery of man. As the valley of the Mississippi, though vast, is simple in its great outlines, and as the river that drains it

---

5   Nathanael Emmons (1745-1840), an American theologian, was born at East Haddam, Connecticut, developed an original system of divinity, somewhat on the structural plan of that of Samuel Hopkins, and, in Emmons' own belief, contained in and evolved from Hopkinsianism. While by no means abandoning the tenets of the old Calvinistic faith, he came to be looked upon as the chief representative of what was then known as the New School of theologians. His system declared that holiness and sin are free voluntary exercises; that men act freely under the divine agency; that the slightest transgression deserves eternal punishment; that it is through God's mere grace that the penitent believer is pardoned and justified; that, in spite of total depravity, sinners ought to repent; and that regeneration is active, not passive, with the believer. Emmonsism was spread and perpetuated by more than a hundred clergymen, whom he personally trained. Politically, he was an ardent patriot during the American War of Independence, and a strong Federalist afterwards, several of his political discourses attracting wide attention. He was a founder and the first president of the Massachusetts Missionary Society, and was influential in the establishment of Andover Theological Seminary.

is formed of necessity, as it is, by the waters that flow from the descending slopes of the great eastern and western chains of mountains, so the valley of this great river of controversy, that has flowed for ages, is simple, and the river itself has been made, of necessity, by the meeting of the constant streams of thought and feeling that have flowed from these great and opposite mountain ranges of alleged facts on the one hand, and of principles on the other. Nor need we wonder at the depth, intensity and power, of the feelings that have been manifested. The subject involves all that man has to hope or fear in an eternal destiny.

Who can fully conceive of the importance of a thorough and radical regeneration, if the account given of the ruin of man is true? It is a deliverance from eternal pollution, eternal shame and eternal woe, the magnitude of which overwhelms the mind, and eclipses all other deliverances. Hence, to the deeply experimental Christian, no evil can appear greater than the dissemination of false or superficial views of the depravity and ruin of man. To such, the flippancy and levity and self-exaltation which so many exhibit, who are ignorant of their own utter ruin, is unutterably mournful and repulsive. Hence, we need not wonder at the earnestness and zeal with which experimental Christians, such as Augustine, the Reformers, the Puritans, Edwards, and others of a like spirit, have defended the doctrine of depravity; nor at the deep sufferings which they have endured, when errors have prevailed affecting vitally the eternal welfare of their fellow-men.

But this is not the only just ground of earnest intellectual activity and deep suffering. Who can estimate the importance of true views of honor and right, in reference to the character of God?

All that is great, glorious and praiseworthy, in the Creator,—all that is valuable or desirable in His eternal kingdom, all that makes existence itself in any degree a blessing,—nay, all that prevents it from becoming a most fearful curse, is at stake. There is no other interest, of which the mind can form a conception, that deserves for a moment to be compared with the interest that every created being has in the character of God. Not only individual non-existence, but much more universal non-existence, is to be preferred to existence under a God the measures of whose administration should violate the fundamental and eternal principles of honor and of right.

This estimate of the importance of this great controversy is not exaggerated. Nor is it so regarded by any competent judge. Hence,

Wiggers,[6] in his history of Pelagianisin and Augustinism, justly remarks, "Among all the doctrinal controversies in the Christian church, the Pelagian certainly take the first place, if we regard the consequences, and the importance of their results to Christian doctrine." Ranke, too, in his History of the Popes, says of the question, debated by Molina,[7] concerning grace, free will, good works and predestination,—which is but the necessary development of the Pelagian controversy,—that, throughout the whole range of theology, Catholic as well as Protestant, it is, and ever has been, "the most important, and the most pregnant with consequences."

---

6   Gustav Adam Friedrich Wiggers (1777-1860), a German theologian.

7   Luis de Molina (1535-1600), a Spanish Jesuit priest and a Scholastic defender of human liberty in the Divine grace and human liberty controversy of the Renaissance (Molinism).

CHAPTER II: THE POINT OF VISION

I SHALL not, in my restricted limits, undertake anything like a full history of so great a controversy. I shall merely attempt to develop the principles, and sketch the general course of the conflict.

It is happy for us, however, that there is a mountain-top so situated that to it we can easily ascend, and from it distinctly and accurately survey the course of this whole conflict. This lofty mountain-top is that eminent Christian father and divine, *Augustine*, Bishop of Hippo.

It will be conceded, by all competent judges, that the most momentous and influential crisis in the whole of this great theological conflict occurred during the fifth century, in the eminently radical and able controversy between him on the one hand, and Pelagius, Celestius and Julian, on the other.

If it is any honorable evidence of intellectual greatness to be able to control, from age to age, the theological speculations of the profoundest and most experimental minds in the church, and, after the eminently able discussions of the present day, to become once more the master spirit, towards whom many leading minds are beginning to gravitate, as a center of revolution and of light, that honorable evidence clearly belongs to *Augustine*.

In an able article on *The Doctrine Of Original Sin*, in the *Christian Review* for January, 1852, of which Professor Shedd,[8] of Auburn, is the author, there is an open and avowed return to the fundamental positions of Augustine, as essential in order to maintain the true depth and vitality of the doctrine. Of Augustine he says, "In two traits he never had a superior,—depth and penetration." Again, refer-

---

8   W.G.T. Shedd (1820-1894) was both a Congregational and, later a Presbyterian pastor. He was a Professor of English Literature before coming to the theological seminaries at Auburn Seminary in Andover and later at Union Seminary in New York. He is best known for his three-volume *Dogmatic Theology, Calvinism: Pure & Mixed, Sermons to the Natural Man* and *Sermons to the Spiritual Man*. He also wrote *The Doctrine of Endless Punishment*.

ring to the theory that all men sinned in Adam's sin, he says: "Augustine, although the first to philosophize upon this difficult point in order to bring it within the limits of a doctrinal system, has, nevertheless, as it seems to us, not been excelled by any of his successors in the profundity and comprehensiveness of his views." He considers that as the most profound theological period in which all the evangelical churches stood together on his ground; and seems to anticipate a speedy return to it, as the opening of an age of deeper and more vital theology. These views were set forth in the organ of the great orthodox Baptist denomination of our country, and were received by them, so far as I know, with universal applause. Certainly, so it was with *The Watchman and Reflector*, of Boston, one of the most influential papers of that denomination. The editor of that able paper speaks of it in the following terms:

> "It is an article discussing at considerable length, and with metaphysical acumen and logic seldom surpassed, a doctrine of theology necessarily fundamental. The writer takes ground that back of consciousness, and of all outward manifestations, there is in man an evil nature,—a corrupt fountain, forming the source of whatever is sinful in his life."

The editor, moreover, is manifestly a convert to the opinions of Prof. Shedd, and anticipates the final triumph of his views, for he proceeds to say: "We do not see how the force of the writer's reasoning can be evaded. He belongs to the school of Augustine, Turretin and Calvin, though bringing to the investigation of his subject more of the fruits of Scripture philology and of philosophy than were furnished to the hand of those distinguished defenders of the faith. He regards the scientific statement of the doctrine of original sin as having made no advance since the framing of the Westminster Catechism in 1643, and sees no prospect of advance for the future in this department of theological inquiry.

> "Remarking of 'those ages of controversy, the sixteenth and seventeenth centuries,' he says: 'Those who held the doctrine of a sinful nature, and of a sinful nature that is guilt, stood upon one side, and stood all together; and those who rejected this doctrine stood upon the other side, and also

stood all together. The Christian church was divided into
two divisions, and no more. And this, because the controversy was a thorough one, owing to the profound view of
sin taken by the disputants on the Augustinian side; the
metaphysical rather than the merely psychological aspect of
the doctrine being uppermost.'

"Since the period here alluded to, various systems of theological belief and denial have come into existence. Socinianism has flourished on the continent, in England, and in
this country. The same may be said of Arminianism as the
distinguishing element of Methodism, and as having largely
permeated the Episcopacy, the Lutherans, the General and
Free Will Baptists. Under the lead of Rev. C. G. Finney,
Drs. Taylor, Barnes and others, a system of what is sometimes called 'New Divinity' has also come into vogue. The
denial of original sin, as held by these men, and at the time
referred to, is a marked feature of each of these systems;
while, of course, there is great general diversity between
them. We cannot help thinking that a true or a false theory
of original sin exerts a vital influence upon theology, either
to preserve it pure, or to corrupt it. It would not be surprising again to see men holding to the doctrine of a sinful nature, and that nature guilt, standing upon one side, and all
standing together; and those rejecting the same doctrine
standing on the other side, and all standing together. There
are tendencies toward this issue, which it is not difficult to
mistake. And when that issue is fairly reached, there will be
fewer hiding-places of error than now exist."

Again, in a notice of this number of the *Christian Review* he says :

"The opening article, on the doctrine of original sin, by a
writer who chooses to withhold his name, is a rare contribution to the metaphysical side of that profound subject.
'Sin a nature, and that nature guilt,' is the running title, and
indicates the writer's position,—just the position which harmonizes with scripture and with consciousness. and establishes man's need of the redemption which is in Christ. In
the main coinciding with Edwards, it differs from him on
points pertaining to the will, and will furnish to the metaphysical student some views on those points which will spe-

cially arrest his attention. It may be doubted whether a more profound or more valuable theological article has lately been given to the public."

The *Puritan Recorder*, a prominent organ of the orthodox Congregationalists, says of the article: "It treats of a subject that is destined to occasion no little discussion; and it treats of it in a masterly manner."

I mention these things as striking signs of the times, and as a proof that it is not needless once more to look thoroughly into the opinions of Augustine. By many it is thought that his views have become as lifeless as the entombed remains of the antediluvian and ante-Mosaic ages. E. H. Sears,[9] in a recent able and deeply interesting work, entitled *Regeneration*, thus expresses his views: "Pleasing omens already indicate that this form of belief is ceasing to become active. We lay it off, then, in the persuasion that it is taking its place among the fossilized remains of a former theologic world, which old convulsions had turned up and left bare to our wondering and curious gaze." It is obvious, however, that the views of Augustine are not destined to lose their hold on men of eminent piety and intellectual power, at least until they have been once more thoroughly reviewed and reconsidered. Nor ought we to wonder at this. His mind was one of uncommon scope, richness and power. His works are, in all parts, full of the seeds of thought. They were, during the middle ages, the great encyclopedia of the theological sciences. We rarely, if ever, find a profound Christian and an eminent divine, from Gregory the great to Luther and Calvin, who had not been molded by the study of Augustine. Among the scholastic divines, Neander[10] says, "The dogmatical bent of Augustine exercised the most decided influence on the minds of the age." Of Anselm of Canterbury, Neander remarks that "he was the Augustine of his age;" and that "he exerted the most important influence on the

---

9 Edmund Hamilton Sears (1810-1876), a Unitarian parish minister and author, was conservative and not in sympathy with either "broad church" or "radical" Unitarians. He wrote a number of theological works influential among liberal Protestants, inside and outside the Unitarian fold. Sears' fame is due to his composition of the Christmas carol, "It Came upon the Midnight Clear."

10 Johann August Wilhelm Neander (1789-1850), was born at Göttingen as David Mendel. His father, Emmanuel Mendel, is said to have been a Jewish pedlar; he adopted the name of Neander on his baptism as a Protestant Christian, whose theological position can only be explained in connection with Schleiermacher, and the manner in which he modified and carried out those principles.

theological and philosophical turn of the twelfth century." Yet, "the works from which his mind derived all its nourishment, and which, as he continually studied them, gave an impulse to all his inquiries, were the Bible and St. Augustine." In addition to his rich and creative intellect, the deep piety of Augustine enabled him thus to draw to himself the great evangelical leaders of each successive age. In addition to this, it ought to be said that the discussion of the great questions concerning the moral character and relations of man has never been so much more comprehensive and thorough, at any one time since Augustine, than it was in his day, that any subsequent age has been fully and properly qualified to sit in judgment upon him. The more that great original controversy is examined, the deeper will be our conviction of the extent and profundity of the discussion. Pelagius, Celestius, and especially Julian, were men of uncommon ability. They left few new modes of assailing the views of Augustine to the ingenuity of their successors. Nor did the indefatigable mind of Augustine shrink from their encounter on any point. The question, also, as to preexistence, was at that time more an open question than it has ever since been, or is now; and was not overlooked in the discussion, as it has generally been from that time to this. The question as to the proper interpretation of the last part of the fifth chapter of Romans, which is the chief passage relied on for disclosing the relations of Adam to his race, was then more an open question than it has ever been since that time. In short, the highest issues of this whole discussion were then first made, and were so deeply discussed that no subsequent generation has ever reached a point of vision high enough to enable them thoroughly to reconsider them.

It is not, therefore, without reason that I have selected this as the point of view,—the lofty mountain-top from which to review the whole discussion.

CHAPTER III: THEOLOGICAL SPECULATIONS BEFORE AUGUSTINE

THIS period includes about four centuries, extending from Christ nearly to the fall of the western Roman empire. In it occurred the earliest and most exciting discussions as to the Trinity. These, however, I shall not notice, but shall fix my attention solely on the great conflict that is now before us.

It is a striking peculiarity of this period that it opened under the influence of no human systems of theology. The sources of theology were in the possession of all, but had not been explored. The Old Testament was in existence, and Christ and His apostles had taught and written. The Holy Spirit had descended, and Jews and Gentiles had been convinced of sin, and, being united to Christ by a living faith, had learned the mysteries of a Christian experience. Without any metaphysical theory as to the origin of sin, they were convinced by facts on every side, as well as by the Word of God, of the deep depravity of all men. Of the moral state, both of the Jewish and Pagan world, Paul had given a dark picture in the first chapters of the epistle to the Romans. Besides all this, in every true convert a Christian experience, without any theological theory, disclosed the deep depravity of the heart. Yet, for many years, these abundant materials were wrought up into no system. No great theologians followed the apostles. An immense chasm separated the apostolical fathers from them. The men whom God inspired tower upwards like mountains. Their uninspired successors at once sink down to the dead level of the plains below.

As years rolled on, however, assaults were made upon various doctrines of the Word of God by different classes of errorists, or else attempts were made to undermine or corrupt them by mixtures of erroneous systems. It thus became necessary to define the real doctrines of Christianity, and to sustain them alike against open assaults and insidious corruptions.

Which of the two moving powers of Christianity should have the ascendency in these opening theological movements would, of course, depend upon the nature of the attacks made, and of the defense which was thus rendered necessary.

The defense of the divine origin of Christianity against Jews and Gentiles was the first work of the church. But they were called, very soon, to repel attacks on the character of God, charging Him with having violated the principles of honor and of right in His dealings with men, both as to their natures and powers, and His action upon them. Of course, this rendered necessary and called forth defenses of God, in which the principles of equity and of honor were recognized, and arguments were presented to prove that God had always and perfectly regarded them.

It is plain, from what I have before said, that such a course of events would lead to such statements concerning the constitution and faculties of man, and the freedom and power of his will, as would tend to superficial views of human depravity. Accordingly, when we take a general view of the main course and logical drift of the discussions on the moral character of man and the grace of God which preceded Augustine, obvious facts authorize us to say that they did finally result in superficial views of human depravity. I do not mean that the doctrine that all men are sinners, and that they need to be saved by the grace of God through Christ, was ever denied. On the other hand, it was universally maintained. But the sinfulness of man was not so developed as to tend to those views of innate depravity which produce the deepest forms of Christian experience,—those forms in which there is a keen sense of the utter moral weakness of man, and of his entire dependence on the grace of the regenerating and sanctifying Spirit. Instead of this, there was a development of those forms which make prominent the energies of the human will, as free and competent to fulfill all the demands of the law and of the gospel. Accordingly, the final result was that the errors of Pelagianisrn were developed from these tendencies carried out to their extreme issues.

It is well known that the whole church, with one voice, maintained the freedom of the will before the discussions of Augustine and Pelagius. Especially was this true of the oriental church. The Greek fathers carefully excluded from their theological system the idea of a nature depraved and punishable before action. According to them, no man was a sinner until he had voluntarily transgressed the laws of conscience and of God, and this no man was under any necessity of doing. We are now prepared to understand and to believe Neander, when he says that "Pelagius was a diligent student of the oriental church teachers; and the form in which he found Christian anthropology exhibited in those writers corresponded with the peculiar development of his own inward life" (Torrey's Neander, II. p. 573). The great idea of his experience, the same eminent historian states to be, to determine "how far man might advance towards perfection, by a self-active development of the germs of goodness lying in his own moral nature, by the superior energy of the will, by self-control."

I have already stated, in general terms, how it happened that the first development of the church was in this direction. I remarked that it originated from the nature of the first great controversial attacks to which the early Christians were exposed. The nature and form of these attacks I shall now more particularly consider. One of the most important proceeded from the Gnostics. The assaults, also, of the Manicheans, and of the philosophers who inculcated the doctrine of fate, tended in the same direction. Gnosticism, it is well known, developed itself in a systematic and concentrated attack upon the Old Testament.

The Gnostics, holding that matter is in its own nature essentially evil, and productive of sin, sought to explain the evils of this world as the result, not of the action of the supreme God, but of a deity called the Demiurgus, or world-maker, who, from preexisting elements, had formed this material system, and in it involved in the bondage of matter spirits of divine origin from the heavenly regions, who thereby were rendered sinful and corrupt. This Demiurgus they asserted to be the God of the Old Testament; and most of them regarded him as an evil and malignant being, whom Christ was revealed to destroy, in order to deliver men from bondage to him and to matter. In proof of these assertions, they appealed to his acts, as recorded in the Old Testament. This, of course, resulted in an attack on the real God of Christianity, which the church was called on to repel. They alleged, in particular, his despotic and unjust conduct, in punishing children for the sins of their fathers, and in violating the free will of man; as, for example, in the case of hardening Pharaoh's heart, and, in general, by his arbitrary and irresistible decrees. Is there any reason, then, to wonder that, in defense of God and of the Old Testament against such charges, the early fathers should have concentrated their energies in a full development and defense of the doctrine of the freedom of the will, and in the exposition of those bold passages which represent God as hardening men and turning their hearts to evil in such a manner as to consist with the laws of honor and of right, and with just views of human responsibility? Moreover, as the Gnostics taught that only one out of the three classes into which they divided men had natures capable of a holy development, is it to be wondered at that the church should earnestly seek to demonstrate that no man had a nature essentially evil and sinful before action, and as such incapable of a right and holy choice of God and of His kingdom? Afterwards, the Manichean notion of a nature essentially evil in itself called for a repetition of the same course of reasoning. And, as the doctrine of fate, which had pervaded the pagan world, encountered them on every side, it, of course, impelled them with augmented momentum in the same direction. Accordingly, it is not possible to state in stronger terms than they have abundantly used the great fact of man's perfect free agency, as a capacity of choosing, with the power of contrary choice, in every instance of voluntary and responsible conduct. This is so fully conceded by all writers on the history of dogmatic theology, of any authority, that it is superfluous to produce any documentary evidence of the fact.

It is also evident, beyond denial, that they conditioned God's decree of election upon His foreknowledge of the voluntary conduct of those to whom the offers of mercy should be proclaimed. In addition to this, by their opposition to the Gnostic and Manichean dogmas concerning natures essentially evil, they were, in fact, led definitely to deny the existence of a sinful nature in man. Hence, Gregory of Nyssa, in his work concerning children prematurely removed, says, "The child, free from all sin, finds itself in the natural state, and needs no purification for its health, because it has as yet fallen into no disease of the soul" (Emerson's *Wiggers*, p. 346). Chrysostom also says, "We baptize children, though they have no sin, that they may have holiness," etc. At the same time, they did not deny that all men do in fact sin, and thus, becoming guilty and corrupt, need the atonement of Christ. Moreover, in general they held that the sin of Adam, in some way, had so affected his race that it stood connected with this result. Still, however, they considered the only immediate effects of this sin to be natural death, a higher degree of sensual excitability, and exposure to a higher power of temptation. And yet on these points some of them spoke with great caution, lest they should seem to undermine the idea of a true and real free agency.

Of the fathers, up to the death of Origen, or the year 254, Hagenbach says:

> "The opinions of the fathers were not as yet fully developed concerning the moral depravity of every individual, and the existence of sin in mankind generally, as the effect of the sin of the first man. Many felt too much disposed to look upon sin as the voluntary act of a moral agent, to conceive of a kind of hereditary tendency transmitted from one generation to another. The sinful acts of every individual appeared to them less the necessary consequence of the first sin, than a voluntary repetition of it. In order to explain the mysterious power which almost compels men to sin, they had recourse not so much to original sin, as to a supposed influence of the demons, which, however, cannot constrain any man to trespass."

In the preceding passage, I think, however, that the statement would have been more correct if he had said that some, rather than "many," were disposed to call in question any kind of hereditary tendency to sin. Concerning the Greek fathers down to the time of Augustine, Hagenbach also remarks :

> "Even those theologians, who kept themselves free from the influence of the Augustinian system, supposed that the sin of Adam was followed by disastrous effects upon the human race, but restricted them (as the fathers of the preceding period had done) to the mortality of the body, the hardships and miseries of life, and sometimes admitted that the moral faculties of man had been affected by the fall. Thus, Gregory of Nazianzum, in particular (to whom Augustine appealed in preference to all others), thought that both the voῦς (mind) and the ψυχή (soul) had been considerably impaired by the fall, and regarded the perversion of man's sentiments, and its consequence, idolatry, which the writers previous to his time had ascribed to the influence of demons, as the effect of the first sin. But he was far from supposing the total depravity of mankind, and the entire

loss of the free will. On the contrary, the doctrine of the freedom of the will continued to be distinctly maintained by the Greek church. Athanasius[11] himself, commonly called the father of orthodoxy, asserted in the strongest terms that man has the ability of choosing between good and evil: and was so far from believing in the general corruption of mankind, as to look upon several individuals, who lived prior to the appearance of Christ, as righteous. Cyrill of Jerusalem also assumed that men are born in a state of innocence, and that a free agent alone can commit sin. Similar views were entertained by Ephraim the Syrian, Gregory of Nyssa, Basil the Great, and others. Chrysostom, whose whole tendency was of a practico-moral kind, brought the liberty of man and his moral self-determination most distinctly forward, and passed a severe censure upon those who endeavored to excuse their own immoralities by ascribing the origin of sin to the fall of Adam."[12]

In support of these statements, he quotes many passages, of which I shall omit all except those from Cyrill of Jerusalem. He says,

"We come into this world without sin, and sin of free choice." "The soul has free will, and the devil can suggest temptations, but he cannot compel to sin contrary to choice." "If anyone through his own neglect is not deemed fit to receive grace, let him not censure the Spirit, but his own unbelief" (Cat. IV. 19, 21, and XVI. 28).

Properly to understand these views of the Greek fathers, we must consider against what errors they were aimed, and remember that even those who held that infants were born sinless, as Cyrill, and Gregory of

11 Athanasius of Alexandria (296-373) is remembered for his role in the conflict with Arius and Arianism. In 325, at the age of 27, he had a leading role against the Arians in the First Council of Nicaea. At the time, he was a deacon and personal secretary of the 19th Bishop of Alexandria, Alexander. Nicaea was convoked in 325 to address the Arian heresy that Christ is of a distinct substance from the Father.

12 The tendency of teaching that the mind of man enters this world in a normal and unfallen state to degrade our conceptions of free agency, and of the true original dignity of the nature of man, and to produce superficial views of the reality find guilt of sin, I have not fully discussed in any one place according to its importance, but have viewed it in various aspects during the progress of the general discussion. To enable anyone who desires it to unite these separate discussions in one view, I will refer to the other places where they occur: Book II: Chap. VIII, p. 118; XI, p. 133. Book III: Chap. V, p. 177; VII, p. 188. Book IV: Chap. III, p. 221; X, p. 277.

Nyssa, believed that there was still in the race a universal tendency to sin, and, in opposition to pride and self-conceit, urged the deep actual depravity of man.

It is too plain to need proof that these views of the Greek fathers are based upon a laudable and reverential purpose to defend God against all charges of violating the principles of equity and honor; but it is no less obvious that they tend to superficial views of human depravity. They also tend to a degradation of free agency itself, in the way which has been pointed out in considering the Unitarian and some forms of the New School theology. For it is plain that every effort to account for developments so universally and so deeply depraved as are those of the human race in this world, by regarding them as the natural result of free agency as such, of necessity degrades free agency itself. Moreover, all efforts to prove that free agency, as it exists in this world, is such as God ought in honor and justice to confer on new-created minds, naturally leads to low views of what is possible in the original and upright state of new-created minds. Accordingly, in the Greek fathers we find low views of the state of original righteousness in which man was created. Hence, Neander remarks that

> "the Pelagians, like the older, particularly the oriental church teachers, with whom they, in fact, more especially coincided, compare the state of the first man with that of an innocent, inexperienced child; only with this difference, that, as a thing necessary in order to his preservation, his spiritual and corporeal powers were already unfolded to a certain extent."

Moreover, in comparing the Greek with the Latin church, he remarks,

> "By means of Augustine, whose influence did not extend to the eastern church, the general system of (Western) doctrine took its shape and direction more decidedly from the doctrine of redemption as a center, and from the anthropology (of Augustine) connected therewith. But among the Greeks the case was otherwise. Whilst, in the western church, the Augustinian scheme of doctrine had become dominant, in the Greek church the older and more indefinite mode of apprehending the doctrines of grace, of free will, and of

providence,—a theory bordering on Pelagianism, —had been preserved."

Anyone can satisfy himself of the truth of this view by a reference to John of Damascus, the great systematic divine of the Greek church, who has preserved the oriental system as it was in the days of Chrysostom, excluding all the modifications introduced by Augustine.

In connection with this state of facts let it now be noticed that it is conceded that the religious experience of the period before Augustine did not have that deep Pauline character which was afterwards developed in Augustine, and in those who adopted his views. Hagenbach says:

> "In opposition to the opinion that conviction of sin, accompanied by powerful excitement, which attains to a sense of pardon only after internal struggles, is alone the sure criterion and indispensable condition of the Christian's character, we may safely refer to the primitive church, in which, to say the least, such a notion of sin did not prevail."

His explanation of this phenomenon appears to me singular and inadequate. In days of external martyrdom, he informs us, such an experience was not needed. But, "when persecutions ceased, it became a duty imperative on the church to cultivate the internal martyrdom in opposition to external triumphs." This internal martyrdom, he tells us, "consisted in the subjection of the heart to the power of the Holy Spirit, in the sense of Augustine, which prepared the way for the regeneration of the church in after ages." He thinks that one experience belonged very properly to the childhood of the church, but the other to a period of necessary subsequent development. From this view I beg leave to dissent. Did not Paul live in the martyr-age? Yet he had the same deep experience and self-crucifixion with Augustine; and he inculcated it as a proper and necessary part of Christian experience, in all ages. Moreover, ought not the heart to be subjected to the power of the Holy Spirit, in all ages, as truly as in the ages after Augustine? There are others who account for such cases of deep conviction by the supposition that the subjects of them were men of violent passions, and powerful sensual tendencies, who, like Augustine, for a time wallow in sin, or at least are called to a violent struggle with their appetites and impulses. What, then, shall be said of the case of Edwards, moral, intellectual and refined from his youth up, and surrounded by nothing but pure and intellectual society? How is his deep Pauline and Augustinian experience to be explained, on this theory? To me it is plain that the type of experience before Augustine was, to a great extent, caused by the tendencies of the prevailing doctrinal system, and that the change of doctrine effected by Augustine introduced a deeper style of Christian experience. A striking confirmation of this view is found in the fact that, in the Greek church,—retaining their original system,—the Augustinian experience has rarely, if ever, been found, even to this day. To complete our view, it ought to be added, that during this period the ascetic system, which is based upon the idea that the origin of sin is to be found in matter,—a principle of Gnosticism, with which the church, in spite of her conflicts against that system in general, was early infected,—struck its roots deep in the Christian world, and developed itself in the form of monastic institutions. The tendency of this ascetic system, in all its forms, is to magnify the works of man, and to hide the free grace of God. We shall find in this, in connection with the superficial theology which has already been considered, a sufficient account of the want, at that time, of a deep Christian experience of the same kind which characterized the apostle Paul, as well as the profound Augustine. Here, then, we see that, in accordance with my opening statement, the principles of equity and of honor, in their reaction from Gnosticism, Manicheism and fatalism, have, in fact, given rise to superficial views of human depravity, which are not adapted to produce a deep Christian experience. These, at length, were taken up and carried beyond the prevailing views of the church, even to their extreme results, by Pelagius and his compeers; and thus led to that great reaction which was developed by the agency of that eminent master-spirit, through whom the channels of a profound Christian experience were disclosed and deepened for all coming ages.

All that Pelagius, Celestius and Julian did, was to carry out to their natural results the principles of honor and right, on the supposition that this is our first state of existence. Their doctrine, in brief, is, that man has such a moral constitution and such powers as God ought, as an honorable and just being, to confer on every new-created being. All men receive so much from the Creator, and Adam had no more. Therefore, all men are naturally as well-off as Adam was before the fall. Hence his fall injured himself only, and not his posterity. Herein

Pelagius differed from the early fathers, so far as they held that the fall of Adam injured the moral constitution of his posterity, and produced a hereditary propensity to sin. But he did not differ from them in teaching that all men are free agents, with full power to obey the law of God and the gospel; and that there is in them no sin, and no sinful nature, before voluntary action. Such was the general view of the whole church before his day.

It followed from the views of Pelagius that a man could live without sin, and so be saved by the law, without any need of the atonement. Hence the Pelagian doctrine that the law is as good a means of salvation as the gospel. Hence, too, the idea of Pelagius, that the grace of God consisted in part in making man a free agent, and also in the presentation to him, in various ways, of motives adapted to excite him to a right use of his powers as a free agent; hence, too, his reluctance to admit the absolute necessity of any other grace exerting an interior and decisive power upon the will, such as to deliver it from the bondage of sin, and restore to it true liberty. Pelagius also differed from the preceding fathers by holding that natural death was not the result of Adam's sin, either in himself or in his posterity. He held that death was inseparable from our nature; and that, therefore, Adam and all his offspring would have died, even if he had not sinned.

CHAPTER IV: THE MOUNTAIN-TOP; OR, AUGUSTINE AND HIS EXPERIENCE

FROM what has been said, it appears that up to the time of Augustine there had been no serious controversy among good men on the subject of human depravity. The assaults on Christianity from without, by the Gnostics,[13] Fatalists[14] and Manicheans,[15] had united the whole church in defending the freedom of the will, and the rectitude of God with respect to the original constitution and powers of man. Thus, all things had given to the principles of equity and of honor an ascendency and a preponderance which threatened at length entirely to eradicate the radical and thorough doctrine of human depravity. That such was the tendency, is obvious from the fact that Pelagius, by whom this work was at length consummated, was a

---

13 Gnosticism was primarily defined in a Christian context as "the acute Helleniza-tion of Christianity" per Adolf von Harnack (1885), until Moritz Friedländer (1898) advocated Hellenistic Jewish origins, and Wilhelm Bousset (1907) advocated Persian origins. Consequent discussions of Gnostic Christianity include pre-Christian religious beliefs and spiritual practices argued to be common to early Christianity, Hellenistic Judaism, Greco-Roman mystery religions, Zoroastrianism (especially Zurvanism), and Neoplatonism.

14 Fatalism generally refers to several of the following ideas: 1) Philosophers usually use the word to refer to the view that we are powerless to do anything other than what we actually do. Included in this is that man has no power to influence the future, or indeed, his own actions. This belief is very similar to predeterminism. 2) That actions are free, but nevertheless work toward an inevitable end. This belief is very similar to compatibilist predestination. 3) That acceptance is appropriate, rather than resistance against inevitability. This belief is very similar to defeatism.

15 Manichaeism was a major gnostic religion, originating in Sassanid era Babylonia. Although most of the original writings of the founding prophet Mani (216–276) have been lost, numerous translations and fragmentary texts have survived. Manichaeism taught an elaborate cosmology describing the struggle between a good, spiritual world of light, and an evil, material world of darkness. Through an ongoing process in human history, light is gradually removed from the world of matter and returned to the world of light from which it came. Its beliefs, based on local Mesopotamian gnostic and religious movements, contained elements of Christianity, Zoroastrianism and Buddhism.

diligent student of the early fathers, especially those of the Greek church, and found in their doctrine concerning man views which accorded with his own experience.

We come now to a great and necessary reaction from this mode of thinking and reasoning, the influence of which has not been expended even to this day. It has not, indeed, ever gained the ascendency, so as to unite all good men in one harmonious phalanx; it has never been able to prevent powerful reactions against itself; yet, as compared with what preceded it, it was a great advance, and it has effected a great work for God and for humanity.

Its peculiar and fundamental work was to restore to the church that deep and radical view of human depravity which is found in the Word of God, and without which all efforts to effect the moral renovation of man and of society will be superficial and powerless.

The great instrument of divine providence, in effecting this reaction, was Augustine, a man whom God had fitted, by his own experience, to sound all the depths of a true and Pauline Christian consciousness, and thus to form an accurate conception of what are the original and normal relations of the mind to God, and of what are the corruptions and perversions which have been introduced into it by sin.

He is that spiritual mountain-top upon which I propose to stand, in order to survey this great conflict, from its first development to this day. And, as his influence enters so deeply into all the religious history of the world since his day, I think it important, so far as possible, to establish a Christian sympathy and good understanding between Him and Christians of the present age.

I am the more desirous to do this, as he is extensively misunderstood. He is thought of as the advocate of a System so stern and fearful that he must have been a mere heartless reasoner, ready to sacrifice all the finer feelings of humanity upon the altar of an iron logical consistency,

It is true that Augustine was a logician; but it is no less true that no man ever had a larger, a more tender, a more sensitive heart, or a deeper abyss of profound and glowing emotion. Indeed, it was the great, the final end of Augustine, to love with the whole intensity of his being, and to be loved with an infinite and almighty love, a love such as can be found nowhere but in God. It was this union of powerful logic and deep emotion which gave Augustine such power over the minds of men,—a power to which every age has borne witness, from that day to the present.

These characteristics of Augustine are noticed by Wiggers, as effecting in him a union of scholasticism and mysticism. But, as some of His remarks on the subject of a mystic experience are adapted to produce misunderstanding, I here introduce them for the sake of some remarks.

Concerning him, then, Wiggers thus speaks:

"From all this, the following characteristic of Augustine is manifest. The most distinctive and the most interesting thing, and that by which His individuality is the most strikingly indicated, is the union of mysticism with scholasticism,—that is, the endeavor by feeling to reach the infinite, with the endeavor to reduce the infinite to our comprehension. In this respect, Augustine is altogether remarkable,—a peculiar phenomenon, one might say, of Christian antiquity. Certainly, we find no father in whom we meet with just as many proofs of a mystic way of thinking as of the prevalence of intellect. How can anyone express himself in a more mystical way than to speak of the embraces of God, and of sucking His milk? And how clearly do we hear the mere mental philosopher, when he disputes with the Donatists, and still more when he seeks to prove the servile will in opposition to the Pelagians! The ecstasies also, of which the vestiges are found in His confessions, and which put him in the condition of those who have prophetic visions, show what a dominion fancy, the mother of mysticism, had over him. It might, indeed, be objected that we ought to consider the age of Augustine. But even in His latter age, during His contests with the Pelagians, striking traces are seen of the mystic mode of thinking, particularly in His assertions respecting the grace of God. Fancy, therefore, and sagacity were combined in him in a manner wholly peculiar, without our being able to say that either preponderated over the other. This peculiar combination, by which he was at once a mystic and a scholastic, is the greatest singularity in Augustine. In full accordance with this peculiarity, or sufficiently explained by it, are both his earnest effort for truth and his devout disposition,—his deep religious feeling,

which speaks forth in so lovely a manner, particularly where
he is not acting the polemic, e. g. in the Confessions, and
which must have made him abhor that pride of human
virtue which ascribes a merit to its own works.

"Augustine had by nature an excessive propensity to the
pleasures of sense, of which he often complains himself, and
which was also confirmed by the early errors of his youth.
This propensity must in due time have led him to mysticism. For, when it afterwards became more intellectual, his
fancy must needs have revelled in a world above sense; and
this readily affords a psychological explanation of the fact
that his love to God was never entirely free from a tinge of
sensuous love. As a necessary consequence, the new Platonic philosophy, which, from its mystic tendency, was well
adapted to his mind, confirmed him still more in this mode
of thinking.

"From what has been said, we may readily infer that Augustine possessed much natural kindness, and a delicate sus-
ceptibility for friendship. But the acuteness of his
understanding inclined him freely to admit consequences
from principles once established, even when repugnant to
his moral feeling. Hence was he so formidable a disputant.
The study of Aristotle's works had certainly a very salutary
influence on his consecutive mode of thinking. Against the
justness of his conclusions no objection can easily be made,
if we only admit the principles."

On this I would suggest, that it is, beyond all doubt, possible not
only to mix sensuous love with the love of God, but also to create a
false religious experience, of which God shall be the nominal object,
but all the elements of which shall be sensual. Such an experience
seems to be intimated in the writings of Hafiz, and other eastern mys-
tics. Nor is it uncommon to denote such religious excitement by the
term *mysticism*. The term, I am aware, is also used, in a better sense, to
denote a true and powerful inward experience of the love of God. But
this ambiguity of usage makes it the more important not to leave the
remarks of Wiggers unguarded. If he means that the love of Augustine
towards God was mystical in the sense of being improperly tinged by
sensualism, I beg leave to dissent from his view. It is well known by
all, that God has so made material things that they are analogous to

spiritual things. Is not light analogous to truth, heat to powerful love, water and food to the nutriment of the soul which is found in truth and love, and harmony in sounds to mental harmony among spirits" Is not the relation of God to man set forth by analogies taken from a human father or a mother, or from the sun, or from a rock or a fortress? Is it, then, sensual to think of God, or to love God, by the aid of such analogies? This would condemn the greater part of the religious experience of the Bible; for it is always expressed by means of such analogies. Suppose, then. that we pass from such analogies as these, to another, no less scriptural, and eminently elevated and sacred,—I mean the relation of the lover and the beloved, the bridegroom and the bride, the husband and the wife. This analogy is, in fact, no more material, no more sensual, than those of which I have spoken, and others of the same kind. So far as they are material, they all stand on exactly the same ground. Nor is it any more sensual or material to illustrate the love of God by the relations of the bridegroom and the bride, than it is by the analogies of light, heat, an earthly father, the sun, a shield, a rock or a fortress.

I concede that by the analogy of the bridegroom and the bride an appeal is made to the strongest human passions, and that these are often corrupted. But it is no less true that a love of God may exist so spiritual, so pure, so powerful, that it shall altogether transcend the power of such passions and emotions, and subordinate, purify, regulate, and control them, and impart to them a sanctity unknown before; by using them as the emblems of a higher love. If the higher love is wanting or feeble, the use of such emblems is dangerous; if that love is as it should be, it is safe. That this higher love did exist in full power in Augustine, there is no reason to doubt. It ruled his mind, and subordinated and sanctified all the analogies by which it was expressed. Indeed, he has given us a definite statement of his views and experience upon this point. Appealing to God, he says :

> "Not with doubting, but with assured consciousness, do I love thee, O Lord. ... But what do I love, when I love thee? Not beauty of bodies, nor the fair harmony of time, nor the brightness of the light so gladsome to our eyes, nor sweet melodies of varied songs, nor the fragrant smell of flowers and ointments and spices; not manna and honey; not a corporeal form, beautiful to embrace. None of these I love,

when I love my God; and yet I love a kind of light, and melody, and fragrance, and food, and embraces, when I love my God; the light, melody, fragrance, food, embraces, of my inner man; where there shineth unto my soul what space cannot contain, and there soundeth what time beareth not away; and there is fragrance which breathing disperseth not, and food is tasted which eating diminisheth not, and there are embraces which satiety dissolveth not. This is it which I love, when I love my God" (*Confessions* X. VI. p. 8).

What can more perfectly and beautifully explain the passages to which Wiggers refers as proofs of mysticism? Does it not divest them entirely of all tinge of sensual love in any improper sense? The full passage with reference to sucking the milk of God will show that Wiggers has not done justice to Augustine in so brief a reference. Addressing God, he says: "What am I to my self, without thee, but a guide to mine own downfall? Or, what am I when truly blessed, but an infant sucking the milk thou givest, and feeding upon Thee, the food that perisheth not?" Who, that has heard God saying, "As one whom his mother comforteth, so will I comfort you," or, "I am the bread of life," can take exception to Augustine's touching expression of filial dependence and love towards God? Did not David thirst for God; and when he found him did he not declare that in the enjoyment of his love his soul was satisfied as with marrow and fatness, and that his loving-kindness was better than life? In a similar style, also, does Augustine thus lament his former ingratitude:

"Thou light of my heart, thou bread of my inmost soul, thou power who givest vigor to my mind, and who quickenest my thoughts, I loved Thee not. ... Too late loved I thee, O thou beauty of ancient days, yet ever new! too late I loved thee! ... Thou didst call and shout, and my deafness ceased; thou didst flash and shine, and my blind eyes were opened. Thou breathedst odors, and I have inhaled them, and pant for thee. I tasted, and hunger and thirst. Thou touchedst me, and I burned for thy peace. When I shall, with my whole self, cleave to thee, then I shall no more have sorrow or labor, and my life shall wholly live as wholly full of thee. ... And sometimes thou admittest me to an un-

usual affection in my inmost soul; rising to a strange sweet-
ness, which, if it were perfected in me, I know not what in
it would not belong to the life to come."

And through what process did Augustine pass, in order to reach
such visions of God, and such seasons of heavenly communion with
Him? In this respect, his experience and that of Edwards were the
same. Both had seasons of deep and unutterable conviction of sin; both
learned deeply to loathe themselves, and to long, with intense longing,
to eradicate the roots of pride, that most dangerous and deepest defile-
ment of lofty, highly gifted minds. With regard to this, Augustine says
to his God:

> "Thou knowest, on this matter, the groans of my heart and
> the floods of my eyes. For I cannot learn how far I am ad-
> vanced in being cleansed from this plague; and I much fear
> my secret sins, which thine eyes know and mine do not. ...
> Fain would I that the approbation of another should not in-
> crease my joy for any good in me."

How truly coincident is this last expression with the statement of
Edwards, before quoted,—

> "The very thought of any joy arising in me, on any consid-
> eration of my own amiableness, performances or experi-
> ences, or any goodness of heart or life, is nauseous and
> detestable to me."

Yet was he constantly afflicted by conscious tendencies to pride.
Augustine, in like manner, calls this "his daily furnace," the constant
affliction of his soul. He desired in all things to see and honor God,
and to Him he confessed that he ought to value fame solely for benevolent ends. "Behold, in thee, O Truth, I see that I ought not to be
moved at my own praises, for my own sake, but for the good of my
neighbor." Knowing, as he did, the treachery of his heart, he earnestly
sought the searching of the omniscient eye.

To this brief view of the Christian experience of Augustine it may
be added, that he was naturally a man of genial, humane and tender
feelings. We see in him, therefore, no tendencies to a stern theology,
unless there is in man a sternness of depravity that calls for stern mea-

sures of justice on the part of God, whilst, at the same time, it opens
the way for the interposition of sovereign grace. If such is, in fact, the
character of man, then it is to be expected that one like Augustine
would arrive at a profound and unwavering conviction of the fact.

On the whole, we need not wonder that Augustine has had so
long continued a sway over the human mind. He had the fervor, the
deep passion and the imagination, of an oriental temperament; and yet
with it was combined the keen logic of a western mind. He was master of all the learning of his age that was accessible in the Latin tongue.
Though like Edwards in the union of logical power with a profound
experience, he greatly surpassed him in rhetorical power; for he had
studied rhetoric as an art, and had taught it before he became a Christian bishop. Hence, his style is universally more rhetorical and finished
than that of Edwards.

Is it to be wondered at that such men as Bernard, Anselm, Thomas
Aquinas, Luther, Calvin, Jansenius, and Pascal, should be drawn by a
sympathetic attraction to the profound doctrinal and experimental discussions of such a mind? Or that, from age to age, they should light
their lamps at his fire?

There is in the Agamemnon of Æschylus a beautiful and brilliant
passage, in which Clytemnestra (the wife of Agamemnon) describes
the transmission to herself by signal fires, kindled successively on
mountain-tops, of the intelligence of the downfall of Troy. If we will
substitute in it the idea of time instead of space, we may use it as a
lively image of the mode in which the fires of Christian doctrine and
experience have been transmitted from Augustine down the tract of
time, kindling upon one mountain-top after another, till they reach
the remotest ages.

I give the passage in the translation of Potter. Though slightly in-
accurate, it is equally good for my purpose. In reply to the inquiry
what herald conveyed the news, Clytemnestra answers:

> "The fire, that from the height of Ida sent
> Its streaming light, as from the announcing flame
> Torch blazed to torch. First Ida to the steep
> Of Lemnos: Athos' sacred height received
> The mighty splendor; from the surging back
> Of the Hellespont the vigorous blaze held on
> Its smiling way, and like the orient sun

Illumes with golden-gleaming rays the head
Of rocky Macetas; nor lingers there,
Nor winks unheedful, but its warning flames
Darts to the streams of Euripus, and gives
Its glittering signal to the guards that hold
Their high watch on Mesapius. These enkindle
The joy-announcing fires, that spread the blaze
To where Erica hoar its shaggy brow
Waves rudely. Unimpaired the active flame
Bounds o'er the level of Asopus, like
The jocund moon, and on Citheeron's steep
Wakes a successive flame; the distant watch
Agnize its shine, and raise a brighter fire,
That, o'er the lake Gorgopis streaming, holds
Its rapid course, and on the mountainous heights
Of Ægiplanctus huge, swift-shooting spreads
The lengthened line of light.
Thence onwards waves
Its fiery tresses, eager to ascend
The crags of Prone, frowning in their pride
O'er the Saronic gulf: it leaps, it mounts
The summit of Arachne, whose high head
Looks down on Argos: to this royal seat
Thence darts the light that from the
Idsean fire Derives its birth. *Rightly in order thus*
Each to the next consigns the torch, that fills
The bright succession."

To complete the image, however, we should remember on what mountain and by whom the fire was kindled that first shone on Augustine. It was kindled by Paul and his compeers on Zion, the mountain of our God.

Chapter V: Augustine's Principles Of Equity And Honor

WE have seen that before Augustine all things, especially in the oriental church, had taken such a course that, in efforts to defend God, two results had come to pass. The standard of the original righteousness which God ought to confer on new-created minds was lowered; and, also, that superficial views had been given of the deep original depravity of man. The result was, that neither subject was truly seen. The principles of honor and right were unduly degraded, the character of man was unduly exalted. This is the necessary result of endeavoring to justify God on the assumption that this is our first state of existence. And yet, even so, no available harmony was secured.

It was reserved for Augustine to restore each of these subjects to its true place in the system, and to attempt to effect a harmony between them.

I shall consider, in order, first, what he endeavored to do on each of these great points, the principles of honor and right, the original and deep depravity of man, and then set forth the mode of harmonizing these moving powers of Christianity which he proposed and defended.

In general, then, I remark that he entirely abandoned all efforts to prove that men, as they enter this world, have such constitutions, propensities and powers, as the principles of equity and honor require God to confer on new-created minds. He clearly conceded and fully taught that this was not the fact. To make this plain, it is only necessary to consider his principles of equity and honor, and his views of men as they enter this world.

We come, then, to the fundamental question on which this present discussion turns,—What were the principles of honor and right, as held by Augustine?

I reply, Augustine held that the principles of honor and right demand of the great Creator that He should give to all new-created minds such an original constitution, and such powers, and place them in such circumstances and under such influences, that they should enjoy a full and fair probation, in which they had full power, by their own free will, to secure a permanent confirmation in holiness and eternal life. These principles were not incidentally avowed by Augustine, but were fully, formally and scientifically set forth; not merely in his early writings, but in his last and most mature works, and especially in his treatise, *De Correptione 'et Gratia (Concerning Reproof And Grace)*, addressed to the Adrumettian monks,[16] near the close of his labors in the Pelagian controversy. Without going into any analysis of that or any other work as a whole, I will merely state what pertains to the point now under consideration.

The constitution and powers which he regarded as demanded of God for new-created beings by the principles of honor and right, were such as result in a true and real free will. The influence and circumstances demanded of God are such that this free will shall not be left to its own unaided energies, but shall be so invigorated and sustained by divine influence that the creatures shall be able always so to choose the right, and persevere therein, that the result shall be an eternal confirmation in good.

In accordance with these views, Augustine asserts concerning the angels that they were, when created, endowed with the requisite powers, and aided by the necessary divine influence; and that some of them, by their own free will, revolted, whilst others so persevered in good as to merit final confirmation in holiness and eternal life. A single extract will make this point sufficiently plain:

> "God so ordered the life of angels and men, that in it he
> might first show what their free will could effect, and then
> what the beneficence of his grace and the judgment of his
> justice could effect. Accordingly, certain angels, of whom
> he is the chief who is called the devil, fled from the service
> of the Lord God, by free will. But, thus escaping from his
> goodness, in which they had been happy, they were not

---

16 After Paul's appeal before Herod Agrippa II and Festus to state his case to Caesar in Rome, he was taken by a centurion of the Roman Imperial guard (Acts 27:1) to the harbor at Caesarea, where they found a ship of Adramyttium to convey them to Asia Minor. From Asia Minor, they anticipated finding another ship to Rome (27:6).

able to escape his judgment, by which they were rendered most miserable. But the rest, through the same free will, continued in the truth, and merited and received a certain assurance that they should never fall."

It appears from this that God dealt with angels and men on the same principles. What those principles were will be more clearly disclosed in what he subsequently sets forth concerning God's providential dealings with men. Let us, then, consider on what principles, according to Augustine, God dealt with man:

"So, also, he made man with free will, and, although about to fall, yet happy during his ignorance of it, because he perceived that it was in his power both not to die and not to become miserable. In which state of uprightness and freedom from sin, if through the same free will he had chosen to remain, truly, without any experience of death or unhappiness, he would have received, through the merit of this perseverance, the same fulness of blessedness with which the holy angels were rewarded; that is, that he should never after be able to fall, and that he should have certain assurance thereof."

Thus far, Augustine has spoken in general terms concerning the original powers and free will of men and angels. A more particular view of what was implied in the original state of his mind may be gathered from other parts of his works. He particularly states that God so made man that he had a perfectly faultless and sinless nature. He asks, "Who does not know that man was made sane, and faultless, and furnished with free will, and free power for holy living?" (De Nat. et. Gr. p. 43). His intellect was in the most perfect state. "Such was his power of mind, and use of reason, that Adam docilely received the precept of God and the law of commandment, and might easily have kept them if he would" (Ibid.). He ascribes to him "the most excellent wisdom." He says, also, that in the inward man Adam was spiritual, after the image of Him that created him (De Gen. ad Lit. VI. p. 28.) He asserts the same in the following passage:

"Not only Genesis, but also the apostle, proclaims that man was made after the image of God, when he says man is the image and glory of God (1 Cor. 11:7). And, that it may be clearly understood that he was made in the image of God, not according to his old corrupt and sinful nature, but according to a spiritual constitution, the same apostle admonishes us (Col. 3:10) that we should put off habits of sin, that is, the old man, and put on the character of Christ, which he calls the new man. And, that he may teach that we once lost this, he calls it a renovation; for he thus speaks, "Ye have put on the new man, who is renewed in knowledge after the image of him who created him" (*Contra Adamantum Manich.* p. 5).

It is true that Augustine very often, if not generally, explains the assertion that God made man in His own image, after His own likeness, with reference to His powers of reason, conscience and will, and His rule over the creatures which is based on these powers. But the passages already quoted show that he also included in the image of God true holiness, or the moral image of God. In this passage he clearly combines both ideas.

Accordingly, of His will he says,

"that it was constituted without sin, and that no passion resisted it, and that it had such power that the decision of perseverance was properly left to such great goodness and such great facility of holy living" (De Cor. et Gr. p. 11).

In another place he says that

"by free will, which then had its powers uncorrupted, they obeyed the law, not only with no impossibility, but even with no difficulty," and "that man had so very free a will, that he obeyed the law of God with great energy of mind" (Op. Imp. VI. p. 8, and IV. p. 14).

Yet, with all this, as man was mutable, and but a limited creature, it was not safe to leave him entirely to himself. God only, the infinite Creator, is above all temptation and all danger of falling. Man, therefore, left to himself, could not always extricate himself from danger, nor insure his own perseverance in good. Hence, it was necessary that God should confer on him an additional divine influence, by way of aid and support; and, accordingly, He bestowed the requisite aid. By this aid, perseverance in good was put entirely within the power of man, and yet still he was not forced to persevere, nor was his free will coerced. Even this aid he could abandon. After describing the nature of this additional aid, he says:

> "It was, therefore, in his power to remain, if he would, because the aid was not wanting by which he could, and without which he could not, perseveringly retain the good which he would. But, because he refused to persevere, truly it was his fault, whose merit it would have been if he had chosen to persevere, as did the holy angels, who, whilst others fell by free will, stood by the same free will, and deserved to receive the due reward of this permanence in good,—that is, so great a fulness of blessedness as is involved in a certain assurance that they shall never fall" (De. Cor. et Gr. p. 11).

We can now decide how high Augustine carried his ideas of the demands of honor and right, by considering whether he regarded this superadded influence as a matter of grace or of debt. Probably those who have not particularly examined the matter will be surprised to hear that he regarded even this aid as a matter of debt, and not of grace. His words are very explicit:

> "If this aid had been wanting either to an angel or to men, when they were first created, their fall would have involved no guilt, since their nature was not made such that without divine aid they could insure their own perseverance in good, even if they would, and the aid was wanting without which they could not insure perseverance."

Augustine says this, as Neander well remarks, on the ground that

> "God is the absolute spirit, without whose fellowship, without whose support and assistance, no creaturely spirit, whether angel or man, can persevere in goodness, in the sound and healthy development of his essential being, which is akin to the divine" (Neander, II, p. 604).

Therefore, Augustine boldly and decidedly takes the ground that if the divine aid which puts such perseverance in good fully into the power of every new-created mind is wanting, then no guilt is involved in the fall of such a mind.

It is deeply interesting and affecting to read such statements as these from the great father of what are considered the stern doctrines of Calvinism. Certainly such sentiments find a response in every generous and honorable mind.

Our moral intuitions declare them to be true. They place in a most striking light the obligations of the great Creator to every new-created mind of men or angels.

And now I do not hesitate to ask, Have any of my statements of the principles of honor and right ever risen higher than this?

By the promulgation of such views, Augustine conferred an unspeakable benefit on the Christian world. He elevated their ideas of the nature and possibilities of free agency, and erected a standard by which to judge fairly of existing facts in the history of man. It rendered possible and enforced more deep and thorough views of human depravity; for, surely, no man can pretend that men as they come into this world develop themselves according to the law of new-created minds, as laid down by Augustine.

The actual influence, too, of these views, has been great. We find a constant reference to them in Anselm and other great thinkers of profound Christian experience during the middle ages. They were recognized and reproduced by the Reformers. They have given form to the language of the Westminster standards. The original righteousness of the new-created man, the fact that he was left to the freedom of his own will, and that his sin was his own free, unforced, and therefore criminal act,—all these are purely Augustinian conceptions, reproduced in almost his own terms, after a lapse of ages.

With such a standard of original righteousness, and with such an experience as Augustine had of the deep depravity of his own heart, the disorder of his passions and appetites, and the moral impotence of his own will,—knowing, too, what he did, by the increasing restoration of his own powers to their normal state, of the original relations of the human mind to God,—can it be wondered at that he took deep views of the depravity of men as they now are? His doctrine is what we should have anticipated from these facts,—that men enter this world with deranged constitutions and disorganized powers of soul and body, their intellectual powers darkened by sin and blind to the true beauty of God and spiritual things, their wills in a state of moral impotence as to that which is holy and good, their propensities, passions and affections, deeply corrupt. Such was man, in his view, as an individual; and, being such, he is also subjected to the power of depraved human society, and of evil spirits.

In these deep views of Augustine, too, we recognize a fountain-head of thought and doctrine for the profound thinkers and experienced Christians of all following ages.

But how could Augustine hold such views consistently with his doctrines of equity and of honor?

In answering this inquiry, we shall see that, although Augustine stood on the verge of truth, and even reached it in the form of his words, yet he failed, through adverse influences which he had not surmounted, to reach it in fact; and, therefore, left the great conflict of the moving powers of Christianity, more fully developed than ever before, to agitate and divide all coming ages.

Chapter VI: Augustine's Theory Of Reconciliation

I HAVE said that Augustine in his theory of reconciliation stood on the verge of truth, and that he even reached it in the form of his words. Let us proceed to consider the development of his theory.

His whole system turned upon the position that all the claims of all men on God, as new-created beings, had been already forfeited, even before they were born. So far, then, Augustine coincided with the theory of preexistence. He escaped from the pressure of his own principles by the great idea of *a forfeiture previous to birth*.

Did Augustine, then, believe in the proper preexistence of men; and that they had sinned each separately, and in his own proper person, before their birth into this world?

We answer *no*. But, nevertheless, he tried, by a different kind of preexistence, to account for and to justify such appalling results as occur in this world. He supposed and believed that all men so preexisted in Adam that they could and did act in his act, and forfeit together all of their rights, in that great and original forfeiture of Adam.

This is, indeed, a kind of preexistence that is available only through the imagination, and not through the reason,—yet it gave to much of his language the form of truth. He spoke of men as if they had preexisted, enjoyed their rights and forfeited them: and this language reacted through his imagination on his feelings, and gave him relief. By the aid of this fiction of the imagination, when men were born into the world he did not look on them as properly new-created beings, or as having the rights of new-created beings, but as beings who were created six thousand years before they were born, and who, at the time of their creation, received from God all the rights of new-created beings; and, soon after, freely and wickedly forfeited them, and so came at that time under his just judgment and condemnation, and have been born under them ever since.

God, he taught, gave to the whole human race a good original constitution, good powers, free will and divine aid, in Adam. But in him they abandoned this aid. This is what Augustine means by the statement,

> "Which aid if man had not forsaken by free will, he would
> always have been good; but he forsook it, and was forsaken.
> For the aid was such that he could forsake it when he chose,
> and in it he could persevere if he chose. … For he had
> power even to persevere, if he would; but that he refused
> proceeded (*descendit*) from free will, which then was so free
> that it could choose both right and wrong. But, now, in the
> case of those to whom this aid is wanting, it is the punish-
> ment of sin; and in the case of those to whom it is given, it
> is given by grace, and not of debt" (De Cor. et Gr. p. 11).

Man, in all these passages, means not merely Adam, but *the race*. Let it be also considered that the fact that men have not now the origi- nal aid, is the penalty of their original forfeiture.

Once more I would call particular attention to the fact that Au- gustine, in his own peculiar way, reached, at least ideally, a theory of preexistence, upon which, after all, the depth and power of his system depended. It enabled him at least verbally to conceive and to speak of every man, as he is born into this world, as a being already fallen by his own act, and who by his sin had forfeited all claims to his original rights as a new-created being, and who had thus fallen under the prin- ciples of just sovereignty.

It is also worthy of special notice that Augustine ascribed to the original free will of man such self-determining power as to exempt it entirely from the decree of predestination. He did not deny, on gen- eral grounds, such freedom of the will. He did not, as has often been alleged, subject it to a fatal necessity on universal principles. He did it merely in the case of fallen *man*. In Adam all men were free, and en- joyed in full perfection the self-determining power of the will. No di- vine purpose interposed to control its use. They were left to the freedom of their own will. That freedom they abused and fell, and in this state the principles of predestination first reached them. Thus, pre- destination did not cause their fall. In Adam, on the other hand, they had perfect free will, and all needed divine aid. Therefore, that first and universal fall was not predestined. It was the result of mere free will; and was, therefore, without excuse. Thus, in words at least, and in appearance, did Augustine reach a theory of preexistence, and by it maintain his principles of honor and right, and vindicate the ways of God to man. Stated in his own words, his theory is,

> "Because by free will he forsook God, he experienced the just judgment of God, that he should be condemned with his whole race; for, since they all were, as yet, existing in him, they also had sinned in him. For, as many of this race as are set free by the grace of God are freed from that condemnation by which they are thus held bound. Whence, also, if no one had been liberated, no one could justly blame the judgment of God."

On these views Neander remarks (Vol. II, p. 265):

> "In this way he could still hold fast at one point to the holiness and justice of God, and to the free guilt of man: could remove the origin of evil from God, and push it back to the originally present, free, self-determining power of man. And, by his supposition of the necessary and incomprehensible connection between the first man and the entire race, the act of the first man may be considered as the proper act of every man; and so, on this ground, the loss of the original freedom is a loss for which all are at fault."

There is not, in the whole history of the human mind, an intellectual phenomenon more remarkable, and in some aspects more sublime, than this.

It is remarkable from the nature of the doctrine propounded,—a doctrine which one would suppose, *a priori,* that no one could ever have believed. It is sublime from the extent and magnitude of the power which it in fact exerted after it had been by Augustine established as an article of belief.

In its logical bearings, of course, it was a wide-reaching theory. And Augustine was not without serious difficulties in some questions of detail in its application. But he was not a man to shrink from the fair results of his own principles. Having adopted the theory and caused it to triumph, he carried it out consistently to all its consequences.

The forfeiture which he alleged he never treated as anything verbal. He regarded it as an absolute and fixed reality. So real was it, that even unconscious infants, who did not gain remission by baptism, were, for it alone, consigned at least to the penalty of endless loss of heaven. Not only did Augustine inflexibly teach this doctrine, but he caused it to be for ages the doctrine at least of the Western church.

Here, now, we have a mountain-summit of thought, from which we can survey this whole great conflict, both in preceding and in succeeding ages. We have, also, a standard of comparison, with which we may compare the various theories of preceding and of subsequent writers. Let us look at Augustine's position.

If the mode of forfeiture which he alleged, and upon which his whole defense of God turned, had been possible and real, then there would have been a place for the element of justice in his system. But, as there was no real preexistence and no real action, it was not possible, and of course was not real; and therefore his whole system was, in reality, devoid of justice. He admitted and insisted upon the very highest standard of judgment, when setting forth the principles of honor and right by which the conduct of God towards new-created minds should be judged; and then, in fact, resorted to a mere verbal evasion of them, by a shadowy and unreal theory of the preexistence and action of the millions of the human race in Adam, thousands of years before they were born.

Yet, shadowy and baseless as is this theory, upon it for centuries the doctrine of the Western church as to original sin, and also all the doctrines which grow out of it, were made to rest.[17]

---

17 Kindly allow me to suggest that Beecher, and many others, do not have an adequate understanding of the Trinity and its application to reality. In the spirit of his age, he wants to discount all mystery, and therefore throws out the proverbial baby with the bathwater. I contend that the doctrine of the Trinity as proposed by Cornelius Van Til, R.J. Rushdoony (in his book *The One and the Many: Studies in the Philosophy of Order and Ultimacy,* Ross House Books; 2nd edition, 2007), James Jordan, Ralph Smith, and myself, may provide a better candidate for the solution to this problem than individual preexistence. There is a sense in which the doctrine of the Trinity provides for an influence upon individuals that is similar to that of preexistence, in that the Trinity provides the context for the existence of the individual, and context has an effect—Ed.

Chapter VII: Response Of The Human Mind To The Theory Of Augustine

IT is often assumed that Augustine developed a doctrine of original sin in which deep thinkers and men of a profound Christian consciousness have agreed with him, in every subsequent age. This Prof. Shedd and others assume; and, to a certain extent, it is true. In the idea of a forfeiture before birth they have agreed with him, and also in the idea that the depravity which precedes action in this life is the result of that forfeiture.

But, as to the mode of explaining the forfeiture itself, which, after all, is the most essential point, the theory of Augustine has not proved satisfactory to the human mind. Indeed, as will soon appear, he experienced great trouble from it himself. One obvious and striking proof that it is not fitted to satisfy even the most orthodox portions of the church, is found in the fact that it has been definitely renounced in this country by the leaders of the great body of Old School Calvinists,—I mean the Princeton divines. Instead of it they have introduced another and a different theory, the nature and validity of which I have already considered. They do not differ from Augustine as to the fact of forfeiture; but as to the mode of it, which is, after all, the great question, they do differ from him to the extent of utter and absolute opposition. Yet they assert that the doctrine taught by them is the true doctrine of the Reformers. Again, Prof. Shedd in his theory differs from them both, and is opposed to them both. Still further, President Edwards in his theory differs from them all, and is opposed to them all. Once more, many of the scholastic divines, and of the Reformers, have advanced another theory, different from all the preceding, and opposed to them all. And, finally, Haldane rejects all existing theories as unsatisfactory and injurious, and declares that the only safe course is to rest on the unexplained assertions of the Word of God. Such, then, has been the response of the human mind to the theory of Augustine, and that, too, after centuries of earnest and profound discussion. And what is the fair import of all this? Is it not that the problem that they have undertaken to solve involves conditions that render it an absurd and impossible problem? What is the problem? It is to show how the human race could have forfeited their rights as new-created minds before they enter this world, without having existed and acted in their own persons before they enter this world. This problem is as if all the algebraic skill of ages were required to be expended on the equation $x^2 + x = -7$ as given by inspiration. It is not likely that they would ever reach any satisfactory results; for the equation is absurd and impossible. Nor would it be any better to say that we must receive it as a profound mystery; for it is within the reach of the human mind, and we can see that it is absurd and impossible.

But, if we may trust the intuitions and unambiguous testimony of all ages, the rights of new-created minds are the clearest and the most momentous realities in the universe of God. And is it to be supposed that such rights can be forfeited at all before the existence of the mind, by the action of which a forfeiture can be made? Is not the whole theory of human rights of every kind a mere mockery, if the great foundation rights can be undermined and evacuated by an alleged forfeiture before existence?

Calvin expressly concedes that nothing is more remote from common sense than that on account of the offense of one man all should be made guilty, and so the sin of one become the sin of all.

> "There being nothing more remote from common apprehension, than that the fault of one should render all guilty, and so become a common sin" (*Institutes* II 1, 5).

The language of Pascal, the devoted and profound Pascal, is even stronger than this: "Undoubtedly," he says,

> "nothing appears so revolting to our reason as to say that the transgression of the first man imparted guilt to those who, from their extreme distance from the source of evil, seem incapable of such a participation. This transmission seems to us not only impossible, but unjust" (*Thoughts*, Part II. ch. 5, § 4).

From such astounding results Pascal found no mode of escape but to discredit the decisions alike of our intellectual and moral intuitions as unworthy of credit, because they are opposed to what he deemed a revealed fact.

Such is a compendious view of the responses of the human mind to the theory of Augustine, in view of every solution that has yet been devised for explaining how a new-created being can come into existence under a forfeiture of its original and inherent rights by an act which it never performed, and which took place ages before it was created. I can say of this nothing stronger than Pascal has said. *Nothing* appears so revolting to our reason. It seems to us not only *impossible*, but *unjust*. And, in view of the action on the human mind of this theory for ages, is there not the best possible reason to believe that it is in fixed and sober reality impossible and unjust? Is the truth wont to act on the human mind as this theory has done? Has it not been tried long enough to disclose its true merits, if it has any? Is it desirable any longer to attempt to base the redemption of the church, and God's eternal glory, on a theory that seems to the purest, holiest, humblest minds, impossible and unjust? Is it safe for the human mind any longer to pursue such a course? Is there no danger of a reaction into universal skepticism, if the most absolute of our intellectual and moral intuitions are thus contemned and trodden under foot as worthless and invalid?

I desire, however, at this point once more to call attention to the fact that this reasoning does not at all affect the great doctrine that men enter this world under a forfeiture, and with innate depravity. This, which is the real element of strength in the system of Augustine, and which has given it all its power, is neither impossible nor absurd. By supposing such a real and intelligible preexistence as I have set forth, all can see that it is both possible and just.

My argument is directed simply against an absurd and impossible theory as to a real and important fact, and not against the fact itself. I should not deem it necessary to say more, did I not know what is the mournful effect upon the human mind of being trained for ages to disregard the most sacred and fundamental intellectual and moral intuitions, under the plea of faith and mystery. The mind seems to be paralyzed and stunned, as if it had been smitten down by a blow, and cannot again, in that particular, react and rally, and recover the use of its powers. Such an effect has been extensively produced on the human mind, for ages, by this result of the discussion under Augustine; for, when the plea of any great moral or intellectual intuitions has been once heard, and, after long, earnest and full debate, rejected, and the course of thought has afterwards rolled on in disregard of them for subsequent centuries under the guidance of ecclesiastical authority, and of the original arguments, in one deep channel, it becomes almost impossible to restore the human mind to the vantage-ground on which it stood when the original conflict began. This effect of the Augustinian debates and decisions was, therefore, like a Waterloo defeat to certain fundamental principles of reason, honor and right; a defeat by which the whole course of events has been changed in every subsequent age, to the present day. Then the great battle for those principles was lost; and never since then have they been able to rally and reunite their scattered forces, and once more to bring them up to the encounter.

I do not mean by this—as is apparent from my previous remarks—that the existence and the just authority of these principles in other important forms was denied. I have clearly evinced that such was not the fact. I do not mean that the results to which Pelagius, Celestius and Julian came were true. In my judgment, they were not. I do not mean that the fundamental facts as to the depravity of man for which Augustine contended were not true. In my judgment, they were. What I mean is, that these true facts were then for the first time fully and authoritatively established upon a theory of forfeiture which was, in the words of Pascal, both impossible and unjust; and that ever since, the human mind has been degraded and crushed beneath the impossible task of vindicating and defending that theory, and has even been urged to the mournful and lamentable extreme of basing the redemption of God's own church and the whole glory of his kingdom upon that false and ruinous foundation, which cannot logically hold it up for one moment from an abyss of infamy and just abhorrence. The human mind cannot be held back from abhorring such a theory, except by the most unnatural violence to its divinely-inspired convictions of honor and of right.

It will be observed that, in the preceding general view of the operation of the theory of Augustine on the mind, I have made some assertions of the truth of which I have not as yet given any formal proof. I have done this deliberately. I desired to arrest attention, and to produce a call for proof. And, since I suppose that call now to be made, I intend to show the truth of the facts asserted concerning the Princeton divines, Prof. Shedd, Edwards, the Reformers, Haldane and others, and thus to prove that the action of the theory of Augustine on the human mind has in all ages been such that we ought to regard it as being in reality what it appeared to be to Pascal—impossible and unjust.

By the theory of Augustine, I mean the theory *that men enter this world under a forfeiture of their rights, without having actually preexisted and sinned, each in his own separate person*. This *is* the general and comprehensive theory. Under it are comprehended all the modes in which different men have attempted to solve a problem that is inherently impossible and absurd.

CHAPTER VIII: DIFFERENT MODES OF SOLUTION

LET us, then, consider, in order, the various solutions of the problem how men can enter this world under a forfeiture of all their rights, if they have not preexisted and sinned, each in his own proper person. We come, then, first, to the solution of Augustine, that all men did exist in Adam, so that they sinned in him in reality, though not in their own separate persons. Augustine, in his *Retractions*, expresses it thus: "Infants belong to the human nature, and are guilty of original sin, because human nature sinned in our first parents." In proof of this, he refers to the Vulgate translation of Rom. 5:12, "*In quo omnes peccaverunt*" (*in whom all sinned*). Augustine, therefore, held to a mysterious unity of all men in Adam, such that in reality they all, as included in him in a common nature, sinned together with him, and thus incurred the forfeiture under which they are born.

Now, that this solution acts on the human mind as if it were false and absurd, is obvious from the fact that the Princeton divines, the leaders of orthodoxy among the old Calvinists, have formally rejected it as such, and introduced another solution in its place. Moreover, they defend this new theory as the true doctrine of the Reformers. In this solution, it is still true that men are spoken of as sinning in Adam and falling with him. But, as Prof. Hodge distinctly informs us, this

> "does not include the idea of a mysterious identity of Adam and his race, nor that of a transfer of the moral turpitude of his sin to his descendants. It does not teach that his offense was personally or properly the sin of all men, or that his act was in any mysterious sense the act of his posterity."

So, also, we are told in the Princeton Review:

"We deny that this doctrine (imputation) involves any mysterious union with Adam, any confusion of our identity
with his, so that his act was personally and properly our act;
and, secondly, that the moral turpitude of that sin was transferred from him to us,—we deny the possibility of any such
transfer" (*Princeton Essays*, I. p. 136).

Indeed, after all the labors of Augustine to defend his solution,
they call in question even the fact that he and his followers ever held to
any such a unity of Adam and his race as we have stated, a union such
as made his sin theirs, truly and properly. They think it incredible that
Augustine ever taught such an absurdity. They admit, however, that
Doderlein,[18] Knapp,[19] and Bretschneider,[20] all assert it; and they might
have added Neander and Wiggers, and, indeed, all others, so far as I
know, who have ever thoroughly investigated the point.

But we need not refer to authority on such a point. The unequivocal testimony of Augustine himself puts it beyond all question. It appears that Jerome[21] had taken and begun to advocate the position that
the souls of all men are from time to time newly created by God, as
fast as they are needed to animate their bodies. Now, this is, at this
time, the general faith of the church, and yet is not looked upon by the
Princeton divines as inconsistent with their view of the guilt of man

---

18 Johann Christoph Döderlein or Doederlein (1745-1792), a German theologian and
   professor of theology at Jena from 1782. He was celebrated for the influence he exerted in guiding the transition from strict orthodoxy to a freer theology.

19 Georg Christian Knapp (1753-1825) was a German Protestant theologian and a
   prominent member of the Pietist movement who represented Biblical Supranatural-
   ism.

20 Karl Gottlieb Bretschneider (1776-1848) was a German scholar and theologian. In
   1820 he published his treatise on the gospel of John, entitled *Probabilia de evangelii et
   epistolarum Ioannis Apostoli indole et origine eruditorum*, where he discussed various
   arguments against Johannine authorship. He then astonished people by announcing
   in the preface to the second edition of his *Dogmatik* in 1822, that he had never
   doubted the authenticity of the gospel, but had published his *Probabilia* only to draw
   attention to the subject, and to call forth a more complete defense of its genuineness.

21 Saint Jerome (347-420) is recognized by the Catholic Church as a saint and Doctor
   of the Church, and the author of the *Vulgate*, which is still an important text in
   Catholicism. He is also recognized as a saint by the Eastern Orthodox Church,
   where he is known as St. Jerome of Stridonium or Blessed Jerome. Practically all of
   Jerome's work in the field of dogma have a polemic character, and are directed
   against assailants of the orthodox doctrines. He is the second most voluminous
   writer (after St. Augustine) in ancient Latin Christianity.

for Adam's sin. Had Augustine held such views as the Princeton divines now set forth, it would have caused him no trouble, just as it
causes them no trouble. Far otherwise was the fact. Augustine regarded it as breaking up that unity of Adam and his race on which his
theory of forfeiture rested. On this assumption, all men were not in
Adam when he sinned. But, if so, he could not conceive how the guilt
of Adam's sin could rest on them, since they could have had nothing
to do with it. How, then, he asks, can they be justly condemned for it?
Does not this imply that he held to a real though mysterious unity of
Adam and all his posterity in his sin? But Augustine shall speak for
himself. Hearing of the views of Jerome, and fearing to arouse him to
controversy by open opposition, in a letter to him he puts himself in
the position of a learner, and seeks to arrest the course of his excitable
and imperious friend by gentle means. Jerome did not see fit, for reasons best known to himself, to answer the inquiries of Augustine.
Hereupon Augustine laid by his letter till after the death of Jerome,
and then made it public. A very instructive letter it is. It clearly shows
that even Augustine could not find undisturbed repose in his own
views. But let us listen to him, as he thus addresses Jerome:

> "Teach me, therefore, I entreat you, what I shall teach, teach
> what I shall hold, and tell me, if souls are created one by one
> for those who are born, when do they sin in the little ones
> so that they need remission of sins in baptism, as sinning in
> Adam, from whom the sinful body is propagated? Or, if
> they do not sin, by what justice of the Creator are they so
> held responsible for the sin of another, when they are intro-
> duced into bodies propagated from him, that they are con-
> demned, if the church does not relieve them by baptism,
> although they have no power to decide whether they shall
> be baptized or not? How can so many thousands of souls,
> which leave the bodies of unbaptized infants, be with any
> equity condemned, if they were newly created, and intro-
> duced into these bodies for no previous sin of their own,
> but by the mere will of Him who created them to animate
> these bodies, and foreknew that each of them, for no fault of
> his own, would die unbaptized? Since, then, we cannot say
> that God either makes souls sinful by compulsion, or pun-
> ishes them when innocent, and yet are obliged to confess
> that the souls of the little ones are condemned if they die

unbaptized, I beseech you, tell me how can this opinion be defended, by which it is believed that souls are not all derived from that one first man, but are newly created for each particular body, as his was for his body?" (Ep. ad Hier.).

Here he does not, indeed, openly avow the generation of souls; nay, he elsewhere says that he would be glad, if he could, to believe in their creation. But he saw no way of removing the objection stated by him. Nor is there any. And, in fact, there is little reason to doubt that he really believed in the generation of souls. Does not the fact that he started such a difficulty, and could not solve it, prove, to a demonstration, that he held to a real unity of all men in Adam as the ground of their sinning in him and falling with him? But this is but a small part of the evidence that exists to prove this point. We do not believe that anyone, after a careful examination of Augustine, will call it in question. Nevertheless, now, the Princeton divines earnestly renounce this theory as absurd, and substitute another in its place. But this only the more clearly shows that the ground on which Augustine fought his great battle, and which is repudiated by them, is really untenable and defenseless.

In place of this, however, they still defend, in another form, as we have seen, the idea of a forfeiture in Adam of all the rights of new-created beings. To effect this, they introduce the idea of federal headship and representation, and teach that, though we did not exist, and, of course, did not act, when Adam sinned, yet that, in virtue of the divinely established representative headship of Adam, God regarded his act as our act, and withdrew from each individual of the race those divine influences which are essential to his proper moral development; in consequence of which, his nature inevitably becomes corrupt, and develops nothing but actual sin.

The validity of this solution I need not now consider, as it has already been fully discussed; and to that discussion I refer.

But, although the Princeton divines set forth such views as those of the Reformers, there is clear evidence that, to say the least, many of them held to still another and opposite solution of the great problem of forfeiture. They held that, by imputation, the sin and guilt of Adam were made to be the real sin and guilt of all his posterity; not, indeed, their personal sin and guilt, but still their real sin and guilt. If this implies that which the Princeton divines declare to be absurd and impossible,—that is, a real transfer of sin and moral turpitude from Adam to all his posterity,—it is, nevertheless, a doctrine of some of the Reformers, and of some of the Schoolmen before them. Indeed, it is but a natural result of the decision of the church and of most of the Schoolmen in favor of Jerome's view, that the souls of all men are created by God, and not derived from their parents, and thus from Adam. In this they forsook Augustine, who plainly held that the sin of Adam was really the sin of all his posterity, because all his posterity were really in him when he sinned. But they were still desirous of agreeing with Augustine in the fact that Adam's sin was the real sin of the race. Therefore, having given up Augustine's basis of the doctrine,—that is, the derivation of souls from Adam,—they would be naturally led to seek out a new basis. This they found in a system of federal headship and representation, in which, by God's constitution, ordinance or decree, the sin of Adam should still be made the real sin of his posterity. Hence Whitby[22] concedes to Bishop Davenant[23] that, so far as the authority of certain of the scholastic divines is concerned, they do teach "that, by the decree of God, Adam sustained the person of all mankind; and that, by the same decree (or ordinance), his posterity are guilty of his first

---

22 Daniel Whitby (1638-1726) was a controversial English theologian and biblical commentator. An Arminian priest in the Church of England, Whitby was known as strongly anti-Calvinistic and later gave evidence of strong Arian and Unitarian tendencies. He was engaged in refuting the Calvinistic positions of Jonathan Edwards. In 1710 he wrote his *Discourse on the Five Points* which eventually drew Calvinist responses from English Baptist John Gill in his *The Cause of God and Truth* (1735) and American Congregationalist Jonathan Edwards in his *Freedom of the Will* (1754).

23 John Davenant (1572-1641) was an English academic and bishop of Salisbury from 1621. When French Amyraldians attempted to garner support, citing the views of members of the British delegation to the Synod of Dort, Davenant offered a reply by way of clarification in his tract, "On the controversy among the French divines," in which he appears to make a distinction between his own views and those of the Amyraldians. On the topic of predestination, he engaged in controversy with the Arminian Anglican Samuel Hoard. In an undated letter to Samuel Ward he endorsed the idea that all baptized infants receive the remission of the guilt of original sin in baptism and that this constitutes their infant baptismal regeneration, justification, sanctification, and adoption. In his view, this infant baptismal remission, which involves the objective status of the infant apart from subjective operations of grace, does not suffice for justification if the child does not later come to faith. Nonetheless, he goes on to argue that this poses no contradiction to the doctrine of the perseverance of the saints as articulated by Dort, since the "perseverance" intended there presupposes subjective grace.

sin, but not of his other sins,"— but he attaches no weight to their authority. This view of the origin of the theory of the federal headship of Adam is confirmed by Knapp, who says that

> "this theory was invented by some Schoolmen, and has been adopted by many in the Roman Catholic and Protestant churches since the sixteenth century."

That by Owen,[24] Turretin, the Westminster divines and others, the sin of Adam was regarded as being really the sin of his posterity, though not personally, is proved at great length and beyond dispute in an article in the *Christian Spectator* for September, 1831, in answer to the *Princeton Review*,—an article to which no reply was ever made, and to which I refer for a more full view of this aspect of the case. It appears, then, that of the doctrine of the federal headship of Adam there are two forms: the more ancient one, that of those who hold that Adam's sin by imputation becomes ours truly, so that, though it is not our personal sin, it is yet our real sin, for which we are truly guilty; the other and more modern one, that of those who, with the Princeton divines, assert that God merely regards and treats it as our sin, though in fact it is not, and we are entirely innocent in our own persons, and free from all the moral turpitude of the sin.

It hence appears that, in making out the result aimed at,—that is, a forfeiture in Adam by the race of all the original rights of new-created minds,—very different courses have been taken. First, a forfeiture by a real existence and action of the race in Adam; then a forfeiture by the representative action of Adam, which by imputation becomes really their sin; then a forfeiture by the same representative action, regarded and treated as their sin, though in fact it is not.

The view of Prof. Shedd differs from either of these. He holds, with Coleridge, that there is no sin, or sinful nature, that is anterior to a free, self-determined act of the will. The sinful nature that he asserts to exist in man is merely such an act of the will; not, indeed, a mere specific volition, but that main and controlling determination that carries with it all the powers and energies of a man, and devotes them to some object as the ultimate end of living. He speaks of the sinful nature of man as "that central self-determination, that great main ten-

---

24 John Owen (1616-1683) was an English Nonconformist (Congregational) church leader, theologian, and academic administrator at the University of Oxford.

dency of the will to self and sin as an ultimate end." This, of course, must be a personal act, of which every man is the author. This self-determination of the will to sense and sin he regards as the fall of every-man's will. Of it he says

> "that the fall of the will unquestionably occurs back of con-sciousness, and in a region beyond the reach of it. Certainly, no one of the posterity of Adam was ever conscious of that act whereby his will fell from God."

Further, he holds that this region beyond the reach of conscious-ness was in Adam.

> "All men were, in some sense, co-agent in Adam; otherwise they could not have fallen with him."

This view is not the view of Augustine, for he held that the com-mon nature of all men sinned, and not that all men sinned together, each as an individual, and by a self-determining act of his own will. Prof. Shedd concedes that such unconscious action in Adam is a mys-tery. He also ascribes his theory to the Westminster divines. In this he is directly at war with the Princeton divines; for they assert that there was no such mysterious action of all men in Adam, and that the Re-formers and Westminster divines did not believe that there was.

The theory of Edwards is different from all these. I shall more fully state it hereafter. It is enough now to say that he held that God estab-lished a personal identity between Adam and all his posterity with re-spect to Adam's first sin, but not with respect to any other. Thus, the first sin of Adam is truly and properly the sin of every man, since with reference to that sin each is the same person with Adam. I need not undertake to prove that this view differs from and opposes all the rest. The thing speaks for itself. Still, the language used by those who hold either of these theories is in so many particulars the same with that of those who hold the others, that it is sometimes hard to tell on which of these various grounds any writer stands, unless he fully defines and carries out his system.

All of these solutions seem to have been given by different indi-viduals since the Reformation. Sometimes writers use the language which belongs to two of them, or even to all of them, in a confused manner. This is not wonderful, for the mind of man has been so made by God that it cannot see any rational way in which the result which they aim at in common can be gained,—that is, the alleged forfeiture of the original rights of the whole human race by the act of one man. Therefore, any solution designed to explain such a result naturally tends to confuse the human mind, and to destroy its powers of discrimination.

The more modern solutions, I think, have no advantage over that of Augustine. On the other hand, so far as he approximated to the idea of preexistence, there was at least an appearance of depth and reality in his theory, which is entirely wanting in the more modern views.

Haldane, however,—a most eminent and devoted Christian, and honored by God as the instrument of a great revival of religion on the European continent,—at last takes the ground that the sin of Adam is as truly ours as it was Adam's. He also holds that it is not made ours by imputation, but is imputed to us because it is ours. Still, he refuses to enter into any explanation. Prof. Stuart had argued against imputation, as implying that God regards a sin as the sin of all men which is not theirs really and in fact. In reply to this, he says that

> "Adam's sin is imputed to his posterity because it is their sin in reality, though we may not be able to see the way in which it is so. Indeed, we should not pretend to explain this, because it is to be believed on the foundation of divine testimony, and not on human speculation, or on our ability to account for it." "In opposition to all such infidel reasonings, it is becoming in the believer to say, I fully acknowledge, and I humbly confess, on the testimony of my God, that I am guilty of Adam's sin." "The difficulty that some persons feel on this subject arises from the supposition that, though the sin of the first man is charged on his posterity, yet it is not theirs. But the Scriptures hold it forth as ours in as true a sense as it was Adam's." "Can God impute to any man anything that is not true? If Adam's sin is not ours as truly as it was Adam's sin, could God impute it to us? Does God deal with men as sinners while they are not truly such?" "He also maintains that this view is not contrary to reason, though mysterious. A thing may be very disagreeable and far beyond the ken of human penetration, which is not contrary to reason. We are not entitled to pronounce anything con-

trary to reason which does not imply a contradiction. A contradiction cannot be true; but all other things may be true, and, on sufficient evidence, ought to be received as true."

According to this, it may be true that God has lied, or been malevolent; for neither implies a contradiction. But, if it be said in reply, that to do so is contrary to his holy and righteous nature, and morally impossible, I reply the same is true as to any act contrary to those moral principles which God has made the human mind intuitively to perceive as true. Therefore, whatever opposes these is contrary to reason, even though not a contradiction.

Of God's alleged dealings in this case, he says that they are

"not such as to be vindicated or illustrated by human transactions. The union of Adam and his posterity is a divine constitution. The grounds of this constitution are not to be found in any of the justifiable transactions of men; and all attempts to make us submit by convincing us of its propriety, from what we are able to understand upon a comparison with the affairs of men, are only calculated to impose on credulity, and produce unbelief. We receive it because God says it, not because we see it to be just." "Those who have endeavored to vindicate divine justice in accounting Adam's sin to be ours, and to reconcile the mind of man to that procedure, have not only labored in vain, but actually injured the cause they meant to uphold."

Haldane, as usual, regards his views of this matter as those of the Westminster divines and the Reformers. It is plain, however, that he is directly at war on this point with the Princeton divines, who teach that the sin and the moral turpitude of Adam are not, and cannot be, actually and in reality those of his posterity, but are only regarded as such, and that this is the uniform doctrine of the Reformers.

I am not sure that I have gathered up all the modes of solving the great Augustinian problem stated at the outset of this discussion,—that is, to show how men can forfeit their original rights before they are born into this world, as long as a real personal preexistence and real sin are denied. What I have produced, however, is enough to furnish evidence that the problem does, in fact, as Pascal says it seems to do, involve both an impossibility and injustice. Certainly, the human mind never acted under a system of truth as it has acted under the system which demands the solution of such a problem. The mind of Augustine never was at rest under it. His successors have never been at rest, but have fluctuated from view to view; and yet no view has ever been proposed which has not been condemned by as sound orthodox and godly divines as have ever existed. Such, I do not doubt, are the Princeton divines; and yet, even they are logically involved in Haldane's charge of "infidel speculations" for they deny that the sin and guilt of Adam are, or can be, as truly and properly ours as they are Adam's.

After reading and carefully considering multitudes of statements, from Augustine down to this day, I cannot find any time or place in which all orthodox divines—as alleged by Prof. Shedd—stood on one side, and that Augustine's side, except in two particulars,—that is, that all men are born into this world under a forfeiture of their original rights, and with inherent depravity. But, denying, as they have done, a real personal preexistence and sinfulness of all men before birth, they have done nothing after this but multiply unsatisfactory solutions of an absurd and impossible problem.

Before I close this chapter, since so much advantage is taken of the prestige of the name of Augustine, I will give a statement of his theory of our sinning in Adam, by a celebrated advocate of his doctrine. I have stated it as his theory, not that we sinned in him as coexistent and co-agent individuals, with each a self-determining will, according to the theory of Prof. Shedd, but, that in him human nature sinned *as a great totality*, which was afterwards distributed into the individuals of the race. This is clearly the view set forth by Odo or Udardus of Tournay,[25] afterwards Archbishop of Cambray. Being by nature prone to philosophical speculation, he became eminent as a teacher, but was devoid of piety. He was at length recalled from a worldly spirit by the power of a deep conviction of sin, wrought in him by the writings of Augustine, and ever after sincerely devoted himself to the service of God. For the sake of a specimen of the thinking and style of an emi-

---

25 Odo of Cambrai (Odoardus, also Odo of Tournai, 1060–1113), born at Orléans, was
    a Benedictine monk, scholar and bishop. His treatise *De peccato originali* in three
    books, composed between 1095 and 1105, discuss the problem of universals, and of
    genera and species from a realist viewpoint.

nent divine of the middle ages, I will give his views; first in his own
words, and then in a translation. The title of his work is as follows :

> "*Odonis ex Abbate primo Tornacensi Episcopi Camera-censis
> Ecclesise de Peccato Originali libri tres*" (Bib. Vet. Pat., vol.
> xxi. p. 230).

He thus propounds and answers the question to be considered :

> "*Quid distat naturale peccatum et personale?*
>
> "*Dicitur enim duobus modis peccatum personale et nat urale.
> Et naturale est cum quo nascimur, et quod ab Adam trahimus, in
> quo omnes peccavimus. In ipso enim erat ariima mea, specie non
> persona, non individua sed communi natura. Nam omnis hu-
> manae animoe natura communis erat in Adam obnoxia peccato.
> Et ideo omnis humana anima culpabilis est secundum suam nat-
> uram, etsi non secundum suam personam. Ita peccatum quo pec-
> cavimus in Adam, mihi quidam naturale est, in Adam vero
> personale. In Adam gravius, levius in me; nam peccavi in eo non
> qui sum sed quod sum. Peccavi in eo non ego, sed hoc, quod sum
> ego. Peccavi homo, sed non Odo. Peccavi substantia non persona,
> et quia substantia non est nisi in persona, peccatum substantiae
> est etiam personae, sed non personale. Peccatum vero personale
> est, quod facio ego qui sum, non hoc quod sum ; quo pecco Odo,
> non homo; quo pecco persona, non natura; sed quia persona non
> est sine natura, peccatum personae est etiam naturae, sed non
> natu rale*" (p. 233).

Of this peculiar passage I subjoin a translation:

> "How does the sin of nature differ from personal sin?"
>
> Two kinds of sin are spoken of, that of nature and per-
> sonal sin. The sin of nature is that with which we are born,
> and which we derive from Adam, in whom we all sinned.
> For my mind was in him as a part of the whole species, but
> not as a person; not in my individual nature, but in the
> common nature. For the common nature of all human
> minds in Adam was involved in sin. And thus every human
> mind is blamable with respect to its nature, although not
> with respect to its person. Thus the sin by which we sinned

> in Adam is to me a sin of nature,—in Adam a personal sin.
> In Adam it was more criminal, in me less so; for I, who am,
> did not sin in him, but that which I am. I did not sin in him,
> but this essence which I am. I sinned as the *genus man*, not
> as the individual *Odo*. I sinned as a substance, not as a per-
> son; and because my substance does not exist but in a per-
> son, the sin of my substance is the sin of one who is a
> person, but not a personal sin. For a personal sin is one
> which I, who am, commit, but this substance which I am
> does not commit; a sin in which I sin as *Odo*, and not as the
> genus man; in which I sin as a person, and not as a nature;
> but, because there is no person without a nature, the sin of a
> person is also the sin of a nature, but not a natural sin."

If all this is not, by this time, perfectly clear, even to the lowest capacity, certainly it is not for the want of suficient pains on the part of
the distinguished archbishop. The difficulty must rather lie in making
that intelligible to the human mind which is, in the nature of things,
absurd and impossible. Yet this elaborate view of the archbishop is
merely an expansion of the definite statements of Augustine, upon
whose ground so many eminent men among us are emulously declaring themselves determined to stand.

In addition to the passage from the *Retractions of Augustine* already
quoted, in which he asserts that it was human nature which sinned in
our first parents, the following statements, as quoted by Wiggers, are
very express:

> "In that one all have sinned, as all died in him. For those
> who were to be many in themselves out of him, were then
> one in him. That sin, therefore, would be his only, if no one
> had proceeded from him. But now no one is free from his
> fault in whom was the common nature" (Ep. 186, c. 6). "In
> Adam all have sinned, as all were that one man" (De Pec.,
> Mer. I. 10). "Those are not condemned who have not
> sinned, since that sin has passed from one to all, in which
> we all have sinned in common previously to the personal
> sins of each one as an individual" (Ep. 194, c. 6).

The statement of Odo, then, is clearly but an expansion of the
doctrine of Augustine. Moreover, his idea that the sin of nature is in

each individual less criminal than his personal sin is a truly Augustinian idea; for, though Augustine held that even those who died before committing any other sin than that of nature would be punished, still he held that they would be punished more mildly than any others. This is owing, at least in part, to the fact that the immense guilt of the great common sin of nature is not charged to each individual, but only his due proportion of it. For Augustine is careful to inform us that

> "there comes not on individuals what the whole apostate creature has deserved; and no individual endures so much as the whole mass deserves to suffer, but God has arranged all, in measure, weight and number, and suffers no one to endure any evil which he does not deserve" (Op. Imp. n. 87).

In still another form he expresses the same idea of a common sin of that all-embracing nature of man which was in Adam, and was afterward divided up and distributed into individuals, each bearing his share of the common guilt.

> "We were all in that one, since we were all that one who fell into sin by the woman who was made from him before sin. Not as yet was the form created and distributed to us singly in which we were individually to live; but there was that seminal nature from which we were to be propagated. This, by reason of sin having been corrupted, and bound by the bond of death, and brought under just condemnation, no man could be born of man in a different condition" (De Civ. Dei, xin. 14).

Neander, regarding Anselm as coinciding with Odo in his exposition of the doctrine of Augustine, represents him as holding "that as entire human nature was only expressed and contained, as yet, in this first exemplar (Adam), entire humanity, therefore, became corrupt in him, and the corruption passed from him to his posterity." Accordingly, Anselm says: "The whole of human nature was so in Adam that no part of it was without him." Neander adds, "He therefore distinguishes *peccatum naturale* from *peccatum personale*. ... This connection of ideas is exhibited with remarkable distinctness in the work of Odo of Tournay."

It is not uncommon at this day for writers, otherwise of great ability, to overlook the fact which I have stated and now prominently repeat, that men may agree with Augustine in the general idea of a forfeiture and of inherent depravity before action in this world, who yet radically differ from him, and directly oppose him, in his solution of the mode of forfeiture. Nevertheless, I cannot but think that if any man desires to be in reality a profound thinker, he ought to discriminate the things that differ, and not collect together a mass of warring solutions of an impossible problem, and call the self-repellent compound the Augustinian theology; or to attempt to represent men as standing together on one side, who, though in general on one side, are yet, while there, engaged in mortal conflict with each other.

I have stated at least six dissimilar and conflicting solutions of the alleged forfeiture of rights by the human race in Adam. If any man holds either of the five that are opposed to Augustine's, whether his view is true or false, he is certainly not on the ground of Augustine. Finally, all of these solutions cannot be true; but all of them can be, and, in my judgment, are false, as designed to explain and justify what is impossible and unjust.

Chapter IX: Disquiet Of The Human Mind

I HAVE given a general view of the import of the response of the human mind to Augustine's solution of the mode of forfeiture. It has proved so unsatisfactory that the leaders of Old School orthodoxy in this country have not only repudiated it, but even denied that Augustine ever held it.

I have also taken a general view of the principles of the other solutions which have been devised to take its place, and seen that these, too, are unsatisfactory, and mutually destructive of each other.

We are now prepared to hear without surprise that such a state of things has never conducted the Christian church to a haven of rest. Beneath the hard outside shell of these discussions there has ever been the profound abyss of deep emotion in view of the vast and eternal interests involved, and of the sacred principles of equity and honor, and their bearing on the character of God.

Let us now attempt, for a few moments, to look into the interior of this vast world of conflicting thought and deep emotion.

I have already said that the principles of honor and right towards new-created minds, set forth by Augustine, have been ever since fully recognized and affirmed. I have given the testimony of Turretin, Wesley, Watts, and the Princeton divines, to this effect. The Princeton divines also testify that the views of the Reformers were the same. I will add a statement from Pictet[26] to illustrate these remarks. He says,

> "The corruption which we bring from the womb of our mothers is a very great evil, for it is the source of all sins. To permit, then, that this corruption should pass from their fathers to their children is to inflict a punishment.

---

26 Benedict Pictet (1655-1724) was a Swiss Reformed theologian who sought to revive the old orthodox theology, but was unable to prevent the Genevan Company of Pastors from adopting a new formula of subscription in 1706. He was also known as Christian poet, some his hymns being included in French hymnals.

But how is it that God should punish men, if they had not sinned, and if they were not guilty?"

This is an avowal of the great principle that God is bound to give all new-created beings upright moral constitutions and tendencies, if they have not previously forfeited their rights. According to Pictet, this forfeiture was effected by Adam, whose sin God imputed to all his posterity, and considered as their sin, before they had existed or acted. Similar evidence is abundant; but, as no one denies the fact, so far as I know, it is needless to adduce more proof.

All who thus hold to a forfeiture in Adam as a justification of God in bringing men into this world with depraved natures, and strong and controlling propensities to evil, are wont to set forth in the strongest terms the injustice of dealing thus with men on any other ground. Though they regard God as the immediate creator of souls in every generation, yet, by the aid of the theory of imputation, they speak of all men as sinning in Adam. Then, by the aid of the imagination, they conceive of human nature as corrupted in Adam, and thus speak of the human race as not having such natures as God at first gave them, and then declare that it would be impious to regard God as originally giving such natures to His creatures. For example, Wesley says :

> "Highly injurious, indeed, is this supposition to the God of our nature. Did He originally give us such a nature as this? So, like that of a wild ass colt! so stupid, so stubborn, so intractable; so prone to evil; averse to good. Did His hands form and fashion us thus? No wiser or better than men at present are? If I believed this, that men were originally what they are now,—if you could once convince me of this,—I could not go so far as to be a Deist; I must either be a Manichee or an Atheist. I must either believe there was an evil God, or that there was no God at all."

Dr. Watts says:

> "And methinks, when I take a just survey of this world, with all the inhabitants of it, I can look upon it no otherwise than as a grand and magnificent structure in ruins, wherein lie millions of rebels against their Creator under condemnation to misery and death; who are, at the same

time, sick of a mortal distemper, and disordered in their minds even to distraction. Hence proceed those numberless follies and vices which are practiced here; and the righteous anger of an offended God, visible in ten thousand instances."

Again, after a survey of the sinfulness and misery of man in all ages, he proceeds to say:

"If we put together all these scenes of vice and misery, it is evident that creatures lying in such deplorable circumstances are not such as they came out of the hands of their Creator, who is wise, holy and good. His wisdom, which is all harmony and order, would not suffer Him to frame a whole race of beings under such wild and innumerable disorders, moral as well as natural. His holiness would not permit Him to create beings with innate principles of iniquity; nor his goodness, to produce a whole order of creatures in such circumstances of pain, torment and death.

"Could the holy and blessed God originally design and frame a whole world of intelligent creatures in such circumstances, that every one of them coming into being according to the laws of nature, in a long succession of ages, in different climates, of different constitutions and tempers, and in ten thousand thousand different stations and conditions of life,—that every one of them should break the laws of reason, and more or less defile themselves with sin? That every one should offend his Maker,—every one become guilty in his sight? Everyone expose himself to God's displeasure, to pain and misery and mortality, without one single exception? If men were such creatures as God at first made them, would not one man, among so many millions, have made a right use of his reason and conscience, and so have avoided sin and death? Would this have been the universal consequent of their original constitution, as framed by the hand of a wise, holy, merciful God? What can be more absurd to imagine than this? Surely, God made man upright and happy: nor could all these mischiefs have come directly from our Creator's hand."

From what has been said, it is apparent that in the formation of the various theories of forfeiture which have been considered, men have been actuated by the noblest impulses of their nature; they have desired to find a basis on which they might found a reconciliation of God's actual treatment of the human race with the demands of the highest principles of honor and right towards new-created minds.

As we have said, if the forfeiture alleged could be made out by any of their schemes, it would be a relief; but, as it cannot, it is no relief. Of this fact some even of the most eminent of the advocates of such theories seem to have had uncomfortable surmises. Augustine, as we have seen could discover no reason to rest in the doctrine of a forfeiture, except on the assumption that all human souls came from the soul of Adam; but this theory Jerome rejected, and was followed by most of the Schoolmen. These same Schoolmen, however, originated another theory of forfeiture,—that of federal headship,—of which this new theory was a desire to escape the objections of Augustine was clearly the moving cause. But this theory also has failed to give rest even to its most decided advocates.

Dr. Watts, for example, though an earnest and zealous defender of it against Dr. J. Taylor, says: "I am not fond of it. No, I would gladly renounce it because of some great difficulties attending it." The reason for not renouncing it which he assigns is, that, in his view, there are greater difficulties attending every other scheme. He held to the common theory that souls are newly created, and one of his chief difficulties lay in reconciling it with the goodness and justice of God that new-created souls should be placed in bodies in and by which they were sure to be morally corrupted in consequence of the sin of Adam. After laboring for some pages to effect such a reconciliation, he does not seem to be at all confident that he has succeeded; nay, he betrays an inward apprehension that he has not, for he says:

> "I am doubtful whether this solution sets the matter in such a sufficient light as to take away all remaining scruples from a curious and inquisitive mind. I confess it is the most probable hypothesis I can think of, and shall be glad to see this perplexing inquiry more happily answered. But, if the case itself be matter of fact, that souls are defiled and exposed to pain by being united to human bodies so vitiated, we are sure it must be just and equitable, because God has thus or-

dered it, though we should not find out a happier solution
of the difficulties that attend it in this dark and imperfect
state."

His difficulties were the same which were felt by Augustine of old,
and which have never as yet been removed. He could not but feel that
new-created minds, who had nothing to do with Adam's sin, since
they did not exist when he sinned, were hardly dealt with in being
treated as if they had forfeited all their rights as new-created minds by
that act. This is not to be wondered at. It is a difficulty so obvious that
the wonder is that any man can overlook it, or, if he does not, can
think that he has removed it. This difficulty lies on the very face of the
solution of the problem attempted by Turretin (L. 9, Q. 12, § 10). He
holds, with Jerome and the church generally, that God creates souls to
animate bodies, but creates them devoid of original righteousness,

> "of which man had rendered himself unworthy in Adam.
> For God is under no obligation to create minds with origi-
> nal righteousness; nay, he may most justly deprive them of
> such a gift, as a punishment of the sin of Adam."

Here, then, we are told that it is most just for God to punish a
new-created soul, in the very act of its creation, for an act which took
place thousands of years before its creation,—that is, to punish it by
creating it without original righteousness,—although, without this, its
moral development is certainly corrupt and ruinous, so that this deprivation is, in the words of Prof. Hodge, "of all evils the essence and
sum." He proceeds to add

> "that this destitution is blamable on the part of man, because
> it is a destitution of the righteousness that ought to be in
> him; but as it respects God it is not blamable, since it is an
> act of vindictive justice in punishing the first sin."

That is, a new-created mind is punished for a sin which it did not
commit, by being created devoid of righteousness, and yet is criminal
for not having that righteousness the possession of which did not depend upon itself at all, but solely on the creative act of God. Moreover,
God is just in all this, because He is thus punishing Adam's sin, which

the new-created mind did not commit. To complete the result, a mind thus defectively created is then put into a body such that the sympathy of the two inevitably calls into action and develops its depravity. If, now, the moral sense recoils from this as anything but a satisfactory vindication of God's conduct towards the new-created souls of the human race, the fault lies more in the theory from which it springs than in Turretin. He calls it "a most obscure question;" and, to use the words of Dr. Watts, resorted to "the most probable hypothesis he could think of."

But, as Dr. Watts suggested a doubt whether his hypothesis "set the matter in a sufficient light to take away all remaining scruples from a curious and inquisitive mind," so, in fact, it has happened with the hypothesis of Turretin, and all others aiming at the same end. The simple fact is, that the problem of defending such a forfeiture is insoluble, except on the ground of a real preexistence. On that ground it can be defended in perfect accordance with the principles of honor and right, and on no other.

It is not, therefore, to be wondered at that in all ages the theory of a forfeiture of rights in Adam has been unsatisfactory to multitudes, who concur with the great mass of Christian divines in rejecting preexistence.

Nor is it wonderful that finally Haldane should try to find rest by refusing to think at all, and, on the authority of God, as he assumed, declaring that Adam's sin is our sin as really and as truly as it was his, and that this is the end of all dispute.

But, when things come to such a pass, it becomes necessary to be quite sure that God has, in fact, said so, before we rest in the doctrine of Mr. Haldane; and this raises a question of interpretation, which neither he nor any one else can evade. Mr. Haldane, then, as well as the rest, has not been able to conduct even the most pious man to a haven of rest.

Finally, when we consider that this theory of a forfeiture in Adam is made the basis of the redemption of the church, and that to justify it is essential to any sense of the mercy of God, and that yet to Pascal it appeared "impossible and unjust," and to Calvin "the most remote of all things from common sense," and to Prof. Hodge a "profound and awful mystery," and that Dr. Woods is "perplexed and confounded" by it, and that the advocates of it mutually neutralize each other by their contradictory solutions, we ought not to be surprised that in successive ages men have been found who have sought relief by the entire rejection of the theory itself. And yet the results of this rejection have not been such as to furnish the desired relief. It is my next object to consider these results.

CHAPTER X: FIRST RESULT OF DENYING A FORFEITURE BEFORE BIRTH

BUT, when the idea of a forfeiture before birth is rejected on such grounds as have been stated, then but two general courses remain, which we shall consider in order. The first is to declare that men are born such and in such circumstances as the principles of honor and right demand; and, of course, we land at once and directly in Pelagianism as implied in this general statement,—that all men are as well off, both as to constitution and powers, as Adam was before his sin. For God, in making Adam, of course gave him all that was due to a new-created mind, and He gives the same to all men as fast as He creates them. This at once cuts up by the roots all ideas of a fall in Adam; or, indeed, in any other way. It regards all men as well created by God, and by nature in full possession of all the powers which, as a practical matter, are needed perfectly to obey Him.

Let no one be surprised at this statement; for, so long as the opposite view of a fall is defended and justified only on the ground of a forfeiture in Adam, it is plain that so long as the principles of honor and right—as the defenders of that theory have ever promulgated and maintained them—are regarded as true, there is no logical middle ground between a just forfeiture of rights and Pelagianism. We say this on the assumption that it is not for a moment to be supposed that God ever has disregarded, or ever will disregard, in His dealings with new-created minds, their just claims according to the laws of honor and right. What those claims are we have seen. If they have not forfeited them, then, of course, they have them, and are made, as they ought to be, with well-ordered powers, free from sin, and in the image of God.

This general course of reasoning we have already illustrated, and the experience to which it gives rise in the case of Dr. Channing. Substantially the same course of reasoning was pursued by Pelagius and his followers in the fifth century, by the Socinians in the sixteenth, and by Dr. John Taylor and his followers in the eighteenth century. It is true that Pelagius did not see the logical relations of his views to the rest of the system. He still retained and defended the doctrine of the Trinity, and of the incarnation and atonement of Christ; and, in a certain sense, of the influences of the Spirit. But, as Dr. Channing well remarked, these doctrines find a consistent development only in a system based on the doctrine of original depravity. The power of the church system prevented this logical development in the days of Pelagius. But, soon after the opening of the Reformation, the power of that system was so far broken, and consistent and free thought had so much more scope, that the whole system was so modified as better to accord with the fundamental principles of the Pelagian theory of human nature. The same was true in the case of Dr. John Taylor. The doctrine of the Trinity was dropped in each case. Yet, at first, the whole system was not reduced to its natural and consistent level. Socinus still retained the worship of Christ, and persecuted Davides[27] for dissenting from his views. Dr. J. Taylor approximated as near to the Trinity as the Arianism of Dr. S. Clarke would allow. He also did not remove from his doctrine all the language which belonged to the orthodox doctrine of the atonement. It was not until the close of the last and the beginning of the present century that the principles of the Pelagian theory were fully and consistently developed in modern Unitarianism.

No one, we think, who holds to the principles of honor and right, and denies a forfeiture of rights in Adam, or by preexistence, ought to censure this ultimate development of the principles of Pelagianism as illogical or inconsistent. The principles of honor and right to which they have ever appealed have never, so far as we know, been formally denied by any orthodox body. Indeed, the most orthodox have had the highest standard. They have been simply evaded by the plea of a forfeiture in Adam. To this the Pelagians and others have objected that it is irrational, unscriptural, at war with the intuitive perceptions of the human mind, and unjust.

---

27 Transylvania had for a short time (1559-1571) enjoyed full religious liberty under an anti-Trinitarian prince, John Sigismund. The existing ruler, Christopher Bathori, favored the Jesuits; it was now Biandrata's object to limit the Judaic tendencies of the eloquent anti-Trinitarian bishop, Ferenc Dávid (1510-1579), with whom he had previously co-operated. A moral charge against Biandrata had destroyed his influence with Dávid. Hence he called in Socinus to reason with Dávid, who had renounced the worship of Christ. Socinus used orthodox terms in an heretical sense.

If so, then the logical development of the system according to the highest orthodox principles of honor and right is, that men are created by God with well constituted and holy minds, tending powerfully to all that is good. They are not morally weak or impotent. They do not come under the delusive and controlling power of evil spirits. Indeed, there are no evil spirits. Moreover, the predominant and natural developments of men, in all ages, are holy and good. There is no predominating tendency to selfishness, dishonesty, violence, wrong, war, conquest and oppression. There is no prevailing tendency to idolatry, lust, sensualism and pollution. All men, as a universal fact, develop a benevolent and holy character, loving God supremely and their neighbors as themselves, and manifesting it in all the organizations of society, and in all the business and duties of life.

These results, however, are so much at war with facts, that they react upon the principles from which they flow. The result commonly is that lower views are adopted of what is possible in new-created minds. Some theory of free agency is adopted which excludes the idea alike of original sin and original righteousness. Men are regarded as free agents, beginning life ignorant and inexperienced, exposed to temptation, with powerful appetites, passions and propensities, and yet able by free choice to form a holy character. If they do this, they are holy from the beginning, and are saved by obedience to the law of God. That this could be done, and had been done, was taught by the Pelagians. Hence their doctrine that men can be saved by the law as well as by the gospel; and that some, in fact, have lived perfectly holy lives. If, on the other hand, men fall into sinful habits,—as they admitted to be the case to a lamentable degree,—they needed, not regeneration by special and supernatural grace, but repentance and reformation, in view of the motives of the law and of the gospel. Moreover, the proper sphere of the grace of God is found in the presentation of these motives. The gospel exceeds the law simply as a more powerful presentation of motives.

It appears, then, that the highest views of the principles of honor and right are modified and reduced, because, according to them, men would be better than even Pelagians, in view of facts, can maintain them to be. For, looking at the history of this world, men have, in fact, sinned with so much power, and energy, and perseverance, that it does not at all look rational to suppose that they are born in the image of God, understanding it to denote a powerful bias to good, and real ho-

liness. They, therefore, resort to a theory of mere free will, not implying either sin or holiness, but a power to practice either. Starting from
this point, they deduce varieties of character from the use made by
men of their free will. This is, certainly, the best view that facts will allow them to take of man. To assert that he is born with original righteousness and a strong bias and impulse towards holiness, would be too
palpably at war with facts.

Of course, these views react upon their ideas of the original condition and character of Adam. Denying that men are now in a fallen
state, of course they cannot admit of any marked contrast between
them and Adam. Hence they regard all the glowing statements which
we have set forth as to the original perfection of his constitution and
powers, and the energy of his holiness, as irrational exaggerations.
Adam, though created full-grown, was only an inexperienced free
agent, who, like all others, needed to form a character by the exercise
of his free will, either in sinning or in obeying God.

A tendency to depreciate the original powers and perfection of
Adam is, therefore, the natural and necessary result of any theory
which, denying preexistence, represents the present condition of man
as his natural state, and not a fallen condition. The more Adam is exalted, the greater is the evidence of a fall from his state to the present
condition of man. The more he is depressed, the less is the evidence of
such a fall. Hence, the final result is, that our ideas of free agency itself,
and of the possible capacities of created minds, are seriously lowered.
The operation of such a view—assuming the facts of human depravity
really to be as I have stated them—is as if a, diseased man, who had
lived only in a hospital, among diseased attendants and patients, should
form his ideas of the normal state of the powers of the body, and of
good health, from such specimens; and should justify God in so making them, by saying that they were as well made and organized as
could reasonably be expected, in view of the fact that all created things
are necessarily limited and imperfect.

We have already remarked that there has been in all ages a large
body of Christians whose deep experimental knowledge of their own
sinfulness, and of the need of a thorough supernatural regeneration,
have led them earnestly and decidedly to reject these views, and to retain the theory of a forfeiture in Adam, notwithstanding its inconsistency with the first principles of reason and of morals. Of the facts for
which that theory proposed to account they were certain. In words, at

least, that theory did account for them; and it appeared to be Scriptural. Therefore they adopted it. The arguments of the Pelagians against the alleged forfeiture of rights were never answered, and never can be. Yet still the power of Christian consciousness was so great that it trod them down, for the sake of a theory which had at least this merit, that it seemed to explain the great facts of human depravity and ruin. The same has been true in every subsequent conflict. In a large body of Christians, Christian consciousness has prevailed.

In accordance with these views, Neander has well remarked, concerning the condemnation of Pelagianism in the days of Augustine, that, although Pelagianism succumbed to an outward force of the civil power, yet there never was a subsequent and violent reaction, since

> "that doctrine conquered which had on its side the voice of the universal Christian consciousness, and which found a ready point of union in the whole life and experience of the church, as expressed in its prayers and in all its liturgical forms." (II, p. 599).

And yet the principles for which the Pelagians contended were of the highest and noblest kind. They contended, as did Dr. Channing, for the honor of God. Neander says of Julian of Eclanum, "He maintained that the highest object of the Christian faith itself, the doctrine concerning God, was essentially compromised;" for the Pelagians and their opponents did not agree even in their doctrine concerning God. The God of their opponents "was not the God of the gospel." Accordingly, Julian says to Augustine,

> "The children, you say, do not bear the blame of their own, but of another's sins. What sort of sin can that be? What an unfeeling wretch, cruel, forgetful of God and of righteousness, an inhuman barbarian, is he who would make such innocent creatures as little children bear the consequences of transgressions which they never committed, and never could commit? God, you answer. What god? For there are gods many, and lords many; but we worship but one God, and one Lord Jesus Christ. What God dost thou make the malefactor? Here, most holy priest, and most learned orator, thou fabricatest something more mournful and frightful than the brimstone in the valley of Amsanctus. God himself,

say you, who commendeth his love towards us, who even
spared not his own Son, but hath given him up for us all, he
so determines,—he is himself the persecutor of those that are
born. He himself consigns to eternal fire, for an evil will,
the children who, as he knows, can have neither a good nor
an evil will."

Dr. Channing, contending for the same great interests, expressed
himself with less excited vehemence and personal severity, and therefore in better taste. But his conceptions of the discord of the facts alleged with the character of God were no less keen than those of Julian.
Hence he said,

> "They take from us our Father in heaven, and substitute a
> stern and unjust Lord. Our filial love and reverence rise up
> against them. We say, Touch anything but the perfections
> of God. Cast no stain on that spotless purity and loveliness.
> We can endure any errors but those which subvert or un-
> settle, the conviction of God's paternal goodness. Urge not
> upon us a system which makes existence a curse, and wraps
> the universe in gloom."

It was also in view of the theory of the imputation of Adam's sin
that Whelpley, in the name of New England divinity, said:

> "The idea that all the numerous millions of Adam's posterity
> deserve the ineffable and endless torments of hell, for a sin-
> gle act of his, before any one of them existed, is repugnant
> to that reason that God has given us, is subversive of all pos-
> sible conceptions of justice. I hesitate not to say that no
> scheme of religion ever propagated amongst men contains a
> more monstrous, a more horrible tenet. The atrocity of this
> doctrine is beyond comparison. The visions of the Koran,
> the fictions of the Sadder, the fables of the Zendavesta,[28] all

---

28   The use of the expression Zend-Avesta to refer to the Avesta in general is a misun-
     derstanding of the phrase Zand-i-Avesta, which literally means "interpretation of
     the Avesta." "Zoroastrianism is the oldest of the revealed world-religions, and it has
     probably had more influence on mankind, directly and indirectly, than any other
     single faith." - Mary Boyce, *Zoroastrians: Their Religious Beliefs and Practices* (Lon-
     don: Routledge and Kegan Paul, 1979, p. 1). "Zoroaster was thus the first to teach
     the doctrines of an individual judgment, Heaven and Hell, the future resurrection of

give place to this: Rabbinical legends, Brahminical vagaries, all vanish before it."

It were easy to produce similar utterances from Socinus and John Taylor and their followers; for, in fact, the argument has been one and the same, from age to age. It has ever been a bold, earnest and eloquent protest, in the name of the immortal principles of honor and right, against the imputation to the God of the universe of such acts as would conflict with justice, fatally obscure His glory, and fill the universe itself with mourning and gloom.

---

the body, the general Last Judgment, and life everlasting for the reunited soul and body. These doctrines were to become familiar articles of faith to much of mankind, through borrowings by Judaism, Christianity and Islam; yet it is in Zoroastrianism itself that they have their fullest logical coherence...." - Mary Boyce, Op. Cit. p. 29.

CHAPTER XI: SECOND RESULT OF DENYING A FORFEITURE BEFORE BIRTH

WE now come to consider the second general course that can be taken by those who reject the idea of a forfeiture in Adam, and do not hold to preexistence. They can still in theory retain, in all their integrity and fullness, the facts of human depravity, and resolve them into the sovereign dispensations of God.

This development is an important part of New England Theology, and seems to have sprung out of the pressure of the arguments used by Dr. John Taylor in his celebrated work against original sin. In his day, the whole Calvinistic world held to the theory of a forfeiture in Adam, in some one of the forms which have been set forth. Of course, the heaviest artillery of Dr. Taylor was brought to bear against it. And yet his arguments were not and could not be novel. Pelagius, Julian, Celestius, Socinus and many others, had employed them before him, as we have shown. But he bore with especial force upon the great point, that it was inconsistent with all just conceptions of personal identity and of justice to consider and treat the sin of Adam as that of his posterity. He says :

> "How mankind, who were perfectly innocent of Adam's sin, could, for that sin and upon no other account, be justly brought under God's displeasure and curse, we cannot understand. But, on the contrary, we do understand, and by our faculties must necessarily judge, according to all rules of equity, it is unjust. And therefore, unless our understanding, or perception of truth, be false,—that is, unless we do not understand what we do understand, or understand that to be true which other minds understand to be false,—*it must be unjust.*"

Again,

"That any man, without my knowledge or consent, should so represent me that when he is guilty I am to be reputed guilty, and when he transgresses I shall be accountable and punishable for his transgression, and thereby subjected to the wrath and curse of God; nay, further, that his wickedness shall give me a sinful nature, and all this before I am born, and consequently while I am in no capacity of knowing, helping or hindering, what he doth;— surely anyone, who dares use his understanding, must clearly see this is unreasonable, and altogether inconsistent with the truth and goodness of God. We may call it a righteous constitution, but in the nature of things it is absolutely impossible we should prove it to be so." (S. p. 109).

"Understanding cannot be various, but must be the same in all beings, so far as they do understand. And therefore, if we understand that it is unjust that the innocent should be under displeasure or a curse (and we see it very clearly, as clearly as we see that *that which is, is, or that which is not, is not*), then God understands it to be so too" (p. 151).

This is simply an assertion that the intuitive perceptions of truth and right, given by God to us in the structure of our minds, must accord with the reality of things, and the perceptions of all minds, including that of God Himself.

At the close of his last statement, he says, very much in the spirit of Julian of Eclanum, "And pray consider seriously what a God he must be who can be displeased with and curse his innocent creatures, even before they have a being" (p. 151).

The younger Edwards informs us that "in their day Drs. Watts and Doddridge were accounted leaders of the Calvinists." They, in this great emergency, put forth their energies to defend the received doctrine of a forfeiture in Adam. The celebrated John Wesley united his energies with theirs in the defense of this common ground. He says to Dr. Taylor:

"In your second part you profess to 'examine the principal passages of Scripture which divines have applied in support of the doctrine of original sin; particularly those cited by the Assembly of Divines in their Larger Catechism.' To this I never subscribed; but I think it, in the main, an excellent

composition, which I shall therefore cheerfully endeavor to
defend, so far as I conceive it is grounded on clear scripture"
(Doc. of Orig. Sin. p. 132).

He also quotes a large portion of the work of Watts on the same subject.

Edwards had seen and studied the work of Watts before he wrote;
for he makes strictures on some of its positions. Nor did he deem it a
sufficient defense,—otherwise he would not have written his own. But,
in his reply to the arguments of Taylor against the current theory of a
forfeiture in Adam, he was so hard driven by the argument from the
diversity of personal identity, the amount of which he thus states, that
"Adam and his posterity are not one, but entirely distinct agents," that
he took the ground that there is no such thing as identity or oneness in
created objects existing in successive moments, "but what depends on
the arbitrary constitution of the Creator" (p. 224, vol. I).[29] Hence it all
"depends on *God's sovereign constitution.*" This he proves by the consideration that preservation or upholding of objects, or persons, is a mere
series of new momentary separate creations, which are united as the
same identical existence, not by the nature of things, but by God's will.
And so the objection that Adam and his posterity are not and cannot
be one and the same agent, or justly be treated as such,

> "is built on a false hypothesis; for it appears that *a divine con-
> stitution* is what *makes truth* in affairs of this nature." (The
> italics are as Edwards left them.)

Thus Edwards, in a way unthought of by Augustine, or Watts, or
Turretin, made out and defended his theory of a forfeiture in Adam,
by resolving personal identity itself into an arbitrary sovereign constitution of God, thus opening the way to make Adam and his posterity
all one person by such a constitution. In order to complete his explanation, Edwards ought still further to have shown how, after God had
thus made Adam and his posterity as really and truly one and the same
person as a man is during the different portions of his life, it did not
follow that all the sins of Adam, and, indeed, of all other men, are our

---

29 It is at this point that we need to consider the arguments of John Williamson Nevin,
    The Mystical Presence, 1846; and Ross, Phillip A. *The True Mystery of The Mystical
    Presence*, Pilgrim Platform, 2011, regarding union with or in Christ.

sins. There is no way to avoid this consequence but to limit the operation of "the arbitrary constitution of the Creator" to only one of
Adam's sins, and to exclude from its operation all the sins of other
men. This certainly would merit in the highest degree the name of an
arbitrary constitution. It only the more clearly shows to what straits
Edwards was reduced in attempting to defend the doctrine of a forfeiture in Adam against the divinely-given and intuitive convictions of
the human mind on the subject of personal identity. This theory of
Edwards is at war with the theory of Prof. Shedd. Yet he eulogizes this
reasoning of Edwards as profound and true. Nevertheless, it appears to
have been too much for Hopkins to receive. He seems to have thought
that here Edwards had strained his metaphysical bow until it broke.
Nor was he ignorant of what the European divines had said to defend
the theory of a forfeiture in Adam. He had also carefully studied John
Taylor, and had, no doubt, examined the argument of Dr. Watts in reply to him; and, on the whole, he concluded that the theory of a forfeiture was not defensible on any ground, and he abandoned it, and
threw himself simply upon divine sovereignty.

What, then, is the real significance of this position? It is, in brief,
this,—although men did not sin in Adam, and thus forfeit their claims
as new-created beings, yet God, in fact, treats them as if they had.
There was no forfeiture, and yet God treats men as if there had been.
He does not enter into communion with them, as they come into existence. He does not bestow upon them a divine influence which secures the right development of their moral characters. On the other
hand, he has in some way, by a divine constitution of things, established such a connection between the sin of Adam and his posterity
that it will infallibly secure a wrong development of character in them,
amounting to total depravity and utter ruin. Moreover, this depravity
is so strong that no power short of the almighty energy of the Holy
Spirit can overcome it.

This theory, as commonly stated, involves, first, a denial of the
doctrine of the imputation of Adam's sin, and of a forfeiture of rights,
and an exposure to punishment by it; and, secondly, the existence of a
fixed and infallible connection between Adam's sin and the depravity
of his posterity. Thus, Dr. Hopkins states his views as follows:

> "It is not to be supposed that the offense of Adam is imputed
> to them to their condemnation, while they are considered as

in themselves in their own persons innocent; or that they
are guilty of the sin of their first father, antecedently to their
own personal sinfulness." "It is carefully to be observed that
they are not constituted sinners by his disobedience as a
punishment, or the penalty of the law coming upon them
for his sin" (Vol. I, p. 318).

Again,

> "All that is asserted as what the Scripture teaches on this
> head is, that, by a divine constitution, there is a certain con-
> nection between the first sin of Adam and the sinfulness of
> his posterity; so that, as he sinned and fell under condemna-
> tion, they, in consequence of this, became sinful and con-
> demned" (Ibid.).

This was, in the circumstances, a bold step for a Calvinist. But the
younger Edwards, Dwight,[30] Emmons, and other leading New England divines, followed in his steps. Bellamy, it is true, still defended the
ancient view; but it has long since ceased to be any proper part of
New England theology as distinguished from old Calvinism. The
younger Edwards,[31] in his views of the improvements in theology effected either by his father or by his followers, says, on this point,

> "The common doctrine has been that Adam's posterity, un-
> less saved by Christ, are damned (condemned) on account
> of Adam's sin; and that this is just, because his sin is imputed

---

30 Timothy Dwight (1752-1817) was an American academic and educator, a Congregational minister, theologian, and author. He was the eighth president of Yale College (1795–1817), He was also the leader of the evangelical New Divinity faction of
Congregationalism—a group closely identified with Connecticut's emerging commercial elite. Although fiercely opposed by religious moderates—most notably Yale
president Ezra Stiles—he was elected to the presidency of Yale on Stiles' death in
1795.

31 Jonathan Edwards, Jr. (174-1801) was an American theologian and linguist. His
fame came from his reply to Charles Chauncy regarding the salvation of all men,
where he defended the traditional evangelical doctrine, his reply to Samuel West's
Essays on Liberty and Necessity, in which he largely modified his father's theory of
the will by giving it a liberal interpretation, and upon his sermons on the atonement. A great deal of religious controversy raged in New England during his lifetime. His works were published at Andover (1842), in two volumes, with a memoir
by Tryon Edwards.

or transferred to them. By imputation, his sin becomes their sin. When the justice of such a transfer is demanded, it is said that the constitution which God has established makes the transfer just. To this it may be replied, that in the same way it may be proved just to damn (condemn) a man without any sin at all, either personal or imputed. We need only resolve it into a sovereign constitution of God. From this difficulty the followers of Mr. Edwards relieve themselves, by holding that, though Adam was so constituted the federal head of his posterity that in consequence of his sin they all sin or become sinners, yet they are damned (condemned) on account of their own personal sin merely, and not on account of Adams sin; as though they were individually guilty of his identical transgression" (Vol. I. p. 487).

Dr. Dwight simply says,

"The corruption of mankind exists in consequence of the apostasy of Adam." "I do not intend that the posterity of Adam are guilty of his transgression." "Neither do I intend that the descendants of Adam are punished for his transgression." "By means of the offense or transgression of Adam, the judgment or sentence of God came upon all men unto condemnation; because, and solely because, all men, in that state of things which was constituted in consequence of the transgression of Adam, become sinners."

Of the mode in which this effect results, he says,

"I am unable to explain this part of the subject. Many attempts have been made to explain it; but I freely confess myself to have seen none which was satisfactory to me; or which did not leave the difficulties as great, and, for aught I know, as numerous, as they were before."

Emmons no less distinctly denies sinning in Adam and imputation in every form. In the train of these the majority of the divines of New England have followed, as well as a large party in other parts of the United States.

They differ, indeed, in their mode of accounting for the universal sinfulness which results from the fall of Adam: some, as we have seen, resolving it into no natural causes, but into a stated mode of divine efficiency, called a divine constitution; others resolving it into the natural operation of the laws of procreation and descent, transmitting a deteriorated constitution and sinful propensities.

But, meantime, the question naturally arises, How are these things consistent with the demands of the great laws of honor and right in reference to new-created minds? These laws have been stated, and we see that they have been held for ages, as the intuitive moral perceptions of the mind. Are they not so? If they are,—if new-created minds have rights, and there has been no forfeiture of them,—then how can God be justified in the course alleged? It is not enough to resort to the idea of sovereignty. God, as a sovereign, has no authority to disregard the original rights of his creatures. Does any one resort to the law of generation? This is a mere ordinance of God. The question still arises, How is He to be defended in establishing and maintaining it? On this point, Dr. Watts says,

> "This natural propagation of sinful inclinations from a common parent, by a law of creation, seems difficult to be reconciled with the goodness and justice of God (that is, without a previous forfeiture). It seems exceeding hard to suppose that such a righteous and holy God, the Creator, who is also a being of such infinite goodness, should, by a powerful law and order of creation, which is now called *nature*, appoint young, intelligent creatures to come into being in such unhappy and degenerate circumstances, liable to such intense pains and miseries, and under such powerful tendencies and propensities to evil, by the mere law of propagation, as should almost unavoidably expose them to ten thousand actual sins, and all this before they have any personal sin or guilt to deserve it."

In a note he adds:

> "If it could be well made out that the whole race of mankind are partakers of sinful inclinations, and evil passions, and biases to vice, and also are exposed to many sharp actual sufferings and to death, merely and only by the origi-

nal divine law of propagation from their parents who had
sinned; and, if the justice and goodness of God could be
vindicated in making and maintaining such a dreadful law
or order of propagation through six thousand years, we
have no need of further inquiries, but might here be at rest.
But, if the scheme be so injurious to the goodness and equity of God as it seems to be, then we are constrained to
seek a little further for a satisfactory account of this universal
degeneracy and misery of mankind."

These, as we have seen, are also the views of the Princeton divines;
paid, indeed, of all who hold the old system of a forfeiture in Adam.
With them the Unitarians coincide. Nor is any relief found by resolving the results in question into a stated mode of divine efficiency, instead of a law or order of propagation. Indeed, this view seems less to
accord with the principles of honor and right than any other which
has yet been considered.

We come, then, once more to the final result, that every theory of
forfeiture before birth that denies preexistence has failed, and must fail,
to give permanent rest to good men. Moreover, the results of entirely
rejecting the theory of a forfeiture before birth are equally unsatisfactory, and are often in the highest degree injurious. We have also seen
that this fact is owing to the existence of a real conflict between the
actual facts of this system, and the principles of honor and right, on the
assumption that this is our first state of existence. We have also seen
that, by assuming the theory of a real preexistence, this conflict can be
entirely removed, and all the powers of the mind find rest. It follows
that the existing system has thus far acted as if it had been deranged by
a falsehood. It remains to be tried whether the system that I propose
will not act as if it had been properly readjusted by the truth. Certainly, the first view has had a fair trial. Is it not time, at least, to give
the other a fair opportunity to develop its genuine results?

CHAPTER XII: OTHER INEFFECTUAL EFFORTS FOR RELIEF

WE have considered the Augustinian doctrine of a forfeiture in Adam of the rights of new-created minds by the whole human race, and of the conflict existing between it and the principles of equity and honor. We have also set forth the results of an entire rejection of the doctrine of such a forfeiture in any way, and have seen that there is no available relief to be found in this course.

It remains that I consider some other ineffectual efforts to find relief by those who hold the common doctrine of forfeiture. It will be remembered that the doctrine, as held by Augustine, exalted the original rights of new-created minds to a very high point, and then represented the effects of the forfeiture through Adam as very disastrous. In consequence of it, man inherits a nature so deranged and sinful that he has lost free will and the power of doing good works, or of saving himself by repentance and faith. Of course, as man has not the power to accept the offers of mercy, God could not foresee that any would accept of them, nor predestinate them to life on that ground. Hence the doctrines of absolute and unconditional predestination, of passive regeneration, and of irresistible grace.

As was to be expected, this view was early assailed by the Semipelagians, under Cassian, as at war with the character of God, and a return to the exploded errors of fatalism.

Nevertheless, in the case of a large portion of Christians in every age, this assault has not led to a rejection of the doctrine of a forfeiture in Adam, but to a modification and softening of the Augustinian form of that doctrine. This has been attempted in two ways:— the first, by giving a milder view of the effects of the forfeiture itself; the second, by introducing the idea of a gracious ability restored by Christ to all the race, after their original ability had been entirely destroyed by the fall. By the first of these methods, the Roman Catholic church, though at first they condemned the Semipelagians. at last, revolting from Luther, and under the guidance of the Jesuits, decided, in the Council of Trent, in direct opposition to Augustine, that free will was not wholly extinguished by the fall, although they conceded that it was debilitated and depressed (*Decree on Justification*, Chap, I). They also decided that man, in the work of moral renovation, is not passive, and that grace is not irresistible; but that man, when acted on by God, freely cooperates with the divine influence, and has at all times the power to resist it (Chap, V). The fifth and sixth anathemas, which follow the *Decree on Justification*, are also directed against all who shall deny these positions. At the same time, they continue to announce the doctrine of the forfeiture in Adam, in the most decided terms. They assert that

> "infants derive from Adam that original guilt which must be expiated in the laver of regeneration, in order to obtain eternal life,"

and that

> "Adam lost the purity and righteousness which he received from God, not for himself only, but also for us" (*Decree on Original Sin*, Chaps. II and IV).

In view of these decisions, the *Catechism of the Council of Trent* says,

> "The pastor, therefore, will not omit to remind the faithful that the guilt and punishment of original sin were not confined to Adam, but justly descended from him, as from their source and cause, to all posterity."

Hence, it is added, "a sentence of condemnation was pronounced against the human race immediately after the fall of Adam" (p. 37, 38, Baltimore edition). In taking their ground as to free will, the Roman Catholic church coincided with the Semipelagians, who, in opposition to Augustine, held that there still remained in man, after the fall, some power to perform good works, and to cooperate with God in effecting their own salvation. The Semipelagians also still further maintained that God's decree of election and predestination was based upon a foresight of the use which men would make of this power. This form of the doctrine of predestination, however, has never been formally established within the Roman Catholic church, but has been, from age to age, the subject of fierce controversies. It was held by the followers of Duns Scotus,[32] Molina, and others. The Augustinian doctrine on this point, however, has always had its earnest defenders in that church. Although Wiggers regards Semipelagianism as being the predominant system in the middle age to the time of Luther, yet it was so rather in its fundamental principles as to free will and power, than in an ultimate development of them in the form of a conditional predestination.

The second mode of modifying the Augustinian doctrine is that of Arminius, in which he is followed by Wesley, Watson, and other leading divines of the Methodist denomination. By these divines the same view is given of the effects of the forfeiture in Adam as was given by Augustine and the Reformers. They hold to the entire destruction of free will in all men by the fall. Arminius, as quoted by Watson, says

> "that the will of man, with respect to true good, is not only wounded, bruised, inferior, crooked and attenuated, but it is, likewise, captivated, destroyed and lost; and has no powers whatever, except such as are excited by grace" (Watson's Theol. List. Vol. II, p. 46).

Watson also says that on this point the true Arminians agree with the Augsburgh Confession, the French Calvinistic churches, the Calvinistic church of Scotland, and Calvin himself, (p. 47). He adds, that in the doctrine of the corruption of our common nature, and man's natural incapacity to do good, the Arminians and Calvinists so well agree, "that it is an entire delusion to represent this doctrine, as is often done, as exclusively Calvinistic" (p. 48). Hence Wesley joined with Watts, against Dr. J. Taylor, in its defense, as we have seen. As to the extent of the forfeiture in Adam, Watson says that

---

32 John (Johannes) Duns Scotus, O.F.M. (1265-1308) was one of the more important theologians and philosophers of the High Middle Ages. He had considerable influence on Roman Catholic thought. The doctrines for which he is best known are the "univocity of being" (that existence is the most abstract concept we have and is applicable to everything that exists). He made a formal distinction between different aspects of the same thing, and the idea of haecceity (the property supposed to be in each individual thing that makes it an individual). Scotus also developed a complex argument for the existence of God, and argued for the Immaculate conception of Mary.

"the death threatened as the penalty of Adam's transgression
included corporeal, moral or spiritual and eternal death, and
that the sentence included the whole of his posterity" (p.
61).

There is also an entire coincidence between the arguments of
Wesley, Fletcher and Watson, to prove the doctrine of original sin,
and those of Watts and Edwards.

The modification of the Augustinian system introduced by
Arminian divines is effected by their doctrine that, in consequence of
the death of Christ, a gracious ability is restored to all men in a sufficient degree to enable them to embrace the gospel. This is called by
Fletcher[33] "a gracious free agency;" and Watson says that by it is com-
municated "a power of willing to come to Christ, even when men do
not come,—a power of considering their ways and turning to the
Lord, when they do not consider them and turn to him" (p. 377).
Upon the foreseen use of this power they base the eternal decision of
God as to man's salvation, and thus arrive at the ancient doctrine of
conditional predestination, although in a different way from the
Semipelagians and the early Greek church.

It is not my purpose to enter into a discussion of the points at issue, between the Arminians and the Calvinists, with reference to this
doctrine. I will only say, that, under a system of real preexistence there
is an important truth which is very nearly related to the doctrine of
gracious ability, though not identical with it, but which I have not
space now to develop.

But my main object is to say that, so long as the idea of a forfeiture in Adam is retained, and real preexistence is denied, neither of the
modifications which I have described is effectual to meet the demands
of the principles of equity and of honor.

As we have seen, Wesley places the demands of these principles as
high as Augustine, Dr. Watts, or any of the Reformers.

According to these principles, God is bound to give to every new-
created being a sound and healthy moral constitution, perfect free will,

---

33 John William Fletcher (originally *de la Fléchère*, 1729-1785), was an English divine,
    born at Nyon in Switzerland. He was a contemporary of John Wesley, a key inter-
    preter of Wesleyan theology in the 18th century, and one of Methodism's first great
    theologians.

and predominant tendencies to good. Accordingly, Wesley perfectly accords with Augustine, Turretin, Watts, and the Reformers, in holding that to make new-created beings either neutral, or with a preponderance towards evil, would be highly unjust and dishonorable in God. Unless these rights have been forfeited, it is in the highest degree dishonorable in God to disregard them.

Now, that men are born without such constitutions and propensities, and not in such circumstances as these principles demand, is conceded by Roman Catholics, Semipelagians and Arminians, as well as by Calvinists. True, the Roman Catholics and Semipelagians do not regard free will as annihilated by the fall. Nevertheless, they concede that it is weakened and depressed, and that the mind is full of corrupt propensities, all strongly tending towards evil, so that without divine grace man will surely perish. It follows that man is as truly wronged as on the Augustinian supposition, even if not to the same extent. There is, in principle, no difference in the two cases, and this modification of the system furnishes no relief.

On the other hand, the Arminians allege that by divine grace, through Christ, free agency has been restored to all men. Even if this were conceded, it does not bring them up to the point demanded by the principles of equity and honor; for they still have depraved natures, and are full of propensities to evil, which are certain to ruin them if God does not interpose. But this is contrary to the demands of the laws of honor and right with reference to new-created minds, as set forth by Wesley and the Reformers.

But, if, even notwithstanding gracious ability, men are wronged, still more are they wronged by being created in a state of such entire depravity and inability as to need such a restoration of power. They ought to have had it from the outset; and the restoration of it is not grace, but only a partial and inadequate compensation for the original wrong.

The same reply may be made to the allegation of some high churchmen, that God is justified in his dealings with men through Adam, by providing for them the opportunity of baptismal regeneration in infancy. For, according to the principles of equity and honor, God ought not to have created men in such a state as to need such a remedy,—even if it were one, which it is not. Moreover, this alleged remedy did not exist till the days of Christ, and since then has been inaccessible by the majority of the human race.

After all, in every one of these cases, and in all equally, if we would defend God, we are driven back to the problem which I have already considered at length,—that is, to show how men can forfeit their original rights, as new-created minds, before they are born into this world, as long as a real personal preexistence and real sin are denied. A necessity of solving this problem lies at the foundation of all these systems alike. If it is, as I have endeavored to show, absurd and impossible, then no modification of a system, so long as it rests on such an alleged forfeiture as its basis, can furnish any relief.

Undoubtedly the motive of the Roman Catholic divines, in their doctrine of free will, was to vindicate God from dishonor with reference to the origin of sin and the ruin of man. This Möhler distinctly affirms, and makes it prominent in his defense of their theology. So, also, no one who has read Wesley, Fletcher and Watson, can doubt that the Arminians aimed at the same end in their doctrine of the restoration of ability by grace and conditional predestination. But the difficulty lay too deep for either of these expedients to reach. It is not peculiar to the Lutheran, to the Calvinist, to the Roman Catholic, to the Arminian or to the Episcopalian. It is found in the common foundation of the system of each and all.

After laying such a foundation, the evil cannot be remedied by any improved mode of building upon it. A system based on injustice cannot be so developed as to become a just system.

CHAPTER XIII: ESTIMATE OF THE CONFLICT

IN my introductory remarks I made the following statements:

> "The conflict of which I propose to write is, and ever has
> been, in its deepest recesses, *a conflict of the heart.* Not that
> gigantic intellectual efforts have not been abundantly put
> forth, but that the deepest and most powerful impulses
> have ever been those of the heart."

I also remarked that

> "the merely logical encounters of powerfully developed
> intellectual systems tend rather to irritation and alienation
> than to sympathy and confidence. Nevertheless, beneath
> every man's intellectual efforts on this subject there has
> been a deeply affecting personal experience, which, if
> known, would show, in a manner adapted to awaken
> deep sympathy, why he has reasoned as he has. Indeed,
> there is a great heart, not only of natural honor, but, still
> more, of sanctified humanity, which, from beginning to
> end, underlies this momentous controversy, the deep
> workings of which must be developed and appreciated
> before the controversy can be properly understood. No
> honorable mind can see these workings uncovered, and
> not be touched with deep emotion in viewing the strug-
> gles of our common humanity, in endeavoring to resolve
> the deepest and most momentous problems of the present
> trying and mysterious system."

I also declared that

> "it is my aim to unfold this experience, and thus, if I may,
> to create on all sides a feeling of sympathy and mutual in-
> terest, by pointing out those benevolent and honorable

impulses, and that regard for truth,—mixed, it may be, with other motives,—by which the various parties have been actuated, and to produce a candid and united effort to eliminate error, and to develop the whole truth."

To some extent I have been able, in the general survey which I have now completed, to unveil the workings of the hearts of our fellow Christians of different ages, from the beginning. My chief regret has been that, on account of my narrow limits, I have not been able to do it more fully. I deeply feel the importance of such an exhibition. We are too prone to forget that all redeemed and holy men of every age are still our brethren, and one with us in Christ. We are too prone to forget their circumstances and trials, and the real and great works which they have performed, each in his age, for God and for man. We are too much inclined to think of their works as collections of dry and dead dogmas, forgetting that they were once filled with the warm emotions of living hearts, and that their authors still live, and, if we are Christians, still love us, and delight to receive from us fraternal tributes of love and esteem.

The most affecting thought to my mind, in making this review, has been that God, who knows all truth, should have permitted men who truly loved Him and communed with Him to remain involved in so great and so injurious errors. But facts show that God has not seen fit to connect infallibility with eminent piety. Indeed, had He done it, He must have entirely changed His administration of this world. The mysterious developments of this system, such as the great apostasy, and the long reign of ecclesiastical despotism and of brute force, could not have taken place as they have, if God had from the first given infallibility to all holy men. One result of the course pursued by God has been, to rebuke, in all ages, the spirit of man-worship. Nevertheless, He has never designed by it to destroy the spirit of brotherly love and of mutual respect among Christians of different ages; and the time will come when they will know, love and respect each other, as they have not done in the dark ages of the past conflict. It will be seen, too, that the final end and highest aim of this great conflict has been in all ages simple and sublime.

The regeneration of man has been the practical work to be done; but, as he is regenerated for God, the final end and highest aim has been to find a full, consistent, and perfect view of a glorious God. This is the highest necessity of a holy mind. It awakens its strongest desires, and is essential to its perfect peace. The voice of every holy soul in all ages has been, "O God, thou art my God; early will I seek thee; my soul thirsteth for thee; my flesh longeth for thee, in a dry and thirsty land where no water is, for thy loving-kindness is better than life" (Ps. 63:1). "With thee is the fountain of life; in thy light shall I see light" (Pd. 36:9). "One thing have I desired, that will I seek after, that I may dwell in the house of the Lord all the days of my life; that I may behold the beauty of the Lord, and inquire in his holy temple" (Ps. 27:4).

It will nevertheless be seen, as I think, that, in some way, dark clouds have been made to arise and to eclipse the glories of God, so that in the most absolute sense it has been true that, logically viewed, He has dwelt in the thick darkness. Many things received and taught and defended concerning Him by the best of men, have ascribed to Him acts more at war with the fundamental principles of equity and honor than have ever been imagined or performed by the most unjust, depraved and corrupt of created minds.

Nothing, in fact, can be conceived of which is more dishonorable and unjust than the deeds which have been ascribed to God, and made the basis of the whole work of redemption,—that greatest of all His works.

It is no doubt true that this has always been done unconsciously and unintentionally. No Christian divine has ever for a moment admitted that the real reigning God of the universe ever has, in fact, ceased to make honor and right the foundation of His throne; yet it is nevertheless true that systems of theology have been framed which, in reality, have represented Him as so doing, and that these systems have been supposed to be based upon the explicit statements of God. These statements have sometimes been received as the decisions of an infallible church as to the sense of the Bible; at others, as the opinions of the great body of believers, in all ages, as to that sense.

These are the things which, in fact, have been done; and, under the influence of such systems, honorable and ingenuous minds have been, and still are, liable to be exposed to an inconceivable amount of suffering. Fearing to call in question what is regarded as sustained by the assertion of God, or is believed by an infallible church, or by the great body of Christians,—prevented by Christian consciousness from taking refuge in infidelity, and yet unable to exterminate the principles of honor and right implanted by God in their souls,—they cannot see around them anything but a universe of terror and gloom, in the lurid light of which a just and honorable God cannot be seen, and in which the soul faints, and it seems better to die than to live.

Others may have defended themselves against coming into such a state, by entirely suspending the exercise of the logical power, from respect to the supposed statements of God, or from a regard to the decisions of a church supposed to be infallible, or to the opinions of the main body of Christians in all ages. Of the truth of the great features of the system they are assured; and, if they meet with positive contradictions of fundamental principles of equity and honor, they will not look into them. Thus, to use a metaphor, though by faith they swallow them, still they do not logically digest them, and thus the poison does not directly enter into their mental circulation.

But with an increasing number of minds such a course will not always be possible. This is especially likely to be true of those who have been disciplined in the higher departments of a properly conducted system of education, and yet have a deep Christian experience. One great end of a true education is to discipline the mind for the candid and unprejudiced pursuit of truth. It teaches the honest Christian to renounce all pious fraud, and not to think that it can ever be for God's glory that we should lie for Him. Moreover, it teaches that it is for the interest of all to know the truth, and that it is a duty to be faithful to it at any sacrifice of reputation or property, or personal ease and enjoyment. It also recognizes the truth which is taught by the structure of the human mind, by the material universe, and by providence, as a part of the revelation which God has made to man as really as the Bible, and does not feel at liberty to suppress any truth taught by God. The future, at least, will develop the result of such views.

But, even if education has not been in all past ages such as it ought to be,—and we do not pretend that it has,—still, even when imperfectly developed, its higher grades have naturally tended to produce free thought, and to give power to that thought. But it has ever led to peculiar trials; for, since the mind is limited and wakes up in this world under the influence of the opinions of the existing generation, and the system of God is vast and manifold in its relations, it is extremely difficult and laborious for a single mind so to grasp and comprehend it as to study out and adjust all its parts, relations and bearings. And if it has had elements wrought into it that bring one part of it into conflict with another, and these remain undiscovered, then the logical tendencies of different minds will impel them in different directions, according as circumstances or the constitutional temperament fix the attention on one part or another of the system. Those who feel deeply toward one part of the system try to carry that out logically. Others, who feel another part, try to do the same with that. Hence arises at once the tendency, already illustrated, of one part of the system to destroy another, to which it has been put in opposition. Hence divisions arise, and extreme parties are formed,—each urging one part of the system so far as to destroy another. In view of these conflicts intermediate parties arise, each trying to retain both of the opposing parts of the system, but differing in the modes in which they endeavor to harmonize and adjust them; but all alike failing in the effort.

Nevertheless, on the scale of ages, the principles of honor and right will finally predominate and have the advantage, whatever may be the purposes or wishes of those who hold the system; and if, by any false theory, they have been put in opposition to any fundamental facts of the system, either those facts will be generally dropped, or they will be so modified as to lose their real nature and import, or else the false theory will be repudiated by which the opposition has been produced.

Now, all the wide field of history which I have sketched is but a collection of instructive illustrations of these tendencies of the mind under the common system; and, after ages of conflict, the time seems to be drawing near in which one or the other of the last-mentioned results must be anticipated. Either the principles of honor and right will generally destroy or render unmeaning the great facts as to the ruin of man, or else that theory will be renounced by which those principles have been arrayed in opposition to these facts.

Thus have the reality of the alleged conflict, its causes, and a possible remedy, been considered, and the importance of its speedy application. The final question now arises, Shall the theory of a previous existence be received as true?

In answer to this three things have been said: There is no evidence of its truth; it merely shifts the difficulty, but does not remove it; and it is inconsistent with the Word of God. These allegations I shall consider in the following book.

BOOK V

The Argument

Chapter I: The Mode Of Proceeding

WHEN it is asserted, as has been stated, that the doctrine of pre-existence—to which I have resorted as alone effectual to harmonize the conflicting powers of Christianity—is a mere theory not sustained by any proof, the question naturally arises, What is meant by this assertion? Is it that it is nowhere in express terms asserted in the Scriptures? The truth of this assertion I have conceded; for I have only assumed "that God has so presented to us this system, taken as a whole, that by a careful study of it we may learn the great law of its harmonious action; and that the Bible has said nothing designed to foreclose this mode of inquiry, or to confine us, by express verbal revelation, to any particular theory on the subject" (Book III Ch. 2, p. 165.)

If, however, any one is disposed to call in question the validity of this mode of reasoning, I would simply ask him, Have any texts of Scripture before you the authority to prove that there is a God, and that the Bible is His inspired Word?

If not, then you must prove those fundamental truths,—the being of a God, and the divine origin and inspiration of the Bible,—by the kind of reasoning which I propose to use to prove preexistence; that is, reasoning from divinely implanted intellectual and moral intuitions, and from the facts of the system. If, therefore, this mode of reasoning is sufficiently valid to be the original basis of all religion, is it not also valid enough to sustain the doctrine of preexistence? Moreover, by what other mode of reasoning can the truth of the Newtonian theory be proved? But I shall say more upon this point in another place.

But, if anyone shall concede the validity of the mode of reasoning, but shall assert that by it nothing can be proved in favor of the doctrine of preexistence, then I reply that this is a mere gratuitous assertion, and no argument. Before conceding any weight to such an assertion, it is at least expedient first to hear the arguments which this mode of reasoning will furnish in favor of the doctrine in question.

The same reply may be made to the allegation that it merely shifts the difficulty, but does not remove it. This, also, is an unproved assertion; and it would be well, before giving any credit to it, to consider carefully and thoroughly and to weigh well the true and logical bearings of preexistence on the difficulties of the system.

But, before proceeding to consider either of these main points, it is indispensable at the outset to meet the third assertion,—that the doctrine of preexistence is opposed to the statements of the inspired volume.

It is natural and proper, in view of such an assertion, to ask, What are those statements? Are they those which teach merely the fact that men are born depraved, and are by nature the children of wrath? Certainly these do not deny or disprove preexistence. For, if men preexisted and fell before they entered this world, it would of course result in these very facts. Therefore, when the Bible asserts the existence of these facts, it does not deny preexistence. Nay, more, so far as preexistence accounts for these facts, in consistency with the character of God, better than any other system, so far does the statement of them in the Bible create a presumption of its truth. The same also is true as to the inspired statements of the magnitude and totality of human depravity.

To disprove preexistence from the Bible, then, it is necessary to produce not merely texts to prove native depravity, and its development in a life entirely sinful, but also passages that shall particularly state that these facts originated in this world, and not in a previous state of existence.

To meet this point, there is, so far as I know, but one passage on which any general reliance is placed; but still that one is enough, if it really does meet and decide the point. That one passage is the celebrated comparison of Adam and Christ, which occurs in verses 12-21 of the fifth chapter of the epistle of Paul to the Romans.

I need not say of this that it has been in all ages and still is relied on by many eminent Christians, as proving that the sinfulness of the human race was caused by the sin of Adam, either by imputation, or by natural causation, or through divine efficiency, or in some other way. But, if so, then, of course, it was not caused by a fall in a preexistent state.

It is necessary, therefore, before proceeding to any general course of reasoning, first to inquire what is the true import of this celebrated passage. Indeed, I think that practically the whole of the present discussion turns more upon this than upon any other point. For, if it had not been for the belief that this chapter proves such a doctrine of forfeiture as I have considered,—a doctrine that appears impossible and unjust,—it could never have gained credence, or sustained itself for a single hour; nor would it have ever been believed that the sin of Adam could or did in any way produce the terrific depravity which has been exhibited in this world ever since his creation and fall.

But so long as it has been supposed that God has asserted these things, it has been felt to be a duty to overrule even those intuitive moral and intellectual convictions which He has implanted in the soul, rather than to distrust His Word. Much as I respect the spirit of faith and of submission to God from which this course of conduct has proceeded, still I cannot but lament that the proper laws of interpreting such a passage had not been more thoroughly studied before coming to such painful and injurious results.

It is evident, therefore, from what has been said, that the proper interpretation of this passage is the first point which demands our attention.

It is plain, also, that this is a point of peculiar moment, since the whole Scriptural question depends, in fact, upon this text. If this fails to sustain the common opinion, there is no other. This will probably strike some with surprise. They have been wont to regard the Bible as full of proof of the fall in Adam. The reason is, that they have regarded all proof of native depravity and the fallen condition of the race as virtually proof of the fall of the race in Adam. It is, however, as we have said, no proof at all of this point. It is proof of a fall at some time, but whether *in* Adam or *before* Adam it does not decide. It suits alike either hypothesis. Let us, then, come to the solitary passage on which the common doctrine is wholly-based,—Rom. 5:12-19.

If it shall appear that no valid argument can be derived from this passage against the doctrine of preexistence, then the way will be fully prepared to take up and to develop the general argument for that doctrine, on the principles which have been already stated; and also to answer such objections as have been alleged against it in those superficial discussions of it to which I have previously referred.

Chapter II: General View Of The Various Interpretations Of Rom. 5:12-19

No other passage of Scripture can be mentioned, the interpretation of which has so seriously affected the human race. Indeed, from the magnitude and universality of its effects, an aspect of sublimity must ever invest it to the thoughtful mind.

From age to age, the millions of a depraved race had filled this world in successive generations. At length a great Redeemer came. He came to redeem a church, to destroy the kingdom and works of Satan, and to reorganize the universe of God. But whence originated the evil which He came to remedy? What was it that plunged the human race in ruins? What caused the infinite emergency to meet which none was adequate in the wide universe but an incarnate God?

Questions like these are full of interest to all worlds, but above all to us; for we are the race from which the church is to be redeemed, and all of our race not included in this redemption are to perish forever.

Need we wonder, then, that theologians and poets, philosophers and kings, as well as unlettered men in all the walks of common life, have listened with deep interest to these teachings of the apostle; that Milton, in his immortal epic, designed to justify the ways of God to man, should make it the burden of his song; that learned expositors and divines should expend volumes on it; that it should become the basis of systems of theology, sermons, catechisms and hymns; that it should tinge all the scenes of domestic life, rise before the mind in the sacred hour of marriage, or as any new-born heir of immortality enters the world, or as death closes the scene;— in short, that it should lie at the basis of all religious thought and emotion in the evangelical Christian world?

Are not, then, the moral aspects of the interpretation of this passage truly sublime? Has it not given character to the intellectual and moral atmosphere into which each successive generation is born, in which their powers are unfolded, and under the influence of which their eternity is decided? And, if it is much to shape one ingenuous youthful mind, like that of Bacon, Burke, Milton, or Washington, in which are the elements of all that can affect and interest our deepest sympathies, how much more so, to shape the minds of all such for eighteen long centuries,—to take whole generations of minds, of all grades and in all ranks, and mold them from the cradle to the grave?

But, if these things are so, need I say, what everyone must see and feel without my saying it, how unspeakable and inconceivable is the importance of a right interpretation of such a passage?

What, then, is the fundamental idea of the common interpretation? It presupposes that this is our first state of existence, and that the guilt and depravity of man are not the result of a fall in a previous state of existence, but are in some way the result of the first sin of Adam.

Various have been the attempts to unfold the mode in which this alleged fall in or through him took place. Some teach that, in some mysterious way, we existed in Adam, were one with him, sinned in him and fell with him, and thus corrupted the common generic nature of the race, and that hence natural death and a depraved nature descend through physical generation; and that all men being born in fact sinners, and with corrupted natures, are under the wrath of God; and that the guilt of Adam's sin is imputed to them, because it is truly and properly theirs.

Others deny any mysterious unity with Adam before we were born, and our actual commission of his first sin, but say that, as Adam was our natural and federal head, God imputes his sin to us, and thus makes it really ours, though not personally; or else that, by a divine judicial constitution, He regards it as ours, though it is not, and holds us liable to punishment for it, independently of and before our own acts; and that, on one of these grounds, as a punishment of that sin, we forfeit His favor, and that accordingly He withdraws from us divine supernatural influences, so that we are born devoid of original righteousness, and, as a necessary result, with natures corrupt and sinful, anterior to choice or action, and leading to actual sin, and deserving of eternal death.

Others do not retain the doctrine of imputation at all, and yet believe that the ruinous consequences of Adam's sin do come upon us;

and that, on account of it, we are born with depraved natures before choice or action, which are properly sinful.

Others, denying a depraved nature anterior to choice, and holding that all sin is voluntary, ascribe to a stated exercise of divine efficiency the fact that all men sin.

Others only affirm that our natures have been so changed, in consequence of Adam's fall, that in all the appropriate circumstances of our being in this world we sin as soon as moral agency commences; and, although the mere nature of man before volition cannot be strictly sinful, yet, in a popular sense, it may be called corrupt, depraved and sinful,—that is, always leading to sin.

Augustine, as we have seen, originally developed the first view, and the others are different stages of recession from it, caused by the pressure of arguments derived from the principles of honor and right, and the character of God. But still, all have one idea in common,—that our original guilt and sinfulness were not caused by our own action in another state of being, but by the sin of Adam.

The interpretation of Augustine rested very much on the false translation of verse 12 in the Latin Vulgate, "*in quo omnes peccaverunt*," which means "in whom all sinned," instead of "for that (or because) all sinned." Hence he often says, that all men were one in Adam, and that Adam, though one, was all men. His philosophical notions, according to Neander, Hagenbach and others, also favored this view. His realistic mode of thinking, as Hagenbach alleges, led him to confound the abstract with the concrete, and so to consider the human race as originally a concrete totality, in which the individuals were merged, instead of a mere collection of distinct and successive individuals, represented by a generic term.

This interpretation was to some extent held during the Middle Ages, and by some at the time of the Reformation, and even since then, it has been defended. So long as it was supposed to rest on the testimony of revelation, its advocates could repel any protest of reason on the grounds of faith and mystery. And it is instructive to notice how wide may be the influence of a wrong translation or exposition of even one word of the inspired oracles; and therefore it is well for all to feel the responsibility, even at this day of translating or expounding a passage like this.

The second exposition, or that of those who derive the doctrine of imputation from this passage, is distinguished by this peculiarity, that it denies absolutely and unequivocally that the apostle here asserts that men became actual sinners, or even received a depraved nature through the sin of Adam. Not only, say they, the passage does not teach this, but it is entirely against its scope and main end. It teaches simply that, as all men were condemned to death for Adam's sin, so all who belong by faith to Christ were justified by Christ's righteousness. By death, they understand penal evils of all kinds. They hold, indeed, that human depravity resulted from this condemnation, since God forsook the condemned race, and took away His Spirit, and depravity followed of course. But all that the passage directly teaches is the condemnation of all for the sin of Adam, and the justification of believers for Christ's sake. The sense is altogether judicial. This is at present the proper Old School view.

The New School divines, on the other hand, consider the passage as teaching not that all men were condemned for Adam's act, but that they all became sinners in consequence of it in some way, without defining alike in what way it was. For saying this, they are charged by their Old School brethren with overlooking the entire scope, end and aim, of the passage.

There was originally, and for four centuries, still another view of this passage; that of the Greek church, which regarded the death spoken of in it as merely natural death. Before Tertullian[1] and Augustine, this was also the view of the Latin church. Ireneus,[2] the great opponent of heretics, knew nothing of anything but physical death in this passage. In favor of this view the authority of the Greek fathers is uniform and unbroken. Muenscher[3] gives passages in proof of this statement,

---

1   Tertullian (160-225), a prolific early Christian author from Carthage in the Roman province of Africa, and the first Christian author to produce an extensive body of Latin Christian literature. He was an early Christian apologist and a polemicist against heresy. Tertullian has been called "the father of Latin Christianity" and "the founder of Western theology." Though conservative, he did originate and advance new theology to the early Church. He is perhaps most famous for being the oldest extant Latin writer to use the term *Trinity*.

2   Irenaeus (d.202) wrote *Against Heresies* (180) is a detailed attack on Gnosticism, which seriously threatened the Church, and particularly against the system of the Gnostic, Valentinus. As one of the first great Christian theologians, he emphasized the traditional elements in the Church, especially the episcopate, Scripture, and tradition.

3   Joseph Munchler, a 19th century German theologian who wrote on hermenuetics, the principles of biblical interpretation.

from Justin Martyr.[4] Athenagoras,[5] Tatian,[6] Theophilus Antioch,[7] Clemens Alex.,[8] Origen, Athanasius, Chrysostom, Cyril Hierosol.,[9] Titus of Bostra,[10] Basil the Great,[11] Gregory Naz.,[12] Gregory Nyss.,[13]

4   Justin Martyr (103-165), was an early Christian apologist. He first studied at the
    school of a Stoic philosopher, who was unable to explain God's being to him. He
    then studied with a Peripatetic philosopher but was put off because he was too eager
    to be paid. Then he went to hear a Pythagorean philosopher, who demanded that he
    first learn music, astronomy and geometry, which he did not wish to do. Then he
    was drawn to Platonism. Finally, he met an old man on the sea shore who told him
    about Christianity, and he converted. He was influenced in this by the fearless con-
    duct of the Christians facing execution.

5   Athenagoras (133 -190) was a Father of the Church, a Proto-orthodox Christian
    apologist who lived during the latter half of the 2nd century. An Athenian philoso-
    pher, a convert to Christianity and, likely, a Platonist before his conversion.

6   Tatian (120–180) was an Assyrian Christian theologian of the 2nd century. His theol-
    ogy involved a strict monotheism which becomes the source of the moral life. He
    believed that the human soul originally possessed faith in one God, but lost it with
    the fall. In consequence man sank under the rule of demons into the abominable er-
    ror of polytheism.

7   Theophilus, Patriarch of Antioch, succeeded Eros c. 169, and was succeeded by
    Maximus I c.183, but these dates are only approximate. He died about 183-185. He
    was the earliest Christian to use the word *Trinity*, but he did not refer to the Father,
    Son and Holy Spirit.

8   Clement of Alexandria (150-215) was a Christian theologian who taught at the Cat-
    echetical School of Alexandria and a convert to Christianity. He was well-educated
    and familiar with classical Greek philosophy and literature who was influenced by
    Hellenistic philosophy to a greater extent than any other Christian thinker of his
    time, and in particular by Plato and the Stoics.

9   Cyril of Alexandria (376-444), Patriarch of Alexandria from 412 to 444, came to
    power when the city was at its height of influence and power within the Roman
    Empire. Cyril wrote extensively and was a leading protagonist in the Christological
    controversies of the later 4th and 5th centuries.

10 Titus of Bostra (Bosra, now in Syria, died c.378) was a bishop and is one of early
    church writers claimed as an early Universalist because he taught that the immortal
    souls of the dead would be purified in purgatory until all were saved.

11 Basil of Caesarea (329-379) was the Greek bishop of Caesarea Mazaca in Cappado-
    cia, Asia Minor (modern-day Turkey). He was a great admirer of Origen and the
    need for the spiritual interpretation of Scripture.

12 Gregory of Nazianzus (329-390) was a 4th century Archbishop of Constantinople.
    As a classically trained orator and philosopher he infused Hellenism into the early
    church. His most significant theological contributions arose from his defense of the
    Nicene doctrine of the Trinity. He is especially noted for his contributions to the
    field of pneumatology, theology concerning the nature of the Holy Spirit.

13 Gregory of Nyssa (335-395) was bishop of Nyssa from 372 to 376, and again from
    378 until his death. He is venerated as a saint in Roman Catholicism, Eastern Ortho-
    doxy, Oriental Orthodoxy, Lutheranism and Anglicanism. He was an erudite the-

Nemesius,[14] Epiphanius.[15] Moreover, it is remarkable that Pelagius took the lead in denying this position, and in defending the doctrine that the death here spoken of was spiritual death.

In John of Damascus, who, at a subsequent date, gave form to the theology of the Greek church, the early doctrine of that church reappears; and still later Greek writers, as Theodoras Studaita,[16] Theophy-

---

ologian who made significant contributions to the doctrine of the Trinity and the Nicene creed. His philosophical writings were influenced by Origen, and he is generally considered to have believed in universal salvation.

14 Nemesius (390-?), Bishop of Emesa (in Syria), was a Christian philosopher, and the author of *On Human Nature*. He compiled a system of anthropology from the standpoint of Christian philosophy, and was a physiological theorist. Much of his writing was based on the work of Aristotle and Galen. He also developed a five-theory hierarchy of Divine Providence based on an earlier Platonic theory. He was one of the earliest advocates of the idea that different cavities of the brain were responsible for different functions. His Doctrine of Ventricle localization of Mental Functioning is a reconciliation of Platonic doctrines on the soul with Christian philosophy and also emphasized Greek scientific interpretation and knowledge of the human body. This doctrine was attributed to Gregory of Nyssa, and was not recognized as the work of Nemesius until the 7th century.

15 Epiphanius of Salamis (310/320-403), bishop of Salamis at the end of the 4th century, is considered a saint and a Church Father by both the Eastern Orthodox and Catholic Churches. He gained a reputation as a strong defender of orthodoxy. He is best known for composing a large compendium of the heresies up to his own time, full of quotations that are often the only surviving fragments of suppressed texts, and for instigating, with Tychon (Bishop of Amathus), a persecution against the non-Christians living on Cyprus, and the destruction of most of their temples. His best-known book is the *Panarion* which means "medicine-chest" (also known as *Against Heresies*), presented antidotes for those bitten by the serpent of heresy.

16 Theodora I (500-548), empress of the Roman (Byzantine) Empire and the wife of Emperor Justinian I. Like her husband, she is a saint in the Orthodox Church. She is perhaps the most influential and powerful woman in the Roman Empire's history. Her contemporary, John of Ephesus, wrote about her in his *Lives of the Eastern Saints,* and mentioned an illegitimate daughter not named by Procopius. From an early age she followed her sister Komito's example and worked in a Constantinople brothel serving low-status customers. Later she performed on stage earning her living by a combination of her theatrical and sexual skills. She made a name for herself with her portrayal of Leda and the Swan, where she stripped off her clothes as far as the law allowed. During this time she met the wife of Belisarius, Antonina, with whom she would remain lifelong friends. At the age of 16, she traveled to North Africa as the companion of a Syrian official named Hecebolus when he went to the Libyan Pentapolis as governor. On her way back to the capital of the Byzantine Empire, she stayed for a while in Alexandria, Egypt, where she met Patriarch Timothy III, who was Monophysite. She then converted to Monophysite Christianity. She worked against her husband's support of Chalcedonian Christianity, and in spite of Justinian being an Orthodox Christian, Theodora founded a Monophysite

lact[17] and Euthymius Zigabenus,[18] repeat it. They all teach that Adam's sin brought natural death on his posterity, but do not teach the propagation of a depraved nature, nor any connate guilt of Adam's sin. Indeed, as we have seen, earlier fathers explained the fact that men do uniformly sin, rather by the influence of evil spirits, than by a reference to the fall of Adam. Some, however, admitted that the moral faculties of man had been weakened by the fall; but none thought of denying the free will of man, and the voluntary nature of all sin. Cyril of Jerusalem,[19] according to Hagenbach, as we have seen, regarded men as born in a state of innocence, and that a free agent alone can sin. Ephraim the Syrian, Gregory of Nyssa and Basil the Great, take the same view. Chrysostom most earnestly advocated the liberty of man and his power of moral self-determination, and severely censured all who endeavored to excuse their own immoralities by ascribing the origin of their sin to the fall of Adam.

---

monastery in Sykae and provided shelter in the palace for Monophysite leaders who faced opposition from the majority Orthodox Christians, like Severus and Anthimus.

17 Theophylactus of Ohrid (1050/60-1108), born on the Greek island of Euboia, near Athens, was a Byzantine biblical scholar and exegete. He was educated at Constantinople by the finest teachers of literature and rhetoric of his time, and was appointed professor of rhetoric at the patriarchal academy and tutor to the emperor's children. He was consecrated as bishop and sent, against his will, to Ochrid, where he was the Metropolitan of the Church in Bulgaria for twenty-five years.

18 Euthymius Zigabenus (d. after 1118) was a 12th century monk and commentator on the Bible. He was a friend of the Byzantine emperor Alexius I Comnenus, for whom he wrote a lengthy work on heresies, *Panoplia Dogmatica,* which began in the apostolic era and continued down to the Bogomils, some of whom he personally examined.

19 Cyril of Jerusalem (313-386) was venerated as a saint by the Roman Catholic Church, the Eastern Orthodox Church, and the Anglican Communion. In 1883, Cyril was declared a Doctor of the Church by Pope Leo XIII. He is also highly respected in the Palestinian Christian Community. He adhered to the Nicene orthodoxy, even if he did avoid the debatable term *homooussios,* and expressed its sense in many passages, which exclude equally Patripassianism, Sabellianism, and the formula "there was a time when the Son was not" attributed to Arius. In other points emphasises the freedom of the will, the *autexousion* (αὐτεξούσιον), and his imperfect realization of the reality of sin. To him sin is the consequence of freedom, not a natural condition. The body is not the cause, but the instrument of sin. The remedy for it is repentance, on which he insists. Like many of the Eastern Fathers, he has an essentially moralistic conception of Christianity.

From this general view of the interpretation of this passage, one thing is plain,—that no one exposition, ancient or modern, can claim the sanction of universal authority.

CHAPTER III: THE TRUE INTERPRETATION OF ROM. 5:12-19

WE have considered some of the various modes in which this passage has been interpreted.

I shall next proceed to state what appears to me to be the true interpretation.

In my opinion, then, the interpretations of the Old School party and of the Greek church contain each an element of the true interpretation, to which must be added a third, found in neither, in order to combine all the parts of the true system.

The element of truth in the Old School system is, that the sense of the passage is judicial, relating to condemnation and justification, and not to the causation of sin or holiness in the race.

The element of truth in the Greek system is, that the death spoken of is simply natural death.

The element to be added, however, is one of more importance than either of the preceding, and must control the whole interpretation of the passage.

It is this,—that all the language, in this passage, which is commonly understood to assert that the sin of Adam exerted a causative power upon the condition and character of his descendants, need not be understood to denote *real* causation, but may, if any good reason calls for it, be held to denote only *apparent* causation; and that a good reason does call for this view; and moreover that such a sequence of apparent causation was established solely in order to make Adam a type of Christ.

The passage, then, thus viewed, teaches that God was pleased to establish immediately on the sin of Adam, and through that sin, the sequence of condemnation to natural death upon all men; a sequence linked to Adam's act by no causative power, but established solely as a type and illustration, both by similitude and antithesis, of the sequence of justification and life eternal from the obedience of Christ. — a sequence in which there is a real and glorious causative power.

315

Such a sequence, in itself devoid of causative power, but established for typical purposes, I call a merely *typical sequence*. It is one not founded in the nature of things, but in a positive arrangement, designed for typical (or typological[20]—Ed.) effect.

To illustrate my idea. When an Israelite, bitten by a fiery serpent, in accordance with the Word of God, looked up at the brazen serpent erected by Moses on a pole, he was immediately healed. Here, then, was a fixed sequence established by God. And yet all admit that there was in the brazen serpent no healing power. It was then a sequence of apparent causation, and not of real causation. But God was pleased to establish it for typical purposes, to illustrate the healing of the soul, mortally wounded by sin, that follows looking by faith to Christ.

Here, then, is a case of a merely typical sequence. There is apparent causation, but no real causation; and the sequence is established to typify another, in which there is a real and glorious causative power.

In like manner, that the sequence of condemnation and death coming on all men through the sin of Adam was a merely typical sequence, established to illustrate a causative sequence of justification and spiritual life through Christ, is the position which I lay down as the key of this whole.

So important a position will, of course, demand a radical investigation. Such an investigation will require us to consider two questions:

1. Is the sequence in this case, whatever it may be, one that is merely typical?
2. What is the sequence?

Of these two, the first, as we have said, is the fundamental question. Certain things are, in this passage, said to have been done by or through one man. What they are, as we have seen, is not agreed. Some

---

20 Whenever Beecher uses *typical* he means *typological*. Interpreting the Bible typologically means emphasizing literary analysis and the flow of the overarching story through each of the smaller, individual stories. This method of interpretation has been around since the Early Church Fathers, and writers such as Geerhardus Vos and other 19th century Presbyterians. In the 20th century, it was fleshed out by David Chilton and Meredith G. Kline, but especially by theologian James B. Jordan, whose books on typology (such as *Through New Eyes*), and the commentaries of Peter Leithart. Also see the works of Sidney Greidanus, Christopher J. H. Wright, Richard Gaffin, N. T. Wright, Stanley Hauerwas, George Stroup, Richard Hays, Rikk Watts, Willard Swartley, Sylvia Keesmaat, Ben Witherington, J. Ross Wagner, Don Garlington, Craig Evans, Steve Moyise, and David Pao.

say that by him natural death came on all men. Others, that penal retributions in general came on all men. Others, that universal sinfulness
came on all men.

Now, without at present deciding which of these sequences is
meant in the passage, I will merely assume that a sequence is meant of
some sort, and ask: is it, or is it not, a sequence of real causation?

To this I have replied that it is not, by any necessity of the case. I
admit that the language used to denote actual causation is used. So far
as the mere words are concerned, they may bear that sense. But there
is no necessity of it. It is equally in accordance with the laws of language and the usages of Scripture to suppose that the sequence is one
of merely apparent causation; so that the sin of Adam, in fact, exerted
no influence whatever on his race, but it and its sequences were
merely ordered so to stand in relation to each other as to make, at the
very introduction of the human race into this world, a striking type of
the coming Messiah, by whom the race was to be redeemed. On this
latter supposition, the fallen condition and depravity of the race are assumed as having been already in existence, and the doctrine is that the
events connected with the introduction of the race into this world by
one man were such as to form a type of the relations and acts of the
coming Messiah in redeeming the church.

Those interpretations which assume a causative sequence make the
sin of Adam really to cause either natural death, or condemnation, or
depravity to all the race, and so to do it as to be a type of the coming
Messiah.

The interpretation which I propose makes it a divinely established
antecedent, without causative power, but designed to make in the
opening scene of this world's history a sublime, impressive and beautiful type of the coming Messiah. The truth of this view, as I have said,
is the fundamental question of the whole discussion. It is also a question the importance of which cannot be overestimated. It is also a
question, so far as I know, never thus raised or discussed before. It has
been generally assumed that, whatever it is that followed the act of
Adam, it was linked to it by the power of a real causation. No one
seems to have thought that any law of language, or any usage of Scripture, gave us our choice here between real and apparent causation. All
seem to have felt themselves shut up to one mode of understanding the
language of causation here used.

However great, therefore, might be the objections from the nature of things, or from the principles of honor and right, to such an understanding, it has been felt that we have no right to give them any weight in opposition to the express statements of God.

It is my purpose, therefore, to show that the laws of language and the usages of Scripture do not shut us up to such a mode of interpretation; that the mode which regards the sequence as merely apparent and typical is in perfect accordance with Scripture usages, and the just laws of interpretation.

1. I say, then, in the first place, that nothing is more common in Scripture than to describe sequences of apparent causation in the same language as is used to describe real causation.

2. Secondly, in the case of types in particular, the sequences are very often those of apparent causation, and yet are always spoken of in the same language which is used to denote real causation.

3. Thirdly, that, in the case of any type, if there is in the nature of things a valid objection to the admission of real causation between the antecedent and the consequent, we have a perfect right to resort to the interpretation which assumes apparent causation.

4. By thus presenting to the mind a choice between the two modes of interpretation, objections to the first mode cease to be objections against the assertions of God, and become appropriate means of deciding what his language means, and thus what his assertions are.

Before proceeding to confirm my statements by proof, I would remark that the fundamental nature and the supreme importance of the inquiry will authorize more detail of Scripture and other proof than I should otherwise employ.

If, therefore, I multiply proofs and examples, it will be for the sake of impression, and to countervail long-established associations by the full exhibition of the laws of language, and the usages of the Word of God.

CHAPTER IV: USE OF LANGUAGE IN DESCRIBING SEQUENCES OF APPARENT CAUSATION

WE come now to consider the truth of the propositions which I have laid down. And, in the first place, I say that there are in the Word of God many sequences of merely apparent causation, not only in types, but elsewhere. And in all such cases both Scripture and the common usages of language, without hesitation, denote these sequences by the same forms of speech which are used to denote real causation. Of this we may find striking illustrations in the case of miracles, where the causative power is in God alone, and yet is apparently exerted by second causes. For example, Moses, by the direction of God, employed a rod, called the rod of God (Ex. 4: 20, and 17: 9), in producing the plagues of Egypt, in dividing the Red Sea, and in bringing water from the rock. Hence God speaks as if the rod had a causative power,—Ex. 4:17. "Take this rod, where with thou shalt do signs." Hence, also, without hesitation, men say that *by* the rod of Moses the water of Egypt was turned into blood, thunder and hail were brought from heaven, and swarms of locusts were summoned to devour the land. So also they say that by the rod of Moses the Red Sea was divided, and water was brought from the flinty rock.

In like manner, so far as language is concerned, a causative power to work miracles is by God ascribed to Moses himself; for, in Num. 20:8, God says to him, "Thou shalt bring forth to them water out of the rock; so shalt thou give the congregation and their beasts to drink."

So also it is said (Acts 5:12), "By the hands of the apostles (that is, by the apostles) were many signs and wonders wrought among the people." God also said to Moses, "Lift thou up the rod, and stretch out thine hand over the sea and divide it" (Ex. 14:16).

This mode of speech is natural to man, and almost universal. If we will read commentators, and the sermons even of the most eminent divines, we shall find that they speak as if miracles were in fact wrought by second causes; that is, they speak according to the appearance of things. Thus they freely say that handkerchiefs or aprons from the body of Paul, or even his shadow, healed the sick, or that the sick were healed by them (Acts 19:12). So also they say that by an ointment made of Christ's spittle and clay, and by washing in the pool of Siloam, the eyes of the blind man were opened; and also that by washing in the Jordan the leprosy of Naaman was healed.

So also it is said that by a stick of wood thrown into the water the lost head of the axe was made to swim; and that the bad water near Jericho was healed by salt that was thrown into it; and that the bitter water of Marah was made sweet by a branch of a tree thrown into it.

In like manner it is said that Elijah and Elisha divided the Jordan by smiting it with their mantle; and that the same river was again divided by the feet of the priests, and the ark of the covenant; that Elisha made iron to swim by a stick of wood, and that by the blowing of horns and a shout the walls of Jericho were thrown down.

Also, in describing all these facts, the mode of expression is often varied, and the apparent cause is said directly to do that which follows it. The rod of Moses is said to have divided the sea, and the mantle of Elijah the Jordan. Salt healed the waters of Jericho, a stick of wood made iron to swim, and a branch of a tree rendered sweet the bitter waters of Marah.

As an example of the general usage in question, we will quote Dr. Smalley:[21]—

> "The Red Sea was divided by Moses' rod, and the river Jordan by Elijah's mantle. It was by smiting the flinty rock in the wilderness that the waters were made to flow out of it like a river. It was by throwing a stick into the river that the young prophet's axe was made to swim, and by washing seven times in the Jordan that Naaman was healed of his leprosy."

---

21 John Smalley (1734-1820), Minister of the Gospel in Berlin, wrote *The law in all respects satisfied by our Saviour, in regard to those only who belong to him; or, None but believers saved, through the all-sufficient satisfaction of Christ,* and a sermon at Wallingford, with a view to the universalists, etc.

He is here endeavoring to show that men are not regenerated by any causative efficiency of the truth; and, to explain such statements as that men are "born again by the Word of God" he regards it as a case of merely apparent causation, spoken of in the same language that is used to denote real causation, and quotes these instances as parallel cases. Whether he is correct or not in denying that the Word of God is a real cause in regeneration, he is certainly correct in his recognition of the law of language which I have stated. Cases of apparent causation, he clearly saw, are often described by the same language which is used to describe real causation.

In like manner, what is said to be done by the rod of Moses, or by the mantle of Elijah, or by the salt, or the branch of a tree, or the stick of wood, is at other times said to be done by Moses or Elijah or Elisha themselves, although they did not do it any more than the material instrument which they used. There is no need of more numerous quotations to illustrate and prove these usages; they are so abundant that anyone can find them for himself at pleasure.

I now proceed to another connected usage of language which is worthy of special notice. I refer to the common and almost universal practice of forming illustrative comparisons by means of these sequences of apparent causation. It will be noticed that, in such cases, there is on one side a sequence of apparent causation to illustrate a sequence of real causation on the other. Thus Henry says of Elisha,

> "He was a man of great power; he could make iron to swim, contrary to its nature; God's grace can thus raise the stony iron heart, which is sunk into the mud of this world, and raise up affections naturally earthly to things above."

Here apparent and real causation are expressed in the same language, and one is used to illustrate the other. He says of Naaman,

> "His being cleansed by washing put an honor on the law for cleansing lepers,"

He says of Elisha,

> "He cast the salt into the spring of the waters, and so healed the streams and the ground they watered. Thus the way to

reform men's lives is to renew their hearts; let those be sea-
soned with the salt of grace, for out of them are the issues of
life."

Here, too, are the elements of a typical (or typological—Ed.) comparison. As Elisha, by casting in salt, healed the fountains of water, so
God by His grace heals the fountains of spiritual life in the soul. In this
case there is on one side apparent, on the other real causation, similarly
expressed. Scott says that at Marah a tree was pointed out to Moses,
"by means of which the waters became sweet and wholesome." Henry
says,

> "The Jews' tradition is, that the wood of this tree was itself
> bitter, yet it sweetened the waters of Marah; so the bitter-
> ness of Christ's suffering and death alters the property of
> ours."

Here again apparent and real causation are expressed alike, and
one is used to illustrate the other. Of Elisha, Henry says, "He was possessed of Elijah's power of dividing the Jordan." Also, speaking of "the
influence which the rod of Moses had upon the battle with the
Amalekites," he says,

> "to convince Israel that the hand of Moses (with whom they
> had just now been chiding) contributed more to their safety
> than their own hands, his rod than their sword, the success
> rises and falls, as Moses lifts up or lets down his hands."

Again, comparing Moses and Elijah, he says, "As Moses with his
rod divided the sea, so Elijah with his mantle divided Jordan." With
reference to the passage of the Jordan under Joshua, he says, "These
waters of old yielded to the ark, now to the prophet's mantle."

In some of the preceding examples, when no comparison is
formed, it will be seen that the strongest language of real causation is
used to describe sequences which are known to be entirely devoid of
causation. In the last comparisons the sequences on both sides are those
of apparent causation.

CHAPTER V: USE OF LANGUAGE IN DESCRIBING APPARENT CAUSATION IN TYPES

UNDER the general laws of language as to sequences of apparent causation comes that which it is my main purpose at this time to consider. I refer to typical sequences without any causative power, but established merely for the purpose of illustrating other sequences, in which there is real causation. Such sequences are merely typical sequences. They have no foundation in the nature of things. I do not mean to assert, of course, that a sequence in which there is real causation cannot be a type, but only that there were sequences that had no causative power, and were therefore merely typical. They were merely positive institutions for typical purposes. In the acts of David as king, in which he was a type of Christ, I do not deny that he exerted real and causative power; as, for example, in defending the people of God and defeating their foes. In other cases, however, if they were not established for the sake of making a type, the sequences would not have existed at all, for they have no foundation in the existing nature of things. A sequence of this kind I call a merely *typical sequence*; it is a sequence of merely apparent causation, established for the sake of a typical illustration of another sequence of real causation.

In this case the same laws of languages exists as in any other sequence of apparent causation; that is, the language of real causation is used. It is the more important to observe this, inasmuch as a neglect of these laws is the main cause of the misinterpretation of the passage in question.

For example, God ordained that after certain sacrifices sins should be remitted. This is a sequence of merely apparent causation, for it is impossible that the blood of bulls and of goats should take away sins. But when the sacrifice of Christ is followed by the remission of the sins of the believer, the causation is real. Moreover, the first of these sequences was established for the sake of foreshadowing the second. It is, therefore, a merely typical sequence.

God also ordained that the sprinkling of the blood of the paschal lamb on the doorposts of the houses of his people should be followed by exemption from the stroke of the angel of death. Here, too, the blood had no causative power to save. It was a sequence established to illustrate the power of Christ's blood to avert the blow of divine justice. Yet of this blood Scott uses the following remarkable language: "The blood of the paschal lamb, sprinkled on the lintel and doorposts, was the *only security* to the Israelites from the destroyer who smote the Egyptians; and under that protection they must abide during the whole night, if they would be secured from destruction. Thus must we abide in Christ by faith to the end of our days." In like manner the sacred writers habitually speak according to the appearance of things; and express a typical sequence, in which no causation exists, by the same terms in which they express a sequence of real causation in the antitype.[22] Accordingly, the Mosaic sacrifices are said, in the Word of God, times without number, to take away sins, to make atonement for sins, to confer the pardon of sins, etc.; the very modes of expression that are used in describing the effects of the efficient atoning power of the blood of Christ. For example, the man who was guilty of fraud as to a trust or in fellowship, or of violent robbery, or of deceit, or of appropriating what had been found and was known to belong to another, and swearing falsely to conceal it, was commanded first to make restitution, and then to bring a ram as a trespass offering unto the priest, and then the following unequivocal language is used: "And the priest shall make atonement for him before the Lord; and it shall be forgiven him for anything of all that he hath done in trespassing therein" (Lev. 6:1—7). The same kind of language is repeated, in various cases, in the preceding chapter. This usage of language is most impressively exhibited in the sixteenth chapter of Leviticus, in the account of the great annual expiation made by the High Priest in the holy of holies for the whole people, by the sprinkling of blood upon and before the mercyseat. He is expressly said to make atonement, by the sacrifice of the scapegoat, for himself, and for his household, and for all the congregation of Israel, and to take away all their iniquities, as fully as this is ever said to be done by the atonement made by the

---

22 Antitype: A person or thing represented or foreshadowed by a type or symbol; especially a figure in the Old Testament having a counterpart in the New Testament.

blood of Christ, of which this great annual expiation was the most striking type.

I am aware that Socinus and others have asserted that the Mosaic sacrifices were offered only for certain lighter offenses and sins of ignorance, but not for sins in general. In reply to them, Turretin, referring to the passages just quoted, and to numerous others, clearly proves that they were offered for sins in general, even of the most atrocious kind. He asks, "When God, in Lev. 16, mentions iniquities and rebellions, nay, all their sins, does he mean only infirmities and sins of ignorance? No sane man can believe it." He shows that the sins for which these sacrifices were offered were designated by the same names as the greatest and most intentional and voluntary sins, and then adds,

> "Since the sins for which these sacrifices were offered are expressed by all these names, without any restriction,—nay, since the expiation is expressly extended to all sins, of whatever kind,—he would do injustice to the Holy Spirit who should limit them to sins of a particular kind" (Turretin, Disp. XIX. *On The Atonement of Christ*, § 9 and 4).

He also freely speaks of these sacrifices as making atonement for all these sins, in language as full as is ever used concerning the atonement of Christ; and he adverts to the same use of language in the Scriptures.

The substitution of the victim, the imposition of hands, the confession of sins, the shedding of blood, the deprecation of divine anger, and the effects of the whole transaction, he refers to as proving that by these sacrifices an atonement for real and great sins was made. "For," says he,

> "if the sacred rites were duly performed, and the victim was declared to be accepted, and to be a sweet smelling savor, then the consequences were the forgiveness of sins and the liberation of the criminal. Hence, repeatedly you may read in Lev. 4, 5, etc., 'the priest shall make atonement for him, and his sins shall be forgiven'" (Disp. XVIII. §7).

He also illustrates this view by a reference to cases in which it is said that an atonement was in fact made and accepted, and God appeased by it (Disp. XIX. § 6), and then adds,

> "Thus, in innumerable other cases, as often as the anger of
> God against the sins of men is appeased by sacrifices, so of-
> ten is it intimated that these sacrifices are offered not for
> some particular and lighter sins, but for all in general, unless
> in any case particular exceptions are made in the law."

The existence of some such specially exempted cases he admits.

Yet, in other places, the same Turretin no less distinctly declares
that these sacrifices had no power to purify the conscience by a real
atonement, or by any real efficiency to take away sin. He expressly
states and proves the following proposition:

> "The victims and sacrifices of the law neither expiated nor
> could expiate any sin, properly speaking; they could only
> expiate certain corporeal and ceremonial impurities" (Disp.
> XIX. § 18).

Hence he says,

> "There are various modes of speaking concerning these vic-
> tims that seem to be contradictory; for at one time it is de-
> nied that they have the power of atoning for sins, and at
> another time it is asserted. But these statements are easily
> reconciled by making this distinction: we deny to them the
> power of expiation considered in themselves and in their re-
> lations to the law" (that is, the causation is *merely apparent*);
> "but we ascribe it to them viewed as connected with Christ
> in the covenant of grace, and in their relations to the mys-
> teries of the gospel, of which they were the types and repre-
> sentations" (Disp. XIX. § 26).

That is, viewing them as types, we use this language just as if the
causation were real, though in fact it is *in Christ* only.

All, then, that I have stated, concerning the laws of typical language, is, in fact, recognized by Turretin, and would be true if it were
not. There was in the sacrifices a merely typical sequence, designed to
represent a real and causative sequence, effected by the atonement of
Christ; but the language used to describe each sequence was the same,
so that, although the sacrifices had no power to make atonement for

sins, yet, as types of the great atonement, they were again and again said to make such atonement.

A very striking case of a similar sequence of apparent causation is found in the history of the rebellion of Korah (Num. 16:46, 47). Wrath had gone out from the Lord, and the plague had begun. Moses said to Aaron, Go,

> "take a censer, and fire, and incense, and make an atonement for them. And Aaron ran into the midst of the people, and behold the plague was begun; and he put on incense and made an atonement for the people, and he stood between the dead and the living, and the plague was stayed."

On this Scott says,

> "This success was a decisive proof of the efficacy of his priesthood." "By his burning of incense the plague was instantly stayed." "In this he was an eminent type of Christ, and his intercession, by which his atonement is rendered effectual to our salvation."

Here is a striking typical illustration of the kind which I am describing. On one side is a merely typical sequence, devoid of causative power; on the other, a causative sequence of real and glorious power. Yet God says that Aaron made atonement, and the plague was stayed. Concerning this same scene, Henry says, "The cloud of Aaron's incense, coming from his hand, stayed the plague." Yet did he suppose that there was in the incense any real power to heal so fatal a pestilence? It ought here to be attentively noticed, that as now by incense, so in the case of the passover by the sprinkling of blood on the door posts in Egypt, temporal death was averted. But by Christ's blood and intercession spiritual death is averted.

But, when sacrifices and incense are said to atone for sin, does the language ever mislead an intelligent reader? He knows that blood and incense cannot thus atone. He knows equally well that there is no power to remit sins but in the great atoning sacrifice of Christ, and that the remissions following Mosaic sacrifices were, in fact, effected by the power of that great atonement, as foreseen.

Indeed, this use of causative language is so natural that we fall into it spontaneously and abundantly. For example, though we know that a brazen serpent had no power to heal one who had been bitten by a venomous fiery serpent, yet we as naturally speak of the serpent lifted up by Moses as healing those who looked to it as we do of Christ as healing those who look to him. Scott says, "The sight of the brazen serpent healed the people." Henry says,

> "That which cured was shapen in the likeness of that which wounded." "A serpent of brass cured them." "Jesus Christ came to save us by healing us, as the children of Israel that were stung by fiery serpents were cured and lived by looking up to the brazen serpent."

Peers, speaking of this type, says,

> "The tremulous eye of infancy, or the feeble sight of old age, if only directed to its proper object, alike experienced its salutary energy; and the obscure and imperfect faith of those whose natural faculties may be insufficient to comprehend the mysteries of the kingdom, or even to explain the nature of their belief, yet if humbly directed to the author of life, shall experience his power to save equally with their more highly gifted brethren." "As each sufferer must himself look to the brazen serpents or his cure, so must every repenting sinner believe (in Christ) for salvation."

Yet he well knew, for so he says, that the healing efficacy was not in the serpent, but in God. Newton says,

> "From guilt and condemnation there is no relief, till we can look to Jesus, as the wounded Israelites did to the brazen serpent; which was not to give efficacy to medicines and plasters of their own application, but to heal them completely of itself by looking at it."

Yet he knew that in reality it had of itself no healing power. No stronger language can be used to denote a causative sequence than is here used to denote a sequence not causative, but merely typical. Edwards says,

"The way that the people were saved by the brazen serpent was by looking to it, beholding it, as seeking and expecting salvation from it. And faith and trust in the Messiah are often spoken of as the great condition of salvation through him."

Calvin says,

"Christ was to be lifted up that all might look to him. Of this there was a type in the brazen serpent lifted up by Moses, the sight of which was a saving cure for those who were mortally wounded by the bite of serpents."

Turretin says,

"If a living serpent bit anyone, a dead serpent cured him, and that merely by the sight of it."

Yet elsewhere he says that neither the serpent nor the act of looking to him had any healing power. He then asks, "Why was the serpent lifted up as a remedy for the wounds of Israel? Why did a sight of it heal?" He answers, "Because the serpent was a divinely ordained type of Christ, and his power to heal the wounds of sin." Doddridge, in his paraphrase, says.

"As Moses lifted up the brazen serpent on a pole in the wilderness, to heal those that were dying by the venom of the fiery serpents there, so also must the Son of Man be first lifted up on a cross, and then publicly exhibited in the preaching of the gospel, that sinners may receive by him a far more noble and important cure."

I quote thus largely in order to make the laws of language in such cases familiar, and could easily multiply cases from the usages of language concerning other types. But what I have quoted must be sufficient. In this last case, two things are deserving of very particular notice. One, that a typical sequence, not implying causative power, is expressed in precisely the same way as the causative sequence which it typified. The other, that the type relates to the healing of the body, the antitype to the healing of the mind, just as the sprinkling of blood in Egypt and the incense of Aaron related to averting temporal death, but the blood and intercession of Christ to averting spiritual and eternal death, in accordance with the analogy established by God between things material and things spiritual.

Let us now review what has been proved. It has been shown,

1. That nothing is more common than the existence in types of sequences of apparent causation, established for purposes of typical illustration.

2. That these, in common with all other sequences of apparent causation, are both in scriptural and in common usage described in the very language that is used to denote real causation.

It follows that, if in the case of any type there is a valid objection to admitting a sequence of real causation, we have a perfect right in interpretation to assume that the language denotes a sequence of apparent causation.

That the justice and honor of God forbid a sequence of real causation in the case of Adam, has, I think, been shown, and will more fully be shown. The inference is self-evident.

CHAPTER VI: APPLICATION OF THE PRECEDING PRINCIPLES TO ROM. 5:12-19

I COME now to apply the principles which have been illustrated to the passage which is the main subject of our present consideration. The passage in question is as follows:

> "12. Wherefore as by one man sin entered into the world, and death by sin; and so death passed upon all men, for that all have sinned. 13. (For until the law, sin was in the world; but sin is not imputed when there is no law. 14. Nevertheless, death reigned from Adam to Moses, even over them that had not sinned after the similitude of Adam's transgression, who is the figure of him that was to come. 15. But not as the offense, so also is the free gift. For if through the offense of one many be dead, much more the grace of God, and the gift by grace, which is by one man, Jesus Christ, hath abounded unto many. 16. And not as it was by one that sinned, so is the gift. For the judgment was by one to condemnation, but the free gift is of many offenses unto justification. 17. For if by one man's offense death reigned by one; much more they which receive abundance of grace? and of the gift of righteousness, shall reign in life by one, Jesus Christ.) 18. Therefore, as by the offense of one judgment came upon all men to condemnation, even so by the righteousness of one the free gift came upon all men unto justification of life. 19. For as by one man's disobedience many were made sinners, so by the obedience of one shall many be made righteous."

So far as the relations of Adam to his race are concerned, this passage, as it stands, asserts (v. 12) that by one man sin entered into the world, and death by sin, and so (that is, by one man) death passed upon all men, for that all have sinned; v. 15, through the offense of one the many have died; v. 16, the judgment was by one to condemnation; v. 17, by one man's offense death reigned by one; v. 18, by the offense of one, judgment came upon all men to condemnation; v. 19, by one man's disobedience the many were made sinners.

Tholuck refers to Chrysostom, Theophylact, and Grotius,[23] as taking the expression "all have sinned," in v. 12, to mean "all have been treated as sinners." He also concedes that the original words παντες ημαρτον may have that sense, and so does Professor Stuart. Storr and Bloomfield[24] adopt it. Knapp also gives to the word ἁμαρτία (sin) the sense, "the guilt of sin," and Schleusner[25] "the guilt and punishment of sin." These judicial senses of these words are still further authorized by the highest authority, as will appear hereafter.

Accordingly, I shall take the expressions "all have sinned," v. 12, and "many were made sinners," v. 19, to mean "were made liable to penalty as sinners;" and "sin," v. 12, to mean "liability to penalty as a sinner." Thus understood, these verses coincide in idea with the statement of verse 16, that "the judgment was by one to condemnation;" and of verse 18, that "by the offense of one judgment came upon all men to condemnation."

It is plain also that the sinful act of Adam, and the condemnation that followed it, are set forth as, in a general view, typical, by way of similitude and antithesis, of the righteousness of Christ, and of the justification of believers thereby.

The main questions in the interpretation of this passage, thus viewed, are, what is the import of the condemnation or judgment on the human race which is said to be by the offense of Adam, and what

---

23 Hugo Grotius (1583-1645) was a jurist in the Dutch Republic. With Francisco de Vitoria and Alberico Gentili he laid the foundations for international law, based on natural law. He was also a philosopher, theologian, Christian apologist, playwright, and poet.

24 Samuel Thomas Bloomfield (1790-1869) was an English clergyman and Biblical textual critic. His Greek New Testament was widely used, in England and the United States.

25 Johann Friedrich Schleusner (1759-1831), a German Protestant theologian who was the fourth professor of theology at the University of Wittenburg, with the associated positions of provost of the Wittenberg Castle Church and assessor at Wittenberg consistory. He was rector of Wittenberg University in the winter semesters 1798, 1804 and 1808. In 1805 he became the third theological professor. In 1817, the government established a post-graduate seminary at Wittenburg, appointing Carl Ludwig Nitzsch as its head and Schleusner as second director.

is the real connection between Adam's sin and this condemnation or judgment;— is it *causative*, or only *typical* (typological—Ed.)?

In reply to these inquiries, I say, in view of the principles already set forth, that when a certain sinful act of Adam, and its sequences, condemnation and death, are set forth as antithetically typical of the righteousness of Christ, and its sequences, justification and life, there is good reason for insisting that the sequence in the case of Adam does not involve a causative power. It should clearly be regarded as merely typical, and not causative. Moreover, the fact that the sequence to the righteousness of Christ is spiritual,—that is, eternal life,—is no proof at all that the typical sequence to the sin of Adam is not natural,—that is, corporeal death,—in accordance with the same laws of analogy which we see observed in the case of bodily wounds healed by the brazen serpent, as a type of mental wounds healed by Christ. On these principles, the sequences would stand thus: As by the transgression of one (Adam) condemnation and natural death came on all naturally related to him, so by the righteousness of one (Christ) justification and eternal life came on all spiritually related to him.

The passage, thus viewed, simply teaches that Adam was a typical person; and that his transgression, and the events consequent thereon, were so arranged as to be typical events; and accordingly were so ordered by God that the condemnation of the race to death for his offense, and its sequences, should, both by way of similarity and also of antithesis or contrast, be a striking foreshadowing of the justification and life of all who trust in the great Savior, by whom the church was to be redeemed out of our race; and that what is said to be done by Adam, or by his offense, to his posterity, denotes a merely typical sequence, and not a sequence of causation.

Let us, then, consider more in detail the truth of these statements.

First, then, as to the typical character of Adam, it is asserted in express terms. He is said to be a type of Him who is to come (τυπος του μελλοντος) that is, of Christ. Nor is this the only place, as we shall see, where this typical character is asserted or assumed.

His typical character is, in this passage, developed by points of similarity, modified and limited by points of contrast. Let us first consider the points of similarity.

1. One point of similarity lies in the fact that in each case there is unity of headship in reference to those related to each. God

might, if he had seen fit, have introduced the human race into this world by many heads. But, if he had done so, then it would not have foreshadowed the one great redeeming head of the church, who was to come. Hence he introduced them by one head. For this reason, Adam is prominently set forth as the one who is the sole head of his natural posterity, and thus, as a type of Christ, as the one who is the sole head of believers in Him. On this unity of headship, in each case, the whole comparison turns. As by *one* came condemnation and death, so by *one* came justification and life.

2. In each case the relations of each head were not limited and national, but catholic, extending to men of all nations. The pride of the Jews conceived of a Messiah whose highest favors should be peculiarly and exclusively their own. As a conquering king, he was destined to exalt their nation above all others. This exclusive idea Paul rebuts by saying that, as the first Adam (the type) was not national in his relations, but universal,—as through him all men were sentenced to natural death, —so must the second Adam be the universal head and Savior of all men of all nations who believe in him, justifying alike all who believe,—making, in this respect, no distinction between Gentile and Jew.

3. Another point of similarity is that in each case there is a judicial act in consequence of what is done by each head. This idea enters deeply into the whole structure of the passage, from beginning to end. The preceding discussion of Paul relative to the effects of the atonement of Christ had been judicial. Justification is a judicial act, flowing from something done by Christ, the antitype. So also is condemnation a judicial act, flowing from something done by Adam, the type. The entire spirit of the passage is judicial. It speaks of acquitting and condemning, and not of making holy or sinful; and, as before remarked, the judicial act flowing from the conduct of each head extends to all connected with him. Condemnation and death, flowing from Adam's act, extend to all men. Justification and life, flowing from Christ's act, extend to all of whom He becomes the head by faith. There is, therefore, in each case a judicial sequence, of which the reality is asserted;

while it is of necessity clear that there is no efficient causation in the case of the type. Such are the points of similarity.

The points of dissimilarity and contrast, by which these are modified and limited, are,

1. That the action of one head was sinful; of the other, righteous.
2. That the judicial act in one case was just condemnation; in the other, gracious acquittal.
3. That in one case the result of the judicial act was the penalty of natural death; in the other, the free gift of spiritual and eternal life. This I shall more fully prove.
4. That the acquittal greatly transcends in the results of grace the results of the condemnation, inasmuch as it justifies and confers eternal life notwithstanding many sins, whereas the condemnation was based on one sin and resulted in natural death.

Now, if this is the true view of the passage, it decides nothing but this, respecting our relations to Adam, and his influence on the race, namely, the fact that the sentence of condemnation to natural death which was passed on him when he sinned was intended to include, and from age to age actually to come upon, the whole human race; and that accordingly such have been, and ever will be, the sequences of his act of sin. But any efficient or causative power of Adam's act to produce such results it does not imply. For, as we have seen, the use of causative language in typical sequences by no means implies any causative power, but merely a sequence established by God for the sake of illustration and impression. And certainly, in the present case, the actual preexistent sin of the human race, each for himself, is a rational ground for passing such a sentence; but the single sin of the first man, a sin in which they neither did or could act at all, is not either a reasonable or just ground of such a sequence.

Chapter VII: Appeal To Authorities

I HAVE mentioned, as worthy of notice, that the judicial view of this passage, independently of what I have just said of the nature of typical sequences and the interpretation of language applied to them, excludes the interpretation which is so common among the New School divines who deny imputation, namely, that the sin of Adam exerted an influence to make all men actual sinners, or that all men are caused to become actual sinners in consequence of it.

The Old School divines teach, that, whether the sin of Adam made all men actual sinners or not in fact, at all events, this passage does not teach that doctrine. If to any this seems to be a surprising and dangerous position, to such I would say that it is nevertheless the openly avowed position of those who are in the highest repute for orthodoxy, and who consider themselves as peculiarly devoted to its vindication and defense. As this is a very important point, I will state an outline of the course of reasoning pursued by Prof. Hodge, designing to avail myself not only of the weight of his authority, but of his logical and exegetical power, to sustain the judicial view of the passage which I have given, and all its legitimate consequences.

The main scope of his argument is to prove that throughout this passage; "the very point and pith of the comparison" are not this,—that, as the sin of Adam was the cause of a corrupt nature in us, or of our actual sin and entire depravity, so the obedience of Christ is the cause of the restoration to us of true holiness, either in nature or in action:— but this,—that, as through the sin of Adam a condemning sentence was passed upon all men, so, through the obedience of Christ, a sentence of acquittal or justification is passed on all who trust in Him. In accordance with this view, he holds that in verse 12 the words "by one man sin entered into the world, and death by sin, and so death passed upon all men, for that all have sinned," do not refer to actual sin, or a corrupt nature, but to the great fact that through the sin of Adam all men were rendered liable to the same sentence of death which was passed on Adam. He thus states the different views of leading authors on this point:

> "1. Many, not only of the older, but also of the modern commentators and theologians, understand sin here to mean corruption; so Storr, Flatt, Bretschneider, etc. This clause, then, teaches that Adam was the cause of the corruption of our nature, which all men have derived from him. 2. Others, taking the word *sin* in its ordinary signification, understand the passage as teaching that Adam *was the cause or occasion of all men's being led to commit personal or actual sin*, either from the force of example or circumstances, or divine constitution. 3. Others understand the declaration that 'through Adam all men became sinners' to mean that on his account *all men are regarded and treated as sinners*."

He then proceeds to state the arguments against the first and second opinions, and in favor of the third. Against the first he reasons as follows:

> "1. It assigns a very unusual, if not an unexampled sense to the words,—the word rendered *have become corrupt* not occurring elsewhere with this signification. 2. It destroys the analogy between Christ and Adam. The point of the comparison is not, 'As Adam was the source of corruption, so is Christ of holiness;' but, 'As Adam was the cause of our condemnation, so is Christ of our justification.' 3. It is inconsistent with the meaning of vs. 13. 14. which are designed to prove that the ground of the universality of death is the sin or offense of Adam. 4. It would require us, in order to preserve any consistency in the passage, to put an interpretation on vs. 15, 16, 17, 18, 19, which they will not bear. *Although the sentiment, therefore, is correct and scriptural, that we derive a corrupt nature from Adam, as it is also true that Christ is the author of holiness, yet these are not the truths which Paul is here immediately desirous of presenting*."

His objections to the second view are presented in the form of arguments for the third. The main course of argument I approve, but not every particular argument.

1. The words translated "sin," and "have sinned," in v. 12, may, in strict accordance with scriptural usage, have the sense of liability to condemnation, or penalty, or of becoming liable to penalty, so as to be regarded and treated as sinners. On this point his argument is clearly conclusive. It is as follows:

> "The word translated *have sinned* may, in strict accordance with usage, be rendered have become guilty, or regarded and treated as sinners. Gen. 44:32 is in Greek, 'I shall have sinned' (ἡμαρτηκὼς ἔσομαι), which expresses the same idea as the English version of the passage; 'I shall bear the blame to my father forever,' that is, 'I shall always be regarded as a sinner.' The same phrase 34 occurs in Gen. 43:9, 'Then let me bear the blame,' the precise idea of being regarded as a sinner; 1 Kings 1:21, 'I and my son Solomon shall be sinners,' that is, *regarded and counted as such*. In our version, therefore, it is correctly rendered, 'Shall be counted offenders.' (In Greek, καὶ ο υιος μου σαλωμων αμαρτωλοι). In Job 9:29, 'If I be wicked' is the opposite idea to 'thou will not hold me innocent,' v. 28, and therefore means, 'If I be *condemned or regarded* as wicked.' Indeed, there is no usage more familiar to the student of the Bible than one nearly identical with this. 'He shall be clean,' 'he shall be unclean,' 'he shall be just,' 'he shall be wicked,' are expressions constantly occurring in the sense of 'he shall be *so regarded and treated*.' (See Storr's *Observationes*, p. 14.) The interpretation, therefore, which has been given of these words, instead of being forced or unusual, is agreeable to one of the most common and familiar usages of scripture language. Even Wahl, in his Lexicon, so explains them, 'άμαρτάνω to bear the blame of sin, Rom. 5:12, coll. v. 19, ubi (questionable. see the original—Ed.) αμαρτωλοι κατεσταθησαν. Ita Lxx. חטא, Gen. 44: 32.'"

His argument on the expression *were made sinners* (v. 19) is as follows:

> "It is in accordance with one of the most familiar of scriptural usages that the words *to make sinners*, are interpreted as

meaning to regard and treat as such. This interpretation, which is demanded both by the usage of the terms employed (see on Rom. 8:4) and the antithesis in this verse, is now almost universally adopted by all classes of commentators. (See Wahl's Lexicon under the word ἁμαρτάνω.) Thus, to make clean, to make unclean, to make righteous, to make guilty, are the constant scriptural expressions for *regarding and treating* as clean, unclean, righteous or unrighteous. (See on v. 12.)

"The expressions, *to make sin*, and *to make righteous* occurring in a corresponding sense, illustrate and confirm this interpretation. Thus, in 2 Cor. 5:21, Christ is said to be 'made sin,' that is, regarded and treated as a sinner, 'that we might be made the righteousness of God in him,' that is, that we might be *regarded and treated as righteous*, in the sight of God, on his account. The word (γενωμεθα) rendered *were made*, in its ground form signifies *to place*, and is often equivalent very nearly with the simple verb *to be*. James 4:4, 'Whosoever, therefore, will be the friend of the world, is an enemy of God;' see also 3:6. It also signifies to constitute in the sense of *appointing to office*, Luke 12:14, Acts 7:10, etc., etc.; or in that of making a person or thing something. In this case it may be rendered simply *they are*. 'By one man's disobedience many are sinners,' or are constituted such, or are made such? The idea is the same. The antithesis is here so plain as to be of itself decisive. 'To be made righteous' is, according to Prof. Stuart, 'to be justified, pardoned, regarded and treated as righteous.' With what show of consistency, then, can it be denied that 'to be made sinners,' in the opposite clause, means *to be regarded and treated* as sinners? If one part of the verse speaks of justification, the other must speak of condemnation."

2. In v. 12, a comparison is begun, which is resumed and completed in vs. 18 and 19.

"It will be seen that those verses teach that 'judgment came upon all men on account of the offense of one man;' that 'on account of the disobedience of one man all were regarded as sinners.' To this corresponds the plain declaration of v. 16. 'We are condemned for one offense.' If, then, these verses express the same idea with v. 12, as is freely admitted by Prof. Stuart and others, *we are forced to understand verse 12 as teaching, not the acknowledged truth that men are actual sinners, but that they have been treated as sinners on account of one man.*"

3. The connection of v. 12 with those which follow demands this interpretation; for vs. 13, 14 are designed to prove the assertion of v. 12 in the sense which is claimed, and are inconsistent with any other sense.

4. It is assumed in vs. 15-19 that the truth of v. 12 has been proved, in this sense, as a proper basis of reasoning and illustration.

5. "This interpretation is required by the whole scope of the passage and drift of the argument. The scope of the passage, as shown above, is to illustrate the doctrine of justification on the ground of the righteousness of Christ, by a reference to the condemnation of men for the sin of Adam. Not only does the scope of the passage demand this view, but only thus can the argument of the apostle be consistently carried through. We die on account of Adam's sin, v. 12; this is true, because on no other ground can the universality of death be accounted for (vs. 13, 14). But, if we all die on Adam's account, how much more shall we live on account of Christ (v. 15)! Adam, indeed, brings upon us the evil inflicted for the first great violation of the covenant, but Christ saves us from all our numberless sins, v. 16. As, therefore, for the offense of one we are condemned, so for the righteousness of one we are justified (v. 18). As on account of the disobedience of one we are treated as sinners, so on account of the obedience of one we are treated as righteous (v. 19). The inconsistency and confusion consequent on attempting to carry either of the other interpretations through, must be obvious to any attentive reader of such attempts."

6. Scripture and experience confirm this interpretation.

7. It accords with the views of the Jews at the time of the apostle and afterward.

8. "This interpretation, so far from being the offspring of theological prejudice, or fondness for any special theory, is so obviously the true and simple meaning of the passage required by the context, that it has the sanction of theologians of every grade and class of doctrine. Calvinists, Arminians, Lutherans, Rationalists,[26] agree in its support. Thus Storr, one of the most accurate of philological interpreters, explains the last words of the verse in the manner stated above. 'By one man all are subject to death, because all are *regarded and treated* as sinners; that is, because all lie under the sentence of condemnation.' The phrase *all have sinned* (v. 12), he says, is equivalent to *all are constituted sinners* (v. 19); which latter expression he renders '*sie werden als Sunder angesehen und behandelt*,' that is, they were *regarded and treated as sinners*. See his *Commentary on Hebrews*, p. 636, 640, etc. (Flatt renders these words in precisely the same manner.) The Rationalist Ammon[27] also considers the apostle as teaching that on the account of the sin of Adam all men are subject to death. (See Excursus C. to Koppe's *Commentary on the Epistle to the Romans*.) Zacharise,[28] in his *Biblische The-*

---

26 Proponents of some varieties of rationalism argue that, starting with foundational basic principles, like the axioms of geometry, the rest of all possible knowledge can be derived. The philosophers who held this view most clearly were Baruch Spinoza and Gottfried Leibniz, whose attempts to grapple with the epistemological and metaphysical problems raised by Descartes led to a development of the fundamental approach of rationalism. Both Spinoza and Leibniz asserted that, in principle, all knowledge, including scientific knowledge, could be gained through the use of reason alone, though they both observed that this was not possible in practice for human beings except in specific areas such as mathematics. On the other hand, Leibniz admitted that "we are all mere Empirics in three fourths of our actions" (*Monadology* § 28, cited in Audi 772). Rationalism is predicting and explaining behavior based on logic.

27 Christoph Friedrich von Ammon (1766-1850) was a German theologian who sought to establish a middle position between rationalism and supernaturalism. He called it "rational supernaturalism," and contended that there must be a gradual development of Christian doctrine corresponding to the advance of knowledge and science. But at the same time he sought, like other representatives of this school of thought, such as K.G. Bretschneider and Julius Wegscheider, to keep in close touch with the historical theology of the Protestant churches.

28 Karl Salomo Zachariae von Lingenthal, (1769-1843), German jurist, was born at Meissen in Saxony, the son of a lawyer and was the father of Karl Eduard Zachariae. His writings deal with almost every branch of jurisprudence; they are philosophical, historical and practical, and relate to Roman, Canon, German, French and English law. The first book of much consequence which he published was *Die Einheit des Staats und der Kirche mit Rücksicht auf die Deutsche Reichsverfassung* (1797), a work on the relations of church and state, with special reference to the constitution of the

ologie, vol. vi. p. 128, has an excellent exposition of this whole passage.
The question of the imputation of Adam's sin, he says, is this:
"Whether God regarded the act of Adam as the act of all men, or,
which is the same thing, whether he has subjected them all to punishment on account of this single act." This, he maintains, the apostle asserts and proves. On this verse he remarks, "*The question is not here
immediately about the propagation of a corrupted nature to all men, and of
the personal sins committed by all men, but of universal guilt* (Strafwür-
digkeit, liability to punishment), in the sight of God, which has come
upon all men; and which Paul in the sequel does not rest on the personal sins of men, but only on the offense of one man, Adam (v. 16).
Neither the corruption of nature, nor the actual sins of men and their
liability on account of them, is either questioned or denied; but the
simple statement is, that on account of the sin of Adam all men are
treated as sinners. Zachariae, it must be remembered, was not a
Calvinist, but one of the modern and moderate theologians of Göttingen.[29] Whitby, the great advocate of Arminianism, says, on these
words,

> "It is not true that death came upon all men *for that* or *be-
> cause* all have sinned. (He contends for the rendering *in
> whom.*) For the apostle directly here asserts the contrary,
> namely, that the death and the condemnation to it, which

---

empire, which displayed the writer's power of analysis and his skill in making a
complicated set of facts appear to be deductions from a few principles. He attempted
to find a new theoretical basis for society in place of the opportunist politics which
had led to the cataclysm of the French Revolution. This basis he seemed to discover
in something resembling Jeremy Bentham's utilitarianism. His last work of importance, *Vierzig Bücher vom Staate*, compared to Montesquieu's *L'Esprit des lois*, and
covers much of the same ground as Buckle's first volume of the *History of Civiliza-
tion*. Its fundamental theory is that the state had its origin, not in a contract
(Rousseau-Kant), but in the consciousness of a legal duty. What Machiavelli was to
the Italians and Montesquieu to the French, Zachariae aspired to become to the
Germans; but he lacked their patriotic inspiration, and so failed to exercise any permanent influence on the constitutional law of his country.

29 Göttingen is a university town in Lower Saxony, Germany. Prior to the period of
German romanticism, a group of German poets that had studied at this university
between 1772 and 1776, formed the "circle of poets." Being disciples of Friedrich
Gottlieb Klopstock (1724–1803), they revived the folksong and wrote lyric poetry
of the Sturm und Drang period. Their impact was essential on romanticism in the
German-speaking area and on folklore in general. Schiller and Goethe were artisti-
cally indebted to him.

befell all men, was for the sin of Adam only; for here it is expressly said that by the sin of one man many died; that the sentence was from one, and by one man sinning to condemnation; and that by the sin of one death reigned by one. Therefore, the apostle doth expressly teach us that this death —this condemnation to it—came not upon us for the sin of all, but only for the sin of one; that is, of that one Adam in whom all men die (1 Cor. 15:22.) Such extracts might be indefinitely multiplied from the most various sources. However these commentators may differ in other points, they almost all agree in the general idea, which is the sum of the whole passage, that the sin of Adam, and not their own individual actual transgressions, is the ground and reason of the subjection of all men to the penal evils here spoken of. With what plausibility can an interpretation commanding the assent of men so various be ascribed to theory or philosophy, or love of a particular theological system? May not its rejection with more probability be attributed, as is done by Knapp, to theological prejudice? Certain it is, at least, that the objections against it are almost exclusively of a philosophical or theological, rather than of an exegetical or philological character."

That I do not agree with Prof. Hodge in the extent of meaning which he assigns to the word *death*, is apparent from what I have previously said. On this point I shall soon speak more at large. But this does not affect the general question, whether the words *sin, to sin* and *to make sinners*, in vs. 12, 19, are to be taken in the judicial sense, as he asserts, or in one of the senses which he opposes. Indeed, many of those to whom he appeals as authorities in behalf of the judicial sense of the terms restrict the words *die* and *death* to natural death, in the passage in question. Setting aside, therefore, this point, I regard it as plain that Professor Hodge is right on the main question; that is, he is right in holding that the words *sin, to sin* and *to be made sinners*, in vs. 12 and 19, are to be taken, in the judicial sense, to denote subjection to the condemning sentence of the law violated by Adam, and a consequent liability to death, the penalty annexed; and that to this reference is had in the "judgment by one to condemnation" of v. 16, and the "coming of judgment upon all men to condemnation by the offense of one" of v. 18. Thus the main idea of the passage is simply this: as through Adam came condemnation, so through Christ came justification.

As in this particular, therefore. I stand on old and generally acknowledged ground, I do not feel that I need to put forth any special efforts in its defense. So clear is the evidence in favor of this mode of interpretation, and so ably has it been developed by Professor Hodge and others, that I do not see any present demand for a new laborer in this field.

At the same time, I do not admit the existence of anything but a merely typical sequence in the case of Adam. Though, so far as the form of the language used is concerned, it may express a causative sequence, yet I adopt the same principles of interpretation as I do when it is said by Turretin that "a sight of the brazen serpent healed;" or by Calvin, that "it was a saving cure for those who were mortally wounded;" or by Edwards, that "the people were saved by the brazen serpent, by looking to it;" or when the Scripture says that sacrifices or incense atoned for sin. Such language describes divinely ordained sequences, according to the appearance of things, and not according to such real laws of causation as connect justification with faith in Christ.

And now, before I leave this part of the subject, I would once more call special attention to the great fact, so often and so clearly asserted by Professor Hodge, that, if the main idea of the passage is what has been stated, then it does not teach that "the sin of Adam was the occasion of our sins, for which we are condemned" (p. 202); nor "that the offense of Adam was the means of involving us in a multitude of crimes, from which Christ saves us" (p. 203); nor "that Adam's sin was the occasion of our sinning, and thus incurring the divine displeasure" (p. 210); nor "that the sin of Adam was the occasion of all men's being placed in such circumstances that they all sin, and thus incur death" (p. 199); nor "that, by being the cause of the corruption of their nature, it is thus indirectly the cause of their condemnation" (p. 199, 200). On the other hand, such a mode of interpretation "destroys the analogy, and causes the very point and pith of the comparison to fail" (p. 185). "That we have corrupt natures, and are personally sinners, and therefore liable to other and further inflictions, is indeed true, but nothing to the point" (p. 185).

The force of the reasoning by which Prof. Hodge sustains these statements I fully admit. I regard it as perfectly unanswerable against the idea that this passage teaches that the sin of Adam was the cause either of our actually sinning or of a corrupt nature in us. I, therefore, most fully concede that which is so earnestly and ably maintained by the highest Old School authority; I concede that, though it is true that we have corrupt natures, and are personally sinners, and therefore liable to other and higher inflictions, yet these things are not asserted *in this passage* to have been caused by the sin of Adam, and that any such assertion would be nothing to the point of the argument, but directly opposed to it. Moreover, I concede that leading scholars of all parties confirm this view. But, if these things are not asserted in this passage to have been caused by the sin of Adam, then plainly they are not asserted to have been caused by it at all, in any part of the Word of God; for there is no other passage of Scripture in which it can be even pretended, with any show of plausibility whatever, that these things are asserted. It appears, then, as the final result of these well-sustained premises, that the doctrine that our depraved natures, or our sinful conduct, have been caused or occasioned by the sin of Adam, is not asserted in any part of the Word of God.

Nor is this result peculiar to the Old School Calvinists. It is found; at least substantially, in one section of the New England divines. I refer to Dr. Emmons, and other advocates of the scheme of divine efficiency, so called, who, with equal clearness, deny any causative power of Adam's act to produce either a depraved nature or actual sin. It is, according to them, a mere condition on which God suspended His decision, that He would exercise His power in causing sinful volitions in all men from the beginning of free agency. Moreover, it was God who caused this condition itself to occur.

The theory of Prof. Hodge, Turretin and others of like views, as to the real origin of human depravity, does not in principle differ from this view of Dr. Emmons. True, they deny God's direct efficiency in causing sinful volitions by reason of Adam's sin; but they do clearly teach that on that ground He creates the soul without original righteousness, and withdraws from it those divine influences which are essential to prevent the corruption of nature and entire sinfulness in action. According to each theory, therefore, the sin of Adam exerted a direct influence, not on his posterity, but on God. It caused him to change his mode of action towards new-created minds, and thus directly or indirectly to cause their depravity, either of action only, or of nature and action both.

Moreover, the whole evidence even of this indirect influence of Adam's sin on his posterity, through God, is derived solely from the sense which is attached to the word *death* in this passage. It is assumed that it does not denote merely natural death, but penal evils of all kinds, natural and spiritual, temporal and eternal. Assuming this sense of the word, they proceed to unfold, as above stated, how God inflicts the penalty in this broad sense. The grounds of this view claim a care-ful consideration.

Chapter VIII: Import Of The Word *Death*, In Rom. 6: 12-19

THAT the interpretation of the word *death* last referred to—that is, as including the death of the soul—is not based on any sound critical grounds, can be shown with great ease.

1. In the first place, that it is not its obvious sense is plain from the fact that four centuries passed away, after the epistle to the Romans was written, before the word was ever here interpreted in this broad sense. Nor was that sense ever adopted by the Greek church at all. Is it not to be supposed that the Greek fathers were capable of judging what was the true sense of so plain and so common a word, as here used by a writer of Greek?

2. In part of the passage natural death is plainly and confessedly meant, as when it is said "death reigned from Adam to Moses," and consistency demands the same sense through the passage.

3. The facts referred to by Paul as recorded in the Old Testament, and on which his reasoning is based, demand this view. He refers to a certain typical transaction as well known, and assumes, as terms of comparison, certain events. These are recorded in Genesis, Chs. 2 and 3. Let us briefly recapitulate them.

In Gen. 2:16, 17, is contained the law or rule of conduct prescribed to Adam, allowing him in general to eat of the trees of the garden, but forbidding him to eat of the tree of knowledge of good and evil. The penalty threatened, in case of disobedience, was death. On the day thou eatest thereof, thou shalt surely die.

In Gen. 3:6-7, the specific act is related by which the law was violated, called "the offense of one" and "one man's disobedience." Af-

347

ter Eve had taken of the fruit of the forbidden tree and eaten, she gave
to Adam and he did eat. This act of Adam is pointedly characterized in
Rom. 5:16 as being one offense, in opposition to many offenses; and in
vs. 15, 17, 18, 19, as the offense of the one man, whose grand peculiarity is, that he is the one through whom, as a type of the coming Messiah, God was about to introduce into this world the whole human
race.

In Gen. 3:14-19, is narrated the passing of the sentence on all the
offenders. On the serpent eternal degradation, eternal hostility between him and his seed, and the woman and her seed, and final defeat,
at the expense of incidental suffering to the Messiah. On the woman,
great sorrow and pain in childbirth, increased dependence on man,
need of his aid, and entire subjection to him.

On man, a curse on the ground, rendering the support of life
more difficult and laborious; and finally, natural or temporal death,
"Dust thou art. and unto dust shalt thou return."

Thus, all parts of the penalty are minutely and fully developed,
without the remotest allusion to spiritual and eternal death. In a transaction so plainly typical such a penalty would have been out of place.
At all events, the import of the death threatened is here fixed. It denotes merely natural death. Besides these, no facts are on record as the
basis of the comparison in Rom. 5:12-19. Paul refers, therefore, to
these alone, and by reference to these we must interpret his language.

It also appears that the sentence of death was intended to include
the race. The mode of address is, as Edwards well remarks, as much
suited to include the race as that in Gen. 1:27-29, which enjoins on
Adam and Eve fruitfulness, subjugation of the earth and rule over it,
and confers on them vegetables for food,—a mode of address which
obviously includes the race. Moreover, all parts of the sentence, on
both Adam and Eve, come of necessity on men of all ages. The curse
on the ground reaches all generations; for it began at once, and has extended to this day. This part of the sentence, then, was at that time denounced on all men, and meets them in all ages. So pains of child-
birth, need of the aid of man, and subjection to him, come on all
women in all ages. Finally, natural death comes on all men in all ages.

Hence, the words "offense" and "disobedience" refer to one well-
known act of one man, followed by a well-known sentence, which
sentence in its scope includes the whole race, and is, in fact, executed
on all. Hence "the judgment" and "condemnation" relate to this well-

known sentence and condemnation, as left on record, and the death
referred to is natural death. In view of these facts, it is plain that, in
making out the parallel and antithesis between Christ and Adam, a
strict adherence to the Old Testament required Paul merely to say that
this particular, definite, well-known sentence came on all men in all
ages; for the passage in Genesis actually means no more. Hence his
language ought not to be made to mean more, in Rom. 5:12-19, than
is involved in the facts to which he refers. We ought to interpret
"death" in Romans by the sentence in Genesis; and this says nothing of
spiritual and eternal death. It refers to temporal death, and that only.
The words are, "Dust thou art, and unto dust shalt thou return."

The main argument for the extended sense of death (that is, all
kinds and degrees of penal evil) is taken from the fact that on the other
side of the antithesis life is taken in the full and highest sense, and not
to denote natural life. But, as I have already abundantly shown, the
type is often in the natural world, and the antitype in the spiritual, as
when the brazen serpent healed bodily wounds caused by serpents, as a
type of Christ's healing the mental wounds caused by sin and Satan;
or, as when deliverance from natural death by the blood of the paschal
lamb typified deliverance from spiritual death. Indeed, the whole system of material types is but a carrying out of this principle. Hence, Edwards says,

> "Not only the things of the Old Testament are typical, for
> this is but one part of the typical world. The system of cre-
> ated beings may be divided into two parts, the typical world
> and the antitypical world. The inferior and carnal,—that is,
> the more external and transitory part of the universe, that
> part of it that is inchoative, imperfect and subservient,—is
> typical of the superior spiritual and durable part of it. which
> is the end, and, as it were, the substance and consummation
> of the other. Thus the material and natural world is typical
> of the spiritual and intelligent world, or the city of God.
> And many things in the world of mankind, as to their ex-
> ternal and worldly state, are typical of things pertaining to
> the city and kingdom of God."

Now, if this is so, and if natural life and death are typical of spiritual life and death, how appropriate, how impressive, how worthy of
God, to make the sentencing of the whole human race to natural death

through the offense of Adam a type, by way of antithesis, of the restoration of spiritual and eternal life, the justification of all who believe in Christ!

In addition to this, it is clear, from 1 Cor. 15, that Paul elsewhere looks on the sentence as denoting simply natural death, and does not take the more comprehensive view. "For since by man came death, by man came also the resurrection of the dead. For as through Adam all die, even so through Christ shall all be made alive." It is, then, in perfect accordance with his habits of thought, that Paul should in Romans also regard the sentence which came through Adam as a sentence of natural death. There is, therefore, in view of all that has been said, nothing arbitrary or forced, or against the general practice of the Scriptures, in this view. On the other hand, it is in perfect accordance with the nature of things and the general practice of the Holy Spirit. It is merely a case of illustrating spiritual things by things natural and material; and need I say that this pervades the Bible? Natural health and life and light on the one hand, and disease and death and darkness on the other, are the standing scriptural illustrations of spiritual health, life, light, or spiritual disease, death and darkness. Nay, what is the whole Mosaic system of material types, but a carrying out of this principle?

If, then, as we have shown, the facts of the Old Testament demand this view,—if in a part of the passage the word *death* clearly denotes natural death,—if this sense accords with Paul's known habits of thought, and the prevailing usage of the Bible in such cases,—there can be no doubt that the view which I defend is true and unanswerable.

The passage, therefore, teaches nothing but the pronouncing of a sentence of condemnation to natural death on all men, through the sin of Adam, as a type and illustration, both by similitude and antithesis, of justification and life eternal through the righteousness of Christ.

To complete this view, however, it is necessary to repeat the statement which I have already made, that, even as it respects natural death, the sin of Adam exerted no causative power to effect the condemnation of his race. It did not involve them in any real guilt whatever. I admit, indeed, without hesitation, that the established sequence of condemnation and death on all men, from the one sin of the one man, Adam, is set forth in forms of language exactly like those which denote the sequence of justification and life from Christ, *in whose acts there was causative power*. Nevertheless. I hold, on grounds already stated, that, according to the laws of typical language, the sequence in one case is *merely typical* (or typological—Ed.) and illustrative, and not causative; in the other, it is antitypical and causative. *Adam no more brought real guilt on his posterity than the brazen serpent really healed those who looked at it, or sacrifices really made atonement.*

It is perfectly plain that, so long as the great laws of language, which I have developed as pervading the Bible, and the common usage of all interpreters and divines remain, it is impossible to overthrow this position. For, if the strongest forms of language that can be used to denote causative sequences are, as I have shown, abundantly applied to denote sequences in which there is confessedly no causative power at all, and if this is eminently so in typical sequences, then plainly in the case of Adam, who is expressly declared to be a type of Christ, no causative power can be proved by any mere forms of language, however strong. They are not and cannot be stronger than those forms which are applied to typical sequences in other cases, in which there is no causation whatever.

I am now prepared to advance another step, and to say that, even if the words *sin, to sin*, and *to make sinners*, in vs. 12 and 19, were to be taken in the sense claimed by the New School divines, or others, as referring to actual sin or a corrupt nature, still, even so, it would be impossible to prove by this passage that the sin of Adam exerted any causative power to produce sin or a corrupt nature in his posterity. For, as I have shown, even in that case we are abundantly authorized to interpret all the language of causation as denoting merely a typical sequence of a corrupt nature, or of sin and death after Adam's sin; a sequence devoid of causative power, and established by God for the sake of illustrating the sequence of holiness, and spiritual life from Christ's obedience,—a sequence in which there is causative power.

Moreover, the just power of God to establish such typical sequences, on the system which I advocate, would originate from the fact that, in bringing into this world beings already depraved, that from among them He might redeem His church, He had a perfect right to introduce them, as He did, by one man, and through him to establish such a sequence of sin, and death in connection with his transgression, as should by its typical power foreshadow and predict the coming of that great *one* by whom the church was to be redeemed. As to the principle of interpretation involved, *it matters not whether the sequence be as it is set forth by the Old School divines or by the New.*

At the same time, to my mind it is perfectly clear that the real sequences are these: that through the sin of Adam all men were condemned to natural death, as a type of the justification of the church and her restoration to eternal life, through the obedience of Christ.

This great antithetic comparison lies at the basis of the whole passage. It is, however, as we have seen, modified and rendered more striking by the apostle, in some respects, by pointing out certain particulars in which the antitype greatly transcends the foreshadowings of the type, in its inestimable gifts of grace and glory.

CHAPTER IX: ADDITIONAL EVIDENCE

THUS much, then, I think is clear,—that, so long as the great scriptural laws of typical interpretation stand, no man can be, with any propriety, condemned or censured for understanding this passage in the sense which I have set forth. Nor is this all. Reasons of great power exist for its general adoption. Every form of the common view I have shown to imply injustice and dishonor in God. On the other hand, the whole view which we have taken of this passage is deeply impressive, highly instructive, and in all respects honorable to God. It is also in full accordance with the spirit and practice of the inspired writers. This will more plainly appear, if we now present this type in its relations to the other early types with which it is connected.

All of the events connected with the origin of this world are by the inspired writers treated as types, looking forward to the ultimate and glorious results of a new-created moral system about to be produced by means of the natural creation, and at the same time indicating the character of the materials out of which that moral system should be created.

The earth without form and void, and the darkness upon the face of the deep, are employed by the apostle Paul (2 Cor. 4:6) to symbolize the condition of disordered and darkened minds such as those out of which a new creation was to spring. As the spirit broods upon the abyss, and the light beams forth at the Word of God, we see shadowed forth His action on the mass of ruined minds, and the truth by which He operates. The harmony and beauty of the completed natural creation strikingly symbolized the higher symmetry and beauty of the new creation in the moral world,—the new heavens and new earth, in comparison with which the first shall not be remembered or called to mind (Is. 65:17, 18). So, also, the formation of woman from man typified the formation of the church from Christ; her union to Adam, the marriage of the church to Christ; their exaltation to the head of this natural system, the exaltation of

Christ and the church to the head of the universe. All this the Bible plainly tells us (Eph. 5:23-33, Rev. 3:21, Rom. 8:17, 29. Compare these passages with the remarks in the last chapter on Heb. 2:7—9. 1 Cor. 15:27, 28. Eph. 1:22, 23).

Suppose, now, that in a preexistent state sin had entered and a hostile kingdom had been established, and God created this world in order to take out of that kingdom by regeneration and atonement His church, and to destroy the remainder,—how appropriate so to introduce the fallen race into this world as to shadow forth their ruined state and the great Redeemer of the church,—the great destroyer of Satan!

They are already under sentence of condemnation, but He is to acquit and save the church, and He is one. To typify these things by similitude and antithesis, Adam, the head of the race, is one; he sins, and a condemning sentence of natural death passes on all his race. At last, the second Adam appears; he is one; he perfectly obeys even unto death, and by his obedience and death a gracious act of pardon and eternal life come to all connected with him by faith. What is more appropriate, what is more perfect harmony with the whole of the connected system of types, than this view? In particular the types of the natural creation, even before Adam had been created or sinned, clearly indicate the idea of ruin, already caused, to be repaired; disorder and confusion, already existing, to be restored to order and symmetry; a moral kingdom to be created out of the elements of chaos. According to the view now given, the same idea is carried out in the transactions in Eden. By the sentence of temporal death through Adam, is typically indicated the fallen condition of the materials of the future race; but it is so indicated as to point the eye to a coming Redeemer, by whom unnumbered millions shall be restored. Thus we no longer seem to open the history of earth in the graveyard of a newly fallen world, but to hear a voice from heaven proclaiming aloud,

> "Millions of souls already fallen shall rise to endless life, and the reign of confusion and death shall end. A great deliverer shall come, through whom unnumbered hosts of the fallen shall be justified, and raised to reign on thrones of glory in everlasting life. This system shall add no new sinner to the universe, but millions already fallen it shall restore, and of

those who remain unreclaimed it shall forever destroy the malignant power."

The foundation, then, of all the fatal errors which have sprung out of this passage, is the assigning to the word *death* a spiritual sense,[30] and giving a causative power to a typical sequence, designed merely to illustrate and enforce truths already evolved and established, and not to be the foundation of an immense system of scholastic theology.

The depravity of the human race Paul had already fully and abundantly proved by its own appropriate evidence, and the great system of justification by faith in the Savior He had fully unfolded and established.

Enraptured with its glory, the thought strikes his mind, that, even in the darkest hour, this glorious consummation was fully before the divine mind, and was most strikingly foreshadowed even in the opening scene of the great drama. Through one man a condemning sentence fell on the whole human race, and has ever since gone into execution, from age to age. In all lands and over all generations death has reigned. So, in glorious antithesis, through one has a sentence of acquittal come to all who believe, and a free gift of divine grace abounding to eternal life. For one offense that sentence came and death reigned, but by this grace offenses innumerable are forgiven and endless life is restored.

All this is merely the amplification and enforcement of striking truths by typical illustration. It is the very genius and spirit of Paul. This part of the system he penetrated more deeply and illustrated more fully than any of the sacred writers.

Does anyone ask for another example in which Paul attempts to illustrate and enforce a logical argument by typical illustration. Turn to his epistle to the Galatians. In chapters three and four he argues at length the great question of justification by faith, and the release of Christians from the Mosaic law; and, having proved his points logically, he illustrates and enforces by a type, taken from two wives of Abraham,—one bond, the other free,—and their two sons, the bondage of the system of Moses and the freedom of the system of Christ. In his

---

30 This *death* can also be understood as the *extinction* of Adam's archetype, see *Arsy Varys—Reclaiming the Gospel in First Corinthians* (2006) and *Varsy Arsy—Proclaiming the Gospel in Second Corinthians* (2008), Phillip A. Ross, Pilgrim Platform, Marietta, Ohio.

epistle to the Corinthians and Ephesians, and especially to the Hebrews, he brings out from his full stores abundant illustrations of this
kind; so that nothing can be more after the manner of Paul than to illustrate in this way.

And, now, there is need of no force, no violence; all is free, natural
and easy, if we interpret the passage in this way. Even without a very
powerful reason in the nature of things, this mode of interpretation
would commend itself as the most suitable and natural; for it grows directly out of the facts of the case, and out of the spirit of Paul.

But, when we look at the moral aspects of the case, the evidence is
augmented beyond all estimation. If the character of God is of any
value, if the division of the human mind and of society against God
and itself is any evil, and if its perfect harmony with God is at all to be
desired, then are we not authorized and required utterly to reject an
interpretation at war with every principle of honor and right, and to
adopt one that removes every dark cloud from the character of God,
presents Him in His true glory, and prepares the way for a full reunion
of the human race to Him in sweet and unmingled love?

Chapter X: Case Of Melchizedek

BY reviewing the argument thus far, it will be seen that the state of the case is this: That, according to the principles of equity and honor, the assumption that the sinfulness and ruined condition of the human race were caused by the sin of Adam is liable to unanswerable objections; that it has held its ground only by the force of a supposed assertion of God; but that, on closer examination, it appears that there is no evidence that God has ever made such an assertion. Of course, the assumption is left defenseless, to encounter the full weight of the reprobation of the principles which it outrages, and to perish before them.

But there may be those whose associations have so long connected a causative significance with the language concerning Adam, that they cannot at once reduce it to a mere description of the appearance of things, as presented by a typical sequence designed for an illustration and foreshadowing of the coming Messiah. They may even be affected by it as if it were a kind of irreverent treatment of the Word of God, adapted to enervate its force and empty it of its meaning.

If any feel thus, it can be only because they have without reason based too great consequences on these words, and have never been accustomed to notice how very common and how highly approved is this very mode of interpretation with reference to the language applied to other types. I will illustrate my meaning by a single case. We will suppose that things had taken such a course that a doctrine which was regarded of fundamental moment had been formed concerning Melchizedek, purporting that he was not a mortal, but a self-existent and eternal person. We will also suppose that on this doctrine great practical questions depended.

Here great consequences would depend upon an unsure basis; and yet, so far as words are concerned, no doctrine admits of easier and more irresistible proof. Is it not expressly said of him (Heb. 7:3) that he is "without father, without mother, without genealogy, hav-

ing neither beginning of days nor end of life, but abiding a priest forever, like unto the Son of God?" Is he not, according to v. 8, contrasted with men who receive tithes and yet die, as being one of whom
it is witnessed that he liveth? What can be stronger than this language,
so far as the form is concerned? And yet, the large majority of the most
judicious commentators hold that he was a mortal man, who had a father and a mother, and was born and lived and died like other men.

On what principles, then, do they interpret this language, so
strong and so definite, so as to consist with these views? They adopt
this principle,—that, since Melchizedek was a type of the coming Messiah, the language of Paul concerning him is to be interpreted as having reference to the appearance of things, as providentially ordered. It
was so ordered that there is on record no account of the parents, birth,
genealogy, life or death, of Melchizedek. As we look at the picture of
him presented by Scripture, none of these things appear on the canvas,
and therefore as a type he is spoken of as being without them. This is
but one in stance of the great law, that, in speaking of a large part of
the types of the Bible, we regard merely the appearance of things, and
speak accordingly. Even if this view of the statements of Paul is regarded by any as not correct in the particular case of Melchizedek, it
yet shows how clearly the great body of interpreters recognize the
truth of the law itself. Calvin, in his notes on Heb. 7:3, states the principles of interpretation in this case with his usual brevity and felicity.

> "No doubt Melchizedek had parents; but Paul is not here
> looking at him as a private individual, but as representing
> Christ. Therefore he allows himself to see nothing in him
> except what is recorded in the scripture. And, since the
> Holy Spirit introduces a most distinguished king of that
> age, and says nothing concerning his birth, and afterwards
> made no record of his death, is it not, as it were, a figurative
> exhibition of his eternal existence? But that which was thus
> shadowed forth by Melchizedek exists in reality in Christ.
> Therefore we should content ourselves with this common-
> sense view,—that, whilst the scripture represents
> Melchizedek to us as if it were delineating in a picture one
> who was never born and never died, it implies that Christ
> has in reality neither beginning nor end of existence. Here
> Melchizedek is not considered in his private and personal
> character, but only as a sacred type of Christ."

He repeats the same principles with reference to verse eight.

Barnes, in his notes, clearly sets forth and defends similar principles of interpretation.

> "There was no record made of the name either of his father, his mother, or any of his posterity. He stood alone. It is simply said that such a man came out to meet Abraham, and that is the first and the last that we hear of him and of his family."

Of the expression, "having neither beginning of days nor end of life," he says,

> "The obvious meaning of the phrase is, that in the records of Moses neither the beginning nor the close of his life is mentioned. It is not said when he was born, or when he died; nor that he was born, or that he died."

Further, he says that these facts would lead those who should read Psalm 110 "to the conclusion that the Messiah was to resemble Melchizedek in some such points as these." On v. 8, in which Melchizedek is contrasted with priests who die, as one "of whom it is witnessed that he liveth." he says,

> "the fair and obvious meaning is, that all the record we have of Melchizedek is, that he was alive; or, as Grotius says, the record is merely that he lived. We have no mention of his death. From anything that the record shows, it might appear that he continued to live on, and did not die."

Others, as Kuinoel,[31] refer the assertions of the passage rather to the origin and close of the priestly life of Melchizedek, as left without record; but still they retain the same general principle, that the apostle, in speaking of the typical appearance of things, uses language which is expressive of the reality of the things represented. Indeed, all who hold that Melchizedek was a man, who was born, lived and died, as other

---

31 Kuinoel. *Philological Commentary on New Testament*, 1828.

men, as Stuart, Bloomfield, Macknight,[32] Rosenmüller,[33] Scott, Henry, Doddridge, and, indeed, the great body of commentators, are obliged to occupy this ground. Of this opinion concerning Melchizedek, Stuart says that it "lies upon the face of the sacred record in Gen. 14 and in Heb. 7; and it is the only one which can be defended on any tolerable grounds of interpretation."

Notice now the strength of this case. How clear is the verbal statement that Melchizedek had neither father nor mother, neither beginning of days nor end of life; and that, in contrast with dying men, he lives and abides a priest continually. Yet, as he was a type, the main body of commentators agree that he was a mere mortal man, who was born and died like all others; and that the language is taken from and designed to set forth merely the typical appearance of the recorded events of his life, so as to illustrate the great antitype whom God by these providential arrangements in that early age foreshadowed.

In this case we have, although in another form, a striking illustration and confirmation of the great principle that sustains my exposition of the passage in Romans. It is that, in speaking of typical (or typological—Ed.) sequences as if they were causative, we speak according to the appearance of things. On the same principle we speak of Melchizedek. Hence it is evident that the same principle is at the bottom of this mode of speaking which I have set forth as underlying other types, and which all men recognize in their common modes of speech. We have seen how strongly numerous writers have asserted that the brazen serpent healed those who looked at it. Yet, in fact, it did not heal them at all; it only appeared so to do. Their language, therefore, expresses the typical appearance of the case, as if it were a reality. It expresses a sequence of *apparent causation*, as if it were real

---

32   James Macknight (1721-?), was a native of Ireland. His father, Mr William Macknight, minister at Irvine where his ancestors, descended from the family of M'Naughtane, in the Highlands of Scotland, had resided for more than a century. His last and greatest work on the *The New Translation of the Apostolical Epistles, with a Commentary and Notes* was published in 1795, in four volumes, after laboring on it for almost thirty years. His *Harmony of the Gospels* was an esteemed a work of standard excellence for the students of evangelical knowledge. His *Truth of the Gospel History* also deserves notice.

33   Johann Rosenmüller (1736-1815), a German divine and professor of theology, was appointed Professor of Theology at Erlangen in 1773, Primarius Professor of Theology at Erlangen in 1773, Primarius Professor of Divinity at Giessen in 1783, and was called in 1785 to Leipzig, where he remained until his death in 1815. His two sons were Ernst Friedrich Karl Rosenmüller, and Johann Christian Rosenmüller.

causation. The same is true in those numerous cases where sacrifices are said to make atonement for sins. So, also, in the case of Adam.

Do I, then, evacuate the language concerning Adam of its proper and scriptural force, when I apply to it this same all-pervading and divinely sanctioned principle? Do I not rather restore it, from a very injurious perversion, to its proper and scriptural sense? Do I not again bring it into a true harmony with the general analogy of the Word of God?

Nor on this ground will the language lose its proper power and influence on the human mind. The typical system of the Old Testament, by its appeals to the imagination, by its illustrative power, and by its prophetic significance, is peculiarly adapted to interest and affect the mind. All experience shows it. Place this passage on the same ground with the sacrifices, the brazen serpent, and other types, and exclude from it all necessity of solving any absurd and impossible problem in morals, metaphysics or natural generation,—remove from it those dark shadows of injustice which hang over it as it is commonly understood,—let it stand simply as an early sublime and beautiful type of the coming Messiah,—and it will have a joyous fullness of meaning, and exert a thrilling moral power unknown and unimagined before. No dense clouds of injustice will darken the character of God, and involve the universe in lurid shades; but the sun of righteousness will be seen, in full-orbed glory, pouring upon this dark world the refulgent rays of divine wisdom and of redeeming grace!

CHAPTER XI: THE COMPLETION OF THE PICTURE

THE training of the mind which fits for typical interpretation has of late very extensively fallen out of use. It may be a reaction caused by previous indiscretion and excess. Yet, whatever its cause, it is an evil. It unfits us for understanding Paul. Though he was a logician, he was not a mere logician. He had an imagination also, and this he used in vividly representing to himself the typical pictures of the Old Testament. Upon these he gazed with delight, just as we gaze on a picture, a statue, or any other finished product of the fine arts. But his feelings were deeper than any that such products of human skill can cause; for he saw in these pictures the products of divine skill and foreknowledge, reflecting light even from amid the darkness of the remotest antiquity upon those glorious purposes of redeeming love, the magnitude and glory of which filled, enraptured and overwhelmed, his soul. These great purposes he developed on appropriate occasions by intellectual processes which will bear the scrutiny of the keenest logical analysis. Hence Paul has ever been the favorite of logical, generalizing, systematizing minds.

But, when he undertook to pour the illuminating power of his imagination upon these great truths by means of typical pictures, it was a process of entirely another kind.

Such pictures were not made for logical analysis, but to be gazed upon as a whole, and as merely illustrative pictures. True it is that Paul reasons from these pictures. He did so in the case of Melchizedek; but he reasons from them as from pictures. He reasons that that which, viewed as a divine combination of acts or events, they foreshadow, must exist, more fully and perfectly developed, in the antitype. Calvin, in a happy hour, clearly saw and distinctly announced these principles in the case of Melchizedek; but they are no less true and important in all similar cases. If any man, then, would be a good interpreter of Paul, he must be able to conceive of and to reproduce in himself the apostle's mental habits, with reference to typical illustrations. He must learn to look upon the Old Testament as Paul looked upon it, and to reproduce in imagination all its scenes and parts as he reproduced them. Nor must he, as some do, in a patronizing way defend and excuse it, as the result of his Rabbinical training, and fitted, perhaps, to benefit the Jews, although to us, properly enough, it seems strange and unworthy of the serious notice of the logical minds of the eminent scholars of the present age. Why should this particular mode of exercising the imagination be despised as visionary and devoid of solidity, simply because it cannot be reduced to the categories and syllogisms of Aristotle? Has the European world in general come to the conclusion that similes, and metaphors, and comparisons, and other rhetorical figures, for purposes of illustration and impression, are of no practical utility; and that they are unworthy of the notice of logical minds, because they cannot be analyzed, and stated in syllogistic form? Why, then, should that exercise of the imagination by types, which inspiration has peculiarly honored and sanctioned, be singled out for rejection and contempt? On this subject there must be a reaction. Indeed, it has begun; for Olshausen[34] has well remarked, that

> "the elements of forgotten typology are becoming more and more recognized, and cannot, consistently with truly historical exposition, be overlooked in the New Testament."

Moreover, in the able work of Fairbairn,[35] in my opinion the ablest of the age on this topic, we see some of the mature results of this reactionary movement, caused, I can not doubt, by the returning influences of the divine spirit, after the great continental apostasy.

The great thing, in a true interpretation of the passage under consideration, if we would sympathetically feel the force of all its parts, is,

---

34 Hermann Olshausen (1796-1839), German theologian, educated at the universities of Kiel (1814) and Berlin (1816), where he was influenced by Schleiermacher and Neander. In 1817 he was awarded the prize at the festival of the Reformation for an essay that brought him to the notice of the Prussian Minister of Public Worship, and in 1820 he became Privatdozent at Berlin. In 1821, he became professor extraordinarius at the University of Königsberg, and in 1827 professor. In 1834, he became professor at the University of Erlangen.

35 Patrick Fairbairn (1805-1874), a Scottish minister and theologian who wrote *The Typology of Scripture*. MacLehose (1886) noted that this was "one of the most important theological works of its day," and suggested that it "appeared at a time when Scotland was singularly barren in theological scholarship, and gained for its author a great reputation, not only in his own country but also in England and America."

to reproduce in our minds the typical picture, upon which Paul gazed as he wrote, and in which he saw foreshadowed the coming of the sec- ond Adam, the great Redeemer of the human race. We shall then be able to feel the force of the passage, even in its minutest details. Let us, then, as completely as in the case of Melchizedek, divest ourselves of the idea that we are approaching the solution of any mere logical problem, and arouse our imaginations to gaze upon the scenes and persons of past ages, as they rose before the mind of the inspired apos- tle. Having surveyed these, then let us turn and in the light of them read his words.

The fundamental fact which seems to have risen before the eye of the apostle was, that death entered this world not as an event natural and necessary to man, but as a penalty inflicted by the decision of a judge, in view of a violated law. The sentence still stood recorded on the sacred page. He saw accordingly the great ancestor of the human race, as a condemned criminal, yielding himself up to the sentence of death. "Dust thou art, and unto dust shalt thou return."

In this, however, there was nothing to excite surprise; for he had, by a definite act, violated a law clearly revealed, and sanctioned in his hearing with the penalty of death.

But of none of his descendants was it true that they had in person violated the same law that Adam did, or any other of the same kind and sanctioned by the same penalty. Why, then, should the same sen- tence of death be inflicted on them? They had not sinned after the similitude of his transgression;— why, then, should they endure the same penalty?

Once more, then, he looks at the sentence in all its parts. The evils of all kinds therein denounced he sees coming ever since on all men. The form of the language is as much adapted to include all men as God's first address to the new-created pair, which was obviously meant for all men. What reason, then, is there to doubt that the sen- tence of death was designed to include all men? There is none. It is plain that when Adam was sentenced to death all men were sentenced with him, and through his offense. It is plain that by the offense of one man judgment came upon all men to condemnation. Plainly, then, the aspect of the whole transaction was as if all men were held guilty of Adam's sin, and punished for it. This is the great typical picture before his mind, and according to this aspect of the case he speaks.

But, lo! on the other hand, he sees a glorious, a divine personage in human form; in the midst of trials and temptations of the utmost intensity, he still is faithful to God. He is still obedient, yea, even unto death, the death of the cross. Around Him he sees gathered a multitude which no man can number, of every age and clime. With Him they are one by a new life,—the life of faith. Through this faith they apprehend and receive the pardon even of the greatest sins, and the merits of his obedience in the infinite and gracious rewards of endless life. This, then, is the second Adam; and now his all-embracing thought is, as all who sustained a material connection with the first Adam were through his disobedience condemned and sentenced to death, so through the second Adam all who sustain a spiritual connection with Him shall be pardoned and restored to endless life.

But, now, lest any Judaizing opponent should suggest that the law of Moses is the ground of the alleged condemnation, he looks upon the picture again, and sees a long interval during which it did not exist. He sees, moreover, that during this long period there was no law like that of Adam, sanctioned by the same penalty, which had been violated by man, and yet sentence of death came upon them all. It must, therefore, have come, as before stated, through the offense of Adam, and the sentence then passed.

The sense of the whole passage I will now endeavor to set forth in a paraphrase, remarking that I shall substitute for sin, sinned, etc., in vs. 12-19, what has previously been proved to be their sense,—that is, liability to punishment or a state of condemnation,—and also complete the comparison in v. 12.

> 12. Wherefore as by one man that universal subjection to a condemning sentence for sin, under which men now are, was introduced into the world, and death thereby as the threatened penalty, and thus through one man death passed upon all, because through him all were involved in a common condemnation as sinners, even so are all who believe justified and restored to eternal life through Christ.
> 13. It is of no avail to suggest that this state of condemnation has not arisen from the offense of Adam, but from the violation of the law of Moses by each man personally; for it existed in the world before that law was given, and such liability to punishment could not be ascribed to men whilst the law was not in existence on which it depended.

14. And yet death reigned over all men from Adam to Moses; even although they had not, as was the case with Adam, personally broken that original law which threatened this death as its penalty, or any other like it. It is plain, therefore, that the sentence condemning them to death did come on all men through the transgression of that one man, Adam, who is the type of the coming Redeemer.

15. But how great is the disparity and contrast between the results of the offense of Adam and the gracious interposition of Christ; for, if through the offense of one man the multitudes of the human race have been sentenced to so great an evil as death, much more have the forgiving love of God, and the gracious gifts resulting therefrom through the one man Jesus Christ, abounded unto the multitudes of the redeemed.

16. There is also another dissimilitude between the transactions in the case of Adam's sin and the free gift of Christ; for the condemning sentence took its rise from one offense, and resulted in condemnation,—but the free gift has respect to many offenses, and results in justification.

17. For if by one man's offense death reigned by one, much more shall they who receive abundance of grace and of the gift of righteousness reign in life by one, Jesus Christ.

18. Therefore, to resume the general view with which I began, and which I have in some respects modified and limited,—as by the offense of one judgment came upon all men to condemnation, even so by the righteousness of one the free gift came upon all who believe, unto justification of life.

19. For as by the disobedience of one man many were subjected to a condemning sentence, so by the obedience of one shall many be justified.

It will be seen that in verse 12 I make the word *law* refer in both instances to the Mosaic law. Anyone can see that the last clause of the verse can be properly translated "liability to punishment is not imputed when the law does not exist," that is, *before* it exists. This is said on the supposition that the liability in question had been supposed to spring from a violation of the law of Moses. This would involve the absurdity of liability to punishment by a law before it exists. In accordance with this view, De Wette[36] translates the words μη οντος νομου, "where the law is not," and says that the statement of the apostle "is by no means a universal position," but "is spoken respecting the time before the law of Moses."

It appears, also, that those "who had not sinned after the similitude of Adam's transgression" are not a peculiar part of these who lived before the law. Prof. Hodge alleges that this is intimated by the word "even." But we often use that word to set forth a striking common characteristic, to be found in all of whom we speak. Thus we say Christ died for all men, *even* for his enemies, who had forfeited all their rights by a guilty rebellion. So, although not one of those who lived from Adam to Moses had ever sinned as Adam did, still death reigned even over them. So the passage was understood by Chrysostom, when he said that "all men were subjected by Adam to death, although they did not (like him) eat of the tree."

Let it now be borne in mind that, with reference to condemnation through Adam, as truly as in the case of Melchizedek, we are authorized to believe that the ground work of the whole passage is typical illustration by a reference solely to the aspect of things as they were providentially arranged by God to meet the eye, and not to the real and hidden laws of causation which lie beneath this aspect.

If any still, through the force of old associations, do not fully see the propriety and impressiveness of a contrast between natural death on one side, and spiritual life on the other, let them look at such comparisons as these:

---

36 Wilhelm Martin Leberecht de Wette (1780-1849), a German theologian and biblical scholar, described by Julius Wellhausen as "the epoch-making opener of the historical criticism of the Pentateuch." He prepared the way for the Supplement theory and made valuable contributions to other branches of theology. He had poetic talent, and wrote a drama in three acts, entitled *Die Entsagung* (Berlin, 1823). He had an intelligent interest in art, and studied ecclesiastical music and architecture. As a Biblical critic he is sometimes classed with the destructive school, but, as Otto Pfleiderer says (Development of Theology), he "occupied as free a position as the Rationalists with regard to the literal authority of the creeds of the church, but that he sought to give their due value to the religious feelings, which the Rationalists had not done, and, with a more unfettered mind towards history, to maintain the connection of the present life of the church with the past." His works are marked by exegetical skill, unusual power of condensation and uniform fairness. Accordingly they possess value which is little affected by the progress of criticism.

As by the brazen serpent a healing power was exerted on all
who looked to it, so by Christ is a divine energy exerted to
heal all who look to him.

Yet let it not be supposed that there is a perfect correspondence in
the two cases. For, if the healing power of the serpent revealed itself in
delivering sinners from natural death, who merely looked to it by the
bodily eye, how much more shall the healing power of Christ reveal
itself, in averting eternal death and conferring eternal life on all who,
in true faith, look to Him by the eye of the mind! Or thus,

As beneath the protection of the blood sprinkled upon their
doorposts the children of Israel took refuge, and thus escaped the ravages of death, even so are the true Israel of
God defended by the sprinkling of the blood of Christ from
the impending perils and the eternal agonies of the second
death.

But how unequal are the things thus compared! How small was
the value or the power of the blood of the paschal lamb! But, if even
this could defend from impending death, how much more shall the
blood of the divine and eternal Son of God, the true atoning Lamb,
who takes away the sin of the world, avert the higher perils of true believers, and exalt them to eternal life! Or thus,

As Aaron, by the incense which ascended from his censer,
made atonement for those ancient rebels, whose crimes had
excited the anger of God, and thus averted the avenging
sentence of death, even so Christ by his atonement and intercession is powerful in every age and clime to atone for
rebellious man, and to avert from all in whose behalf he interposes the sentence of death.

But how far beneath the great reality was the prophetic adumbra-
tion! For the intervention of Aaron effected but a temporary deliverance from the stroke of death; but the intercession of our great High
Priest in heaven forever averts the second death, and confers eternal
life on all for whom he intercedes.

In all these cases the comparison proceeds from natural death in
the type to spiritual life in the antitype.

Indeed, the apostle Paul has given us a most striking typical comparison of this very kind.

> "For if the blood of bulls and of goats, and the ashes of a heifer, sprinkling the unclean, sanctifieth to the purifying of the flesh, how much more shall the blood of Christ, who through the eternal Spirit offered himself without spot unto God, purge your conscience from dead works to serve the living God!" (Heb. 9:14).

CHAPTER XII: THE ARGUMENT REINFORCED

IN the general statement of the true interpretation of the passage under consideration, given in the third chapter of this book, I adopted the view of the Old School party, that the sense of the passage is judicial, relating to condemnation and justification, and not to the causation of sin or holiness in the human race; and also that of the Greek church, that the death spoken of is simply natural death.

To these I added the position that, in the case of Adam, the type, the sequence, was not causative, but merely one of apparent causation for typical purposes.

The truth of the first of these positions has been rendered so apparent that it needs no further confirmation. But it will not be useless to add some additional confirmations of the other two. For, although the case is at present sufficiently clear, were there no uncommon obstacles to the perception of the truth, yet, considering the power of the association of ideas and of habit, and the tenacity with which the human mind holds on to established opinions, it is better to err by excess of argument than by a relative deficiency,—I mean a deficiency in view of the practical end to be gained. I shall, therefore, subjoin some additional considerations, of no small weight.

It will be seen that thus far I have gone upon the ground that it is as consistent with the laws of typical (or typological—Ed.) illustration to understand the word *death* to mean natural death, as it is to give it the broad sense which includes the whole penalty of the divine law. I have also assumed that it is as consistent with those laws to understand a merely typical sequence of condemnation by the sin of Adam, as to understand a causative one. Supposing these views to stand on equal grounds, I have argued in the first case from the facts of the Old Testament, and in the second from the laws of equity and honor, revealed by God as His own rule of conduct, that we ought to understand natural death and a merely typical sequence to be set forth in the passage.

But I now add that in neither case do the two modes of interpretation, in fact, stand on equal grounds, as I shall proceed to show.

I lay down, then, the position, with reference to the first of the two points just mentioned, that it is more in accordance with the true laws of typical illustration that there should be an antithesis of natural death by Adam, and spiritual life by Christ, than that the idea of death should be carried into the spiritual and eternal sphere. For the great idea of the Old Testament typology is to illustrate the things of the eternal and spiritual sphere by the events of this life, and of this visible material system.

So Paul expressly states the matter, in the ninth chapter of Hebrews. The system of types was "of this creation," ταυτης της κτισεως (v. 11). The great realities belonged to the invisible spiritual system. By the great law of analogy they were set off one against the other, as the typical and the antitypical. I do not say that the type and the antitype are never in the same sphere, for occasionally they are. But, as a general fact, they are in different and analogical spheres.

Nor has this great law escaped the notice of at least some of the writers on typology, though they do not seem to have reflected on its scope. In particular, Fairbairn, to whose able work I have before referred, has given a very clear and impressive enunciation of this law. It is the fifth of his series, and is thus stated:

> "Another rule of interpretation arising out of the principles already established, and necessary to be borne in mind if we would give an enlightened and consistent view of typical symbols and transactions; is, that due regard must be had to the essential difference between the nature of type and antitype. For as the exhibition of divine truth contained in the former was given on a lower stage, or by means only of carnal and earthly concerns, in applying the elements of truth, so taught, to the higher,—that is, the spiritual and heavenly concerns of Messiah's kingdom.— what bore immediate respect to the flesh in the one must be understood as bearing immediate respect to the soul in the other,—while in the one temporal interests only appear, their counterpart in the other must be eternal interests; in short, the outward, visible, and carnal in the type, must in the antitype pass into the inward, spiritual and heavenly."

This rule, he very properly says, enters into "the very vitals of the subject." He admits of only two exceptions to it in the New Testament, and he contends that these are rather apparent than real.

Yet, notwithstanding all this, he is so fully controlled by the common views of the case of Adam, that he does not see that he extends his influence into the spiritual and eternal sphere as truly as that of Christ. According to his own rule, in the case of Adam, "temporal interests only" ought to appear; "their counterpart in the other (Christ) must be eternal interests;" "in short, the outward, visible and carnal in the type, must, in the antitype, pass into the inward, spiritual and heavenly." If we limit the sequences of Adam's transgression, with the Greek church, to natural death, then we do observe this law; but, if we extend them to the spiritual and eternal sphere, then we violate the law; and it is a law which enters into "the very vitals of the subject."

Nor is this all: if we thus extend the idea of death, and give to Adam causative power, it entirely overloads the type, and destroys the truth of the apostle's comparison. The power of Adam, in the spiritual sphere, to produce eternal death, extends to all the race; and, when we reflect that, thus far, Christ being judge, the great majority have, in fact, perished, and that forever, the effect of the comparison is that of an anti-climax. Adam has, in fact, destroyed more than Christ has saved; and their ruin is as complete and eternal as is the salvation of those whom Christ saves. But, if we suppose that Adam has, in fact, ruined no one in the spiritual sphere, but that the sequence of death, in the natural sphere, upon his transgression, is a designed antithetic type of eternal life through Christ, then the antitype, as it ought, towers above the type in its true spiritual magnitude and glory.

In addition to this, if death is taken to mean the full and eternal penalty of God's law, and the sequence is causative, then the penalty of Adam's act is so enormously disproportioned to its demerit, that it tends to make the contemplation unspeakably painful, and to confuse all our ideas of justice and honor. If a penalty is enormously disproportioned to an offense, it loses all its power as a penalty, and produces reaction and disgust, if not indignation. If a king, because of some sin of a viceroy, of which his subjects were entirely ignorant, should send out his armies, and exterminate, with extreme torments, every man, woman and child, in the province of that viceroy, and then should proclaim that he did it to show his indignation against sin, in view of its enormous evils, and his fixed purpose to punish it, what rational human being could be found upon whom such a proceeding would not react, and rather create abhorrence of the king's injustice, than of the viceroy's sin? And yet there would not be, in such a transaction, one millionth part of the horror and the injustice that is involved in the idea of an utter forfeiture, by all the millions of the human race, of the favor of God, and their exposure to his frown, and to all the miseries of endless damnation, by a solitary act of Adam, of which they had no knowledge, and over which they had no control,—and which forfeiture actually results in the endless ruin of the great majority of them. It is not in the power of human language to express, nor of the human mind to conceive, the horror and injustice of such a proceeding. What, then, must be the painful and confounding influence of retaining such a view, on one side of a typical comparison designed to set forth the glories of redeeming love! How must it confuse our ideas of justice and honor! How dark and gloomy will it render the system which rests upon it! With what melancholy shades will this passage of Scripture evermore be veiled!

But, represent this system as a remedy for evil already existing, let it ruin none and save unnumbered millions, remove from Adam the idea of power efficiently to cause evil at all, let the judicial sequence of natural death be ordained as a type to illustrate, by antithesis, eternal life through Christ, and I do not know any passage in the Word of God which combines higher elements of sublimity, beauty, and divine glory.

The value of a type depends, not upon the existence of causative power in the sequence, but upon the fact that God ordained it to illustrate some great and glorious truth, and that it does illustrate it. Hence, the sprinkling of the blood of the paschal lamb, the brazen serpent, the incense of Aaron, lose none of their value because they were not linked to their sequences by causative power. What though they did not, in reality, avert natural death (sic)? It is enough that God made them appear to do it, for the sake of illustrating the real power of Christ to avert eternal death. So, what though it be true that the sin of Adam exerted no power to injure one individual of the human race? It is enough that God so arranged events that, apparently, the human race was sentenced to natural death, through his sin, in order to make a great, glorious and original type of justification and eternal life through the coming Redeemer. In this way it has its legitimate influence and its full power as a type. But, the moment you load it down with a causative power to produce eternal death, you transgress the true laws of typical analogy, veil its radiance in the dense clouds of injustice, and utterly destroy its legitimate power.

And now I cannot but feel that I have adduced sufficient reasons to induce all Christian men, who love the honor of God and the good of man more than any or all other interests, to reject the common interpretations of this passage, and to adopt that which I have proposed.

I know full well the strength of the influence of Augustine, and Calvin, and Edwards, and of the creeds of the Reformation. I know the power of national churches, of great denominations, and of great teachers.

But I know, also, that, after all, these things are but finite, temporary and local. God only is infinite, universal, eternal, all-glorious, and worthy of universal homage and praise.

Before Him the nations are as a drop of a bucket, and are counted as the small dust of the balance. Yea, all nations in his sight are as nothing, and they are counted to Him as less than nothing, and vanity. He pours contempt upon princes; he makes the judges of the earth as vanity. He blows upon them, and they wither, and the whirlwind takes them away as stubble.

The question now at issue does not so much concern the honor of human organizations as the true and unclouded glory of this great God. I have written as I have, because I have felt in my inmost soul, and with deep and long continued sorrow, that He is deeply dishonored, and the energies of His kingdom on earth are fatally paralyzed, by the basis on which His own church has placed His greatest and most glorious work, the divine work of redeeming love. I have believed, and therefore have I spoken.

If it were seen to be so, then there would be but one response from every true child of God. If His honor is at stake, all else must give way. What are creeds, institutions or denominations, in comparison with Him for whose honor they are professedly made, and for whom, alone, they avow a desire to exist?

But the great turning point of the whole question will be, Do they, in fact, dishonor Him?

And now, as before Him, I ask attention to the following considerations:

The first, *the natural, the intuitive convictions of the human mind, with reference to the commonly alleged dealings of God with the human race through Adam, are dishonorable and unjust.*

That this is so has been confessed by men than whom none are more eminent for intellectual power, and for piety. Augustine, Calvin, Pascal and Watts, have virtually or openly confessed it; Dr. Woods, Dr. Hodge and Haldane, have virtually or openly confessed the same.

That they are so, in fact, I have evinced by showing that all efforts to explain and defend them have resulted in inconsistent and mutually destructive theories, every one of which has been, and still is, condemned by some large portion of the true church of God. So true is this, that Haldane has declared that all such efforts have but made the case still worse, and that it is our duty to believe on the naked and unexplained Word of God; and that this must be the final authority in the case.

But, in a case like this, are we to take for granted an interpretation involving such consequences? Or is it, indeed, a self-evident interpretation? History does not seem to imply that it is self-evident, and in fact it is not so.

I have shown, in the first place, that the view which I advocate is, at least, as consistent with the laws of interpretation as any other, and that from the facts of the Old Testament, and from the laws of honor and right, there is a decided preponderance in its favor.

I have next shown that the common interpretations are opposed to the prevailing and almost universal laws of typical (or typological— Ed.) analogy; that they overload the type, and make the passage untrue; that they destroy the moral power of God's displeasure at Adam's sin, by exaggeration; and that they imprison, suppress, and do violence to the deepest convictions of the human mind against dishonor and injustice, which can find no relief till they have been expressed.

I allege that the view which I present is simple, intelligible, eloquent, sublime, beautiful, worthy of God, in perfect harmony with the laws of language, and, in particular, with the laws of typical usage.

But, if these things are so, can anyone fail to see what the conclusion ought to be?

I know that the result is momentous, but is it more than God deserves?

At all events, is it not a duty thoroughly to reconsider this whole question, until a position can be found that shall so present the great

work of redeeming love as not to reflect deep dishonor on the character of God?

CHAPTER XIII: SURVEY OF THE ARGUMENT

IN the opening chapter of this book I remarked that practically the whole of the present discussion turns more upon the interpretation of the last part of the fifth chapter of Romans than upon any other point. For, if it had not been for the belief that this passage teaches such a doctrine of forfeiture as I have considered and exposed,—a doctrine which, in the judgment of Pascal, appeared obviously impossible and unjust,—it could never have gained credence or sustained itself for a single hour; nor would it have ever been believed that the sin of Adam did or could in any way produce the terrific depravity which has been exhibited in this world ever since his creation and fall.

But, so long as it has been supposed that God has asserted these things, it has been felt to be a duty to overrule even those immutable intellectual and moral intuitions which he has implanted in the soul, rather than to distrust His Word.

The effect of this has been to paralyze the intellectual and moral energies of Christians to an extent of which no adequate conception has as yet been formed, and to reduce them to a state of lamentable captivity and bondage. For, though not in close confinement, and thus cut off from all action, yet they have been hemmed in by certain tremendous intellectual enclosures, which they have not dared to throw down or to pass. Moreover, whilst hemmed up within these limits, they have, of necessity, as I have shown, rather expended their energy in mutual conflicts, than in assaults upon their great and common enemy, the god of this world.

The most direct and obvious cause of this state of things has been the almost unanimous rejection of preexistence, the only principle which can give them true liberty, and unite their energies to bring to a speedy close to this spiritual captivity.

It is for this reason that I have felt it to be indispensable to enter as thoroughly as I have into the discussion of this passage, for the sake of developing its true meaning, and of showing that it does not, as is asserted, exclude preexistence, but rather presupposes and requires it.

But, now, that old and terrific apparition of divine authority, which has for so many ages frowned darkly before the church, can no longer be raised to dismay our souls, and to scare us back into our ancient captivity. Thank God, we are free! The wide field of truth is before us, with none to molest us or to make us afraid; let us arise at once, and, by the aid of the divine Spirit, enter and possess it.

The way is now prepared to resume the inquiry proposed at the end of the last book. Shall the theory of a previous existence be received as true? In reply to this, it was answered by its opponents, there is no evidence of its truth; it merely shifts the difficulty, but does not remove it; and it is inconsistent with the Word of God.

The last point having been considered, I shall now resume the other two. I made a few remarks in reply to them at the opening of this book, but shall now subject them to a more full and thorough discussion. In opposition to preexistence, then, as I have set it forth, it is alleged that it is a mere theory, entirely devoid of any proof of its truth.

This remark is not infrequently made in a manner which seems to imply a high regard for truth and evidence, and a rational fear of adopting unfounded and visionary theories. It is sometimes, also, presented as if it were a view of the case so profound and exhausting that nothing more remains to be said. If, indeed, it were true, such might, in reality, be the case. But it is apparent that assertion is not argument, and that it is no legitimate mode of terminating a discussion to take for granted the very point at issue.

But I will not assume that those who make this remark intend thus to beg the question, I will assume that they mean that this is a point that can be known only by revelation, and that it is not definitely revealed in express terms in the Word of God. If so, then they assume that, if it is not expressly and verbally revealed, it must ever be a theory, and admit of no decisive proof.

In reply to this, I have already briefly stated that the most important of all the truths which we hold cannot be thus proved.

But such is the importance of this point that it deserves a more formal and full consideration. I will, therefore, once more call attention to the real and deepest foundations of our religious, intellectual and moral systems, and to the laws of belief upon which they rest.

The great but simple fact, then, with reference to such fundamental doctrines, is this: *that they rest upon certain ideas and intuitive convictions of our own minds, taken in connection with the facts of the system around us.*

Thus, since God has made us in His own image, we derive from our own minds the elements of our idea of a personal God, as a being possessing intellect, emotions and affections, will, the power of choosing ends, forming plans, and making laws, a moral nature, and a sense of what is right and wrong, honorable and dishonorable. We find, also, in ourselves an intuitive belief of the necessary relation of cause and effect. Thus made, we examine our own minds and bodies, and the world around us, and there find facts which require an infinite mind, such as we are enabled to conceive of, through our own minds, as the cause. Thus we arrive at a rational belief of the being of a God. In the language of Paul, "The invisible things of him are clearly seen, being understood by the things that are made, even his eternal power and Godhead."

So, too, when certain books are presented to us claiming to be a revelation from this God, we are obliged to rely upon the same principles for evidence of the truth of their claims. We see that miracles were wrought by their authors, or prophecies uttered by them, or doctrines and a system set forth transcending the intellectual and moral abilities of man. Such things we refer to God as the only adequate cause, and believe those to be His messengers whose claims he attests by such evidences. Till we have done this, their words have no binding power over us.

But what truths are there so important as the being of a God and the fact that the Bible is His Word? Are they not the basis of our whole system of religious belief?

It is plain, then, that there are modes of proof besides express verbal revelation, and that these are the most powerful and trustworthy by which the mind of man can be influenced. Otherwise, God would not have left the whole system to rest on them. Nor is it otherwise in the material system. We fully believe, without express verbal revelation, the Newtonian system, based on the law of gravitation. Our evidence lies in the structure of our minds, and in the facts of the system itself. By the structure of our minds we are led to search for the law of the system, and no less are we led by the same structure to rest in that law which systematizes, harmonizes and explains, all the facts of the system, and unites them in one glorious whole. No text of Scripture proves the Newtonian theory. Nay, the popular phraseology of the Bible, as well as of common speech, seems to oppose it. But, because it unites, explains and harmonizes all facts, we believe it.

Thus, by reasoning on the great law of causation, we first ascend from His works to a knowledge of the great first cause. In the same way we establish the divine authority of His Word, proving by various arguments that it demands God as its cause or author. Nor do we otherwise establish the law of gravitation; for we show that all the facts of the system demand such a law as their cause.

If, then, it can be shown that the facts of this moral and physical system, taken as a whole, are such as to demand a preexistent state in order to explain them, as really and as much as the facts of the material system demand the law of gravitation to explain them, or as much as the facts of the whole system demand God as their cause, then the doctrine of a preexistent state can be proved by the highest possible proof, —proof so clear and so strong that no intelligent being need wish to go beyond it. Let me state a single course of reasoning, which of itself would be all-sufficient. The laws of honor and of right are of God; nor has He ever violated them, nor will He. This is the premise of an argument powerful enough to revolutionize nations and churches, and to shake a world.

Taking, then, this premise, I allege that if the facts and principles which have been already set forth are true, there is a brief argument, entirely within our reach, and comprehensible by all, which of itself is enough to settle the question forever.

If the facts which have been stated concerning the ruined condition of man are true, and if the principles of honor and right have been truly set forth, and if the only passage that seems to teach the common doctrine can, in accordance with the true and well-known laws of typical language, be so interpreted as perfectly to accord with the idea of preexistence, and if the common theory arrays the principles of honor and right against the conduct of God, whilst the other exhibits them as in harmony, then it follows, of absolute necessity, that the common view is false, and that which I advocate is true. If the premises are granted, the conclusion is inevitable; and no argument can exceed this in power. The argument for the being of a God has no superior force. The proof that the Bible is the Word of God is no more conclusive. The proof of the truth of the Newtonian theory is not more powerful, although that is regarded as established beyond any rational doubt. For the mind of man is so made that nothing can do such violence to its most immutable intuitive convictions as the supposition that God can bring to pass results such as exist in this world in a mode that is at war with the principles of honor and right. If there is a mode consistent with those principles, we know, with the highest and most absolute certainty, that this, and not the other, is the mode which God has taken.

For my own part, I am satisfied that the premises are true, and that, therefore, the conclusion is valid. Nor shall I cease to regard this argument as perfectly conclusive till the premises are overthrown. But any attempt to do this must, I think, prove a failure. For the evidence from Scripture, experience and history, in proof of the statement concerning the ruined condition of man, is of such immense power that it admits of no logical reply, and the only real argument ever urged against it has been the appeal to our intuitive convictions of honor and right. But the whole power of that argument is now neutralized by the doctrine of preexistence, which I have assumed. Moreover, the evidence for the principles of honor and right, which I have stated, from the intuitive convictions of the human mind, from the tendencies of regeneration and sanctification, and from the Word of God, is powerful beyond expression, and can never be answered; and the only real argument against them has been an allegation that they were inconsistent with certain well-known acts of God. But the whole power of this argument, also, has now been neutralized by the doctrine of preexistence, which I defend. And, finally, the interpretation of Rom. 5:12-19, which regards the language as denoting, in the case of Adam and his posterity, merely natural death, and typical sequences, and not causative, is not only a possible interpretation, but it is the one which best accords with the well-known laws of typical language, and with the analogy of the Word of God.

But, in addition to this, there is a strong auxiliary argument in support of the same view in the fact that the results of all attempts to explain the connection between the sin of Adam and the ruin of his posterity have been so unsatisfactory as to create a violent presumption that the idea is in itself incapable of vindication or defense. On the other hand, preexistence easily explains all the facts of the case. I will first illustrate this statement by analogous cases. It was once held almost universally that the words "this is my body" were to be taken as denoting a literal truth, as set forth in the doctrine of transubstantiation. Of this truth, of course, the scholastic divines felt bound to produce a philosophical exposition and defense. The result, as was to be expected, was a violent distortion of philosophy itself, and fertile crops of absurd and ridiculous results. The fact is manifest. No exposition and defense of the dogma in question is extant, that does not lead to absurdities. Is it not, then, a fair inference that the thing itself is an absurdity? In like manner, the Roman Catholic dogmas of sacramental regeneration and sanctification, and of the ruin of all who are not in the Roman corporation (church), have never been, at any time, so expounded and defended as to avoid either gross absurdities or else a contradiction of most notorious facts and the most sacred moral principles. Now, though efforts have been made, and still are made, to base these things on Scripture, is there not in history a proof that the things alleged are absurd in each case?

Now, it is worthy of notice, not only that it has been confessed in all ages that any exposition of the influence of Adam's sin to ruin his race is beset with most formidable difficulties, but that all attempts to explain it have failed so completely that not one can be mentioned which has not been pronounced false by eminent Christians in large numbers. Some have resorted to the theory of the transmission of the corrupted soul from generation to generation. But this has been almost universally repudiated by the church in all ages, as leading to materialism, and making the substance of the soul sinful. Moreover, if it were not so, it would not in the least help the case on the score of justice and honor. But, on the theory that God creates the soul, it may well be asked, Does He create a depraved and polluted soul? If not, whence comes its original native depravity? Does it come from the body? What is this but to revive the pernicious Gnostic doctrine, that the origin of sin is matter, and that to escape from sin we must mortify, scourge and macerate, the body. If the body is not the cause, then it may be supposed to lie in God. Does He, then, as some teach, impute the guilt of Adam's sin to a new-created soul, and on account of this guilt, and as a punishment, create it without original righteousness, with draw from it supernatural influences, and leave it a mass of corruption, exposed to a sinful world and to Satan? Can this be defended on any known principle of honor and right? I have already shown that it is confessed that it cannot. No effort is made to do it. All who allege it retreat to the cover of mystery. But I am unable to see any mystery in the case. A new-created being thus treated is by a large portion of the Christian world regarded as, beyond all reasonable grounds of doubt, treated dishonorably and unjustly. With such I coincide. Is the theory of those any better who say that the constitution is so changed, before knowledge or action, as in all cases to lead to sin as soon as moral action commences; and that a being with such a constitution is then exposed to the full power of a sinful world and of Satan? Another large portion of the Christian world regard this, and very properly too, as no more honorable and just than the other alternative. Shall we, then, trace all sin and holiness alike to the efficient agency of God, and hold that He established a constitution such that if Adam sinned he would efficiently cause all his posterity to sin? But, on this theory, even Adam could not sin, unless God caused him so to do; and it results in this,—that God causes all men to sin, because He had previously caused Adam to sin. A very large portion of the Christian world regard this theory as unsatisfactory, and inconsistent with correct views of man's responsibility for his sins, and of God's sincere opposition to sin.

Shall we, then, with Edwards, confound all ideas of personal identity, and insist that God made Adam and all his posterity one person with respect to his first sin, and different persons with reference to all other sins? Few, we think, will engage in so desperate an undertaking.

Shall we, then, with Augustine, resort to the idea of a mysterious unity with Adam, and hold that all men actually existed in him, sinned in his act, and are guilty of it? For ages this view was held and defended, just as transubstantiation was, but with equal violence to the intuitive convictions of the human mind. It indicates, indeed, an admission of the great truth that men ought not to be punished but for their own acts; it led to forms of speech that seemed to teach that all men did in reality apostatize from God at once and together,—and, on this ground, they repelled charges of injustice; and it implies one form of preexistence and action; but in reaching this result they violated all laws of personal identity and distinct personal existence, and involved themselves in unspeakable absurdities. Augustine felt and frankly conceded the difficulties of the subject, and at times confessed his ignorance. Luther did the same. So did Turretin. Möhler, after surveying all the solutions ever offered, declares them utterly unsatisfactory, and retreats to mystery. Is there no presumption, in all this, that this alleged fact is incapable of vindication or defense?

Indeed, it is admitted by Prof. Hodge that the whole difficulty lies in the mere fact alleged, and not in any particular mode of explanation. "It is on all hands admitted," he says, "that the sin of Adam involved the race in ruin. *This is the whole difficulty.* How is it to be reconciled with the divine character, that the fate of unborn millions should depend on an act over which they had not the slightest control, and in which they had no agency? This difficulty presses the opponents of the doctrine (of imputation) more heavily than its advocates." According, then, to Prof. Hodge, *the best possible* ground of justifying God in such an arrangement is to represent him as regarding "an act over which they had not the slightest control, and in which they had no agency" as being, nevertheless, their act, and as withdrawing from them, on account of it, all favor, communion and divine influence, and thus inflicting on them "a form of death which is of all evils the essence and the sum." Is this, then, the best mode of justifying God, in a case so momentous? Certainly it is a hard case, for to many it seems that none can be worse. I, however, do not regard it as the best. Nevertheless, I do agree with Prof. Hodge that all the modes resorted to by those who reject this are as truly and entirely unsatisfactory.

After all, the great difficulty lies in the idea that untold millions of new-created minds should in any way be brought into being by God, for an endless existence, either with positively depraved natures, or natures so deranged, disordered and ruined, as certainly to result in depravity so powerful that nothing but supernatural power can overcome it; and then, with such natures, be subjected to the highest power of temptation to evil through corrupt human organizations, and satanic agency, being moreover from the very first abandoned by God, and under His infinite displeasure. This, I say, is the great difficulty; and no reconciliation of this with honor and justice in God has ever been effected, nor is it, in my judgment, possible to effect it.

But, in addition to this, the mode in which it is said to have been effected by those who ascribe causative power to the act of Adam is obviously entirely inadequate to effect such a result; as much so (or even more) as looking at a brazen serpent is to heal the bite of a poisonous fiery serpent. For, indeed, it is an astounding fact that is alleged when we say that one act, done six thousand years ago, made a whole race so wicked that their depravity defies all but supreme and divine power.

Certainly the theory of baptismal regeneration, or sanctification by the Lord's supper, truly viewed, seems far more rational than the fact alleged in this case. Is it not as possible, and far more reasonable, that consecrated water should, by a divine constitution, regenerate the person whom it actually touches, or the consecrated wafer sanctify the person who eats it, than that either one act of eating, done six thousand years ago, or the sin of that one act, should, to this time, and in all future generations, have power to make the millions of this world, before action, so unspeakably depraved that without a supernatural regeneration they must all forever perish? At all events, if one sinful act of eating, at the beginning of the world, can by any divine constitution be made the cause of depravity so inconceivably great and all-pervading, who has a right to say that it is either absurd or improbable that an act of eating, attended by obedience to God, should in the Eucharist by a divine constitution sanctify the soul and fit it for heaven? Or, even that sanctified water should, by a divine constitution, wash away sin, original and actual? Indeed, Möhler argues, and not unreasonably, from the assumed fact that man fell through a material system, that it is *a priori* probable that God would restore him through a system of material sacraments. Speaking of the seven sacraments, he says,

> "The entanglement of man with the lower world, which since Adam's disobedience hath been subjected to a curse, is revealed in the most diverse ways. Even so diverse are the ways (that is, the sacraments) whereby we are raised up to a world of a higher order in and by the fellowship with Christ."

The design of the sacraments, he says, is, "to raise humanity again up to God, as through Adam it had fallen." Again he says,

> "As man ignominiously delivered himself over to the dominion of the lower world, so he needs its mediation to enable him to rise above it."

Certainly it is more reasonable to suppose man to be raised, through a divine constitution, by oft-repeated and manifold material sacramental acts, than to suppose all men in all ages to be so deeply sunk by one act. Hence, if the whole sacramental system of Rome is rejected as absurd, and the very germ of the papal despotism, why should another theory, still less rational, be retained?

If, now, anyone shall say, *These things, after all, ought not to be said; for they virtually concede that all which Pelagians, Unitarians and Infidels, have said against the doctrine of the fall of the human race in Adam is correct, and it will be received by them with triumph, and be followed by the renunciation of the doctrine of human depravity, and of Christianity itself.*

To this I reply, *The rejection of the common doctrine of the fall in Adam is not in any sense a rejection of the doctrine of the native depravity and fallen condition of the human race in its fullest and amplest sense, nor of any doctrine of Christianity resting on that basis. Nor does it touch the Scriptural or historical or experimental arguments in favor of that doctrine, or any other doctrine of Christianity. If all that is said in the Bible concerning Adam were stricken out, still there would remain a perfectly full and ample proof of the doctrine of depravity, and of every other doctrine of the Christian system.*

Nor is this all. In all ages the strongest arguments of the opponents of that doctrine, and of Christianity, have been derived from the fact that the fall of Adam has been made its basis and originating cause. They have no real arguments against it; they never have had, except such as have been furnished to them by thus making that an essential part of the doctrine which has no logical connection with it, and, still more, which furnishes the only real and valid arguments against it.

Nothing weakens a cause so much as to defend it by unsound arguments, and to refuse to admit the force of true and real arguments against it. By placing the doctrine of human depravity on the basis of the fall in Adam, its opponents have been enabled to array the truth itself against it, yea, the highest, most sacred, and most affecting truth that can be seen or felt by the mind of man. That truth, without which neither the glory of God nor the sacredness of His government can be seen. Nay, it has led to the crippling and degradation of the human mind for long ages, by urging it to do violence to its most sacred and godlike convictions, by repudiating them as wretched and false.

The doctrine of depravity is a real, a momentous, a mournful fact. Scripture, history, Christian experience, unite in its proof. If it were not called on to wrestle even against God and the truth, by an unhappy misunderstanding, it might stand against the world. But how can it ever universally prevail whilst obliged to contend with the sacred principles of honor and right, and to resort to theories indefensible and absurd?

Whether those who have hitherto opposed this doctrine will receive these concessions with triumph or otherwise, has no bearing on the question what is the truth. If, in ages past, they have, in some important respects, spoken the truth, and it has been rejected by the advocates of depravity, that is no reason why we should persist in weakening our cause by doing the same. But I trust that they will not triumph, but receive such concessions with candor, and look at the real arguments in favor of the doctrine with more interest and care, when it is seen that it can be held in its fullest form, and yet conflict with no principle of honor and right.

Is there any danger in making the trial of this course? The other course has been tried for many long centuries. What has been the result? Lamentable division and conflict, and theories none of which has yet been able to satisfy the human mind that it is rational and consistent.

Turn, now, from these conflicting and unsatisfactory attempts to the simplicity and intelligibility of the other theory. It resolves original sin and native depravity into a well-known result of the laws of the mind, which we call habit. This is neither a part of the essence nor an original attribute of the mind. It is a permanent predisposition, or propensity, to a sinful course of action, caused by repeated previous action. The Princeton divines have clearly described what I mean, in rebutting the charge of teaching physical regeneration, which had been alleged against themselves. They say:

> "The main principle, as before stated, which is assumed by those who make this charge, is, that we can only regard the soul as to its substance on the one hand, and its actions on the other. If, therefore, there be any change wrought in the soul other than of its acts, it must be a physical change. And if any tendency, either to sin or holiness, exist prior to choice, it is a positive existence, a real entity. Thus the charge of physical depravity and physical regeneration is fairly made out. We are constrained to confess, that, if the premises are correct, the conclusions, revolting as they are, and affecting, as they do, the fair names of so large a portion of the Christian church, are valid. The principle itself, however, we believe to be a gratuitous assumption. It is incon-

sistent with the common, and, as we believe, correct idea of
habits, both connatural and acquired. The word 'habit'
(*habitus*) was used by the old writers precisely in the same
sense as 'principle' by President Edwards (pp. 380-1), or
'disposition' as used and explained by President Dwight.
That there are such habits or dispositions which can be resolved neither into 'essential attributes' nor 'acts,' we maintain to be the common judgment of mankind. Let us take
for illustration an instance of an acquired habit of the lowest
kind, the skill of an artist. He has a soul with the same essential attributes as other men; his body is composed of the
same materials; and the same law regulates the obedience of
his muscular actions to his mind. By constant practice he
has acquired what is usually denominated skill; an ability to
go through the processes of his art with greater facility, exactness and success, than ordinary men. Take this man
while asleep or engaged in any indifferent occupation,—you
have a soul and body not differing in any of their essential
attributes from those of other men. Still there is a difference.
What is it? Must it be either 'a real existence, an entity,' an
act, or nothing? It cannot be 'an entity,' for it is acquired,
and it will hardly be maintained that a man can acquire a
new essential attribute. Neither is it an act, for the man has
his skill when it is not exercised. Yet there is certainly
'something,' which is the ground of certainty that, when
called to go through the peculiar business of his art, he will
do it with an ease and rapidity impossible for common men.
It is as impossible not to admit that this ground or reason
exists, in order to account for the effect, as it is not to admit
the existence of the soul to account for its exercises. By constant practice, a state of mind and body has been produced
adapted to secure these results, and which accounts for their
character. But this is the definition of principle or habit as
given above. A single circumstance is here wanting which
is found in other 'habits,' and that is, there is not the tendency or proneness to those particular acts to which this
state of mind is adapted. This difference, however, arises not
from any difference in the 'habits' themselves, but from the
nature of the faculties in which, so to speak, they inhere. A
principle in the will (in its largest sense, including all the active powers) is not only a state of mind adapted to certain

acts, but prone to produce them. This is not the case, at least
to the same degree, with intellectual habits. Both classes,
however, come within the definition given by President
Edwards and Dr. Dwight: 'A state of mind,' or 'foundation
for any particular kind of exercise of the faculties of the
soul.' The same remarks may be made with regard to habits
of a more purely intellectual character. A man, by devoting
himself to any particular pursuit, gradually acquires a facility
in putting forth the mental exercises which it requires. This
implies no change of essence in the soul; and it is not
merely an act, which is the result of this practice. The result,
whatever it is, is an attribute of the man under all circumstances, and not merely when engaged in the exercises
whence the habit was acquired.

"But to come nearer to the case in hand. We say a man
has a malignant disposition, or an amiable disposition. What
is to be understood by these expressions? Is it merely that he
often indulges malignant or amiable feelings? or is it not
rather that there is an habitual proneness or tendency to
their indulgence? Surely the latter. But, if so, the principle
stated above, that we can regard the soul only as to its substance or its actions, cannot be correct. For the result of a
repetition of acts of the same kind is an abiding tendency,
which is itself neither an act (eminent or immanent) nor an
'entity.' Here, then, is the soul with its essential attributes,—
an habitual tendency to certain exercises, and the exercises
themselves. The tendency is not an act, nor an active state
of the feelings in question; for it would be a contradiction
to say that a man whose heart was glowing with parental
affection, or filled for the time with any other amiable feeling, had at the same moment the malignant feelings in an
active state, although there might exist the greatest proneness to their exercise. We have seen no analysis of such dispositions which satisfies us that they can be reduced to acts.
For it is essential to the nature of an act that it should be a
matter of consciousness. This is true of those which are immanent acts of the will, or ultimate choices (by which a
fixed state of the affections is meant to be expressed), as well
as of all others. But a disposition or principle, as explained
above, is not a matter of consciousness. A man may be
aware that he has a certain disposition, as he is aware of the

existence of his soul, from the consciousness of its acts, but the disposition itself is not a subject of direct consciousness. It exists when the man is asleep or in a swoon, and unconscious of anything. Neither can these habits be, with any propriety, called a choice, or permanent affection. For in many cases they are a mere proneness to acts which have their foundation in a constitutional principle of the mind. Our object at present is merely to show that we must admit that there are mental habits which cannot be resolved either into essential attributes of the soul, fixed preferences, or subordinate acts; and, consequently, that those who believe in dispositions prior to all acts do not necessarily maintain that such dispositions are of the essence of the soul itself. If it be within the compass of the divine power to produce in us that which by constant exercise we can produce in ourselves, then a holy principle or habit may be the result of the Spirit's influence in regeneration, without any physical change having been wrought."

This I am willing to adopt as a very satisfactory description of the origin and nature of that state of mind which, in my judgment, precedes voluntary action in this world. Man is born with sinful habits, formed by himself, deeply fixed, and unconquerable except by divine grace; and this is the simple account of the whole matter. Let it now be noticed that the result at which these able writers aim is the very thing which is given to them by preexistence, in perfect consistency with the laws of mind and the character of God. But that such evil habits can be concreated is not capable of proof, and is not probable; and, even if it were possible, it is not consistent with the character of God. Moreover, if they were concreated by God, they ought to be viewed rather in the light of an evil unjustly inflicted by him upon man, than of depravity for which man can be justly held accountable. But, on the view which I present, all of these difficulties disappear.

That man is responsible for habits thus formed, and that they fill up the proper meaning of such words as a sinful disposition, bias, taste, inclination, is very clearly stated by Prof. Stuart, in his discussion of the nature of sin, in the *American Biblical Repository* for July, 1839.

"It will doubtless be asked here, What, then.— is there not such a thing as sinful disposition, bias, taste, inclination in men? Are we to abandon all expressions of this sort, so long established by usage, and the common sense of mankind?

"Not at all to abandon them, is my reply. Whenever a disposition, bias, inclination, propensity, or whatever of this nature one may please to name it, is spoken of as being sinful, the phraseology evidently may have two different meanings. In the one case, if by the phraseology in question we mean to designate the bias, or inclination, or propensity to evil, which men have created for themselves by practically indulging in sin, then these words may be taken in their natural and proper sense. It is a known law of our being that the indulgence of forbidden desires and practices strengthens our propensity to evil. The man, then, who is guilty of such indulgence, is truly and properly a sinner, because of his strengthened propensities to evil. All which he has done to augment these propensities has been voluntary transgression of God's law; and for these propensities, as thus augmented or aggravated, he is altogether accountable as a sinner. They are not only the evidence of his sin, but, in as much as he has made them strong and imperious, so far as they have been augmented and made to become imperious by him, they are themselves sinful, because they have been strengthened by voluntary sinful indulgence. Hence the Scriptures so often speak, and truly they may speak, of ἐπιθυμία (*desire*) as being sinful."

If men are born with such habits, thus formed in a previous state of being, then for them they are responsible. And it is worthy of notice that the old writers often call the opposite state produced by regeneration the habit of love, faith, or of any other Christian grace. Thus, by the theory of preexistence, a deep foundation is laid for a thorough doctrine of original sin and total depravity; and yet the guilt rests upon man, and God is clear.

Accordingly, this view has so much verisimilitude, that it has naturally suggested itself to Julius Müller, a man of all intelligent, far-seeing and candid mind, as the only satisfactory explanation of the matter, on a fair view of the facts of the case. Of him Professor Edwards says:

"As a profound and scientific theologian, he has probably no superior among his learned countrymen. His great work

is on the Nature of Sin, and is characterized by profound
investigation, accurate analysis, comprehensive survey of
the entire field, and a systematic arrangement of his materials truly German."

He first establishes the reality of sin, disclosing its nature and its
guilt. He comes to the result that nothing can partake of the nature of
sin, or involve guilt, except the acts of the will, or the results of those
acts on the constitution in the form of sinful propensities and habits.
He resolves all actual sin into selfishness, and herein agrees with Edwards and Hopkins. He then discusses different theories of the origin
of sin, rejecting the idea that it is either the necessary result of a finite
nature, or of the metaphysical imperfection of man; or that it results
from the fact that the mind is connected with the material system by
the body, with its senses and appetites; or that evil is necessary, in order, by its contrasts, to secure a vital development of individuals in human life; and also the Manichean theory of a self-existent principle of
evil.

He traces the origin of sin to the perverted and self-determined
action of free will. He holds that, to originate character, there must be
at the beginning of existence a power of choice between good and
evil, such that, whichever is chosen, the other might have been chosen.
Herein he agrees with Augustine and his followers. By this power of
choice, a character may be formed such that the preponderance either
to good or to evil shall be so strong as to create a certainty that the opposite will never be chosen. In this state of preponderance to evil, he
finds man from the very beginning of his development in this world.
He does not, therefore, come here to form a character, but with one
already formed. The following condensed summary of his views on
this point I take from the abstract of Mr. Robie, in the *Bibliotheca Sacra*
for May, 1849, p. 253, not having myself seen the second volume of
the work.

"If there were, at the commencement of our conscious existence, such an individual act as the stepping forth of the will
out of a state of indecision into a sinful purpose, it would
remain as a dark background in the memory. But who is
able to say definitely when and how he for the first time
acted in contradiction to his moral consciousness? Certainly

our recollection, if our attention is directed sufficiently early
to this point, goes back further than is generally supposed;
and many a one will be able to say when, for example, the
first feelings of hatred and revenge were enkindled within
him, and what a tumult they produced in the soul of the
child. But, if we descend deeper into the shaft of self-recol-
lection, we discover behind these earliest moments of sin
still others by which they were prepared, and which accordingly must have been of the same sinful character; and, if we
seek to fix these, yet other similar emotions loom up in our
memory, and these again, if we seek to hold them fast, lose
themselves in an uncertain twilight. To a pure beginning,
to an original determining act, it is impossible in this way to
attain. The earliest sinful act which presents itself to our
consciousness does not appear as the incoming of an altogether new element into the youthful life, but rather as the
development and manifestation of a hidden agency, the
awakening of a power slumbering in the deep. Sin does not
then for the first time exist in us, but only steps forth into
light. However important the epoch of awakening moral
consciousness may be, it has a past behind it, which is not
without co-determining influence upon the conduct of the
child in that crisis.

"And is it probable that a decision on which depends the
future moral character of an immortal soul would be in-
trusted to the weak hand of a child? Go back as far as we
may, we do not find formal freedom in this life. From the
earliest period of his existence in this world, the moral character of man is already determined. On the ground of a
practical empiricism,—that is, a mode of thinking which
seeks for the circumstances and conditions of the moral actions of men only in what comes under our observation
during this earthly life,—the doctrine of necessity cannot be
refuted.

"To originate one's own character is an essential condition of personality; and since from the beginning of this life
man's character is already determined, we are obliged to
step over the bounds of time to find the source of his freedom of will, to discover that act of free will by which he
determined himself to a course of sin. Is the moral condition, in which, irrespective of redemption, we find man to

be, one of guilt, and a consequence of his own act; is there
truth in the testimony of conscience which imputes to us
our sins; is there truth in the voice of religion that God is
not the author of sin,—then the freedom of man must have
its beginning in a domain out of time. In this domain is that
power of original choice to be sought for which precedes
and preconditions all sinful decisions in time."

We have here the elements of an argument which, if the premises
are sure, is valid. The premises are, sin must be man's own act, guilt
can attach to nothing else. Nor is God the author of sin. Yet man is,
from the beginning of this life, a sinner, and guilty. This is the testimony of conscience and of God. Of course he must have sinned before
entering this world.

He reasons again to the same effect, as follows:

"The problem is, to reconcile the guilt of each individual
with the universality of sin in the race, and thus show the
falsity of the conclusion, drawn from that universality, that
sin is an essential constituent of human nature, or a matter
of metaphysical necessity. On the one side, there is in all
men an innate sinfulness, and, on the other side, wherever
sin is there is guilt; that is, each individual is, by his own
self-determination, the author of his sin. This would be a
manifest contradiction, if there were not preceding our
earthly development in time an existence of our personality
as the sphere of that self-determination by which our moral
condition from birth is affected. And so, from these undeniable facts of human life, we are led to the same idea to
which the examination of human freedom brought us,—the
idea of a mode of existence of created personalities out of
time, and from which their life in time is dependent. Should
we, however, ascribe to all personal creatures in the timeless
state of their being such a perversion of will as is found in
man, we should transfer the same difficult problem to the
sphere in which, we suppose, is found its solution. But here
we are met and relieved by a doctrine which finds a place in
the religious belief of most nations, that a part of the spirit-
world, by their self-determination, founded a moral state of
being in undisturbed harmony with God, and thus elevated

the original purity in which they were created to a free holiness; and that another portion of those beings entirely and
decidedly turned away from God, whereby for their existence in time every inclination to good was excluded."

Who does not see that this distinguished divine, who is confessedly the leader of the German theologians of this day, was led to take
this view by the same mode of reasoning that is deemed conclusive
with reference to the Newtonian system? The solution which he assigns accounts for the facts of the case. No other does or can. The object of his work and his line of argument differ from mine, yet in this
particular I am gratified to see that we come to common results.

It is also an encouraging circumstance that Dr. Hodge, speaking
in the name of the Princeton divines, has referred with approbation to
this work of Müller as one of great importance, and on the right side
of the great question of original sin. We are thus encouraged to hope
that they will adopt his doctrine, that nothing is sin except acts of the
will or their results in evil habits, and logically follow it out to its results.

There is another and more extended form of argument, which requires greater detail and fulness than is consistent with my present limits, if its full power is to be exhibited. It is the argument taken from the
agreement of the phenomena of the system as a whole with preexistence, and also from the tendencies of the system to affect human society, in contrast with the actual effects of the opposite system. I can but
state this argument in outline. Volumes would be required to do it full
justice. But, to prepare the way, I for the present suspend this line of
argument, to meet the remaining allegation against the theory of preexistence.

(Note To Second Edition:— On reading the second volume of Müller,[37] I
find that, though he argues with me in the fact of the preexistence of man, yet
his views of the state in which he preexisted, the reasons of his sinning, and the
influence of sinful habits do not agree with mine.)

---

37 Julius Müller (1801-1878), was a German Protestant theologian. His chief work was
   The Christian Teaching of Sin, 2 vols., 1839, in which he carried scholasticism so far
   as "to revive the ancient Gnostic theory of the fall of man before all time, a theory
   which found no favor amongst his theological friends" (Otto Pfleiderer). Müller's
   other works include *Dogmatische Abhandlungen* (1870), and *Das christliche Leben*
   (1847).

Chapter XIV: The Origin Of Evil

THE remaining allegation against the theory of preexistence is, that it merely shifts the difficulty, but does not remove it. This is thus stated by Dr. Woods (Vol. II. p. 365.)

> "This hypothesis, even if admitted to be true, would still fail of answering the purpose intended. Although it might furnish some plausible account of our innate depravity, it would cast no light on the fact of our having sinned in a previous state, and so would leave the great difficulty untouched. Why moral evil should ever be suffered to exist in beings who are entirely dependent on God and under his control, and how its existence can be accounted for consistently with the infinite perfections of God, is a question to which human wisdom, untaught from above, can give no satisfactory answer."

To this there is a reply obvious, simple and conclusive. The real and great difficulty lies, not in the idea that free agents should sin, but in the idea that God should bring man into being with a nature morally depraved, anterior to any will, wish, desire or knowledge, of his own, or with a constitution so deranged and corrupt as to tend to sin with a power that no man can overcome in himself or in others; and that, in addition to this, He should place him in a state of so great social disadvantage, and, as the climax, expose him, so weak, to the fearful wiles of powerful and malignant spirits. This difficulty preexistence does touch and entirely remove, by referring the origin of his depravity to his own action in another state, and showing that the system of this world is a system of sovereignty established over beings who have lost their original claims on the justice of God.

If now a difficulty is alleged still to exist as to their first sinning in a previous state, it is enough to say that this is not the same difficulty that existed before, but altogether a different one; that is, how beings, created with an uncorrupt moral constitution, and in a spiritual system arranged in the best manner to favor their perseverance in right, could be led to sin. Suppose, then, that this question is not answered, and cannot be (although I do not concede that it cannot)—but suppose it. What then? It merely leaves a *mysterious* fact; but it does not, as in the former case, present an *alleged* fact, which the human mind can see to be within the range of its faculties, and to be positively unjust. It therefore removes a dispensation positively unjust, and, in place of it, presents one that is simply mysterious. But it resorts to mystery in a proper place. For, since the past history of the universe is not revealed in detail, nothing exists to forbid the idea that, whatever were the circumstances in which men sinned, and whatever were the reasons of their sinning, still they were such as in the highest degree to show forth the honor, justice and love of God, and to throw the whole blame on man. What, then, if we cannot state exactly these circumstances and reasons? What if we cannot reconstruct the past history of each man? Still we know nothing, and we see nothing, to forbid a full belief, based on confidence in God, that, in all His dealings with them, He was honorable and just.

But, if it be said we do still know enough to create a difficulty,—we do know that all created beings are entirely dependent on God, and under His control, and it seems inconsistent with wisdom and justice that He should allow them to sin,—I reply, this objection assumes as its basis a theory of the relations of divine power to a system of free agency which is neither self-evident nor in accordance with the Word of God.

It assumes that God, in making and governing a system of created minds, has, at all stages of progress, absolute and unlimited power to secure universal holiness, if He will; and rejects the supposition of a temporary limitation of divine power in the earlier stages of His system, in consequence of the necessary liability of finite minds to unbelief and distrust of God, when exposed to the inevitable trials which pertain to an infinite system, such as befits God, and in which alone He can properly act out Himself. These opposite views are also connected with two unlike views of the character of God, which grow out of and accord with them respectively. On the side of absolute and unlimited power, it is asserted that the will of God in all things is, and ever will be, so completely done, that He is entirely free from all grief, pain or suffering of any kind, from the sins of His creatures. On the other side, it is held that God, in reality, has no pleasure at all in the death of him that dies, but prefers his eternal life, and is really and truly grieved by the sins of His creatures; but that there is a temporary limitation of divine power, originating from the limitation of finite capacities to comprehend God and His ways, and a consequent liability in the first generations of creatures to unbelief, distrust and sin, involving a season of suffering in God, and requiring a full unfolding of truth in act, until God and His system shall be fully disclosed, and the occasion of unbelief cease.

The position that God's power of disclosing Himself and His system and plans to His creatures in their earliest generations is limited, does not diminish but increases our ideas of the greatness of God; for His greatness is the cause of the limitation in question. It is merely the inability of an infinite mind to bring itself and its plans down to the level of a finite mind. Does it exalt our ideas of God, and show the infinite difference between Him and a creature, to assert that He can put Himself and all His plans fully into the mind of that creature? Or, does it. on the other hand, most exalt God to say that He is so vast that no created mind can fully comprehend Him or His plans, and that it is beyond even His power to destroy the infinite chasm that separates creator and creature? But, simple and obvious as is this idea of the vastness of God and His system, and this consequent limitation of finite minds, and obvious and satisfactory as is the solution of the origin of evil which it furnishes, still it has been much overlooked. The causes which have blinded the minds of so many to it are, the inconsiderate ascription to God of the unproved ability to do all things, in a moral system, by naked power, without moral and intellectual motives; want of proper reflection on the disproportion between Him and created minds, and on what is essential in order to act with Him in a universal system, and on the discipline needed to fit created minds for it, and on the trial involved in such discipline; on the ease with which a being so vast in the execution of plans which are infinite and for eternity may be misunderstood, and on the immediate and fatal effects of a loss of confidence in God. It has not been sufficiently considered, that, if the very greatness of God, and the necessary limitation of all, even the highest created minds, render it impossible for Him to disclose fully either Himself or His plans to them, then that He must try them, by acting in view of what He sees, not of what they see; that is, He must ever act in view of considerations unseen and unknown to created minds. He dwells in light to which no created mind can approach; and no eye has seen, or ever will see, but in an infinitely small degree, all that is involved in the full knowledge of God. But, when once these things are well considered, they disclose a satisfactory reason for the origin of evil, and one not dishonorable to God, for to annihilate the infinite distance between Himself and a creature is not in His power. He must act according to His own greatness, and yet under the limitations created by an utter impossibility of transmitting into a finite mind a full knowledge of all that exists in an infinite one. Hence, if He will act with finite minds, on an infinite plan, He must act, at least in the earlier generations, with a necessary liability of being misunderstood; and, if His ways are trying, of losing the confidence of those with whom He acts. But, whoever disbelieves, and distrusts God and departs from Him, departs, of course, from infinite truth and right; and, though God's vastness forbids him to disclose this at once, yet the progress of events, in a course of development, will surely show that such is the fact.

What God needs, then, is not naked power, but calm, benevolent, tranquil patience and time. In this way, the progress of events will cover him with glory, and His enemies with shame.

This view is that which accords with the general spirit of the Bible, and with the views there given of the vastness of His plans, and of His taking counsel of none (Is. 40, Rom. 11). Their impenetrability to created intellects is no less clearly set forth. Clouds and darkness are round about him. The Lord hath said that He would dwell in the thick darkness. Secret things belong unto Him.

Carry back, then, these principles to the early generations, and we find an ample solution of the origin of evil, in the trial of new-created minds, with uncorrupted moral constitutions, and yet not developed by discipline, and needing trial to perfect them, as was the case with Christ, who learned obedience by the things that He suffered, and was thus perfected. Conceive of them as in trial, distrusting God, revolting and taking ground against him, and the system is solved. All else is a system of patient evolution on the part of God, by which the truth is to be revealed, and they are to be exposed, and the power and reign of unbelief are to be forever destroyed, not by direct force, but by truth and justice.

In this account of the matter we rise entirely above any solution which the common system of the fall can furnish. On the other hand,

that discountenances this view, even as respects the first entrance of
sin, by representing God as disowning it in this world. Here, he brings
in sin, by the fall, as an element chosen and desired. He, through one
sin, renders sure the existence of a fallen race, as furnishing the necessary materials for a system of grace,—such materials, and so situated, as
have been described. In this way are created the positive difficulties already considered, and of which there is no reasonable solution.

This, of course, nullifies all theories as to any honorable solution of
the great problem of the primitive origin of evil; for, if God is such a
being that His feelings do not revolt at introducing moral evil into this
world in this way, then there is no reason to look for any better mode
of securing the same result in the first entrance of evil.

It may, indeed, be said that it is of no use at all to speculate as to
the origin of evil; it is a thing that cannot be understood; it is beyond
the reach of our faculties, and to speculate concerning it is presumptu-
ous. Indeed, Dr. Woods has not hesitated to use the following hard
words on the subject:

> "If we should try to make out, by reasoning, that something
> like this (that is, preexistence) must be supposed, in order to
> account for the fact of our depravity consistently with the
> justice of God, our reasoning, instead of proving the fact of
> a preexistent state, would only prove our ignorance and
> presumption."

Is it, indeed, so? And will reflecting men be willing to take such a
ground on the most practical and important of all questions? If the
great end of this remedial system is so to justify God and condemn
man as to lay a reasonable foundation for undissembled and intelligent
penitence, then is it not necessary to take up, not merely the fact, but
the origin, of sin? Are there, in fact, no principles of equity and honor
on this point? Has the church in all ages been mistaken in supposing
that there are? Is it not possible that men may so misinterpret the Bible
as to represent God as introducing sin dishonorably? Are we bound to
receive all that any man chooses on such grounds to assert concerning
God? Is nothing due to the honor of God? If it can be clearly proved
that the common theory of the fall in Adam is at war with God's
honor, and that preexistence is not, because it opens the way for such
an origin of evil as I have described, is there no sound argument in all

this? So far am I from giving way before such a style of dogmatic as-sertion, that I do not hesitate to say that a proper vindication of God in this matter is one great work both of this and of future ages.

All that God is doing, in the present dispensation, is but a part of one great system. We cannot understand this system, unless we con-sider its ends, and the adaptation of means to gain them. One end is, to put down all hostile power, rule and authority, now arrayed against God (1 Cor. 15:24, 25). This is to be done by exposing the nature, criminality, and results of the revolt of Satan and his followers from God. This implies that it may be and must be known that it originated without any good reason, and from no fault on the part of God; and that the creature is to be blamed for its origin, and not the creator; and, in order to see this, it must be disclosed, at least in principle, how and why it did originate.

If its power is to be destroyed by turning the convictions of intel-ligent beings against its authors, then it cannot be destroyed till they are convinced. The same principles apply in the case of man. The Bible nowhere represents the conflict between God and His rebellious creatures as one of mere power. God is to be "justified in his sayings and overcome when he is judged." It is a strife which is to be decided not by naked power, but by good conduct; that is, by benevolent, honorable, and right conduct.

But, as it is a strife between unequal parties, infinitely unequal, there is a sentiment of honor in such a case, imposing the highest re-sponsibilities on him whose power, knowledge and other advantages, are greatest. We see the action of this principle clearly developed in this life. In a moral strife of an elevated, highly-educated clergyman, of great powers and advantages, with an inexperienced boy, whilst we should not excuse sin in the boy, yet we should judge the clergyman by the law,—to whom much is given, of him, also, is much required.

Especially, if, in such a conflict, the original advantages of anyone, for good conduct, depended not on his own will, but on that of one in conflict with him, should we make high demands of honor on the more powerful, not to put his antagonist into a position of needless weakness and disability. In physical conflicts, all admit the force of this principle. If a powerful man should give to a weak antagonist a lead sword and a paper shield, and arm himself with a steel sword and a metal shield, would there be any honor in a victory achieved in such circumstances?

In this wide universe no thought is so affecting as to exist for eternity, and to be called on, in a relatively brief time of trial, to decide the character of that eternity.

In the case of every being who thus exists, the following things do not depend at all upon his will, but solely on God's. The fact that he exists; his original constitution and powers; his circumstances in the system of God, and the influences exerted on him by God, by way of statement, persuasion and motives of all kinds, adapted to secure a right deportment.

In order to justify God, and to condemn His sinful creatures, all the sentiments of an honorable mind demand that it be made to appear that, in all these things, God did all for His creatures that our highest conceptions of justice, honor, magnanimity and generosity, demand; all that was needed to place them in the most favorable position possible, all things considered, for good conduct; and that he earnestly desired their success, and that their misconduct was against reason, honor and right, and no less against the feelings and wishes of God.

If any say that, on such principles, the entrance of moral evil cannot occur, I reply, the statement is very inconsiderate.

What is the standard of the best possible constitution and powers? Is it not an adaptation of the mind to know God, to commune with Him in love, and to act in a system with Him? But this implies, of necessity, vast powers of conception and emotion, powerful impulses to action, and great energy of will. To fit innumerable minds, so constituted, to act together and with God in an infinite system, involves, of necessity, trial, just as it did in the case of Christ, in order properly to develop and perfect them; and such trial involves the possibility, and even the danger, of failure through unbelief.

For, as the preserving power, in time of trial, is a belief of the statements of God as to what is right and wrong, wise and unwise, and as to the certainty of good or evil, as law is observed or violated,—and if none but God knows, or can know, intuitively, all truth, and the full extent and certainty of good or evil involved,—and if He cannot transfer His own infinite perceptions to finite minds, then no course is left but to throw His creatures on *faith*; and, if in trial they will not believe, but will gain, by trial against law, a knowledge of good and evil, then to push on the system to its final results, till the real truth in the case shall be developed by facts; God, meantime, enduring with infinite patience the unbelief and ingratitude of His creatures, till He has fully acted out his own truth and righteousness, and they their falsehood and wrong. Thus would God be "justified in his sayings, and overcome when he is judged."

Such a view of the origin of evil does not imply the necessity of sinning, as a means of moral development. For, under such a system, multitudes have persevered without sin, and been confirmed in holiness. Indeed, no one can show that of the great majority of existing beings this is not true. The decided probability is that it is true.

Nor, in the case of any, was there a necessity of falling; for, though limited in knowledge, still they had the power to believe God, and so to stand steadfast in obedience. In the highest exercises of faith there is always a vigorous exercise of the will; and it was, before evil entered, in the power of all to believe, and thus to live. But they disbelieved, and fell. Of this we see a symbol in the temptation in Eden. Belief of God and eating of the tree of life are connected. Disbelief of God, and a determination to know, by trial, the truth of His statements as to good and evil, is symbolized by a determination to eat of the tree of knowledge of good and evil, in view of the denial of danger and the hope of gain which proceeded from him who well remembered his own guilty fall.

Such a view of the origin of evil is a full defense of God. It also shows that, after creation and the entrance of sin, a system of evolution, with a well-defined end, would, of necessity, arise, presenting something to be done by God, not in the exercise of mere naked power, but in the practical development of all His excellence, in a system in which, according to His own words, he is as really "*tried and proved*" as are His creatures, and in which in a peculiar and infinite degree He develops patience, long-suffering, mercy, grace, self-sacrifice, self-denial, and forgiving love, and finally overcomes and prostrates all His foes by this full development of His real and infinitely tried and proven excellence, in contrast with the unbelief, ingratitude and malevolence, of His enemies.

Not only is this view of the origin of evil better than any that the common theory of the fall in Adam will allow, but it is in striking accordance with the general aspects of the Bible.

That sacred book discloses to us upon its very face a system of evolution (progressive development—Ed.) designed fully to bring out the character of God, and, by so doing, to give him a glorious intellectual and moral victory over all His foes. But the very nature of such a system shows that it was not possible for God to make this disclosure of Himself to finite creatures, by direct power, and without the acting out of principles and attributes in a system. This is a necessary inference from the infinity of God, and is proved by facts; for He now reaches this result at the expense of much misery and the ruin of many of His creatures. By this He makes certain principles so clearly known as to remove all grounds of subsequent unbelief in coming ages. But, if God, by direct power, could have made the universe to know these things just as surely without the facts as with them, then the misery is superfluous and malevolent.

God, also, in certain cases, has recognized the limitation of finite minds from which the necessity of such evolution arises. He says, by Moses, of the Jews, "I said I would scatter them into corners. I would make the remembrance of them to cease from among men, were it not that I feared the wrath of the enemy, lest their adversaries should behave themselves strangely, and lest they should say, Our hand is high, and the Lord hath not done all this;" that is, lest I should be misunderstood by limited minds, if I did not thus disclose myself (Deut. 32:26, 27; also see, also, Num. 14:15).

We notice, also, that the great end of the system, in all who are saved, is, in a peculiar and preeminent degree, to develop and perfect *faith*. Throughout the whole system intense energy is concentrated on this point. I infer from this that here was the weak point where evil first entered, just as if, when a building had fallen into ruins, we should infer that the weakness which caused the fall lay just where the architect was concentrating all his skill to produce peculiar strength in the new building.

So, then, this view falls in with all known laws of mind, and with the leading facts and character of the system.

On the other hand, to ascribe to God unlimited direct power to produce, without evolution (progressive development—Ed.) any amount of knowledge and faith, in an infinite system, makes the introduction of evil not so much a mystery as a needless act of malevolence. For, what if it does give occasion to God to display His attributes? Still, by the supposition, He could have caused exactly the same knowledge, and belief, and feeling, concerning them, without any such evolution (development—Ed.). And it is a self-evident truth that it is malevolent to produce results at the expense of eternal misery that could be produced just as well without it.

Indeed, although Dr. Woods denies this temporary limitation in the power of God, yet, when he is called to defend God, in view of the existence of moral evil, he resorts, in fact, to the same theory.

> "My answer is, it may, in one way or another, be the means of making a brighter and more diversified display of the divine perfections, and thus of giving the intelligent creation, as a whole, a higher knowledge and enjoyment of God. It may be the means of illustrating more clearly the excellence of the law and government of God, and of producing ultimately, through his moral kingdom, a purer and more ardent attachment to his character and his administration; so that his intelligent creatures, by means of the instruction and discipline in this way afforded, may be brought ultimately to a state of higher perfection and enjoyment than they could attain in any other way."

Now, if God had the direct power to give to His creatures the knowledge of Himself and His law and administration which is here spoken of, without any developments, then His creatures could obtain the specified results of that knowledge in another way, and without development.[38] They could obtain both the knowledge and its results by direct divine communication. But Dr. Woods says that they "could not attain them in any other way." He is sustained in this assertion by the best of reasons; for, if God could have communicated them directly, and without such developments of suffering as exist, and will exist forever, then He is malevolent, as before shown.

Hence, all of those who agree with Dr. Woods in defending God on the ground that by moral evil and its results He develops Himself and His government as He could not otherwise do,—and all know how numerous they are,—do, in fact, concede the very principle for which I contend.

Indeed, on this question, there are but two suppositions possible. Either the limitation of divine power in the earlier stages of creation, which I advocate, exists, or it does not exist. If it does not exist, then no man can defend God against the charge of malevolence. If it does

---

38 The idea of development implies time. And it could be useful and interesting to further explore the idea that the revelation of God to human beings requires time (growth and development) because human beings are time limited creatures. The revelation of a timeless being to beings in time requires time.

exist, then there is, as I have shown, a simple and natural solution of the origin of evil. Out of this first origin would naturally arise a system like that in this world, for the redemption of a part of those who had fallen, and the exposure of the rest; the whole resulting in a full development of God, and the removal of all future occasions of unbelief.

If the limitation in question does not exist, if God has unlimited power to communicate knowledge and emotion without development, then there is no reason for the existence of evil. It discloses nothing that could not be just as well disclosed without it. It makes no display of the attributes of God, or of His government, that could not be just as perfectly made without it. The sufferings of the lost are, therefore, so much needless, and worse than needless, misery. This view of the case impeaches the character of God, darkens the whole system, sickens the mind, and renders non-existence more desirable than life.

But we are not left without inspired testimony on this point. We have seen that, of these opposite systems, one implies, and the other excludes, the suffering of God. If, then, the Bible decides the question whether God suffers or not in consequence of the entrance of evil, it, in so doing, decides the question which of these systems is true.

But, if anything is prominent and uncontradicted in the Bible, it is the great doctrine that the entrance of evil has involved a period of long-continued suffering to God. Indeed, it is the grand characteristic of the present system, that all the glorious results to which God is conducting the universal system have been purchased at the expense of His own long-continued and patiently-endured sufferings. In this He gives to the universe the highest possible proof of pure, disinterested, self-sacrificing love.

These disclosures of the Bible settle the question as to the origin of evil. *They no less clearly prove that the origin of the sin of man is not to be looked for in this world.*

We do not find here beings with uncorrupted moral constitutions, nor in the most favorable circumstances. We find nothing which a God, such as the Bible discloses, would be irresistibly moved to confer on new-created minds, in whose death He had no pleasure, and whose eternal well-being He so desired as to be filled with grief at their ruin. In view of such facts, there is but one conclusion to which we can rationally come. We see at once that this world is not the abode of new-created, upright minds. On the other hand, this is a system of sovereignty towards beings who, by sin, have forfeited their rights as new-created minds. The laws of honor and right, towards new-created minds, are not observed in this world, because men are born under a forfeiture of them, and are "by nature children of wrath." By thus running back to a previous state, we can reach a sphere in which those principles were observed towards new-created minds which consist with the character of God, as revealed in the Bible; and, on those principles, we can account for all the native depravity and entire sinfulness of man; and, as no testimony of God confines us to this world for the origin of human depravity, then, if these things are so, the character of God and the general principles and facts of the system prove that sin did not originate here, but that this dispensation is merely a step in the great system of exposure, by which God is to be disclosed, truth and holiness vindicated, and error, unbelief and sin, to be exposed, paralyzed and punished, forever.

Chapter XV: Argument From The System

I AM now prepared to resume and set forth the argument from the agreement of the phenomena of the whole system with the theory of preexistence, and from a view of its relations to education and the social system. I have already said that a full development of this argument will require volumes, rather than a chapter in a single volume. But, to complete the outline of my argument, it is necessary that I state some of the points involved, and indicate the mode of their development. I shall state nothing, however, for the proof of which I am not willing, or rather desirous, to be held responsible.

I allege, then,

1. That a system based on preexistence is the only one which admits and requires such principles as explain what the church of God is, and develops a system of the universe centering in God and the church, according to the Scriptures.

2. It is the only system which demands, or even allows, of a natural and consistent development of that view of God which is peculiar to the Scriptures,—I mean that view in which His attributes of patience and long-suffering are presented as glorious realities, and are not enervated, or rather annihilated, by the assumption that God cannot suffer, which is a doctrine not of the Bible, but of a severe and unscriptural philosophy.

3. It alone so explains the operation of the material system, in the work of redeeming the church, as to unfold the reasons, laws and use, of its symbolical and typological significance, the laws of its action on the mind, and the mode of making it a powerful agent in the cultivation of holiness,—and as thus to cut up by the roots the Platonic, Gnostic and Manichean errors as to this part of God's system.

4. It alone renders possible a system of education that is philosophical and consistent throughout, concealing none of the

maladies of the mind, and furnishing remedies for them all, so as harmoniously to develop, purify, invigorate and perfect all the powers of the body and of the mind in connection.

5. It alone can put an end to that paralysis of social and religious energy which is produced, as I have shown, by a deep and radical division among good men, which is, regarding the present system, without any logical remedy.

6. It alone can present to the human mind a God so correlated to it in all respects that He fills its highest possible conceptions, fully evolve (develop) and perfect all its powers, and lead it, by the full influence of His own example, to a truly humble, unworldly, self-sacrificing, self-denying life.

7. It alone averts the tendency of free thought toward Pelagianism, and ultimately to mere naturalism and infidelity, under an elevated system of education, by rendering a supernatural development the great, fundamental and truly philosophical law of the system,—thus on this point harmonizing reason and faith.

8. It alone leads to such an understanding of the doctrine of future eternal punishments as connected with the previous suffering of God, and properly throws the moral sympathies of all holy minds on the side of God, and puts an end to that reaction which tends to fatally destroy the true and indispensable power of that doctrine.

9. It alone leads to those full and consistent views of God, and that eminent holiness of the church, which renders possible and introduces the predicted marriage-supper of the Lamb.

10. It alone so presents God and His government as to furnish the logical means of effecting in principle and spirit a radical destruction of those despotic civil and ecclesiastical organizations in which is the great stronghold of the god of this world, and which are the chief impediments to the spread of the gospel, and the conversion of the world.

11. It alone can furnish the logical means of binding Satan, destroying His kingdom, converting the world, and reorganizing human society in accordance with the principles of the kingdom of God.

It will, I suppose, be admitted that, if these statements are true, they do furnish all needed evidence of the truth of preexistence.

But, of course, I cannot expect them to be believed without proof. Nor can I, in my present limits, make out a full defense of them all. But I state them as theses or propositions essential in order fully to develop my argument, and which I am willing, at any time and in any proper way, to defend.

At the same time, I shall not leave them all entirely without proof, but shall select some of the most fundamental of them, and proceed to their exposition and defense, reserving to a future time the completion of the work.

It is obvious that, if these general statements are true, the doctrine of preexistence not only removes the main causes of antecedent derangements, but it puts the whole system into working order, and fits it for the present and future exigences of the church. By this I mean, not only that it causes the main moving powers of the system to work together, as already shown, but also that it introduces the principles of harmony into the whole system in all its parts, thereby rendering possible the unity of the church, and preparing the way for the final intellectual and moral victory, which is to be an end of all strife.

It effects this by taking up the great Scriptural facts which have been held without any enlarged and rational principle of connection, and combining them in a plan, simple and sublime, growing out of clear and definite principles, and comprehending the end of the universal system, and its origin, progress, and final state.

The following great facts lie on the surface of the Bible: The fall of Satan, and the existence of a kingdom of evil spirits in conflict with the kingdom of God; also the existence of an opposing system, centralized by Christ, designed to destroy their power and prostrate them forever. The fulfillment of this great design is said to precede and close the present dispensation. Another coincident prominent fact is the redemption of the church through the atonement of Christ, a work the completion of which also coincides in time with the prostration of the kingdom of darkness. Another striking feature of the Bible is that the present material system was created to be subservient to this end, and is destined to a future renovation when this dispensation has closed. Finally, the Word of God presents the church as united to God, at the end of the system, by a peculiar and eternal covenant; as sitting down with Him upon His throne, and inheriting all things, and reigning with Him forever. It declares, moreover, that the great end of all these proceedings is the disclosure of God to present and future generations of intelligent minds in all ages and all worlds; and, in accordance with this end, it develops a full, wonderful, and in some respects unanticipated and peculiar character of God.

The existing theories of the fall in Adam have never allowed all of these great biblical facts to be combined in any simple, natural and consistent system of the universe, growing out of clear and definite principles, each part of which harmonizes with every other, and imparts to it strength; but they have rather been arranged in limited and incomplete systems, always leaving some of the facts the relation of which to each other and to the great end of the system of the universe is unknown.

Indeed, all efforts to form a complete system of the universe have been discouraged by many as adventurous and profitless. So, indeed, they are, if the system is not lawfully constructed out of revealed facts. But, if revealed facts do furnish a simple and sublime system, why reject it? Such a system is a natural want (both *desire* and *lack*—Ed.) of the mind. Towards this end, it has tended in all ages. History is full of theories of the universe. All men, too, at this day, are, in fact, influenced by theories of the universe of some sort,—even those who affect to discourage such theories in others. Such theories may not have been developed by them, and consciously stated and adopted. They exist rather as those elevated reservoirs of water, which few visit, but which nevertheless impel the little streams of water which are used in the varied business of daily practical life. It would, indeed, be quite as rational to scout the idea of elevated and distant reservoirs as expensive and out of the reach of the community, and to advocate the construction of a mere system of water-pipes, without a reservoir, for practical use, as to scout and repudiate theories of the universe. The world is full of them; their influence is felt on every side. All men daily use trains of thinking and reasoning that have flowed from them, even if they have never consciously seen and adopted them. Those who repudiate them are often great admirers of Edwards. But did he aim at no system of the universe? What is his celebrated and eulogized treatise on God's last end in creation, but his system of the universe? What is his "History of the Work of Redemption," but that system of the universe historically exhibited? In particular, near the close of his general introduction, he states, in five particulars, the great outlines of that system; and all of these particulars, so far as they go, coincide with the view revealed in the Bible.

Moreover, in his "Miscellaneous Observations" relative to the angels and heaven, he still more fully illustrates various parts of his system of the universe. So, then, those who eulogize Edwards ought not to deny and under value systems of the universe. In like manner it has been fashionable with many to speak of the question of the origin of evil as a vain and profitless inquiry; and yet many, not to say all, of the practical religious systems of the day, spring directly out of different theories as to the origin of evil. The theory of divine efficiency is at its roots one theory of the origin of evil and of the universe; that of imputation is another; and that of the New Haven divines is still another. And, even if few ascend to these fountainheads of thought, still multitudes, in all parts of the land, are daily drawing and drinking the different kinds of water which flow from them.

It is, therefore, not without reason that Müller, in his great work on sin, says

> "that this great problem has occupied the spirits not merely of the theologian and philosopher, on account of their calling, but of all to whom there has been a deep necessity of finding a rational and intelligible ground of the true significance of human life, *and very properly* so. So certain as the religious ethical interests of the human spirit are the absolute highest, so certainly must a world-opinion which seeks entirely to avoid the question concerning the origin of sin; or to put it aside as a subordinate matter, appear nothing more than in the highest degree empty and abstract" (Vol. I. p. 289. Pulsford's translation).

The origin of evil and a system of the universe, then, are lawful objects of inquiry. Let us, then, inquire what is that system of the universe which the doctrine of preexistence derives from the Word of God.

A true view of the system of the universe demands two things as essential.

First, a solution of the intellectual and moral system.
Second, a true view of the relations of the material system to it.

That theories as to the material system have great power over the doctrinal development of the moral system, all experience shows. The facts of greatest interest to be considered in the moral system are, the origin and progress of moral evil, and its final subjugation by the dispensations of God.

But no one needs to be told how extensively the doctrine has prevailed, both in the heathen and Christian world, that the true cause of the origin of sin is to be found in matter. It pervades the Platonic philosophy, the various theories of Gnosticism, the Manichean system, and has also penetrated the various branches of the Christian church. Indeed, Isaac Taylor,[39] in his analysis of the ascetic corruptions of ancient Christianity, does not hesitate to represent this feature of Gnosticism as their primal source; and no well-informed thinker will call in question the correctness of this judgment. Not only, therefore, is the whole theory of sin and holiness, of morals and of practical sanctification, vitally affected by the question of the relation of the material system to the intellectual and moral, but the influence of that relation has extended to the whole theory of the system of the universe. Indeed, from this quarter, it is possible, by a single decision, to control the whole system. It is, then, a matter of the highest practical moment, and not of mere theory, to come to a correct view of the relation of the material to the intellectual and moral system of the universe.

And yet, as we shall soon see, the mere statement of the system, growing out of preexistence, will so adjust the relations of the material world, that all conflict and evil influences from that quarter will cease.

Let us, then, consider in order, first, the solution of the intellectual and moral system of the universe, and then the relations to it of the material system.

The natural and scientific solution of any system requires the discovery of its end (purpose—Ed.), and of the relations of its parts to that end and to each other. Hence Edwards made God's end in creation the subject of a special treatise, in which, as I have said, he gives his system of the universe. He comes to the conclusion that the union of the

---

39 Isaac Taylor (1787-1865), an English philosophical and historical writer, artist, and inventor, who had published a devotional volume, *Saturday Evening* (London, 1832). Subsequently he developed a part of that book into *The Physical Theory of Another Life* (London, 1836), a work of speculation, anticipating a scheme of duties in a future world, adapted to an assumed expansion of human powers after death.

church to God is the final end. In this the system is completed. In this God rests.

The key to the whole system is, no doubt, to be found in correct views of the church, and of her union to God. But the position in which Edwards leaves the matter does not fully satisfy the mind. Other questions will arise, which he does not answer. What is the peculiar idea of the church? For what great end was she redeemed and united to God? Why is her final union to God spoken of as a marriage?

Till these questions can be answered, the mind does not rest in the solution of Edwards as full and thorough. To these questions no satisfactory answer has, as yet, been given. The common system suggests none, and admits of none. That which I advocate does. But, before I produce it, let us consider existing opinions as to the church.

Of all writers on theology, President Edwards the elder thought and wrote the most on the church in her eternal relations. Indeed, it is the grand peculiarity of his theology that it centers around this point. Hence its riches, depth and power. His history of the work of Redemption, as well as his essay on the end of God in creation, are so far correct as they put the union of God and the church in the center of all things. But, the mind at once demands, What is the church, and why this union? Let us, then, consider some common views on this subject, and some which Edwards has more fully developed.

1. It is, then, generally conceded that the church consists of those, and those only, who are redeemed through the atonement of Christ, and regenerated and sanctified through the gracious influences of the Holy Spirit. Indeed, we might almost define the component elements of the church in the words of the apostle Peter, by saying that they are those of the human race who were "elected according to the foreknowledge of God the Father, through sanctification of the Spirit, unto obedience and sprinkling of the blood of Jesus Christ" (1 Pet. 1:2). These in heaven will all sing the same song of redeeming love, and none can sing this song but those thus redeemed from this earth.

2. It is also generally held that, through the redemption of the church, there has been made a peculiar and glorious development of the divine attributes, the influence of which is, or is to be, felt throughout the whole intelligent universe.

For, although this is a small world, and the human race in itself is relatively unimportant, yet, as all created beings in all worlds have a common interest in God, whatever develops his attributes and character has an interest which is universal, and of the highest kind.

3. It is also held that the redemption of the church is effected through a severe and widely extended conflict. That on the side of God are arrayed legions of angels of light; and that against these are arrayed legions of fallen spirits, under Satan, the original author of evil, and the great leader of the existing rebellion against God.

4. It is also admitted, by all who credit the Bible, that when the redemption of the church is completed this conflict is brought to a final close. That then all hostile rule, and authority, and power, shall be put down, and that all enemies shall be put beneath the Redeemer's feet (1 Cor. 15:24, 25.)

5. It is also admitted and taught, at least by Edwards, that the church will not, after her redemption, be merged in the great mass of holy beings who compose the kingdom of God, but will remain forever a peculiar and united body, sustaining peculiar and eternal relations to God and to the rest of His kingdom. Of this the proof is ample.

6. It is also proved and taught by the same great divine, that, through the redemption of the church and her union with Christ, the whole intelligent universe will be brought together and united under one head in Christ; and that of this head, in virtue of her union to Christ, the church shall compose a part. That, in virtue of this union, the church shall be exalted with Christ to sit upon His throne; and that, in consequence of this elevation, her dignity and rank shall exceed those of the angels, and of all other orders of created beings. In short, that the church shall be nearest of all created beings to Him who sits on the throne of the universe, and shall, in union with Him, rule over that universe forever. Of this, too, the scriptural proof is ample.

7. Lastly, it is held by him that the church is the ultimate end of God, not merely as a means, but as what He rejoices in and is satisfied

with most directly and properly, as the bridegroom rests in and is satisfied with the bride. In his own words,

> "They are those elect creatures, which must be looked on as the end of all the rest of the creation, considered with respect to the whole of their eternal duration, and, as such, made God's end,—and must be viewed as being, as it were, one with God. They were respected as brought home to him, united with him, centering most perfectly, and, as it were, swallowed up in him, so that his respect to them finally coincides, and becomes one and the same as his respect to himself."

For his proof of these points, see his treatise on "God's Last End in Creation."

Such, then, are some of the points which are more or less generally conceded by intelligent Christians; and no one will deny that they present to the mind ideas of inconceivable magnitude and interest. Moreover, these views are sustained, in all their great outlines, by the clear and decisive testimony of the Word of God.

Yet thus far enough has not been stated to satisfy the rational demands of the mind as to the system of the universe, and to give it rational repose. Indeed, until a more full account is given of some intelligible ulterior end of these proceedings, they have to the mind an aspect of something exaggerated and incredible.

Why is one part of God's creatures thus made the end of the creation? Why so valued, honored and exalted above the rest? Especially are these feelings excited, if this union is presented as the ultimate result of all things.

If the holy universe are all created (sic), and God has at length completed His works of development, so that nothing remains but to study and adore what He has done,—moreover, if the Scriptural account of heaven and its joys is taken as nothing but a glowing statement of the enjoyment of the pleasures of holy society and of worship, and of the study of God's works, and if only indefinite suggestions are made of unknown modes of active usefulness,—then the mind is driven back from the future, as if everything of great interest had already been done, and as if the mere ends of study, and enjoyment, and indefinite action, and even of endless worship, did not open before the mind a future equal to what its capacities can comprehend and demand. After a long training on earth to thought, and enterprise, and vigorous action, it needs some more definite and intelligible field for the exercise of its powers, and some affecting and exciting end of action.

There is one simple idea, naturally flowing from the system of preexistence, that will at once effect all this. It is this: *that the work of creating and training intelligent beings to know and love and serve God is but just begun*, and that the main increase and extension of the universe is yet to come; and that by the redemption of the church the universe of God will be brought into such a state that that increase can be made without any hazard of any new entrance of moral evil, and be continued forever,—and especially that the church, owing to the manner of her redemption, and her peculiar training, will be prepared to preside over and to train the successive generations of new-created minds as no others can; and that, for this end, and also as the resting-place of his own highest and most peculiar affections, she will be united to God, and exalted to reign with Him in the manner that has been described. Also, that the relation of this union between the church and God to this increase, is the reason why it is called a marriage.

Viewed in this light, the redemption of the church, as set forth in the preceding statements, derived from the Word of God, loses its aspect of an insulated, exaggerated and incredible transaction. It is at once placed in the center of the system, as a simple and rational means for the attainment of ends so definite, so vast, so momentous, so deeply affecting, that they at once fill and satisfy the mind as worthy of God, and sufficient fully to put in requisition, and that forever, all the affections, intellectual powers, and attainments of the church. The object, moreover, is one of surpassing interest to God, and to all other orders of created minds, forever.

For, if in the redemption of the church God aimed to prostrate Satan and his hosts, and thus to put the universe in such a state that an endless increase could be secured, and also to provide the means of effecting it, and also a peculiar object of his own eternal affections in their highest form, then his whole system is not only perfectly explained, but is seen to involve the highest possible good of the universe. We see the importance to God, and to the whole universe, of the redemption of the church. It fully justifies the use of such means as the incarnation and the atonement. It shows why God created and governs all things with reference to this end. It shows why the advent of the day of the final union of God and the church is an occurrence of such deep interest to Him and to His holy kingdom. It shows why it is such a crisis in the history of the universe,—why to it all things have tended from the beginning, and why from it all things will forever diverge, after the great work shall be finally completed.

It would be a matter of just surprise, in view of all the statements of the Word of God which have been set forth, that this view of the case has never presented itself and been adopted, if the common system did not lead the mind away from it and exclude it, as I shall soon evince.

Yet at one moment the profound and original Bellamy stood on the very verge of the true solution, and even suggested one of its main features. I refer to the sublime idea of the future indefinite increase of the kingdom of God, after the close of this system. But the peculiar relations of the church to this increase he did not discern, nor its intimation by the analogy of the marriage of the church to God. Yet the views which he did advance are worthy of record, as showing what ideas a contemplation of God's system as a whole suggested to his mind, with reference to the ultimate state of the universe.

He is defending his own doctrine concerning the wisdom of God in the permission of sin, on the ground that He must, in all that He does, do what is most for His own glory. To this his opponent, among other things, replies that "God might have brought all possible beings into existence at once, which would have given a greater display of his perfections." To this Bellamy answers that, in his opinion, God knows and has done exactly what was wisest and best in this matter, and therefore most for His own glory. And to this he adds:

> "How know we if God thinks it best to have a larger number of intelligences to behold his glory and be happy in him, but that he judges it best not to bring them into existence till the present 'grand drama' shall be finished at the day of judgment? That they may, without sharing the hazard of the present confused state of things, reap the benefit of the whole, through eternal ages; whilst angels and saints may be appointed their instructors to lead them into the knowledge of all God's ways to his creatures, and of all their

ways to him, from the time of Satan's revolt in heaven to the final consummation of all things. And as the Jewish dispensation was introductory and preparatory to the Christian, so this present universe may be introductory and preparatory to one after the day of judgment, almost infinitely larger. That this will be the case, I do not pretend so much as to conjecture. But I firmly believe that what is best on the whole, that infinite wisdom always has done, and always will do; and here I rest" (Works, vol. II, pp. 142—3. New York, 1811).

This view is brought forward to answer an objection, and is for this end presented as a hypothesis which no man can disprove. Bellamy, therefore, saw the rationality of the idea of endless increase after the day of judgment; but the indications in the system that the church was specifically prepared for that very end, and the manifest intimation of it in the analogy of marriage, entirely escaped his notice. If he had compared this sublime suggestion of his with all that is said in the Bible on the relations of the church to God, he would have found reason to regard it as more than a mere supposition, or a conjecture; he would have found the facts and the language of the Bible relative to the church all tending to this result, fully explained by it, and incapable of any other satisfactory explanation.

The idea of increase after the day of judgment is also the basis of Pollok's *Course of Time.*[40]

Two youthful sons of Paradise are introduced as walking high on the hills of immortality,

> "Casting oft their eye far through
> The pure serene, observant if, returned
> From errand duly finished, any came,
> Or any, first in virtue now complete,
> From other worlds arrived, confirmed in good."

One such they saw approaching the place where they stood. This place is the residence of God, the center of the universe. Of it the poet thus speaks:

---

40 *The Course of Time* is a ten-book poem in blank verse, published in 1827 by Robert Pollok.

"Mountains of tallest stature circumscribe
The plains of Paradise, whose tops, arrayed
In uncreated radiance, seem so pure,
That naught but angel's foot, or saint's elect
Of God, may venture there to walk here oft
The sons of bliss take morn or evening pastime,
Delighted to behold ten thousand worlds
Around their suns revolving in the vast
External space, or listen the harmonies
That each to other in its motion sings.
And hence, in middle heaven remote, is seen
The mount of God in awful glory bright.
Within, no orb create of moon, or star,
Or sun gives light; for God's own countenance,
Beaming eternally, gives light to all;
But further than these sacred hills his will
Forbids its flow—too bright for eyes beyond.
This is the last ascent of Virtue; here
All trial ends, and hope; here perfect joy,
With perfect righteousness, which to these heights
Alone can rise, begins, above all fall."

Of himself he thus speaks:

"Virtue, I need not tell, when proved, and full
Matured, inclines us up to God and heaven,
By law of sweet compulsion strong and sure;
As gravitation to the larger orb
The less attracts, through matter's whole domain.
Virtue in me was ripe.—I speak not this
In boast, for what I am to God I owe,
Entirely owe, and of myself am naught.
Equipped, and bent for heaven, I left yon world,
My native seat, which scarce your eye can reach,
Rolling around her central sun, far out,
On utmost verge of light: but first to see
What lay beyond the visible creation,
Strong curiosity my flight impelled."

On his way he saw the hell to which had been consigned the lost of the human race, and, full of wonder and astonishment, pressed on towards Paradise for an explanation. Such an explanation the youthful sons of Paradise could not give, and therefore conducted him to another teacher.

"Something indeed we heard before,
In passing conversation slightly touched,
Of such a place; yet rather to be taught,
Than teaching, answer what thy marvel asks,
We need; for we ourselves, though here, are but
Of yesterday—creation's younger sons.
But there is one, an ancient bard of Earth,
Who, by the stream of life sitting in bliss,
Has oft beheld the eternal years complete
The mighty circle round the throne of God;
Great in all learning, in all wisdom great,
And great in song; whose harp in lofty strain
Tells frequently of what thy wonder craves,
While round him gathering stand the youth of heaven,
With truth and melody delighted both;
To him this path directs, an easy path,
And easy flight will bring us to his seat."

The sum of the reply is thus given by the ancient bard:

"The place thou sawst was hell; the groans thou heardst
The wailings of the damned, of those who would
Not be redeemed, and at the judgment day,
Long past, for unrepented sins were damned.
The seven loud thunders which thou heardst, declare
The eternal wrath of the Almighty God.
But whence, or why they came to dwell in woe,
Why they curse God, what means the glorious morn
Of resurrection, these a longer tale
Demand, and lead the mournful lyre far back
Through memory of sin and mortal man.
Yet haply not rewardless we shall trace
The dark disastrous years of finished Time,
Sorrows remembered sweeten present joy.

> Nor yet shall all be sad; for God gave peace,
> Much peace, on earth, to all who feared his name."

The narrative of the bard occupies the remaining books of the poem.

Here, then, as in Bellamy, we have the idea of endless increase, but the relation of the church to it is not seen.

Indeed, the moral education of the youth of heaven, in various worlds, is represented as often, if not always, completed without the knowledge of the history of this world and of the church. Even some of those in Paradise do not know enough of it to instruct a newcomer.

And yet the poet thus sets forth the result of the history of this world. At the close of the judgment, and of the burning of the earth, angels and saints, chanting songs of praise, ascend with the Redeemer to the eternal gates.

> "Thus sung they God, their Savior: and themselves
> Prepared complete to enter now, with Christ,
> Their living Head, into the Holy Place.
> Behold! the daughter of the King, the bride,
> All glorious within, the bride adorned,
> Comely in broidery of gold! Behold,
> She comes, appareled royally, in robes
> Of perfect righteousness, fair as the sun,
> With all her virgins, her companions fair, —
> Into the Palace of the King she comes,
> She comes to dwell forevermore! Awake,
> Eternal harps! awake, awake, and sing! —
> The Lord, the Lord, our God Almighty, reigns!"

He sees the universal and unchangeable system opening as a wedding, resulting in the endless covenant union of God and the church. He also believes in an indefinite increase and education of new-created minds, and yet sees no peculiar relation of the church to so great a work. Edwards, also (Vol. II, p. 605), holds that some in heaven will be a kind of ministers in that society,—"ministers to their knowledge and love, and helpers of their joy, as ministers of the gospel are here;" but he does not intimate the relation of the church as in a peculiar sense the teacher of new-created minds, although he notices that "the glorification of the church, after the last judgment, is represented as the proper marriage of the Lamb." He also teaches that they possess all things

> "in their Head, who has the absolute possession of all, and rules over all, and disposes all things according to his will; for by virtue of their union with Christ, they also shall rule over all. They shall sit with him in his throne, and reign over the same kingdom."

It is, therefore, the more remarkable that the idea of an endless increase of new-created minds, to be educated and trained by the church in coming ages, does not appear ever to have occurred to the mind of Edwards as implied in the analogy.

And yet, it is the less to be wondered at, because the common system tends to lead the mind away from such a result. In that system the redemption of the church is looked on as merely a work of divine manifestation, not growing by any temporary limitation of divine power out of the antecedent history of the universe, but merely acted out for the benefit of orders of beings already in existence, who look on as spectators, just as if the universe were already nearly or quite infinite, and as if, although the redemption of the church is an act eminently honorable to God. yet, in the words of Chalmers,

> "It is but an ephemeral doing in the history of intelligent nature; and that there remains time enough to him for carrying round the visitations of as striking and peculiar a tenderness over the whole extent of his great and universal monarchy."

But, if it is the redemption of the church which both marks and causes the subjugation of moral evil for the universe, and if it prepares the way for an endless increase of new-created beings to be trained by the church, then it is not one of many ephemeral transactions, but is the great event to which all things tend from the beginning, and from which all things again diverge through all future ages.

To a king it is not, surely, an ephemeral transaction, when he obtains and is united to a royal bride, who, during his life, is to preside with him over his kingdom, and educate and train his children to be princes in his empire. It is a peculiar arrangement, which affects his whole life and reign, and all the interests of his empire, as none other can. Moreover, it awakens emotions higher and more peculiar than any other relation or event.

If, then, the final and eternal union of the church to God is something analogous to this,—if the love by which they are united is peculiar in its nature and intensity, if the union opens the way to an endless increase of the family of God, and if all new-created beings are to be trained by the church for stations of influence and honor in the kingdom of God,—then it is a peculiar arrangement, which affects his whole existence and reign in all future ages and in all worlds, and all the interests of his empire also, as none other can. It is the key to the system of the universe.

We now see at once, as before stated, a sufficient reason why the redemption of the church should be God's great end during this dispensation, and why he manifests an interest so peculiar in all pertaining to this result.

But, it may be said, What has preexistence, or the fall in Adam, to do with all this? Why may not the same system be reached, on either supposition?

I answer, because such a system as I have developed, centering in the church, presupposes and rests upon principles, with reference to the origin of moral evil, which preexistence calls for and admits, but the opposite view does not call for, but excludes. And, so long as they are not called for, but excluded, it is not possible to see any necessity of a church, any crisis calling for her redemption, anything peculiar to be effected by her, any reason for a peculiar union between her and God, any peculiar work for her to do. Let us once more consider these principles.

I have already stated two theories of the relations of divine power to a system of free agency: one assuming that God has absolute and unlimited power at all times to secure universal holiness, if He will; the other teaching a temporary limitation of divine power in the earlier stages of creation, in consequence of the liability of finite minds to unbelief and distrust of God, when exposed to the trials which inevitably pertain to an infinite system, and which are necessary to their own development and perfection. These opposite views are also logically connected with two opposite views of the character of God. One asserting that the power of God is at all times so unlimited over minds that His will has been, is, and ever will be, so completely done, that He is, and ever has been, entirely free from all grief, pain or suffering of any kind, from the sins of his creatures.

On the other hand, it is held that God in reality, as he asserts, has never had any pleasure at all in the revolt and ruin of any of His creatures, but has been truly grieved at it; and has altogether preferred their eternal life. But that a temporary limitation of divine power, in the earlier stages of creation, owing to the liability of the first generations to unbelief and sin, has involved a season of trial and suffering to God, the result of which will be such a full unfolding of His character and truth in act (history—Ed.) as shall at length remove from all future generations the causes and the occasions of unbelief.

On these principles, we see that there never has been any occasion for God originally to introduce sin of set purpose; and that His character and feelings, His sense of honor and right, are such that He could not do it. All that His own benevolence and sense of equity and honor would allow him to do would be to create the first generation of beings with such powers and faculties as would best fit them to be in union with Himself, at the foundation of an eternal system, destined ever to increase, and then to subject them to such a system of probation and education as should be best adapted to develop, elevate and perfect, their characters. Even so did Christ, though sinless, learn obedience by suffering; and thus was He made perfect.

If, then, in consequence of the temporary limitation of His power, caused by the want of antecedent history and developments, a part of them distrusted him, and revolted in the hour of trial, and afterwards, from successive generations, seduced others to join them, thus organizing and extending a hostile kingdom, then another step would become necessary to God, and that is, to prepare for Himself an order of beings whose love to him should be so all-comprehending and immutable that neither trial nor exaltation should ever lead them to revolt; and who should be peculiarly prepared to train others, and who should, therefore, be fit to be with Him at the foundation of an eternal kingdom, and, at the same time, in the process of preparing these, disclose so fully, through trial and suffering, His own glorious character and truth, as to avert the occasions of unbelief in all future generations of created beings.

It is obvious, then, that these principles not only explain what the church is, and what is her place in the system, but also show that, from the beginning of the creation, all things tended to such an issue. In short, that the redemption of the church and her union to, God, as a preparatory step to the endless increase of the universe, is but a natural and perfectly intelligible development of the principles which I have stated.

Of course, the opposite view, which denies these principles, cannot furnish any such solution of existing facts. On the other hand, the real existence of such facts as flow from and are accounted for by these principles, is a strong argument sustaining their truth.

But we do find disclosed in the Bible a state of things exactly corresponding to what would result from such principles, and which, in the light of such principles, receives a glorious and satisfactory solution, disclosing a system worthy of God, and meeting and filling the highest possible conceptions of the human mind. Is there not, therefore, the best possible reason to believe that both the principles and the system are true?

These presumptions are carried up to an absolute certainty, when we consider that the God disclosed in the Bible has the character which is demanded by this system, and is repudiated by the other.

The character of the God of the Bible is definite and strongly marked. Among all of His characteristics, none is more strongly marked than His sensibility to the appropriate causes of pleasure and pain to benevolent, honorable and upright minds. This sensibility is asserted in every form of language, and nowhere denied.

He is, therefore, represented as peculiarly sensitive to the existence and developments of sin. It is at war with every impulse and desire of His nature. It causes Him great and long-continued suffering. Indeed, the true energy and the highest glory of His character cannot be conceived till we understand that such is the fact, and yet that no impatience, or bitterness, or malignant resentment, or spirit of unholy revenge, has ever been or ever will be disclosed. In the midst of the highest trials of His patience, He is entirely tranquil and self-possessed. He is the very God of peace. No conception of God presents His moral power in so striking a light. Moreover, in this view, God Himself being judge, His highest glory lies. Such is the system of the universe, with respect to God and the church, which naturally grows out of the doctrine of preexistence as I have set it forth, and which evinces its truth by assigning to God His true character as presented in the Bible, and taking up and combining in a harmonious and glorious plan the leading facts of the Bible,—a thing which the opposing system can never do.

For, in perfect accordance with the doctrine that God has at all times unlimited power to produce holiness and exclude sin, it represents Him as having first, without any necessity, permitted and ordered its introduction by Satan, and then deliberately called into existence, in addition, all the sin that is in this world, by a system designed and adapted to produce just such an amount of sin. A fallen race was needed in order to exhibit His attributes in a work of redemption; and therefore God arranged a system to secure such a race, composed entirely of new-created beings, all of whom should be so affected by the act of the progenitor of the race as either to be born sinners, or else so deranged in their moral constitution that they certainly would sin, and be so entirely and deeply depraved that no power but that of God could bring them into a state of holiness. All this, too, is effected and rendered sure by an act over which they had not the slightest control, and in which they had no part. Certainly, no one can properly describe this as anything but a plan (to be sure, for alleged benevolent ends) to produce sin on a great scale, and in all the generations of men.

Out of this sinful race thus produced a church is to be redeemed; but, on such principles, what is the church? for what end redeemed? why united to God? Of what importance is it to the universe?

Can it at all augment the power of God to arrest the progress and destroy the sway of moral evil? Not at all. That was always infinite and unlimited. Can it put the universe into a state any more favorable for the increase of new-created beings, to be kept from sinning and perfected in holiness? Not at all; for the power of God to produce and perfect such was always unlimited. Can it make any manifestation of God, adapted to control minds, that invests him with new moral power, that could not otherwise have been exerted? Not at all; for the power of God to control minds, on this theory, has always been full, infinite and unlimited. There is, therefore, no occasion for a system designed to augment that power by removing from it temporary limitations. In short, there is no significance to the church as the central idea of the system of the universe; no satisfactory explanation of the importance to God of her redemption, nor of His deep interest in the work, nor of His amazing sacrifices to effect it, nor of His joy in its completion.

Nor is this all; it not only renders it impossible on such grounds to combine the great facts of the Bible into any consistent system of the universe, springing out of intelligible principles, and carrying them out into glorious results, but it represents the great central measure of the system as founded on a transaction which many, even of its advocates, are constrained to admit, cannot be defended on any principles of honor and right which the mind of man was made to form, but must be shrouded under the veil of faith and of mystery. How can a proceeding of this kind be made the part of any intelligible system of the universe? How can it exalt our conceptions of God, or do any good, if it needs to be defended by an appeal to mystery, against our intuitive convictions of equity and honor, and must be sustained by blind faith rather than sustain faith by its own power?

It is important, however, to discriminate the views which I have presented from others with which they may be confounded.

There is a theory which makes the essential nature of free agency such that the limitation of divine power is not temporary, and confined to the earlier generations of creatures, but is eternal. Such was the theory of Origen. Accordingly, he held that, after fallen spirits had been restored by a material system, and it had been destroyed, they and others would again fall, and another similar system be needed; and thus that there would be an eternal succession of such systems, and of redemption through them. From this view Augustine very properly revolted. But it is not the necessary or natural development of preexistence, and is no reason whatever for rejecting it, although Augustine presents it as such. Origen had plainly no idea of the nature or design of the church. He did not see that God by her would exclude any future entrance of sin. He based his theory, as Mosheim has clearly shown, on the false philosophy of Ammonius Saccas, and not upon the great and leading facts of the Word of God. There is nothing in unperverted free agency that cannot be forever controlled by moral means, after the full disclosure of God has been made through the redemption of the church; so that moral evil will never again enter, and no work of redemption, like the present, ever be needed or undertaken again.

Nor are the views which I have presented to be confounded with the opinions of those who apply to this world the principles which I apply to a previous state. In explaining the origin of evil in this world, it is alleged by some that there may be a limitation of divine power such that God could not exclude evil from a moral system; or, at least, that He could not exclude it, or the present degree of it, from the best moral system, because such is the nature of free agency that, for aught that we can prove, it may enter. In order so to accord with facts as to justify God, these principles ought to be applied to a system and a state of things in which God gives to new-created minds the best constitutions and circumstances. If, in such circumstances, evil enters, it implies the limitation assumed; and this justifies God.

But to the state of things in this world these principles do not at all apply. The system of this world is obviously a system of sovereignty towards fallen minds, and not a system designed to illustrate the principles of equity and honor towards new-created minds. Men do not enter this world with the best possible constitutions, and are not placed in the best possible circumstances. For new-created minds God could do and ought to do much more than to give them such constitutions and circumstances as are found in this world. Hence, the principles which can be easily and consistently applied to a preexistent state do not at all apply to this world. If there is a limitation of God's power, the proper place to illustrate that principle is a state in which new-created beings do receive the best possible constitutions and are placed in the most favorable circumstances. If out of such a system sin springs, and a kingdom of evil is formed, then there would naturally be formed a system of sovereignty like that in this world, composed of fallen beings, who had forfeited their original rights.

Chapter XVI: The Material System

THE union of mind with matter is the great peculiarity and the great wonder of the present system; and nothing is more important than to know why God established this union, and how He designed it to operate. Surely the influence on the mind of a material system so vast and powerful cannot be neutral. If rightly viewed and used, immense good must result; if otherwise, immense evil. Such is the testimony of facts. Platonism and Gnosticism regarded matter as the cause of sin, and refused to ascribe it to the original free choice of the mind in a spiritual sphere. The mind, in itself, is pure and well-disposed, but is, unfortunately, linked to a degrading and corrupting material system. Notice now the results: false conceptions of holiness and sin, a spurious religious experience, torpor of the moral sense, an entire perversion and subversion of the system of grace, the introduction and undue honor of celibacy, penances, bodily austerities and other ascetic practices, monasteries, nunneries, and a universal corruption and derangement of the whole social system.

Thus the effect of these and similar systems has been to turn away the eye from the original entrance of evil in the spiritual sphere, and to throw off the blame and guilt of sin from sinners upon the material world, and thus to derange the entire operation of the system of God.

On the other hand, the doctrine of a preexistent fall, not only, as I have shown, combines the great facts of the Bible relating to a spiritual world into a simple and sublime system of the universe, growing naturally out of clear and definite principles, but it also so adjusts the relations of the material world to it as to remove all the pernicious results which have been introduced in past ages, by false views of the relations of the material to the moral system.

It does this in a manner simple, thorough and effectual. It throws the primitive origin of all moral evil out of this world, into a spiritual system. It thus at once simplifies the problem, and accounts for the origin of all moral evil on the same spiritual principles. It exculpates matter, and throws the whole responsibility, where it ought to rest, upon minds. It not only excludes the possibility of ascribing the origin of sin to this material system, but enables us to show that it was designed and adapted to aid in the great work of moral renovation. It was made with the express design of illustrating, by powerful analogies, the character and system of God. If properly used, it is adapted to destroy the moral torpor of the mind by its pungent illustrations, and to give vividness and power to its conceptions of spiritual things. The intense and quickening energy of the language of the Bible is greatly owing to the divine skill with which this principle is employed. Light, darkness, heat, cold, summer and winter, seed-time and harvest, day and night, sickness, health, life, death, marriage, and all the incidents and affections of the family state, food and raiment, and all the lawful employments of life, are parts of a material system, planned with wisdom so divine, that, if intelligently used, they arouse and stimulate the torpid soul with a quickening and renovating energy. Of such materials our Savior's parables are framed. From such sources he drew those short and pungent statements, which, once heard, are never forgotten, but ever after burn like fire in the soul. This material world, in all its beauties, in all its sublimity, in all its powers and terrors, symbolizes God, and both allures and warns. God meanwhile suspends the full action of His emotions, which man could not endure, and beseeches him to become holy, to escape those spiritual terrors the emblems of which surround him on every side. Thus the whole system is one of mercy, patience and forbearance, on the part of God, and of wise and powerful adaptation to renovate the depraved mind of man. The Lord, in wisdom, founded the earth, and established the heavens; and wisdom cries aloud and utters her voice in the streets.

Thus at a blow does this system cut off the very roots of Platonism, Gnosticism and Manicheism. and of the ascetic systems and social abuses which have arisen from these errors, and also the systems of sacramental regeneration and sanctification, on which the great religious despotisms of ages are based.

On the other hand, the doctrine of the fall in Adam tends directly to introduce a system of virtual Gnosticism. For, if, as the church teaches, the soul is created by God, and the body alone descends from Adam, then it is natural to regard the body as the cause of sin. And this tendency has developed itself in extensive results, in the Roman Catholic church, in the Lutheran and in the Calvinistic churches.

I am aware that the system of divine efficiency, which teaches that God causes all men to sin by His direct energy, because Adam sinned, avoids this difficulty,—but it is only by a peculiar system as to the necessity of divine agency in all volition, which does not accord with the general and intuitive convictions of man. Moreover, this system furnishes no satisfactory explanation of the redemption of the church, and her relations to the universe. For, if no man can choose except through divine efficiency, and if this efficiency is competent to produce whatever choice God pleases, then there is no need of any system of development in order to accumulate moral power such as has been described in explaining the relations of the redemption of the church to the universe ; nor is there any valid reason for the existence of evil, or of redemption at all.

I am also aware that the system of imputation endeavors to avoid Gnosticism, by ascribing sin to the necessary consequences of God's creating the soul without original righteousness, and the withdrawal of supernatural influences from man as a punishment of the sin of Adam, leaving him to become necessarily corrupt and depraved. But this does not at all relieve the matter; for it virtually destroys the guilt, and even the nature, of sin, by ascribing it to the mere fact that a new-created moral agent exists without a righteousness and a divine influence, the enjoyment of which does not at all depend on his own will. Even Augustine has virtually decided that there would be no criminality if sin were to originate from such a cause. Möhler also repudiates this theory, as implying that in a mere finite nature, as such, there is a necessary sinfulness. He says,

> "The question before every other is, to account for the wounds of the spirit, especially for the perversity of the will. Would the spirit of man, because it is an essence distinct from God, when considered in itself,—that is to say, as void of the gift of supernatural grace, and as a bare finite being,— be found in that attitude of opposition to God in which man is now born? Then man, merely as a finite being, would be of himself disposed to sin, and would not be so merely through the abuse of his freedom."

He saw that if man, merely as a creature, is opposed to God, then God would be the author of sin.

Hence the most natural and obvious theory of explaining the fall of Adam has been, in all ages, a reference to the influence of the material system on the soul; and thus the doctrine of the fall in Adam tends strongly and directly to Gnosticism, and all its pernicious results.

Hence the extensive tendency to interpret the statements of Paul, John and others, concerning "the flesh," and "the body of sin," as referring to the material system, and not to the internal and original depravity of the spirit. The radical erroneousness of this interpretation has been thoroughly exposed by Edwards, Müller and Möhler; and yet the common theory of the fall in Adam directly tends to originate and confirm this Gnostic mode of exposition. Möhler, on the supposition that sin is transmitted through the body, asks, with great force,

> "How could the infusion of such a corporeal poison convey to the soul the germs of all which, in the most comprehensive sense, constitutes self-seeking,—to wit, revolt against God, arrogance and envy towards our fellow-men, vanity and complacency in regard to ourselves? If so disordered a spiritual condition, if so distempered a moral state, could be engendered by the connection of the soul with the body, it would be then certainly very difficult to uphold the notion of moral evil."

On the other hand, the doctrine of preexistence teaches not only that the material system does not cause human depravity, but that it was created and arranged to aid in the work of sanctification and redemption. It explains, on this ground, its analogies to the spiritual system, and its typical significance; also the principles of the formation of language, and the proper mode of so using the material system as to produce the highest sanctifying results. It can transform this whole world into a temple of God, and all the lawful acts and duties of life into a system of worship through types of higher spiritual things, and the family state into a little miniature of the universal system.

Having thus constructed that high and copious reservoir from which the lower systems of thinking, feeling and action flow, let us look at the quality and the effects of the streams that flow from it.

Or, to resume our original figure, having disclosed the end and restored to harmonious action the moving powers of the system, and

exhibited the relations of its parts, let us next look at its practical working in some of its details.

Chapter XVII: Results And Practical Tendencies

THE preceding discussion is an ample defense of the doctrine of preexistence against the charge of being a mere theory, of no practical moment. It has evinced that this doctrine is not devoid of proof elevated, dignified and logical in its nature, and certain in its results. It has also shown that it can do what nothing else is able to effect; it can rescue Christianity from its present perilous position without injury, and with great benefit to the depth and power of all its doctrines. By its present perilous position, I mean a position in which it has no real defense against the charge of imputing the highest conceivable injustice and dishonor to God.

I have often wondered at what has appeared to me to be a strange temerity among good men on this subject. One would think that the natural feeling of their hearts would be to shrink sensitively from even a possibility of imputing the least dishonor and injustice to God, and much more so from the fearful hazard of imputing them to him on the highest conceivable scale. One would think that, if any portion of Scripture seemed to imply such dishonor to God, a cautious and thorough investigation of the laws of interpretation would be first made, to see if another view of the passage were not possible. And yet this has not been the case. It has been conceded repeatedly that the acts ascribed to God, in His dealings with the human race through Adam, do appear dishonorable and unjust, according to any principles of equity and honor which God has made the mind of man to form. And yet, simply on the basis of Rom. 5:12-19, and without any adequate search for a more legitimate mode of interpretation, they have for ages gone on to ascribe these acts to God. When I think who God is, and what the redemption of the church is, and how inconceivable is the injury of basing this great work on an act of infinite dishonor and injustice, I cannot but feel that a more hazardous and tremendous risk was never run by intelligent Christian men.

Look, for a moment, at the facts of the case. Review the principles of honor and of right, as I have stated them in the first book. Weigh well the fulness and power of the concessions of the truth of these principles made by the church, from age to age. Think of the great fact that God has so made the human mind that it cannot but recognize their truth. Think of the profundity and power of the feelings which were made to respond to them. Think of the great fact that God made them to be, beyond comparison, the ruling feelings of the soul, and that the principles to which they respond are at the very basis of His government, and then think, if you can, how much dishonor to God, and evil to man, is involved in placing the whole system of Christianity on a basis that, in the utmost conceivable degree, does violence to all these feelings and principles.

Notice, then, the full confession of the great body of the church, that the only defense against the charge of doing this has been the theory that all men had forfeited their rights as new-created beings, by "an act over which they had not the slightest control, and in which they had no agency," and which took place before they existed: and also the confession of Calvin, that nothing is so remote from common sense as this defense; and of Pascal, that nothing appears so revolting to our reason, and that it seems to be impossible and unjust; notice, also, that the great body of the church has decided, and that justly, that there is no defense of the acts ascribed to God in the plea of His rights as a sovereign,—and the fearful state of the case becomes too painfully apparent. And to this the facts of history, as I have set them forth, correspond.

I do not hesitate, therefore, to say that the human mind cannot conceive of a more dangerous mode of representing the acts and defending the character of God than this; and unless it can be shown that my interpretation of Rom. 5:12-19 is erroneous, then still to retain it will, to say the least, be in the highest degree perilous to religion, and that in a case of the utmost conceivable, moment. But I am well assured that the erroneousness of my interpretation cannot be shown. And, indeed, there is no reason to wish that it could be. Who ought to desire to continue such a mode of representing and defending God, if another and a better mode is possible, or even conceivable? What can be worse than the representations that now exist in the church, and the pernicious influence of which, for centuries, I have endeavored at least in part to set forth?

And, now, is it nothing practical that preexistence can deliver the church at once from such a state of things? Is it nothing practical that it places the redemption of the church on a basis in the highest degree honorable to God? Is it nothing practical that it brings experimental, spiritual and supernatural Christianity, as set forth by Paul, Augustine and Edwards, into sympathy with the principles of equity and honor, those powerful and all-pervading elements of humanity, from which it has been alienated, and the operation of which has so constantly tended to create a strong repulsion against it? Is it nothing practical that the deep misunderstanding of the divine character which it has always produced should cease? Is it nothing practical that the real God of the universe should be seen as He is, and not with His real feelings of long-suffering, compassion, sympathy and grief, misrepresented or denied, and His glories obscured by dark clouds of injustice, changing the whole universe into a system of sadness and gloom, if not of horror?

These are the questions at issue, as I have repeatedly shown; and they are real questions, they are *practical questions*, and not visionary speculations. A God who was seen and felt to avow and act on the principles of honor and right which I have laid down, and to manifest the feelings which I have set forth, would exert inconceivable moral power; for the mind of man is made to be acted on by such feelings and principles, clearly apprehended in such a being as God, with inconceivable energy. There is no power like it, or to be compared with it. It can agitate the nations, and shake the globe.

All this power Christianity now loses, and encounters an equal and all-pervading repulsion. This is the great, the main reason why the energy of Satan on earth is so immense. Here is the secret of His strength; here is the hiding of His power.

There is, therefore, a power of emotion in the human heart hitherto entirely undeveloped on the great scale by Christianity. As now presented, it can never develop it. Nay, more, as I have shown, it directly tends, as education and moral culture increase, to division and paralysis. Never—I say it confidently—never will Christianity bring out the whole power of human emotion in sanctified forms, till it is based upon preexistence.

To what has been said I would now add that the Scriptural exposition of the system of the universe, as centering in the union of God and the church, inasmuch as it implies and is based on the doctrine of preexistence, still further takes that doctrine out of the region of mere abstract speculation, and *gives it a practical embodiment in the great central measure of the kingdom of god*. A measure which is the main subject of the inspired oracles of God from beginning to end; for the sake of which the material system was organized, and to execute which the providence of God is administered.

There is no way in which principles are so clearly and surely taught as by a practical embodiment in a working system. The laws and powers of steam, as well as the principles of mechanics, are practically, definitely and clearly embodied in a steam-engine. When the raging ocean-waves had swept away Winstanley[41] in the lighthouse which he had constructed on the Eddy stone rocks, it was plain that he had not embodied in it the principles of architectural strength which the case required. When Smeaton,[42] after a second wreck and ruin had occurred, at last constructed a lighthouse which could defy every wind and wave, then, in that structure, he did practically reveal, in an embodied form, what were the laws of architectural strength in such a case. There is no kind of revelation clearer than this.

In like manner, to illustrate great things by small, the whole of the present dispensation is a system of sublime measures, embodying principles and aiming at a glorious result. The result is an imperishable spiritual structure, including the universe, under God and the church

---

41   Gerrard Winstanley (1609-1676) was an English Protestant religious reformer and political activist during the Protectorate of Oliver Cromwell. He was one of the founders of the English group known as the True Levellers for their beliefs, based upon Christian communism, and as the Diggers for their actions because they took over public lands and dug them over to plant crops. They self-identified as True Levellers, while the Digger name was coined by their contemporaries. He published a pamphlet called *The New Law of Righteousness*, which advocated a form of Christian communism. The basis of this communistic belief came from the Book of Acts 2:44-45. He took as his basic texts the Biblical sacred history, with its affirmation that all men were descended from a common stock, and with its skepticism about the rulership of kings, voiced in the books of Samuel and the affirmations that God was no respecter of persons, combined with Paul's doctrine that there were no masters or slaves, Jews or Gentiles, male or female, in the New Covenant. From these and similar texts, he interpreted Christian teaching as calling for what would later be called *communism*, and the abolition of property and aristocracy.

42   John Smeaton, FRS, (1724-1792) was an English civil engineer responsible for the design of bridges, canals, harbors and lighthouses. He was also a capable mechanical engineer and an eminent physicist, and was the first self-proclaimed civil engineer, and often regarded as the "father of civil engineering." The lift equation used by the Wright brothers was due to John Smeaton's work.

as the head. The measures are the formation of the material system, the introduction of the human race into it, the incarnation of God, the atonement, the redemption of the church and her union to God, and the prostration of the empire of Satan. In all this there is no theory; it is simply the actual present working system of the universe. Such a course of things is not arbitrary; it implies principles, it grows out of reasons; and these principles and reasons are, therefore, embodied in the system.

Is it not, then, plain, even to a demonstration, that whatever is thus embodied is taught with a certainty, definiteness and power, that nothing can surpass?

Now, that the idea of preexistence is thus embodied in the system of the universe, I have undertaken to show; and I think that I have shown it. I have considered the character of God and the system of the universe, not as imagined in speculation, but as revealed in the inspired oracles. I have surveyed its parts, and their relations and combinations, and their great end as a whole. And I have asserted that the great idea of preexistent sin, as I have set it forth, is clearly and definitely embodied in the system as a whole.

Now, with regard to this mode of reasoning, it will be conceded, I think, that it is, as I have said, in its nature elevated and dignified, and, if my doctrine is properly made out by it, sure and absolute in its results.

To the power of this course of reasoning we are also to add the argument derived from the fact which I have proved, that nothing but the assumption of preexistence can vindicate the character of God, and prevent the great moving powers of the system from so conflicting with each other as in a great measure to paralyze the energies of the church, and afflict her with innumerable evils.

That such modes of reasoning, if legitimately used, must lead to sure and infallible results, no rational man will deny. The only course that remains is to show that my use of them has not been legitimate.

It is worthy, therefore, of the more particular attention, that the argument against the doctrine of preexistence is not, like the argument in its favor, based upon legitimate general principles, and the intellectual and moral necessities of the system. It cannot be shown that the doctrine of preexistence tends to any evil. It tends neither to subvert nor to weaken any fundamental doctrine of the gospel. Nay, rather, it gives strength to them all. It does not tend to divide or paralyze the church; on the other hand, it tends to union and strength. The opposition, then, relies on no general views, except the allegations, which have been fully considered and refuted, that it cannot be proved, and that it does not avail to remove any difficulties. Besides these allegations, there is nothing except certain alleged positive statements of the Word of God. Of these, I have thoroughly considered Rom. 5:12-19, the only one that is adapted to exert any great power. Besides this, a few incidental statements are appealed to, with reference to which a few words are all that is necessary. The assertion in 2 Cor. 5:10 "that (at the judgment) everyone shall receive the things done in his body, according to that he hath done," is said to imply that there had been no previous sin, other wise that also would be judged.

But, if we sinned and came under a forfeiture in a previous state, there is no need of an additional judgment, as to that state. By the supposition, if that state had continued, we were lost. All our hopes depended on a new life in this world. Of course, our acts here are the only proper basis of a decisive judgment.

To this it may be added, that even if there should be, in fact, a reference to our conduct in our previous sphere of action, it would not conflict with this passage. For the very foundation of a new probation in this world is to obliterate the memory of a former state, and to speak only of this life. On this plan, it would be right to assert merely that we shall be judged for our deeds here, and to say no more; neither affirming nor denying anything as to a previous state.

It is also asserted that God created Adam's spirit when it entered his body, on the authority of Gen. 2:7. But, even if it were so, and if Adam was made upright, and fell, it would not follow that the continuance of the race was not effected by means of spirits who had already fallen. But, to meet this latter idea, an appeal is made to Zech. 12:1, as proving that God creates the spirits of men as they enter the body. But the verse, of necessity, teaches no such thing. A very proper sense of the verse is that God is the Creator of the spirit of man that is in him,—which would be the truth, at whatever time God created that spirit. The stretching forth the heavens, and laying the foundations of the earth, which in that verse are ascribed to God, were in past time; and, therefore, Dr. Noyes[43] very properly translates the three verbs in past

---

43 John Humphrey Noyes (1811-1886) was an American utopian socialist. He founded
    the Oneida Community in 1848, and coined the term *free love*. In his second year at
    Yale he made his first theological discovery. He was trying to determine the date of

time, and thus makes the creation of spirits a past event, and not one which takes place daily.

But, even in the case of Adam, the creation of his spirit is not asserted in the words "God breathed into his nostrils the breath of life," but merely the gift of natural life,—that which unites spirit and body. If natural life ceases in man, his spirit does not cease to exist, but leaves his body; and God can call it back again, and reunite it by natural life, as in the case of Lazarus. In such a case the language of Genesis may properly be used; we may say God again breathed into him the breath of life; but, certainly, He did not create his spirit. So as to Adam it is asserted that God gave bodily life, but not that He then created his spirit. The apostle Paul, in 1 Cor. 15: 44-49, expressly applies the passage to the life of the body, and thus sanctions the view which I have taken.

Appeal is also made to the statement that Adam was created in the image and likeness of God. I have already said that, if this were true of Adam, even in a moral sense, it would decide nothing as to his posterity, but would merely prove that the spirit of Adam was not fallen when it entered his body. But there is no proof that these words are to be taken in a moral sense with reference to Adam. This passage in Genesis has in Paul a divine expositor. In 1 Cor. 11:7, whilst setting

---

the second coming of Christ, and determined it had already occurred. His conclusion was that Christ's second coming had taken place in 70 A.D., and that "mankind was now living in a new age." With this in mind he became increasingly concerned with salvation from sin and with perfection. He began to argue with his colleagues that unless man was truly free of sin, then Christianity was a lie, and that only those who were perfect and free of sin were true Christians. This internal religious crisis brought about a religious conversion. From there he began to proclaim that he "did not sin." The idea of Perfectionism—that it was possible to be free of sin in this lifetime—caused his friends to think him unbalanced, and he began to be called a heretic by his own professors. From the moment of his conversion Noyes maintained that, because he had surrendered his will to God, everything he chose to do was perfect because his choices "came from a perfect heart". His theory centered around the idea that human will was divine because it came from God, that all that God created was perfect. The only way to control human will was with spiritual direction. And Noyes proclaimed "it was impossible for the Church to compel man to obey the law of God, and to send him to eternal damnation for his failure to do so." He claimed that "his new relationship to God canceled out his obligation to obey traditional moral standards or the normal laws of society." As a result Noyes started acting on impulses from his intuition rather than giving thought to the actions or consequences. On February 20, 1834, he declared himself perfect and free from sin. This declaration caused an outrage at his college, and his newly-earned license to preach was revoked.

forth the typical (or typological—Ed.) significance of God's creative acts, he asserts that man, as man, and as the head of the little microcosm, the family, is the image and glory of God; and that woman, who represents the church, is the glory of man. We see, then, that God, in forming man and woman, and the family, so did it as to represent symbolically Himself, the church and the universe, as an infinite family under one head, composed by the union of God and the church.

It appears, also, from the context of the passage in Genesis, that man, as rational and intelligent, and ruling over this material system, is also regarded as in the image and likeness of God. This view is almost exclusively the one recognized by Augustine and the fathers. And, in this sense, men and women alike are spoken of as in the image of God now as much as Adam was. James accordingly says of men in every generation that they "are made after the similitude of God" (James 3:19). On this ground, also, the law against murder in all ages is made to rest. "Whoso sheddeth man's blood, by man shall his blood be shed: for in the image of God made he man" (Gen. 9:6). This law is obviously based on a reason that exists in all men, in all ages. All are in the image of God.

There is also another view in which man is recognized by Paul as the image of God in a typical sense, and it is one of great sublimity and interest. At the creation, Adam and Eve were exalted to be at the head of the universal new-created system. In this Paul saw a designed type of the exaltation of Christ and the church above all things, as the great and final result of the present moral system of new-creation. Of this the proof is conclusive. His reasoning from the assertion that God put all this natural world under the feet of man, Ps. 8:6, cannot be explained or defended on any other ground. The Psalmist there refers to the original creation. The "all things" spoken of are "all sheep and oxen, yea, and the beasts of the field, the fowl of the air, and the fish of the sea, and whatsoever passeth through the paths of the sea;" and these were subjected to man at the time of the creation. And yet Paul argues from it that all things, God only excepted, are to be subjected to Christ and to the church in Him. On the principle of reasoning from type to antitype, this reasoning is sound, but on no other. (See Heb. 2: 5-9. 1 Cor. 15:27, 28. Eph. 1:22, 23.) I freely admit that man was made in the image of God to the full extent that is implied in all these divine testimonies. But no inspired expositor has ever said that the passage in Genesis has any reference to the moral image of God. The views

which they have given of the passage are enough to exhaust its significance, and no man can prove that it was designed to mean anything
else.

If any should inquire whether I do not hold that all men were
originally made in the image of God, I answer, yes, I hold it much
more consistently and firmly than it is possible to hold it on the common view. I hold, according to Ecc. 7:29, that "God made man (that is,
all men) upright, and they have sought out many inventions." The
preceding course of remark shows that the only design of the writer
was to throw the guilt of that great and general corruption, of which
he had been speaking, off from God, upon men. He therefore states of
man, meaning all men,[44] that God made them upright, but they have
sought out many inventions. Here is merely a general fact stated,
without any details of time or manner, and stated solely for the sake of
defending God.

The truth of this statement is much more apparent, on the supposition of preexistence, than on any other; for, according to that, all
were created upright, individually; but, according to the common
doctrine, men are now created, but not upright, and, therefore, they
never have been upright at any time or place. To say that God made
all men upright in Adam, is merely trying to cover up the common
view of the facts of the case with the fig-leaves of words; for it is
maintained that God creates spirits now, and that He does not make
them upright. Of course, they never were made upright. Nor is it any
better to say that souls are generated, and not created; for, at all events,
even so they are not generated upright, and never were upright.

As to the statement that "God saw everything that he had made,
and lo! it was very good" (Gen. 1:31), it would have been perfectly appropriate in view of a system made to redeem fallen souls, such as I
have set forth. The word *good* does not mean *holy*, for it includes the
newly-organized world, and animals as well as man. And if it was a
material system, made to remove existing evils, then, though sinful
spirits were introduced into it, yet still it would be true, in the highest
sense, that it was all very good,—that is, *perfectly adapted, as a system,*

---

44 Again, at this point the doctrine of the Trinity comes into play in the sense that man
or humanity is simultaneously both individual and corporate. And there is a significant sense in which the wholeness of the corporate character of humanity provides
the context of the individual, and this context might play a similar role in Edwards
theory as his idea of preexistence.

for the ends for which it was made. And, in this respect, it was all the better for the existence of fallen souls in it; for, on any other supposition, it could not gain its great end.

But it is asserted that God's intercourse (conversation—Ed.) with Adam implies that he was at first holy, and afterwards fell into sin. But, in reply to this, it may be very properly alleged that even if sinful propensity was in Adam and Eve. Yet, before a trial and test, they would naturally be unaware of it. But, as soon as they were tried, their real character was disclosed to their own apprehension, and fear and shame came over them.

As to God's intercourse with Adam, all that we know is, that He brought the beasts to Adam, and that Adam named them, and that God made Eve out of his side. But it is a most significant fact that, on the first trial, both of them sinned. What proof, then, is there from facts that they were holy before?

The truth concerning this whole portion of Scripture is, that it has been looked at from a wrong point of view. Its import is wholly typological. So is it everywhere regarded and treated in the Scriptures. The common mode of viewing it has introduced into it the elements of a theological theory, of human devising, which has entirely overlaid and obscured the true, simple and scriptural view, and is entirely out of place. Christ, and the church, and sin, and condemnation, and righteousness, and redemption, and the nature and results of the future system, are here set forth in types. Moreover, the act of Adam was typological, and not that of Eve. The sentence which followed the offense was designed, as I have shown, to be typological, and to include all the race. So was the exclusion from Paradise typological. That the act of Adam alone was typological is plain; for on no other ground can we explain it that Paul takes no notice, in Rom. 5 (though he does elsewhere), of the fact that the woman first sinned, and not Adam, and thus sin entered into the world by her. But as the woman was not the type of Christ, but Adam, as ruler and head of the race, so it was upon his sin, and not upon hers, that he regards the sentence of death as based. If we look upon these transactions as merely typological, all is plain. If we look on them as causative, then they naturally lead to all the puzzling questions which Albert the Great and other scholastic divines have discussed through weary folio pages; as, for example, what would have been the character of the children, if Eve had sinned and not Adam, or Adam and not Eve, and what would have been the law of child-birth on various suppositions, etc. The simple truth, however, is, that God so ordered events as through Adam to set forth a type of the relations of the redeemed to Christ.

The doctrine of preexistence has also been opposed on the ground that infants do not manifest as much intelligence as they ought, on that supposition. But this is a mere matter of opinion. No one can say that the nature and effect of the union of the mind with the body is not such that the highest created mind would be by it reduced to infancy such as we see. It would be the very object of such a system to deliver the mind from the influence of the memory and associations of a past existence. To effect a radical change of character, the proud spirit would be reduced to a state of weakness and dependence; all things would be made to seem new,—new analogical knowledge would be communicated, new motives and hope would be made to open on the soul.

An effort has also been made to prove that the fallen angels and men are different orders of beings, and that all of the fallen angels were condemned without hope, as if this were fatal to the doctrine that the spirits of men had fallen in a previous state of existence. But this, if true, has no force, except on the assumption that between the original fall of Satan and his angels, who kept not their first estate, and the introduction of man into this world, there was no subsequent extension of the kingdom of darkness. Certainly, those who hold that Satan and his angels have had power to plunge in ruin the millions of the human race, and who know that they have so much range as to come with the sons of God into His presence, as the book of Job teaches us, ought not to take the ground that these same angels have not been able in past ages to seduce other orders of beings from their allegiance to God. But on this point I have already said enough, in the eighth chapter of the third book (see p. 193).

Occasionally, also, someone has been found to appeal to Rom. 9:11, where the apostle refers to God's decision concerning Jacob and Esau before they had been born, or done good or evil. But in this case the reference is so manifestly to action in this life, that, for the most part, all intelligent opposers pass it by as nothing to the purpose; and very properly, for the action referred to and denied is manifestly action subsequent to birth.

On surveying this reasoning of opposers, it is striking how entirely devoid it is of great principles and sublime views. All these are against them. Their reasoning is merely an effort to shut up the mind, by disconnected and incidental scriptural statements, to a system which in its main drift and general influence is, as I have shown, at war with moral principle, dishonorable to God, and injurious to man.

On the other hand, the view which I present is embodied in the great central measures of the system, and is demanded by its revealed spirit and principles. No incidental passage has ever been produced against it, or can be, that does not admit of a legitimate interpretation in perfect coincidence with it; and in such a case the main current of principle and of the system must decide the interpretation in my favor.

To this I would add that the whole spirit of the Bible is in sympathy with my views. It is a book the great idea of which is a supernatural creation, from the very depths of depravity and satanic power, by almighty sovereign grace. It is not possible to conceive of new-created minds as coming, in the manner commonly supposed, into such a state as is thus implied, without doing violence to the moral nature, and exciting compassion for them as wronged. But God nowhere regards the human race as unfortunate or wronged, but always as exceedingly guilty. And no man can properly regard the dictates of his moral nature, and yet come up to the tone of the Bible on this point, except through the doctrine of preexistence. Nor will any man otherwise ever have a consistent view of the depth and power of human depravity in this world, nor of those abysses of wickedness which our Savior calls the depths of Satan, and which he regards as so profound as not to be easily understood.

As to the beneficial intellectual and moral tendencies of the views which I have advocated I think that there can be no doubt. Even the mere fact that they may be true will open, as I have already had cheering occasion to know, to many a tempest-tossed mind a haven of rest. As I have said in my introductory remarks, they will show that from the greatest difficulties there is always a possible relief.

They also tend powerfully to diminish the rigor and acerbity of theological controversy on this subject, and to effect a change in the intellectual and moral temperament of the church. They rationally demand such a suspension of former judgments, on the points at issue, as shall at least so admit the possibility that the modern churches of Christ are expending their energies in a fruitless effort to work effectually with an ill-adjusted system, and that their painful divisions and alien-

ations on this subject have sprung from this fact, as shall lead to a new
and candid reinvestigation of the whole subject.

They evince, also, that the various parties to this controversy deserve from each other a higher degree of sympathy and respect, in
view of the causes which have led to their supposed or real errors, than
has been conceded. Under an ill-adjusted (misunderstood—Ed.) system, as I have shown, the best and most honorable impulses of a Christian's mind may lead to real and injurious errors. The impulses that
have led the Old School divines to the adoption of the idea of a forfeiture in Adam are honorable impulses, although the result is by so
many regarded, and, as I think, justly, dishonorable to God and injurious to man. So also the rejection of such a forfeiture, and of the doctrine of depravity with it, by the Unitarians, is the natural and logical
result of the noblest principles and impulses of the human mind, as the
system now is, though the result is in the highest degree calamitous
and dangerous. So, too, the impulses of the various classes of divines
who have tried to find a middle ground between these extremes are
honorable, and worthy of our highest sympathy and respect.

If this should but be duly recognized as the ground of mutual respect and sympathy, and the certain assurance of former decisions be
for a time suspended, it would be possible to review the whole ground
once more with the prospect of mutual benefit and progress in the
truth. The character of this discussion in past ages has been, at least on
the surface, too sternly unsympathizing. I say *on the surface*; for, after
all, Augustine, and Pascal, and others like them, have had tender
hearts, and have had many a struggle to suppress the impulses of their
own honorable principles and emotions. And yet, under the control, as
they supposed, of divine decisions, they overruled them, and sternly
enforced their convictions. So acting, they could not afford to be tender, and to yield to their feelings. They must be unnaturally stern to
maintain their ground at all. Accordingly, in the hour of battle who
was more stern than Augustine? And yet even he, when he opens his
heart to Jerome, reveals the sympathies of a tender spirit, that sought in
vain to find repose for his noblest feelings upon views which, after all,
he felt constrained to adopt and defend. If those who discuss this question could but afford to look into each other's hearts, and see and respect the honorable feelings and impulses that exist there, it would
soon be found that love and mutual sympathy can do what mere argument can never effect.

At the same time, argument and profound discussion are necessary, in order to come to any intelligent and harmonious results. For depravity is a reality, as much as bodily disease; and the mind cannot be happy till it is healed; and yet the principles of honor and right are no less a reality, and the mind must suffer till they are recognized and honored in all their legitimate relations both to God and to man.

But, preeminently, the great want (both *desire* and *lack*—Ed.) of the age is the infusion of a new and powerful spirit of sympathy and love into the discussion of this great question. Nothing else can so enlarge and give dignity to the intellect. Nothing else can lead to that candor and patience and comprehension of views which are indispensable to the profitable discussion of so vast and momentous a theme. Nothing else can avert those premature, superficial and passionate committals, which fatally arrest all progress in true knowledge, and forever shut up the soul in a narrow circle of predetermined ideas, without enlargement and without progress.

And does not the time call for such an increase of sympathy and love? Is there not an urgent necessity, unknown before, of a deeper and more powerful development of Christian experience? Can anything else resist the tendencies to Naturalism, Deism, Pantheism and Infidelity, which on all sides pervade the community? A superficial doctrine of depravity, and a feebly-developed Christian experience, can never meet the great crisis of the age which is coming on. The church needs to be strengthened with all might by the Spirit in the inner man, to be rooted and grounded in love, and to be able with all saints to comprehend the height and depth and length and breadth of the love of Christ, that surpasses knowledge, and to be filled with all the fulness of God. But, without that deep and thorough purification which results from deep conviction of sin, and self-loathing in the sight of a holy God, this is impossible. And now, with all humility, I would say that my deep interest in the views which I have presented arises from a profound conviction of their adaptation, and of their necessity to produce this result. On any other grounds, I should care for them but little, for this is the great interest of the age. But a careful observation of the experiences and the discussions of the present and of past ages has led me to my present convictions.

I cannot but hope that God, in his providence, is preparing the way for a more profound and universal consciousness of the deep depravity of man. Experience is proving, more and more, the superficial-

ity of Pelagianism to disclose and to heal the deep depravity of the human soul. And I cannot but joyfully recognize the hand of God in the
fact that the work on Regeneration, by E. H. Sears, of which I have
before spoken, distinctly discards the Pelagian theory, and adopts a
deeper and more radical view. Of Pelagianism he thus speaks:

> "May we suggest that it is a survey of human nature only
> upon the surface, without sounding its mystic and troubled
> deep? Hence those who adopt it so often recede from it, as
> the mysteries that lie within successively reveal themselves.
> Hence a church formed around this as one of its central
> principles will seldom retain that class of minds whose
> habits of thought are ascetic or introspective, or whose deep
> and surging sensibilities demand some potent voice to guide
> and to soothe them, some light to explain their dark and
> terrible on-goings. Its recruits come from the side of the
> world; not from those who had before left it, and are pass-
> ing on to deeper experiences."

These deeper experiences he proceeds to delineate in a most affecting and impressive way. He utters an earnest and long-needed
warning against the spurious religionism that springs from the intoxi-
cation of pride, in which "self-contemplation is the highest devotion,
and self-worship the daily ritual." He gives a striking description of
conviction of sin, in the light of the divine law.

> "The eternal law shines down through our being, and
> shows our desires and aims, in opposition to its own sanc-
> tity. It is the hatefulness of the selfish will in the presence of
> the All-Pure. Doubtless, the revelation is at first humiliating
> and painful. In that hour of self-conviction, the burden of
> our most inherent corruption hangs heavy on our souls.
> Two ideas, for the time, take sole possession of our minds,
> and fill the whole scope of our vision. Our inmost self how
> alienated! The divine nature how dazzling and dreadful in
> its holiness! ... He who before was complacent and satisfied
> with the shows of a seeming morality is startled and dis-
> mayed, as a light from out of himself is let down through
> the central places of his being, and reveals the secret corrup-
> tion that lurks through all its winding recesses. How false

has been his standard of right, how low have been his aims, and what impurities have tainted the springs of his conduct! 'I thought myself alive without the law,' said the great apostle; 'but when the commandment came, sin revived, and I died.' When the eternal law shone forth, the sin that was in me came full into the range of my consciousness, and instead of spiritual life I found there a mass of death. ... What we have now described is sometimes called 'conviction of sin.' But it is more than that. Sin pertains only to what is wrong in our volitions and actions. But now the sources of sin, lying deeper than all volition and action, are shown to us; for the vain disguises of our self-love having withered away under the beams of the divine countenance, the diseased mass whose hidden motions had swayed our volitions and conduct is disclosed, and makes us cry, 'Who shall deliver us from this body of death?'" (pp. 149, 150).

His description of the process of regeneration is no less heart-moving and affecting. I hail these developments of doctrine with deep and undissembled joy; and that joy is increased by the sincerity with which they are sanctioned by the Executive Committee of the American Unitarian Association, as a clear and strong statement of the practical doctrines of Christianity, and of a profound religious experience. The author well says that if any of his reasonings "should not sound like the traditional utterances of denomination, they may yet be just as worthy of attention;" a thought which all men would do well to ponder.

Yet, I am not able to agree with the estimable author in his views of the origin of this depravity of nature that lies beneath the will, and which he does not regard as properly sinful. He ascribes it to tradition, by descent from preceding sinful generations.

"It is an inherited, disordered nature impersonated in each individual." "Adam began the work of the degradation of the species; the balance between good and evil began to dip the wrong way; his successors kept adding to the weight. Sin became more facile with every generation, till the scale came heavily down. And this is *the fall of man.*" "With primitive man began the descending series, and it kept on till the time of Christ. Then the ascending series began, and it will keep on till it comes up to the level of that height where began the march of humanity."

But how does this view agree with facts? Were not men as much, or even more, depraved before the flood, according to the Bible, than they have been at any time since? Will not there be also a revolt immediately after the millennium? Are the children in a long line of holy families in their own consciousness less depraved? Was it so in President Edwards, whose experience we have given? Yet he came from a long line of holy ancestry. Moreover, when I see new-created souls coming under this law, and beginning an eternal existence in depraved society, as men sink deeper from generation to generation, I cannot recognize the justice or honor of God; I cannot admit that such souls have ever had a fair probation. I cannot but apply to this point the remarks of Dr. Watts concerning the law of generation, which I have quoted on p. 290. I admit that certain causes of depravity are transmitted by the material system. But the central elements of a sinful spirit, pride, selfishness, self-will, envy, and the like, do not, in fact, rise and sink in successive generations; nor is it reasonable to think that it is in the power of matter, or of any law of generation, to originate or to remove them. Whilst, therefore, I rejoice in the depth of experience indicated in the work of Mr. Sears, I cannot accord with his views of the origin of human depravity, and of its changing scale. Yet I immeasurably prefer his views to the superficial Pelagianism which he justly rejects.

But to me nothing seems fully to meet the facts of history and of the Bible, the conduct of God in so entirely blaming and condemning man, and the existence of "those masses of sin and misery," of which Dr. Dewey speaks, "that overwhelm us with wonder and awe," and of those "depths of Satan" to which our Savior refers, but the view which I have advanced. To my mind, every view is superficial that cannot sound all of these depths, and analyze history as we find it to the very bottom; and every view is at war with the principles of honor and right which undertakes to go to such depths without preexistence.

The doctrine of the fall in Adam was designed to be the foundation and defense of a radical doctrine of depravity. Yet it is, and has been in all ages, the real, great and logical fountain-head of Pelagianism; and, if we would seek security from these tendencies, and find a system which, in all its parts, tends to deep views of depravity, and a profound Christian experience, we must resort to the doctrine preexistence.

To evince the truth of these statements, let us, for a moment, suppose the system which I have delineated to be true, and that the whole Christian community have adopted it as thoroughly as they have heretofore the doctrine of the fall in Adam. Let us suppose that the reason, the imagination, the association of ideas, have come under its full power; and, now, let us inquire to what results the system would naturally and necessarily tend. We can, in this way, form some judgment of the power of the indirect and collateral evidence which sustains its truth; for a system of falsehood cannot tend to produce the effects of truth, nor a system of truth those of falsehood.

In general, then, I assert that the natural and necessary affect of a full and firm belief of the system, as I have set it forth, is to give the deepest views of human depravity and of original sin, and to make regeneration, or moral renovation, philosophically the great practical end of both the spiritual and the material systems, and to concentrate their united influence, through the various powers of man, upon a profound development of this great change.

I say that it makes regeneration the great practical end philosophically. For, if it is believed that the mind has been so affected by sinful action, previous to birth, as to be born depraved, and full of sinful tendencies, and disjoined from God, its true life,—and, if it is believed that this material system is not the cause of sin, but has been so framed as by its analogies to illustrate regeneration and spiritual life, and to aid in producing them,—then there is nothing in the system to turn away the mind from the great practical end of Christianity. By the very supposition, the thing to be done is not to develop the good tendencies of a new-created mind in its normal state, but to eradicate the evil tendencies of a sinful mind in a fallen state, and to new-create it in holiness. And there is nothing which can logically supplant or supersede this work.

Indeed, this tendency of the system is so obvious that it has never been denied. For this reason, no doubt, it is that the Princeton divines recognize Julius Müller as clearly on the right side of the great question at issue. So, also, in the *Bibliotheca Sacra* he is represented as holding firmly a thorough doctrine of original sin. Augustine, also, saw this result very clearly; and in one of his earlier works,—that on free-will,—when the first freedom of his mind had not been influenced by church authority, was favorably disposed towards this view, and left it optional to anyone who would to adopt it. Hence, Cudworth represents him as having

> "a favor and kindness for it, insomuch that he is sometimes staggering in this point, and thinks it to be a great secret whether men's souls existed before their generations or no; and, somewhere, concludes it to be a matter of indifference, wherein everyone may have his liberty of opening either way without offense."

To me it is highly probable that Augustine would have adopted the doctrine of preexistence, had it not been for the influence of certain decisions of the church on the sacramental system, which had sprung from her Gnostic and ascetic tendencies. Indeed, this is a fair inference from some of his statements; for he found great difficulties, as we have seen, in Jerome's view of the constant creation of new souls from age to age, and no less in the theory of the generation of souls; and not infrequently he said, especially in his book on the origin of the soul, that he could not tell which was the true view. Eucherius,[45] Bishop of Lyons, and Alcuin[46] of old, took the same ground; and Doederlein asserts that Luther, and most other teachers eminent for wisdom, have coincided with them. This, it will be observed, is a virtual confession that, after all, the question is not settled that the common view of Rom. 5:12-19 is correct; for, if it is, the idea of preexistence is excluded, by a divine decision. How different would have been the course of events, had Augustine and other leading men, when the question was first thoroughly discussed, been left unembarrassed by the Gnostic and ascetic dogmas of the church, which had already dishonored marriage, exalted celibacy and monasticism, and laid the foundations of ecclesiastical despotism in the system of sacramental regeneration and sanctification! The spirit of these corrupt systems is opposed to preexistence as I have developed it, since it is at war with

---

45 Saint Eucherius, bishop of Lyon, (380-449), a high-born and high-ranking ecclesiastic in the Christian Church of Gaul, is remembered for his letters advocating extreme self-abnegation. He also attended the First Council of Orange (441) as Metropolitan of Lyon.

46 Alcuin of York (730s or 740-804), an English scholar, ecclesiastic, poet and teacher from York, Northumbria, is the most prominent figure of the Carolingian Renaissance.

Gnosticism, whilst they imply and are based upon the origin of sin through the material system, which is the fundamental principle of Gnosticism. Considering, therefore, the powerful Gnostic spirit and tendencies of the age, and the power of church authority, it is not to be wondered at that Augustine did not succeed in rising above it so far as to adopt and develop the system of preexistence as I have set it forth, —a system which in its principles and spirit would have been utterly at war with Gnosticism in every form.

One thing, however, is clear, from this general view: *that it has been seen and conceded, in every age, that the doctrine of preexistent sin does tend to a deep and thorough view of depravity and regeneration, and is not to be condemned on the ground of any Pelagian or other dangerous tendencies.* The same, however, cannot be truly said of the common doctrine of the fall in Adam; for, though it is meant to be the basis of a deep doctrine of depravity and regeneration, and is commonly supposed to be such, nevertheless it tends at once, and with great logical power, to Pelagianism. The reason of this is plain; for it implies, of course, a denial of preexistence, and an assertion that man enters this world as a new-created being. But in this is, of necessity, contained an unanswerable logical argument for Pelagianism. For it has been conceded on all hands, and *most strongly by the most orthodox*, that the laws of honor and right demand of the Creator to confer on new-created beings natures in a normal and well-balanced state, tending to good, and needing only development in a natural direction. It follows, of course, since God is honorable and just, that He does confer on all new-born minds such natures; and this is neither more nor less than Pelagianism. A more just, natural and logical conclusion was never drawn from any premises whatever. It is perfectly plain, therefore, that, in the common doctrine of the fall of Adam, there are the logical seeds of pure Pelagianism, ready to spring up at all times. This is the reason why it has always been so hard to exterminate this dangerous system. The church has always furnished the premises which led to it, and has thus been obliged to meet it at a logical disadvantage.

I have shown that all this is the result of a false decision, made nearly fifteen centuries ago, under the overruling influence of a church deeply sunk in the spirit and the errors of Gnosticism. Pious as Augustine was, he could not so far rise above the spirit of his age as to introduce a system the logical development of which would, as I have shown, have cut up Gnosticism by the roots. Hence, though he saw the power of preexistence to explain original sin, and at first looked upon it with favor, he yielded to a corrupt ecclesiastical influence, and, by the aid of a false translation, and a false realistic philosophy, he introduced that false decision, concerning the great problem of the forfeiture of rights by the human race, which has been to every subsequent generation the fountain-head of errors and divisions. There is but one true solution of that problem possible, and that is through preexistent sin.

Since then, the general views which he introduced have been sustained against the protests of the principles of equity and honor, by the supposed testimony of God, in Rom. 5:12-19, although the uniform opinion of the church for nearly the four preceding centuries had been that the sentence referred to in that passage was merely natural death. I cannot but believe, however, that anyone who will candidly consider what I have said on that point will see that there is no divine testimony to sustain the doctrine of a forfeiture in Adam, or of a fall in Adam in any way. But. if this supposed testimony falls away, then, unless we admit of preexistent sin, we come once more logically to the result that men, as new-created minds, are in their normal state, and need only culture and development; and this is Pelagianism. and scientifically and logically at once cuts up the doctrine of regeneration by the roots.

But, on the other hand, the view which I present makes regeneration the only logical or philosophical end of the system; and the laws of honor and right, instead of turning man from it, impel him towards it with all their energy. For, if God has not injured man, but has conferred on him undeserved mercy through this system, then every principle of honor, as well as of interest, calls on him to yield to the divine influences, and to comply with the divine injunction to cast away all his transgressions, and to make to himself a new heart and a new spirit, lest he die forever.

But this is not the whole strength of the case. For the view which I present not only unites the reason, and the dictates of equity and honor, in the great work of regeneration, but it also concentrates the united energies of both the spiritual and the material systems, through other powerful faculties of man, upon the great end of regeneration. Man has not only reason, by which he longs after and delights to behold a systematic unity of all things;—he not only can be influenced through his intellectual, logical and moral powers,—but he is powerfully affected through his imagination, and the association of ideas. The work of moral renovation can never be carried to its highest point, if these faculties are arrayed against it, or divided against each other. But, if we derive sin from Adam through natural generation, these powers are arrayed against the work of regeneration. Man finds himself at once bound in a material system, which he is obliged to regard as tending to corrupt the soul,—a system polluting and polluted.

Let anyone read the development of this subject by Turretin, or by Watts, or by Ridgeley,[47] or by Willard,[48] or by hundreds of others, and see if it is not so. Even if any try theoretically to disavow it, it comes practically to this issue. But, if sin comes through generation and the material system, then, as in the Roman Catholic church, marriage is dishonored, and the imagination and association of ideas defile and are defiled. But. if the origin of sin is thrown back into a spiritual state,—if this system is made to aid in regeneration, if all its analogies, properly understood and used, tend to it,—then is marriage honored, and the imagination and the association of ideas are purified at once, and unite their energies in the great work of moral renovation.

Thus the views which I present alone avert all tendencies to Pelagianism, and make a supernatural regeneration the great and philosophical end of the system. They also provide the means of deep and thorough sanctification. Moreover, they present to the sanctified reason that complete unity of the spiritual and material worlds in one intelligible system which meets the highest intellectual and philosophical wants of the mind. They also give a true system of mental philosophy, based on an investigation of the normal state of the mind, the nature and laws of unperverted free agency, the effects of sin on the faculties, and the changes needed to restore the mind to its true and original harmony and life in God.

So, also, they fully develop the idea of God, so as to meet the wants of the mind thoroughly regenerated and purified;— holy and

---

47 Thomas Ridgeley, English Puritan (1667-1734) was the assistant and successor to Thomas Gouge. He is noted for his famous exposition of the Westminster Larger Catechism, A Body of Divinity (1731).

48 Emma Hart Willard (1787-1870), an American women's rights activist who dedicated her life to education. She founded the first school for women's higher education and wrote several textbooks throughout her lifetime, including books on history and geography. She also published a book of poetry, The Fulfillment of a Promise (1831) with her most popular poem entitled "Rocked in the Cradle of the Deep."

just, yet not an unfeeling and arbitrary God, but sympathetic, tender, gentle, patient, condescending, as well as all-wise and all-mighty.

The great end and final result of the system is also one which deeply interests the feelings and excites the imagination. It is the redemption of the church, and her eternal union to God, in infinite love, for the highest and most benevolent ends. Viewed from this point of view, what a history is that of the church! What tragedies of suffering does it involve, but how glorious the final result! It thus opens the way to pure and perfect emotion, in sympathy with God and the universe; for it discloses the great center of God's emotion, and brings the mind into sympathy with Him and with His angels, with reference thereto.

It discloses, also, the great center of spiritual beauty, in the united loveliness of God and the church. Out of Zion, the perfection of beauty, God is seen to shine. It thus explains the analogies of this spiritual beauty, as seen in the highest beauty of man and woman, and in their union, and also in nature. It thus purifies, develops and elevates, the imagination. It also aids, as nothing else can, to subordinate, control and sanctify, the appetites and the senses. It employs the association of ideas to link all things to the glorious and holy ends of the system. In marriage, and in the family, we are constantly reminded of the glorious consummation of all things at the close of this dispensation. The changes of day and night, the revolving seasons, the varied colors of the landscape, and of morning and evening, are linked by spiritual associations and analogies to the universal system. Thus this faculty imparts to all objects and events of this earthly scene a heavenly color and radiance.

Thus this dispensation, truly viewed, gives rise to a system of education which so trains man as to sanctify and unite all his powers, and in no respect to divide the mind against itself. It unites faith and reason, and makes a supernatural development rational. It sanctifies the world and life in all their parts.

It exposes, moreover, the delusive nature of those ideas of progress which are caused by the illusions of pride. It discloses the true end (purpose—Ed.) of this world as a moral hospital, and makes it apparent that humiliation, confession of sin, and purification and pardon, are the final results of the truest and highest progress. Life thus becomes sober, the world is valuable chiefly for its spiritual ends, and heaven is seen to be the true and only home.

It explains God's mode of discipline and culture by trials varied and severe, and the reasons why He so highly values the faith and patience, and other graces of His people thus produced. It enables Christians to understand for what glorious ends God is training them, and for what purposes they will be called on to put forth their powers, as kings and priests to God forever. It thus furnishes the noblest end, the highest standard, and the most powerful motives for self-culture; and makes life, from beginning to end, a constant system of education for eternity.

APPENDIX

THE BRIDGEWATER TREATISES

Debates over the applicability of teleology to scientific questions came to a head in the Nineteenth Century, as Paley's argument about design came into conflict with radical new theories on the transmutation of species. In order to support the canonical scientific views at the time, which explored the natural world within Paley's framework of a divine designer, The Earl of Bridgewater, a gentleman naturalist, commissioned eight Bridgewater Treatises upon his deathbed to explore "the Power, Wisdom, and Goodness of God, as manifested in the Creation." Published from 1833 to 1840, the treatises are:

1. *The Adaptation of External Nature to the Moral and Intellectual Condition of Man*, by Thomas Chalmers, D. D.

2. *On The Adaptation of External Nature to the Physical Condition of Man*, by John Kidd, M. D.

3. *Astronomy and General Physics considered with reference to Natural Theology*, by William Whewell, D. D.

4. *The hand, its Mechanism and Vital Endowments as evincing Design*, by Sir Charles Bell.

5. *Animal and Vegetable Physiology considered with reference to Natural Theology*, by Peter Mark Roget.

6. *Geology and Mineralogy considered with reference to Natural Theology*, by William Buckland, D.D.

7. *On the History, Habits and Instincts of Animals*, by William Kirby.

8. *Chemistry, Meteorology, and the Function of Digestion, considered with reference to Natural Theology*, by William Prout, M.D.

In response to the claim in Whewell's treatise that "We may thus, with the greatest propriety, deny to the mechanical philosophers and mathematicians of recent times any authority with regard to their views of the administration of the universe," Charles Babbage published what he called *The Ninth Bridgewater Treatise, A Fragment*. As his preface states, this volume was not part of that series, but rather his own reflections on the subject.

He draws on his own work on calculating engines to consider God as a divine programmer setting complex laws underlying what we think of as miracles, rather than miraculously producing new species on a Creative whim. There was also a fragmentary supplement to this, posthumously published by Thomas Hill. The works are of unequal merit; several of them are of high stature in apologetic literature, but they attracted considerable criticism. One critic of the Bridgewater Treatises, Edgar Allan Poe, wrote Criticism. Robert Knox, an Edinburgh surgeon and leading advocate of radical morphology, referred to them as the "Bilgewater Treatise," to mock the "ultra-teleological school." Though memorable, this phrase overemphasizes the influence of teleology in the series, at the expense of the idealism of Kirby and Roget.

OVERVIEW OF BEECHER'S ARGUMENT

Beecher began with an analogy from history regarding a steamship with two paddle wheels turning in opposite directions, referring to the classic Christian conflict between God's Sovereignty and human free will, between Calvinism (or Augustinianism) and Arminianism (and/or Unitarianism). His intent was to illustrate the history of Christian theology since Augustine. Augustinianism was the older theology and Unitarianism was the newer. This conflict irrupted again in the midst of America's Great Awakenings, and more decisively during the Second Great Awakening (1820s-1870s) in the battles between the New School (or New Light) and the Old School in Presbyterianism and Congregationalism, which then spread broadly. The conflict is that the heart of the American Experiment in that America was designed as a way to avoid the theological conflicts that destroyed Europe prior to the founding of America.

Beecher identified the conflict as being between the concern for human depravity versus the concern for God's holy character. The Augustinians/Calvinists argued that God's sovereignty means that God creates some people before the foundation of the world for the express purpose of demonstrating the glory of His justice by condemning them to hell, citing verses like Rom. 9:21: "Hath not the potter power over the clay, of the same lump to make one vessel unto honor, and another unto dishonor?"

In direct reaction and opposition to this idea, the Arminians, Unitarians and the Pelegians before them found such an idea to be contrary to the biblical teaching of the holy character of God and antithetical to the idea of biblical justice. Beecher argues that this group believed that God had created human beings in His own image, which meant in part that the human moral ideals of honor and righteousness were reflections of God's character, that God had created human beings with an innate and correct desire for and understanding of honor and righteousness because such is the character of God Himself. This group believed that one person's sin could not be credited to another, citing verses like Ezk. 18:20, "The soul that sinneth, it shall die. The son shall not bear the iniquity of the father, neither shall the father bear the iniquity of the son: the righteousness of the righteous shall be upon him, and the wickedness of the wicked shall be upon him."

Therefore, what offended and/or contradicted such biblical moral ideals was not consonant with God's biblical character, and must be an incorrect analysis. An honorable and righteous God would not endow new-created minds (human beings) with a sin nature that was irresistible. An honorable and righteous God would only create human beings with an innate sense of honor and righteousness similar to His own. To do anything less would dishonor the very idea of honor and righteousness, which originates in God. So, for human beings to be born into sin implies that a sovereign God is responsible for their sinfulness. This is what Pelegians, Arminians, and Unitarians believe.

And in direct opposition to this line of reasoning, the Augustinians and Calvinists point to human history and various Bible verses that clearly demonstrate the horrific and unchecked sinfulness of humanity in every age, and that sin so warped human perception as to deprive human beings of any correct understanding of God prior to their personal regeneration. It appears to Augustinians and Calvinists that the position of the Pelegians, Arminians and Unitarians involves the denial of human history, and the reality and extent of human sin and of various biblical teachings. The Augustinians and Calvinists argue that sin has warped human understanding, and that is why it *appears* that a sovereign God has created new human beings in sin. But, because God is both infinitely good and sovereign, it cannot be true that God is responsible for sin. Therefore, people are responsible for their own individual sin, even though it appears that individuals are born with a fully functioning sin nature. It is not that God is an affront to humanity for something that only God can understand, but that humanity is an affront to God because of our inability to avoid sin.

The conflict involves different ways to understand God's character and the reality of human sin. If God is the epitome of goodness, righteousness and sovereignty, how can the reality of human sin from birth be explained? Or, given the reality of human sin, how can God's character be good and righteous—and sovereign? If God is all-powerful, why can't He eliminate sin? If God is all-righteous, why does He allow sin to exist? Such questions continue to plague people today.

Beecher examined this conflict and its history, and determined that it is unavoidable and unsolvable if the logic and assumptions of both sides are correct, which is why I called attention to the theology of presuppositional antithesis.[1] The issue is not that some people and/or theologies are good and others are evil. Rather the issue is the definition of good and evil. In the final analysis it is a judgment call, not a matter of logic, reason or experience. Whose judgment do we trust? Our own or God's. And it is our trinitarian character or nature through which our judgment and God's judgment can be identified as one. They can be unified, but only in Christ.

In addition, each side goads the other into active opposition because of their commitments to either God's sovereignty or to the honor and righteousness of God's character. According to Beecher, Christianity is locked into a conflict with itself that keeps it from further development by continuing to renew these central arguments in every new generation (new created beings). He determined that Christianity is stuck in a rut, and can make no more progress until it is extricated from the rut.

NEW-CREATED BEINGS

According to Beecher the faulty assumption or idea that causes the problem is the idea that people in every generation come into the world as new-created beings (Book III, Chap V, p. 177). By this he means that they come into existence without any previous inheritance,

---

1   See footnote 1, p. 1.

experience or history. His solution to the problem is the *doctrine of preexistence*,[2] which he believes explains how human beings can be born into sin (with a sin nature) without God being responsible for it. The idea is that people "earned" God's condemnation in some previous state of existence. However, the denial of the traditional doctrine of preexistence is so well integrated into every understanding of contemporary Christianity that it is difficult to counter or oppose, and I believe, rightly so.

If people are born into sin as the Augustinians and Calvinists claim, then God's character is put into question because it is unjust to punish people for something that they are not responsible for. This also puts the doctrine of imputation into question as well. The doctrine of individual responsibility for sin requires that people be judged on the basis of their own beliefs and behavior, and not be charged on the basis of beliefs and behaviors of others, including Adam. This is clearly a biblical teaching (Ezk. 18:4, 20).

Yet it is impossible to deny or ignore the doctrine of innate sin and human depravity. By every measure people are sinners from the very beginning of their existence. It has to come from somewhere!

Beecher shows that preexistence was considered by Origen but rejected by the condemnation of Origen's idea of it as heresy. However, the various conceptions of preexistence at the time pertained to individual souls and lacked an adequate development of the doctrine of the Trinity that insists that individual identity cannot be separated from corporate, cultural and spiritual identity.[3] Beecher himself was not clear of this individualistic idea either, which led him into an exploration of Spiritualism and other ideas of individual preexistence. He did not adopt any Spiritualist ideas, as far as I know—though he seems to have explored it. In my opinion, further exploration in that direction is an error because it fails to take the doctrine of the Trinity into consideration.

TYPOLOGICAL PERSPECTIVE

However, if we think of the idea of human preexistence as being a cultural and social reality rather than an individual reality, some traction may be gained. As I said in the Preface:

---

2   See Appendix: Doctrine of Preexistence, p. 471.

3   See footnote 17. p. 250.

I found myself thinking of it as a kind of antediluvian human cultural remnant out of which God called Abraham.
Abraham's father, Terah (whose Hebrew name means "Ibex,
wild goat," or "Wanderer" and "loiterer") was a priest of a
very ancient religion, possibly related to the god, Sin. Abraham was called out of that culture to create a new culture
that we know as Old Testament Judaism, which was to be a
blessing to all nations, all peoples of the earth (Gen. 12:2-3).
The culture of Judaism got bogged down in self-centered-
ness, whereupon Christ came to liberate the Gospel of God
to once again be a blessing to all nations, all peoples of the
earth. Understanding Beecher requires an understanding of
the "big picture" of God's mission to the world (p. 7).

This is not exactly what Beecher was arguing, but is reflective of
how I understand some of what Beecher said. Beecher was arguing for
a pre-Genesis 1:27 existence of humanity, which is accompanied by a
great many difficulties, both historically and biblically. What I'm suggesting here is more of a typological understanding of Scripture and
history that follows the Apostle Paul, who introduced it, John Nevin,[4]
a contemporary of Edward Beecher, James B. Jordan, a contemporary
of mine, and many others.

These authors, following Paul, taught that God was creating a
New Creation *in Christ* that would supplant the Old Creation *in
Adam*, that this New Creation in Christ constituted a new humanity, a
new race or culture of human beings. The old race, the race or culture
of Adam was destined for extinction because it could not escape the
influence of Sin (the ancient god).[5] Christ had come to put an end to
the culture of Adam by inaugurating the culture of Christ. The death
of the one and the birth of the other issued from the same event—the
life, death and resurrection of Jesus Christ.

Typologically then, in the same way that Jesus Christ came to a
preexistent world, the world of Old Testament Judaism, God had earlier come to Abraham to take him and his seed out of a previous preex-

---

4   Ross, Phillip A. & Nevin, John Williamson. *The True Mystery of The Mystical Pres-
    ence*, Pilgrim Platform, Marietta, Ohio. 2011.

5   Indeed, *extinction* is the meaning of *death* in Genesis 3. Reread Chapter VIII: Import
    Of The Word *Death*, In Rom. 6: 12-19, p. 347. See also *Arsy Varsy—Reclaiming the
    Gospel in First Corinthians*, Phillip A. Ross, Pilgrim Platform, 2008, "Death."

isting world, the world of Terah, the world of the god called *Sin*. This
is the typological pattern.

Abraham provided the new archetype for those who had previously belonged to Sin, as Christ provided the new archetype for those
who had previously belonged to Father Abraham, those we know as
Old Testament Israel. This typological understanding is not as fixed,
not as hard and fast as the precision of science or modern and post-
modern people are used to. Typology deals with patterns and flows
rather than hard details and precise prediction. Typology deals with
cultures and archetypes rather than individuals and beliefs, with patterns rather than facts.

CREATION PERSPECTIVE

Another way that might provide some traction for better understanding and adapting Beecher's idea of preexistence piggybacks on
the typological understanding regarding the creation of a new humanity or a new human race *in Christ*. Here we take the idea of a new creation in Christ as the type of creation found in Genesis 1 & 2. And by
this idea of a "new creation" we mean the creation of a new typology
or archetype of humanity. We might think of it as a kind of human
cultural DNA, where individuals are the building blocks of human
culture (1 Pet. 2:5).

We first use the Old Testament to ground the reality of Christ as
the Son of God and a co-creator of the world (Gen. 1:1-26) by the
power and reality of the Trinity and through Christ's fulfillment of the
Old Testament. Then we read this New Testament understanding of
Christ as co-creator back into the creation accounts of Genesis. And
the fruit of this reading provides an understanding that the creation
accounts in Genesis are typological in the sense that their central purpose is to describe the creation of humanity in the environment in
which humanity finds itself. The creation accounts in Genesis provide
description regarding the creation of a type or culture of humanity in
the same way that Abraham provided the typology and archetype for
Old Testament Israel, and Jesus Christ provides the typology and
archetype for New Testament Christianity. The subject of the creation
accounts is not the creation of the "world" of science—of matter, dirt
and stars, but the "world" of history—of peoples, places and kings. Un-

derstood typologically the creation narratives in Genesis describe and provide for the creation of human culture.[6]

Here God's typological creation *ex nihilo* doesn't necessarily mean that God began with absolutely nothing with regard to the creation of humanity (אדם—from Strong's H119; *ruddy*, that is, a human being, an individual *or the species*, mankind, etc.), but that God began with a blank cultural canvas. If Beecher is right that in some sense humanity had some sort of previous or primeval existence, prior to Adam, and earned or inherited God's condemnation through that state of existence, and God wanted to provide humanity with another chance or further development, then there may be good reasons for God wanting to begin "afresh" with a "new cultural canvas" or human archetype.

There was "nothing" on the canvas—but there was a canvas of some sort! In this case, God may have been creating a human culture *ex nihilo* in the sense of starting fresh, without the baggage of any previous culture or history. Here I'm asking us to read Beecher as if he argued that Adam's Original Sin was a kind of cultural or archetypal carryover, inheritance or "canvas," rather than an individual preexistent soul, from a preexistent human state or culture. Here, the guilt and consequence of that Original Sin could have originated from that preexistent "canvas," perhaps like a kind of DNA. I'm suggesting that we read Beecher sociologically rather than individualistically.

This understanding then allows for humanity, the genus or archetype, to be infected with an innate sin nature that is "normal" (because it exists as an archetypal carryover or "canvas" from a previous period or expression of existence). This way it does not damage the character of God. God did not design a flawed and sinful humanity in the Genesis creation, but humanity earned the consequences of her sin in a previous "world" or "age" (αἰών).

To date there are scant records, history or evidence of such a previous age or existence, but then again it could have been so different that we have no idea what to even look for. Or its destruction could have been so complete that nothing is left to find. Such an existence

---

6 This is not a denial of traditional understanding of the creation narrative in Genesis, but is simply a typological understanding of the literature. Of course, God originally created everything from nothing, but that event is so far back in time that it is inaccessible to humanity. The more we learn about reality and the cosmos in which we live, the farther away the origin of the universe recedes from human understanding.

may have been in a different "place" or "realm" or "world." (Don't make too much of this speculation, but don't deny its possibility, either.) From this perspective all of the classic doctrines of Christianity can be preserved and the classic heresies can be avoided, according to Beecher.

This allows us to understand terms like "sun," "stars" and "heavens" mentioned in Genesis typologically, much as can be done in the book of Revelation, where celestial bodies provide analogies for rulers, kings, governments and the governing aspects of such entities. Thus, the creation and destruction of the heavens and the celestial bodies associated therewith are understood as the various cataclysms associated with the changing of historical *ages* (αἰών), also translated as *world*.

THE HINGES

Beecher's argument hangs on a couple of hinges. The first difficulty is accepting the apparent legitimacy of the Pelegian argument that original sin did not irreparably taint human nature (total depravity) and that human beings are still capable of choosing good or evil, just as Adam was before the Fall. Beecher goes to great lengths to demonstrate that this is a common idea in the history of Christianity, and that many of the great saints have believed and argued some version of this idea. And it cannot be denied that many significant Christians throughout history have believed and argued this point. Yet, the truth that the church rightly branded it a heresy cannot be denied either. So, we might understand Pelegianism to be true from a certain perspective, but inadequate to the fullness of the whole truth of the biblical perspective.

Beecher has set up his argument in such a way that this idea cannot simply stand by itself. We cannot and should not accept or reject this idea on its own merits, but must understand it in its own context and history. In the same way that the Five Points of Calvinism were not taught by Calvin in the way that they were defended at the Synod of Dort, and while the Five Points are valid, they do not actually represent Calvinsim very well. If all a person knows are the Five Points of Calvinism, he does not and cannot actually understand Calvinism.

The Five Points were responses to the teaching of Arminius, and apart from an understanding of that perspective, the Five Points will be over-relied on and alone are not able to communicate the heart of Calvinism. Similarly, Pelegianism (including Arminianism and Unitarianism) according to Beecher are reactions against Augustinianism, and will provide a similarly skewed understanding of Christianity in and of itself/themselves.

A true understanding of Christianity cannot be built upon a reaction to a partial presentation of Christianity, but must take into consideration the wholeness of both presentation and reaction (or response). Christianity is not merely a presentation of information, nor is it merely a response. Rather, the wholeness of Christianity always includes both a presentation of the gospel of Jesus Christ *and* the proper response. Christianity is not a test wherein providing the correct answers produces salvation. Not at all! Thus, similarly, Calvinism is true from a certain perspective, but is but inadequate to the fullness of the whole truth of the biblical perspective.

Calvinists will find this very difficult to actually understand because history has so shaped the Calvinistic argument (as opposed to Calvin's actual theology) as to exclude all suggestions of the credibility of Pelegian, Arminian and Unitarian arguments. Calvinism as it has been argued historically in the conservative Calvinistic traditions in a way that simply cuts the opposing ideas off at their proverbial knees.

However, Beecher is not simply asking Calvinists to eat a little crow. He is also asking the Pelegians, Arminians and Unitarians to also eat their share, because they have all essentially done the same thing as the Calvinists by arguing for the necessity, reality and integrity of goodness of God's character. While those who oppose Calvinism are repulsed by the idea of a God who creates people with an unavoidable sin nature, Beecher argues well that there is no evidence to suggest otherwise.

He argues that Scripture presents a just, loving and honorable God who is completely responsible for all of creation, and at the same time it teaches that human beings are completely and utterly lost in sin. And this is the great conundrum of the Bible. These two ideas cannot both be true, yet the Bible teaches them both. Augustine, and Calvin who followed his lead, argued for one side of the conundrum, and Pelegius, Arminius and Socinus who followed his lead, argued the opposite. And, according to Beecher, all of Christian history has followed in the model of this bifurcation. Therefore, he cites Augustine as the central culprit who is at the heart of this problem, which has dominated both Christianity and human history ever since.

The second hinge that Beecher presents is his reading, correction and understanding of Rom. 5:12-19. The crux of Beecher's argument here falls from Paul's teaching that just "as by one man sin entered into the world, and death by sin" (v. 12), "so by the obedience of one shall many be made righteous" (v. 19). Here we see that the central idea pertains to what Plato defined as the problem of the "one and the many" (Plato's *Parmenides*).

It is important to realize that the Bible itself knows of no such problem, and that Augustine like so many church leaders before him who had been educated in Greek philosophy, simply imposed the categories of Greek philosophy upon the Bible in their analysis. I'm not suggesting that Bible authors (who truly represent God) didn't understand the problem, only that for them it was not an abstract problem that required an intellectual solution.

At its heart the issue of the "one and the many" pertains to the idea of representation. How can one thing represent something else? And particularly, how can one thing represent a category of other (many) things? The Greeks understood the issue intellectually and abstractly, where the biblical authors understood it historically and spiritually.

Beecher's argument is that Paul was not writing about a causal relationship between Adam's sin and human sin, or between Christ's righteousness and human righteousness. It was not that Adam's sin *caused* the sin nature to infect all of his posterity, but that the relationship between Adam and fallen humanity, like the relationship between Christ and redeemed humanity, was/is typological.

Paul himself originated the biblical doctrine of typology in Col. 2:16-17: "Let no man therefore judge you in meat, or in drink, or in respect of an holyday, or of the new moon, or of the sabbath days: Which are a shadow of things to come; but the body is of Christ." Some things foreshadowed other things in history, and these first things were the types or models of what was to come later. Inherent in the idea of typology is the idea of prophecy, of predicting the future or suggesting that certain things necessarily follow from other things—and even logic itself.

What Beecher didn't know or discuss is the relationship of the doctrine of the Trinity and typology, or the Trinity and the problem of the "one and the many."[7] So, while Beecher suggests that the best

---

7   See footnote , 17, p. 250.

solution to the problem he presents is the doctrine of preexistence, it seems to me that a better candidate is the doctrine of the Trinity.

DOCTRINE OF PREESISTENCE

THIS section is provided in order to show how much this doctrine actually impacts religion and philosophy. It is at the very heart of many misunderstandings and fallacies, which means that a proper understanding of it and its context and dynamics could substantially correct a great many of the world's problems. And again, I believe that the doctrine of the Trinity better solves the problems that the doctrine of preexistence intends to answer. It must be assumed that Beecher believed the "traditional" doctrine which is described in brief below.

Pre-existence, preëxistence, beforelife, or pre-mortal existence refers to the idea that each individual human soul existed before conception, and at conception (or later) one of these pre-existent souls enters, or is placed by God, in the body. This idea is also found in varying degrees in the Abrahamic and other religions. Note the individualism of the idea.

CHRISTIANITY

The Bible treats the idea of pre-existence indirectly, i. e., Jeremiah 1:5, Romans 9:10-12, Ephesians 1:4, John 9:2-32.

The earliest surviving Christian writings on the pre-existence are by Origen. Origen posited in a speculative work that the soul was assigned a body as a penalty for its sin of looking downward toward the corrupt earth. The doctrine also derives in part from a repudiation of Greek thought by Tertullian, who argued that a material body was created for each immaterial soul. While orthodox Christian doctrine insists that humanity did not pre-exist, some people postulate that the biblical tradition says otherwise.

LATTER DAY SAINT MOVEMENT

The idea of pre-mortal existence is an early and fundamental doctrine of Mormonism. In 1833 Joseph Smith, Jr., taught that just as Jesus was coeternal with God the Father, "Man was also in the beginning with God. Intelligence, or the light of truth, was not created or made, neither indeed can be" (*Doctrine and Covenants* 93:29). This reference indicates the LDS belief that aside from spirit and body, there is a third aspect of humanity, namely, an "intelligence." It is this intelligence, according to LDS doctrine, that "was not created or made, neither ... can be."

Latter-day Saints believe there was a spiritual creation quite some time before the physical creation, and that the non-created, eternal intelligences of humans were put into the created spirits, which were in turn put into physical bodies. The nature of an "intelligence" is not precisely understood and its difference from spirits largely seems to be an arguable moot point, so far, until further revelation is given (but there are spiritual bodies as well as physical bodies, according to LDS doctrine.)

In 1844, Smith taught:

> "[T]he soul—the mind of man—the immortal spirit. Where did it come from? All learned men and doctors of divinity say that God created it in the beginning; but it is not so: the very idea lessens man in my estimation.... We say that God himself is a self-existent being.... Man does exist upon the same principles.... [The Bible] does not say in the Hebrew that God created the spirit of man. It says 'God made man out of the earth and put into him Adam's spirit, and so became a living body.' The mind or the intelligence which man possesses is co-equal with God himself.... Is it logical to say that the intelligence of spirits is immortal, and yet that it had a beginning? The intelligence of spirits had not beginning, neither will it have an end. That is good logic. That which has a beginning may have an end. There never was a time when there were not spirits; for they are co-equal [co-eternal] with our Father in heaven" (Excerpt from *King Follett Discourse*).

After Smith's death, the doctrine of pre-mortal existence was elaborated by other Latter Day Saints. Although the "mind" and "intelligence" of humanity were still considered to be co-eternal with God, and not created, Brigham Young introduced the idea that the "spirit," distinguished from the "mind" or "intelligence," was created and not co-eternal with God. Young postulated that we each had a pre-spirit "intelligence" that later became part of a spirit "body," which then eventually entered a physical body and was born on earth. In 1857, Young stated that every person was "a son or a daughter of [the Father]. In the spirit world their spirits were first begotten and brought forth, and they lived there with their parents for ages before they came here" (Ostler, Blake (1982), "The idea of pre-existence in the development of Mormon thought," *Dialogue: A Journal of Mormon Thought* 15(1):59–78.).

Among Latter-day Saints the idea of "spirit birth" was described in its modern doctrinal form in 1909, when the First Presidency of The Church of Jesus Christ of Latter-day Saints issued the following statement:

> "Jesus, however, is the firstborn among all the sons of God —the first begotten in the spirit, and the only begotten in the flesh. He is our elder brother, and we, like Him, are in the image of God. All men and women are in the similitude of the universal Father and Mother, and are literally the sons and daughters of Deity" (MFP 4:203).

This description is widely accepted by modern Latter-Day Saints as fundamental to the plan of salvation. However, there are differences of opinion as to the nature of the pre-mortal existence in other Latter-Day Saint denominations.

The LDS Church teaches that during the pre-mortal existence, there was a learning process which eventually led to the next necessary step in the pre-mortal spirits' opportunity to progress. This next step included the need to gain a physical body that could experience pain, sorrow and joy and "walk by faith." According to this belief, these purposes were explained and discussed in "councils in heaven," followed by the War in Heaven where Satan rebelled against the plan of the Heavenly Father.

The Development of the Doctrine of Preexistence, 1830–1844, by Charles R. Harrell, LDS *Religion and Doctrine, Journal*: 28:2

> "Perhaps no doctrine has had greater impact on Latter-day Saint theology than the doctrine of preexistence, or the belief in the existence of the human spirit before its mortal birth. Fundamental concepts such as the nature of man as an eternal being, his singular relationship as the offspring of Deity and concomitant brotherhood with all mankind, the talents and privileges with which he is born into the world,

and his potential godhood are all inextricably connected to the doctrine of preexistence. This distinctive LDS doctrine was not immediately comprehended by the early Saints in the more fully developed form in which it is understood today.

Like many of the other teachings of the Prophet Joseph Smith, it was revealed line upon line and adapted to the Saints' understanding. Moreover, there was a natural tendency to view initial teachings on preexistence in light of previously held beliefs until greater clarity was given to the doctrine. This study traces the early development of the doctrine by examining chronologically the revelations and recorded sermons and writings on preexistence by the Prophet Joseph Smith in light of contemporary commentary by his associates. Seeing how early Saints perceived preexistence enhances our own understanding of the doctrine and leads to a greater appreciation of our theological heritage."

GREEK THOUGHT

Plato believed in the pre-existence of the soul, which tied in with his innatism. Innatism is the idea that the mind is born with ideas and knowledge, and that the mind is not a "blank slate" at birth, as early empiricists such as John Locke claimed. Innatism asserts that not all knowledge comes from experience and the senses. Plato thought that we are born with knowledge from a previous life that is subdued at birth and must be relearned. He saw all attainment of knowledge not as acquiring new information, but as remembering previously known information. Before we were born, we existed in a perfect world where we knew everything. This theory is similar to reincarnation, though there are differences.

ISLAM

In Islam, all souls are thought to have been created as adults before earthly birth at the same time God created the father of Mankind, Adam. The Qur'an recounts the story of when the descendants of Adam were brought forth before God to testify that God alone is the Lord of creation and therefore only He is worthy of worship (Qur'an 7:172), so that on the Day of Judgment, people could not make the excuse that they only worshiped other gods because they were following the ways of their ancestors. God then removed the memory of this event from the minds of humanity, leaving only an innate awareness that He exists and is One. This is known as the *Fitra* in Islam. In addition, God decreed at which point each and every human would be born into the physical world.

JUDAISM

In rabbinic literature, the souls of all humanity are described as being created during the six days of creation (Book of Genesis). When each person is born, a preexisting soul is placed within the body. (Tan., Pekude, 3).

In the *Tractate Sanhedrin*, the question is asked, "When does the soul enter the body of the newborn?" The answer "at birth" is rejected in favor of an intermediate stage within the womb, usually interpreted as forty days after conception, after which it is traditionally believed that a baby is taught Torah by an angel.

Within the Jewish scriptures, the *Tanakh* (or Old Testament in Christianity), there is a passage used to teach that the spirit within humans did not pre-exist, but was created within each person in the womb: "The burden of the word of the LORD concerning Israel. The saying of the LORD, who stretched forth the heavens, and laid the foundation of the earth, and formed the spirit of man within him."

DOCTRINE OF THE TRINITY

JUST as God is identified as Trinitarian, so are His people, and so is His world. We have been created in God's image, and God is fundamentally, essentially and completely Trinitarian. Christians are to understand the world through God's eyes, and God's eyes are Trinitarian. There is nothing outside of or apart from God. God is all encompassing, "infinite in being and perfection" (Westminster Confession of Faith 2:1). The point is that God is ultimately one and at the same time God is ultimately three. In God alone there is ultimate unity and ultimate diversity and/or individuality at the same time.

Let me illustrate and apply this idea. How can I be an individual, a unique whole, and at the same time be part of a distinct individual corporate entity—humanity, a nation and/or state, and the body of Christ? I am who I am as an individual in and of myself, yet my identity as a human being, an American, an Ohioan and a Christian is interwoven with all other human beings, Americans, Ohioans and Christians. I am a Christian *in Christ* as explained by the doctrine of Christian unity. While we use these distinctions all the time, it is quite difficult to provide an ultimate and rational explanation for such definitions and distinctions of personal and corporate identity.

While it is difficult to explain the Trinity, it is at the same time the most ordinary concept imaginable. Everyone intuitively understands that a thing can be both individual and corporate at the same time. Everyone intuitively knows what it means and uses such distinctions every day—everyone, not just Christians. And yet, a complete or comprehensive explanation of what the Trinity means or a survey of its implications is impossible.

We use a lot of things that we don't understand—cars, computers, microwaves, etc. We don't need to understand everything about a thing to use it. Yet, we can live more fully and more effectively

476

when we understand more about how life works, about how reality is ordered. So, how does the Trinity effect our lives and our perceptions of things? Allow me to try to provide an explanation.

Being a Christian means being an individual Christian and at the same time being a member of a group of Christians, a member of a Church—the body of Christ, just as Jesus Christ is a person and a member of the Godhead. An individual person may be a Christian, but he cannot be a Christian by himself because being a Christian is always a matter of corporate identity, which then informs our individual identity. While our individual identity as Christians is dependent upon our corporate identity as Christians, the corporate identity of the church is not dependent upon our individual identity. Christians are called to love, so there must be an other, someone else to love. And apart from that love of others, the love of the fellowship of believers, one is not fully Christian. There's no such thing as a "Lone Ranger Christian." Christianity is always both an individual and a corporate affair.

Becoming a Christian means being born again, being regenerated by the Holy Spirit, who dwells in the hearts, minds and lives of believers. Ask a young Christian under three feet tall how he knows he is a Christian and he will likely tell you "because Jesus lives in my heart." This is deep wisdom, and not mere childishness.

While "me" and Jesus live in the same body (sort of), it is not simply a matter of my own unique individuality because Jesus, who lives in my heart, also unites me with a larger group of people, who also have the same Jesus living in their hearts, so to speak. Jesus also unites me with something beyond my own physical body, something eternal —God. Jesus is the bridge between me and God, and also the bridge between me and His people—the Church or body of Christ.

Paul asks, "The cup of blessing that we bless, is it not a participation (a communion, a fellowship) in the blood of Christ? The bread that we break, is it not a participation (a communion, a fellowship) in the body of Christ?" (1 Cor. 10:16). These are not real questions, they are rhetorical questions. Paul is stating facts about the Trinitarian God. To receive the cup is to participate in or unite with Christ. To receive the bread is to participate in or unite with Christ. Communion is for faithful Christians because it is a *participation* in and/or a union of sorts with Christ. It is an acknowledgment of corporate membership in Christ. It is not a mere memorial or mere assent, but involves all of the

actual spiritual and legal rights and responsibilities pertaining thereunto.[8]

Communion or the Eucharist is not to be received casually or in-
discriminately and especially not unfaithfully. As we see in 1 Cor. 11,
people are to identify themselves as faithful Christians before coming
to the Lord's table, lest they eat and drink judgment on themselves (1
Cor. 11:29). Participation in the body of Christ requires self identification as a Christian and an intention of faithfulness to that identity.

Most translations translate the Greek word κοινωνία as *communion* rather than *participation*, but either will do. Communion is not
simple union, but it is a kind of union. Where union is a kind of
merging or loss of self in something greater, communion is not a loss
of self, but an expansion, a clarification or extension of self. In communion both self and other remain clearly defined in the same way
that God's Trinitarian identities—Father, Son and Holy Spirit—are
clearly distinct, yet identical.

Christians have a unique individual identity, yet an overlap of
common identity with Christ and with the community of Christ here
and in eternity at the same time. There are common elements that belong to the self, to other Christians, and to Christ. The Christian iden-
tifies with Jesus Christ, but He does not become Christ, nor does he
lose himself in Christ. Rather, his identification in Christ makes him—
his self, his individuality—more unique, not less. The sharing of Christian values and Christian character gives his personality increased definition, increased clarity. He becomes more himself in Christ. People
become more in Christ than they could ever be apart from Christ.

To participate in something is to take an active part in it. Participation and communion provide the foundation upon which social
mores are built. Mores are strongly held social norms or customs,
which derive from the established practices of a society or group.
Taboos are a subset of mores that forbid a society's most unacceptable
behaviors. Taboos are things like incest and murder. The word *morality* comes from the same root, as does the noun *moral*. Morality—behavior—is both individual and communal, personal and social. God's
covenant is both personal and social. Being a Christian is both personal
and social. God is both personal and social.

---

8   See footnote 1, p. 165, footnote 29, p. 286, and footnote 4, p. 464.

The point is that participation in the Lord's Supper provides the foundation for social mores and personal morals, which issue from the expression of Christian character through the imitation of Jesus. In other words, the Lord's Supper defines Christians. It defines who we are in Christ. It informs us as it forms us, both individually and corporately. It defines us as Christians and sets Christians apart from non-Christians. It is not magical, but it is mysterious. It is spiritual, but it is also real.

Paul goes on to say that our Christian identity is like the bread that we share. It is one loaf, but it is torn into many pieces. Yet, the tearing does not diminish the oneness of the loaf, but rather it enhances it because the loaf is not merely one loaf of bread, but it represents the one body of Christ. The division of the loaf into parts is an expression of the unity of Christ and actually increases the glory of Christ.

The same thing is true about the cup. It begins as one kind of grape, one vat, flask or bottle of wine. Interestingly, the grapes from which it is made have only a resemblance to the wine itself. And again, the oneness of the vat, bottle or skin in which the wine was carried is not diminished by those who drink from it. It remains one vat, bottle or skin, yet, it too is enlarged by the drinking because it re-presents (presents again) the blood of Christ, the one sacrifice made for the people of Christ. It becomes part of the identity and the unity of the people of Christ. And the glory of Christ is increased with every individual who participates in it whether they ultimately come to salvation or damnation.

In the Lord's Supper there is an intermingling of the elements, an intermingling of the unity and diversity of the elements, and of those who participate in the Supper, in such a way that the sum of the individual parts (or participants) is greater than the unity of the whole. Christ Himself is enhanced and expanded by the participation of His people in the Supper (if we can think of God in terms of size, which of course we can't. Nonetheless, Christ grows with His people, as they grow more mature in the faith and as they grow in numbers.)

Thus, the Trinity, Communion and the body of Christ (the church) are all fused together in the unity of Christ and His people in history. Because people necessarily live in time, this unity in Christ also necessarily exists in time. And because it exists in time, like all things in time it involves a process or development. And its development or maturity necessarily includes all of the various elements and stages of its development. My childhood is as much a part of who I am as a person as my last dying days. My life, our lives, Christ's life includes the wholeness of our unique individual histories and the wholeness of the history of the Godhead. It's all involved with who we are as God's people.

THE TRINITY & PREEXISTENCE

Beecher, being a creature of his own time, had an individualistic understanding of personhood. Indeed, individualism is both root and fruit of the American Experiment. The common understanding in America and the West is that all people are new-created beings at conception or birth. The alternative view is that of reincarnation, where individuals get recycled through history. His use of the language of "new-created beings" is an effort by Beecher to steer his discussion into the corral of individual preexistence.

But Paul argued that God had "chosen us in him before the foundation of the world" (Eph. 1:4). Whatever else this means, it means that God did some predestining with regard to specific individuals. Beecher knew that there was a problem with Christian theology regarding personhood, and this book describes the problem quite well. However, his prior commitment to individualism forced him into the only logical solution to the problem (from an individualistic perspective), the preexistence of the individual. And he argues this soundly. So, if we accept Nineteenth Century individualism, we should agree with his analysis and findings.

The great difficulty that people have with the doctrine of the Trinity is related to the fact that, like the Greeks before us, Christians today are mostly individualists. The doctrine of the Trinity is full of contradictions from an individualistic perspective. But if we can amend our understanding of human identity and personhood from the shallowness of individualism, there may be another—better—solution to the problem that Beecher has presented. If we can understand the idea of corporate preexistence, in the sense of a previous kind or genus of human being that served in some sense as the canvas for God's creation of Adam, then we may be able to better understand and apply Beecher's arguments.

The danger for conservative Christians today will be to distinguish this idea of corporate preexistence from the errant ideas of conservative biblical creation and scientific or Darwinian evolution that dominate today. I'm pretty sure that the Twenty-First Century will significantly alter both the current scientific and the contemporary, conservative biblical ideas of creation.

Anticipating this change, I am suggesting that the doctrine of the Trinity, at least as I understand it, may replace Beecher's idea of preexistence without destroying the essential characteristics of his argument and findings. There is a sense in which the social ethos into which particular individuals are born plays a formative role in the identity of those individuals. I am simply stating what is patently obvious, that the families, neighborhoods and nations in which we are born contribute significantly to our identities as individuals. A citizen of a nation may be born into a warring nation, and find himself at war without any personal prior involvement. Thus, these contextual elements play a kind of preexistent role in our lives in the sense that they have significant involvement in the shaping of our individual characters and identities.

I am suggesting that this fact arises out of the trinitarian character of the world in which we live, that we live in a trinitarian world created by a Trinitarian God for triniarian people who have been created in His Trinitarian image. In addition, the application of the doctrine of the Trinity to Beecher's problem will provide a much more productive solution than to chase down the ghosts of some imagined individualist preexistence.

Thus, Beecher's arguments here are not correct because of this limitation, and this focus on preexistence is a serious error. But correcting his error with a better understanding of the doctrine of the Trinity can transform and correct the issue of preexistence with the context of our human individuality, that context being the corporate character of humanity as an organism. This is an aspect of our trinitarian human character. Beecher's arguments are helpful in that they trace a theological problem that runs through history creating various partial and errant views and solutions that only the wholeness and holiness of the manifest Trinity can solve. And indeed, the establishment of God's Trinitarian character in humanity has been God's mission from before time, which can come to fruition only in Christ Jesus, His only begotten Son. Hallelujah!

INDEX

Aaron's incense............328

Abelard..26, 94, 95, 96, 138

Abelard, Peter....26, 95, 96, 138

Agamemnon of Æschylus 239

Alcuin of York..............454

Alexander, Archibald.....19, 32, 87, 107

Ammon, Christoph von 342

antitype 325, 331, 335, 350, 353, 361, 363, 369, 372, 373, 443

Athanasius of Alexandria 227, 312

Athenagoras..................312

Augustine.4, 43, 52, 53, 57, 83, 188, 215, 218, 220, 221, 222, 229, 230, 232, 233, 234, 235, 236, 237, 238, 239, 240, 241, 242, 243, 244, 245, 246, 247, 248, 249, 250, 251, 252, 254, 255, 256, 257, 258, 259, 260, 261, 263, 264, 266, 268, 269, 270, 271, 274, 275, 282, 287, 293, 294, 295, 297, 310, 311, 375, 376, 384, 393, 429, 433, 438, 443, 448, 453, 454, 455

Babbage, Charles..........198

Basil of Caesarea...........312

Bellarmine, Robert..........38

Bloomfield, Samuel........333

Bretschneider, Karl.......258

Brown, William Lawrence 4

Burnap, George.......45, 64, 120, 121

Calvin, John...4, 12, 22, 23, 54, 55, 218, 220, 239, 253, 295, 330, 345, 359, 375, 376, 437

Celestius...5, 217, 221, 230, 255, 285

Channing.....................282

Channing, William Ellery 102, 103, 105, 106, 111, 112, 115, 117, 128, 129, 137, 150, 156, 158, 191, 278, 279, 282, 283

Clement of Alexandria. 312

Coleridge, Samuel. 42, 147, 262

Cyril of Alexandria.......312

Cyril of Jerusalem.........314

Dávid, Ferenc 279

de Wette, Wilhelm.......368

death, spiritual....31, 42, 57, 58, 92, 147, 296, 309, 313, 331, 334, 343, 345, 348, 351, 356, 365, 367, 369, 371, 372, 373, 375, 382, 385, 445, 456, 465

Dewey, Orville..45, 49, 51, 111, 119, 452

Döderlein, Johann........258

Dwight, Timothy 289, 290, 389, 390

Edwards, Jonathan...52, 67, 78, 79, 80, 81, 82, 134, 136, 142, 173, 190, 214, 215, 219, 230, 238, 239, 252, 256, 263, 287, 288, 290, 296, 329, 345, 349, 350, 375, 384, 389, 390, 392, 393, 413, 415, 416, 423, 424, 434, 438, 452

Edwards, Jonathan, Jr.. 286, 289

Edwards, Pierpont..........75

Emmons, Nathanael.....214

Epiphanius of Salamis...313

Eucherius, bishop of Lyon 454

Euthymius Zigabenus. .314

Fairbairn, Patrick..364, 372

fatalism..........230, 232, 293

fiery serpent. .317, 329, 330

Fletcher, John........296, 298

Foster, Hannah................75

Foster, John....75, 124, 125, 126, 129, 130, 131, 132, 133, 137, 154, 155, 156, 157, 158, 162, 182, 191

French confession...........57

Fuller, Andrew......135, 156

Gnosticism...224, 230, 232, 311, 414, 431, 432, 433, 434, 455

Gregory of Nazianzum 226

Gregory of Nazianzus. .312

Gregory of Nyssa 225, 227, 312

Grotius, Hugo.......333, 360

Hagenbach, Karl..193, 226, 229, 310, 314

Hagenbach, Karl Rudolf 193

Haldane, Robert.....83, 252, 256, 264, 265, 266, 276, 376

Harris, John............154
Hegel, Georg. 121, 122, 152
Hitchcock, Edward178, 195
Hodge, Charles...20, 42, 80, 83, 91, 93, 94, 96, 109, 145, 146, 257, 275, 276, 337, 345, 346, 368, 376, 385, 396
Irenaeus............311
Islam. 83, 138, 283, 284, 474
Jerome.......4, 258, 259, 261, 274, 275, 448, 454
John of Damascus...83, 229, 313
Julian.....217, 221, 230, 255, 282, 283, 285, 286
Knapp, Georg.......258, 262, 333, 344
Kuinoel............360
Leibniz, Gottfried 342
Levellers............439
Lingenthal, Karl............342
Macknight, James..........361
Manichaeism............4, 232
Martyr, Justin.................312
Melanchthon, Phillip.......22
Melchizedek..358, 359, 360, 361, 363, 365, 368
Möhler, Johann.......60, 193, 298, 384, 386, 433, 434
Molina, Luis de............213
Molina, Luis de 216
Monophysite.................313
Moravian confession........58
Müller, Julius.392, 396, 413, 434, 453
Munchler, Joseph............311
Neander, Johann...220, 224, 228, 245, 250, 258, 269, 282, 310, 364
Nemesius.................313
Nettleton, Asahel..142, 143, 145
Nevin, John 287

Norton, Andrews......45, 47, 49, 111, 191
Noyes, John.................441
Odo of Cambrai....266, 268, 269
Old School-New School Controversy..12, 14, 15, 99, 109, 111, 119, 134, 136, 137, 139, 142, 143, 149, 151, 153, 157, 182, 185, 228, 252, 271, 311, 316, 337, 346, 352, 353, 371, 448, 461
Olshausen, Hermann.....364
Origen...209, 226, 312, 429, 464, 471
Owen, John.................262
Pascal, Blaise........26, 94, 96, 138, 239, 253, 254, 255, 256, 265, 276, 376, 378, 437, 448
Pelagius.......5, 99, 184, 217, 221, 223, 224, 231, 232, 255, 279, 285, 313
Pictet, Benedict......271, 272
Pollok, Robert.................420
rebellion of Korah..........328
Ridgeley, Thomas..........457
Rosenmüller, Johann.....361
Ryland, John....75, 124, 156
Schleusner, Johann Friedrich 333
Scotus, John Duns..........295
Sears, Edmund......220, 450, 452
Shedd, W.G.T.......217, 218, 252, 262, 263, 266, 288
Sheppard, John.........75, 125
Smalley, John.................321
Smeaton, John.................439
Socinianism............135, 219
Socinus.................99
Socinus, Faustus......99, 279,

285, 326
Spangenberg, August.......59
Sparks, Jared.............45, 46
Spinoza, Baruch............342
Story, Joseph.................101
Strigel, Victor.................59
Stuart, Moses.....20, 21, 145, 264, 333, 340, 341, 361, 391
Tatian.................312
Taylor, John.................39
Tertullian.................311, 471
Theodora I.................313
Theophilus.................312
Theophylactus of Ohrid 314
Thirty-Nine Articles........57
Tholuck, Friedrich....22, 24, 333
Titus of Bostra.................312
Turretin, Francis.37, 39, 41, 42, 60, 63, 85, 86, 105, 178, 179, 180, 218, 262, 271, 275, 276, 297, 326, 327, 330, 345, 346, 384, 457
Waldensians.................56
Ware, Henry.................103
Watts, Isaac...39, 40, 41, 42, 63, 85, 105, 149, 180, 271, 272, 274, 276, 286, 287, 288, 291, 295, 296, 297, 376, 452, 457
Whitby, Daniel.................261
Wiggers, Gustav...216, 225, 234, 235, 237, 258, 268, 295
Willard, Emma Hart......457
Winstanley, Gerrard......439
Woods, Leonard. 88, 89, 90, 93, 94, 96, 103, 109, 129, 143, 145, 149, 150, 276, 376, 397, 401, 406
Zachariae, Karl.................342
Zoroastrianism.................283

Made in the USA
Monee, IL
24 February 2021